HUNTER'S GUIDE TO LONG-RANGE SHOOTING

Wayne van Zwoll

STACKPOLE
BOOKS

0 11557 03314 4

Published by
STACKPOLE BOOKS
5067 Ritter Road
Mechanicsburg, PA 17055
www.stackpolebooks.com

Printed in the United States

First edition

10 9 8 7 6 5 4

Cover photograph by Wayne van Zwoll
Cover design by Caroline M. Stover

Library of Congress Cataloging-in-Publication Data

Van Zwoll, Wayne.
Hunter's guide to long-range shooting / Wayne van Zwoll.— 1st ed.
p. cm.
ISBN-13: 978-0-8117-3314-4
ISBN-10: 0-8117-3314-9
1. Shooting. 2. Hunting guns. I. Title.
SK37.V36 2006
799.2'13—dc22

2005031362

Contents

Introduction

Wind swept with a hiss over black sage while cloud shadows raced across the red Wyoming earth. I bellied to the gentle crest and peeked. The buck was alone. Slowly I slid the rifle ahead of my face, past a grizzled sage, and snicked off the safety. In the 4x Lyman, he looked very small. I held a foot into the wind and high, and fired. The pronghorn streaked away as I rolled over to cycle the Remington 722. In the scope once again, he slowed and stopped, even smaller now. I held farther into the wind and kept the wire on his back. At the report, he raced for the distant rims; but this time I heard the 90-grain .244 bullet bite into his slats. The buck wobbled, staggered, and fell.

"It's a long shot." Like "flash in the pan" and "set your sights" and "lock, stock, and barrel," this bromide owes its origin to shooters. To label an effort a long shot is to define it as difficult. Long shots are worth betting on or investing in only if the prize offsets the high risk of failure.

Of course, "long" is relative. Can a football team score a winning touchdown with less than half a minute on the clock and 80 yards to go? It's a long shot, but, as with the three-point bucket that clinches a basketball game at the buzzer, no one dismisses the possibility. A bid for the U.S. presidency on a platform of taxation without representation—now that's a long shot!

But perspectives change with time and events. In my childhood, talk of putting a man on the moon drew smirks and giggles. Just a few decades earlier, plans for building a winged flying machine qualified as lunacy. The real long shot has grown more ambitious since hunters used stone-tipped arrows. The advent of gunpowder, then rifled barrels, then smokeless cartridges, jacketed bullets, and high-tensile steels has increased the reach of firearms. Most of these developments, along with optical sights to extend aim, evolved to meet the needs of hunters and soldiers. But much of the recent science that has stretched effective range has come from target shooters.

Shooting contests followed close behind the use of firearms in warfare and hunting. One artist's rendition of a match in Zurich dates to 1504. European nobility sponsored shoots with prizes to encourage marksmanship that could be useful in wartime. In frontier North America, informal contests inspired such paintings as George Caleb Bingham's *Shooting for the Beef* and Thompkins H. Matteson's *Turkey Shoot*. Good shooting brought prestige. It also had everyday utility, as frontiersmen depended on their rifles for subsistence and to defend homesteads. Muz-

The author takes aim with a Mannlicher-Schoenauer rifle with Kahles scope in high European mounts.

zle-loading rifles put a premium on first-shot accuracy. Author James Fenimore Cooper and naturalist John James Audubon wrote glowingly of the rifle.

Target shooting followed immigrants from Europe to our eastern seaboard. German- and Swiss-style Schuetzenfests included beer, sauerbraten, and fine single-shot rifles. The first recorded Schuetzenfest occurred in New York the year after the Civil War ended. Most shooting was done at 200 yards, offhand. The rifles weighed from 12 to 16 pounds, with 32- to 45-caliber bores and sophisticated aperture sights. A common accessory was the palm rest for the forward hand, an extension that allowed a shooter to rest his elbow and the rifle's weight on his hip while keeping the sights on target. Buttstocks on schuetzen rifles had prominent cheek rests and deep hook buttplates. Shortly after 1900, some events were established for shooters using optical sights.

As early as the schuetzen games, there were long-range matches fired prone, with long-barreled rifles resembling those used by buffalo hunters. Remington's Lewis L. Hepburn modified the rolling block in an effort to build a rifle that would beat the Irish sharpshooters who had won at Wimbledon in 1873. The Irish had subsequently challenged any American team to another contest through an ad in the *New York Herald*. The team would comprise six men who would fire three rounds of 15 shots, one round each at 800, 900, and 1,000 yards. Targets would be of standard Wimbledon configuration: 12 feet high and 6 feet wide, with a

3-foot-square bull's-eye. The Sharps and Remington companies soon came up with prize funds and promised to furnish rifles specifically for the event. The Amateur Rifle Club was formed to conduct tryouts for the American team. The fledgling National Rifle Association (NRA) and the cities of New York and Brooklyn put up $5,000 each to build a range on Long Island's Creed's Farm. Deeded to the NRA for $26,250 in 1872, it would be called Creedmoor.

That September, Americans with .44-90 Hepburn-modified rolling blocks upset a skilled Irish team shooting muzzleloaders; the score was 934 to 931. Matches held in 1875 and 1876 were won more decisively by the U.S. team. While international shooting competitions made headline news, spectators flocked to see marksmen test their skills at more accessible events. One match in Glendale, New York, during the 1880s drew more than 600 participants and 30,000 spectators. In 1898, a shooting festival there included $25,000 in cash prizes.

It has been some time since the general public showed such interest in the shooting sports, but there's still a fascination for the difficulty involved. Speed, accuracy, and reach can all impress. In the rifle fraternity—which includes tactical shooters, hunters, and target shooters—reach has become the focus of attention.

This book is about long-range shooting with modern rifles and pistols. Although the science of long-distance marksmanship owes much to military work, this is not a text on sniping. It is a book for sportsmen, beginner and seasoned shooter alike. It details the remarkable histories of the men and the companies that brought us from the patched round ball to the jacketed softpoint bullet traveling three times as fast. You'll learn how the science of ballistics came to be and where you can get data that apply to your favorite load (in fact, it may be in the extensive ballistics tables in chapter 6). From choosing barrels, bullets, and sights to understanding optics, you'll be prepared for that shot you always thought was impossible. And you'll make it.

In this book you'll find a clear distinction between intrinsic accuracy and field accuracy. You'll learn how to make your body a better rifle rest. Notes on wind-doping tell you how to read the breeze and compensate so your bullet's arc bends into the bull's-eye. How do temperature and elevation influence bullet travel, and where do you hold when shooting uphill or downhill? The answers are here—with tips on range estimation and rangefinders. Here you'll learn about precision shooting from the best riflemen on the 1,000-yard line and the most experienced hunters in the field.

You may be asking, is it ethical to shoot long distances? Arguably, it is unethical to shoot at game unless you're sure of making a quick kill. Your shooting position and skill level, the target size and presentation, plus the wind and light conditions all matter. Even big, close targets are difficult if you've just arrived, breathless, at the top of a hill in a ridgetop gale and must shoot right away.

This book gives you the hard information you need to hit more often at long range, whatever your choice of rifle, whatever kind of shooting you do. It will also help you determine your maximum effective range under a variety of conditions. *Hunter's Guide to Long-Range Shooting* is not about hope. It's about making sure shots at distances that demand an uncommon level of marksmanship.

No matter how sophisticated your gear, results at extended range depend mostly on your skill. For that reason, "long-range rifle" is a presumptuous label. It presumes that you can steady a rifle while aiming it at the proper spot and releasing the bullet. It presumes a degree of rifle control that's rare among hunters. Hunting, after all, is the application of skills that put you close to game. Whether you carry a rifle, a handgun, or a shotgun with slugs, shooting long requires a different set of skills. It can be part of a hunt, but it is not hunting. You might even say that it is what you do when you haven't hunted very well. Long shooting entertains and challenges shooters on the target range. In the field, it is an effort of last resort. But to prepare for it makes a lot of sense. Not only is the skilled marksmen better able to make the long shot; he or she can hit more surely, and more quickly, at any distance.

I couldn't have written this book without the help of many bright and experienced people in the firearms industry and the indulgence of fellow hunters and competitive shooters. These people and others have generously shared their time and resources: Tony Aeschliman, Don and Norma Allen, Art Alphin, Pat Beckett, Richard Beebe, Bill Booth, Adam Braverman, Randy and Coni Brooks, Frank Brownell, Kim Cahalan, Ron Coburn, Alan Corzine, Curt Crum, Chub Eastman, D'Arcy Echols, Dave Emary, Rob Fancher, Vic Fogle, Rick Freudenberg, Randy Fritz, Terry Gordon, Scott Grange, Mike Harris, Chris Hodgdon, Jeff and Kristi Hoffman, Wayne Holt, Steve Hornady, Tom Houghton, Kevin Howard, Shannon Jackson, Steve Johnson, Mike Jordan, Ken Jorgensen, Garth Kendig, Sheri Kerr, Mike Kingston, Paulette Kok, John Krieger, Jon LaCorte, Mike Larsen, John Lazzeroni, Torbjorn Lindskog, Karen Lutto, Bill McRae, David Miller, Rich Moncrief, Terry Moore, Jim Morey, Ken Nagel, Jason Nash, John and Bob Nosler, Dan O'Connell, Ken Oehler, Alan Orr, Tim Pancurak, Ed Plummer, Larry and Brenda Potterfield, Linda Powell, Dennis Reese, Brad Ruddell, Dan Shepherd, Jeff Sipe, Charlie Sisk, Mike Slack, David Smith, Eddie Stevenson, Roger Stowers, Larry Tahler, Paavo Tammisto, Hermann Theisinger, Mark Thomas, Paul Thompson, Dwight Van Brunt, Lex Webernick, Larry Weishuhn, Bill Wiseman, and Fred Zeglin.

The Roots of Reach

The fighting grew fierce around Saul, and when the archers overtook him, they wounded him critically.
—1 Samuel 31:3 NIV

A GRAY GOOSE WING

Killing at a distance dates way back. Rocks, then spears enabled men to hunt and fight without physical contact. But not until the development of the bow were missiles given leverage beyond that of the human arm. Early Oranian and Caspian cultures fielded archers 15,000 years ago, and the bow helped the Persians in their conquest of the civilized world. Around 5000 B.C., Egypt freed itself from Persian rule by way of the feathered shaft. Four thousand years later, Persia's cavalry was armed with bows and quivers full of arrows. Short recurve bows (with limbs bent back at the tips to increase cast) date to around 500 B.C. The Turks are credited with sending arrows half a mile in flight contests with sinew-backed recurves. Powerful flight bows were commonly shot by archers lying flat on their backs, steadying the bows with their feet.

When the Greeks started studying ballistics about 300 B.C., little was known about gravity and air resistance, the two main forces acting against a projectile in flight. Later, Isaac Newton, Leonardo da Vinci, Galileo, Francis Bacon, and Leonhard Euler would define these forces and measure their effects. Early on, the arrow's arc demonstrated ballistic principles. But its visibility, so useful for scientific study, was no protection for game animals or opposing armies. For years after gunpowder was invented, archers ruled the battlefields. At the Battle of Hastings in 1066, the Normans drew their English foes into pursuit with a false retreat, then launched volleys of arrows toward the oncoming troops. The English were badly beaten. They soon adopted the "gray goose wing" as their weapon of choice.

Unlike the Turks, who developed composite bow limbs for more thrust, English archers carried one-piece bows. It was called a longbow not for its tip-to-tip measure but for the archer's long draw, with the anchor point at the ear or cheek. Short bows of the day were commonly drawn to the chest. The English became renowned for their accuracy, but in battle, they adopted the Viking and Norman tactic of raining a swarm of arrows into distant troops. Thus, a line of archers resembled one of Swiss pikemen, but with a reach that exceeded 100 yards. Getting past a pikeman, an attacker was instantly inside enemy lines; surviving the first volley of arrows guaranteed nothing but an increasingly hazardous journey into the maw of that line. Well supplied with arrows, trained troops could let loose several flurries a minute. An open assault could expose the enemy to several minutes of hell. Armor would turn some arrows, but it wearied the advancing foot soldiers who wore it. English bowmen aimed for the joints in the armor, and for the exposed head and neck of any man foolish enough to shed his helmet on a hot day. They shot deliberately at horses to make the steeds unmanageable and put hapless riders on the ground, where their chances of survival were instantly reduced. The French felt the longbow's deadly sting at Crecy in 1346 and Agincourt in 1415.

The English "war" bow averaged 6 feet in length, with a flat back and curved belly. Most archers preferred yew over other wood, but Mediterranean yew beat the English variety hands down for purity and straightness. Some of the most effective English bows were made of Spanish yew. After the longbow caused otherwise mighty armies to flee, Spain forbade the growing of yew on the premise that it might find its way to England and then into battle against Spanish troops. The English, desperate for staves, cleverly required that a quota be included with every imported shipment of Mediterranean wine.

England kept its army ready for combat by edict. Conscripts were required to practice with their bows. Royal statutes dictated that anyone earning less than 100 pence a year had to own a bow and arrows, which could be inspected at any time. Poachers in Sherwood Forest were offered a pardon if they agreed to serve the king in battle as archers. This was an appealing offer, as hunters caught with iron arrowheads on the king's hunting ground were summarily hung with their own bowstrings. A contingent of these outlaws won a spectacular victory at Halidon Hill in 1333. Their arrows killed 4,000 Scots in a conflict that cost the English just 14 casualties.

Notwithstanding the longbow's pivotal role in European history, few specimens remain. It became for a time a ubiquitous tool, but when aged limbs lost their spring or were damaged in use, a bow went into the fire. Unlike early firearms and swords, bows were seldom embellished and kept as heirlooms. The small number of well-preserved longbows include unfinished staves in the Tower of London and a bow recovered in 1841 from the wreck of the ship *Mary Rose,* sunk in 1545.

West of the Atlantic, bows varied in shape and construction. Ash and hickory in the American colonies, and Osage orange on the eastern plains, were fashioned into slender bows, rectangular in cross section. Softwoods such as the yew used by Indians in the Pacific Northwest served better in broad-limbed bows. Some tribes favored sinew laminates that protected the back of a bow at full draw. Horn, occasionally applied in strips to the bellies of bows, was chosen for its performance under compression.

North American Plains Indians preferred shorter bows than did eastern tribes, even before horses appeared with Spanish exploration. The first bows on the plains measured about 5 feet long. Mounted warriors soon switched to shorter limbs, like those favored by northwest tribes. Riding alongside bison and elk and shooting several arrows quickly at short range, hunters on the prairie required little in the way of accuracy. Arrow shafts were crude; long fletching steered them. Raised nocks on the arrows of the Plains Indians complemented the "pinch" grip preferred by horsemen shooting quickly. In contrast, arrows of the eastern Indians were long and beautifully made, with short feathers to clear the bow handle during a stalk.

Accuracy was important, because one shot was the rule. All tribes adopted steel heads when white traders made them available. Obsidian (volcanic glass) was as deadly but more fragile, and it took hours to nap out a head. Most big-game heads were small, to penetrate; bigger heads snagged in brush and in small game and were easier to retrieve.

To shoot faster in sequence, a Plains Indian pushed the bow as he pulled the string, using a short draw to his chest. A typical 24-inch arrow might be pulled 20 inches, but that short draw stacked enough thrust from a thick-limbed bow to drive arrows through bison. And the speed with which repeat arrows could be launched made firearms second choice to mounted warriors until Samuel Colt's Walker revolver came along in 1839. "Bigfoot" Walker, a nineteenth-century Texas Ranger and the gigantic pistol's namesake, allowed that he'd seen many men "spitted with 'dogwood switches' . . . [Indians] can shoot their arrows faster than you can fire a revolver, and almost with the accuracy of a rifle at the distance of fifty or sixty yards." From horseback, the bow proved much easier to use than a rifle.

East of the plains, arrows were favored over early flintlock muskets, which, besides making noise and belching smoke that obscured the animal, were inaccurate. Several arrows could be loosed in the time needed to recharge a musket. Arrows could be fashioned in the field, but powder and balls were scarce, expensive, and hard to steal. The bow's effective range matched that of many eighteenth-century long guns.

A FLASH AND A BANG

The beginnings of gunpowder are obscure, but explosive "Chinese snow" appeared in fireworks a couple of centuries before Roger Bacon, an English friar and philosopher, described gunpowder in 1249. Experiments in gas propulsion by Berthold Schwarz set the stage for the first firearms, which came along in the beginning of the fourteenth century. Edward II brandished guns during his 1327 invasion of Scotland.

Initially, gunpowder comprised about 41 percent saltpeter, with equal proportions of charcoal and sulfur. In 1338 French chemists changed the composition to 50-25-25. The English preferred a mix of 75 percent saltpeter, 15 percent charcoal, and 10 percent sulfur. That recipe was commonly accepted until the development of guncotton in 1846. In America, a powder mill at Milton, Massachusetts, near Boston, was built before any gun-making facility. By the start of the Revolution, colonists had produced or purloined 40 tons of black powder. Half went to Cambridge, where it was wasted before George Washington assumed control of the Revolutionary Army. In no time, the Continental Army had no powder, and new mills were top priority. By 1800, U.S. mills were producing 750 tons of black powder annually.

Igniting this sulfurous fuel was easy in the open air, but setting it afire in a chamber to launch a ball challenged gun designers. The first firearms, developed in Europe a century and a half before Columbus sailed for the New World, were heavy tubes that required two attendants. The Swiss called these weapons culverins. The culveriner steadied the tube, while the gougat applied a priming charge and then lit

Modern muzzleloaders like Dudley McGarrity's BPI are simply refinements of the first firearms.

it with a smoldering stick or rope. Shooters favored mechanical rests. Forks could be made to support infantry guns or even used on the saddle of a mounted warrior. Clumsy and inaccurate, culverins often misfired. Ignition even without accuracy could be effective, however; the noise and smoke could unnerve an enemy armed with pikes or even bows. Barrels were often fitted with ax heads to make them lethal in hand combat.

Ignition by fuse worked for stationary cannon, whose muzzles could be aimed at a wall or a gun emplacement. Timing mattered little because the target did not move. Even a mass of soldiers presented a target that was essentially fixed. But gunners on the move could hardly afford to wait while an assistant caught up with a burning wick and then tick off more time while the cannon fuse burned, all the while pointing the muzzle at hostiles. If the enemy was advancing fast or sweeping by on horses, a fuse did not pass muster.

Once guns were trimmed so that one man could easily carry and aim them and torch the charge, a faster firing device became imperative. The first lock was simply a crude lever by which a smoldering wick was lowered to the touchhole in the barrel. The wick was later

This Austrian massif shadows Tyrolean villages where early rifle matches were held.

replaced by a match, assisted by a cord or a long wick that was kept smoldering atop the barrel. The shooter eased the serpentine into the wick until the match caught fire. Then he moved the mechanism aside and lowered the match to the touchhole. Later, a spring kept the match from the touchhole until needed; a trigger adapted from crossbows gave the shooter more control. Such a mechanism was known as a matchlock—a term also applied to guns that featured it. The Spanish arquebus was one. Arquebusiers carried extra wicks smoldering in metal boxes on their belts.

Sixteenth-century German gun designers eliminated the unreliable wick when they developed the "monk's gun." A spring-loaded jaw held a piece of pyrite (flint) against a serrated bar. The shooter pulled a ring at the rear of the bar, scooting it across the pyrite to produce sparks, which showered a pan containing a trail of fine gunpowder that led into the touchhole in the barrel. A more sophisticated version called the wheellock appeared around 1515 in Nuremberg. It featured a spring-loaded sprocket wound with a spanner wrench and latched under tension. Pulling the trigger released the wheel, causing it to spin against a fixed shard of pyrite held by spring tension against the wheel's teeth. Sparks flew. Wheellocks were less affected by wet

Flint ignition followed the matchlock and the wheellock. Pyrite in the hammer jaws strikes a steel plate, or frizzen, which flies forward as sparks shower into the pan, igniting powder that carries flame through the touchhole into the barrel, firing the main charge.

weather than were matchlocks. They also gave quicker ignition and were faster to make ready.

The roles of pyrite and steel were reversed in the lock à la miquelet. The design was, by all accounts, Dutch but was named after Spanish *miquelitos* (marauders) operating in the Pyrenees. Later it would be modified to incorporate a spring-loaded cock that held a piece of flint and swung in an arc when released. At the end of its travel, the flint in the jaws of the cock hit a pan cover or hammer, kicking it back to expose the primed pan. Sparks landed in the pan, igniting a priming charge of black powder that burned through a touchhole in the barrel to the main charge. The cock eventually became known as a hammer, the hammer a frizzen. The mechanism was dubbed the flintlock, a less costly affair than the wheellock, and more reliable.

Matchlock, wheellock, and flintlock mechanisms had a common weakness: exposed priming. Wet weather could render them all useless. And because there was no way to control the direction and intensity of the spark, ignition wasn't certain even with dry priming. Then too, if the priming did ignite, flame might not reach the main charge, yielding only a "flash in the pan." Producing a spark inside a barrel didn't make sense until early in the eighteenth century, with the discovery of fulminates (shock-sensitive salts of fulminic acid, an isomer of cyanic acid). In 1774 the physician to Louis XV wrote about the explosiveness of fulminate of mercury; ten years later, Antoine Fourcroy and Nicolas Louis Vauquelin followed up with experiments. Englishman E. C. Howard discovered in 1799 that adding saltpeter to fulminates of mercury produced a shock-sensitive but manageable explosive. "Howard's powder" may have influenced the work of Scotch clergyman Alexander John Forsythe, who in 1806 demonstrated internal ignition. Two years later, Swiss gunmaker Johannes Pauly designed a breech-loading percussion gun that employed a cartridge with a paper percussion cap at its base. A spring-loaded needle pierced the cap, detonating the fulminate.

Powder fired by a spark in the chamber marked a watershed in firearms development. New types of ammunition and the guns to fire them were quick to follow. In 1818 Englishman Joseph Manton built a gun with a spring-loaded catch that held a tiny tube of fulminate against the side of the barrel and over the touchhole. The hammer crushed the fulminate, and breech pressure blew the tube away. The Merrill gun, 14,500 of which were bought by the British government, employed this mechanism. In 1821 the London firm of Westley Richards designed a percussion gun that used fulminate primers in a flintlock-style pan. The falling hammer opened the pan cover, exposing a cup of fulminate. The hammer's sharp nose pierced it, sending sparks through a touchhole at the cup's base. Two years later, American physician Samuel Guthrie found a way to make fulminate pellets, a convenient alternative to loose fulminate and paper caps.

Although many inventors claimed credit for inventing the copper percussion cap, sea captain Joshua Shaw of Philadelphia probably deserves the honor. In 1814 the British-born Shaw was denied a patent for a steel cap because he was not yet a U.S. citizen. He persevered with a disposable pewter cap, then one made of copper. Between 1812 and 1825 the U.S. patent office issued 72 patents for percussion caps. Only a few of these designs proved workable. Some caps fragmented, spattering the shooter. Others had so little priming mix that they failed to ignite the main charge—or so much that they started the ball before the burning powder could build pressure. In 1822 Shaw patented his own lock. By that time, it was clear that the percussion cap atop a hollow nipple had a bright future. In 1846 Congress awarded the 70-year-old Shaw an honorarium.

Despite the obvious advantages of a closed passage to concentrate the spark directly on the powder charge, percussion rifles and shotguns were slow to catch on. Fulminates were chemicals, and in the early nineteenth century, chemistry was still commonly viewed with suspicion. Also, the first caps were not consistent. Governments, ever wary of new inventions, resisted replacing pyrite with primers. By this time, flintlocks had also been refined; they looked good and performed quite reliably. Shooters who stood by the old system tried to spread some odd myths. For example, percussion shotguns were said to kick harder but deliver less punch downrange. Britain's Colonel Hawker, a firearms authority, fell for the fiction: "For killing single shots at wildfowl rapidly flying, and particularly by night, there is not a question in favour of the detonating system, as its trifling inferiority to the flint gun is tenfold repaid by the wonderful accuracy it gives in so readily obeying the eye. But in firing a heavy charge among a large flock of birds the flint has the decided advantage." Eventually the convenient, weatherproof percussion cap would win over the doubters.

Meanwhile, firearms were changing in profile—becoming shorter and slimmer, with smaller bores and more sensitive triggers. The cumbersome firearms that had come from Europe with the Pilgrims in the early seventeenth century were typically 75-caliber smoothbore flintlocks, 6 feet long. Though rifled barrels had been winning matches since 1498 in Leipzig, Germany, and 1504 in Zurich, Switzerland, rifles were costly to make and slow to load. Early firearms were mostly for military use, and warfare in Europe at that time did not require fine accuracy. More important was quick reloading by green recruits.

In the New World, however, conflict presented no wall of uniforms as a target. The enemy was a wraith, alone and partly hidden behind vegetation. Accuracy mattered on the hunt too, because long shots were common. For these reasons, Americans favored the French-style flintlock that had been popular in Europe at the beginning of the eighteenth century. The jaeger (hunter) rifle that evolved from it had a 24- to 30-inch barrel of 65 to 70 caliber, with seven to nine deep, slow-twist grooves. Most jaegers wore a rectangular patchbox ahead of a wide, flat buttplate. Double-set triggers were common. To conserve lead, frontier gunsmiths built jaegers with 50-, 45-, and even 40-caliber bores. A pound of lead, they reasoned, would yield seventy 40-caliber balls but only 15 of .70-inch diameter. They lengthened the barrel, replaced the jaeger's sliding patchbox cover with a hinged lid, and installed a "crescent" butt to fit comfortably against the shooter's upper arm.

Even though most of the changes were wrought in Pennsylvania by German gunsmiths, their redesigned jaeger became known as the Kentucky rifle. It was much more accurate than the Brown Bess musket issued to British troops during the Ameican Revolution, but the Kentucky rifle was slower to load. Pounding full-diameter balls home against rifling was difficult and made noise that gave away the shooter's position. Mounted hunters and soldiers found loading intolerably troublesome. To speed it up, Americans cast undersize balls and swathed them in greased linen patches that took the rifling. So accurate were these balls, and so fast to load, that the colonists trounced even crack jaeger troops, who charged their rifles with tight-fitting balls. The patched ball quickly gained favor with hunters, who liked the cleaning action of the patch and its protection of the bore against leading. Animal fat was commonly used to grease the patch, but in a pinch, a shooter could use saliva.

RIFLES TO TAME A FRONTIER

By the end of the eighteenth century, hunters in New England south to the Great Smoky Mountains possessed what were arguably the best rifles in the world. Renowned for its accuracy and reach, the Kentucky rifle featured the proven innovations of European gunmakers, modified to meet the demands of the American frontier.

A rifle was an individual project. It would be decades before Eli Whitney and others came up with the practical means for mass production. But while Old World sportsmen got their firearms from established shops in England, Switzerland, and Germany, pioneers pushing west of the Alleghenies had access only to backwoods forges and gunsmiths whose main virtue was resourcefulness. Parts not only had to be made; the steel itself had to be wrought on the gunmaker's anvil.

America's oldest gunmaker, Remington, got its start in 1816 when Eliphalet (Lite) Remington II put his hand to his father's forge in Litchfield, 4 miles from New York's Mohawk River. Lite was 22, living with his wife, Abigail, in his father's stone house on Staley Creek. Borrowing from the jaeger rifle design, Lite made the barrel first, pumping the bellows to heat an iron rod cherry-red. He hammered the rod until it was half an inch square in cross section, then wound it around an iron mandrel that was not quite as big in diameter as the finished bore. Heating the tube until it was white-hot, he sprinkled it with borax and sand. He held one end with his tongs and pounded the other on the stone floor to seat the coils. When it had cooled, Lite checked the 45-

Modern muzzleloader at hand, the author glasses Utah peaks. Pioneers came here with flintlocks.

caliber barrel for straightness and hammered out the irregularities. He ground and filed eight flats to make the tube octagonal, then traveled to Utica to pay a gunsmith the equivalent of a dollar to rifle the bore. Back home, Remington bored a touchhole and forged a breech plug and the lock parts, shaping them with a file. He used uric acid and iron oxide to finish the steel a hazel brown. He made the stock from a walnut plank, his only tools a drawknife and a chisel. He smoothed the wood with sandstone and sealed it with beeswax. Hand-wrought screws and pins fastened the lock parts. Legend has it that Lite took his new rifle to a local shooting match and placed second, prompting the winner to ask him for a rifle just like it. Remington is said to have filled his order in ten days. Price: $10.

Pioneers pushing west soon found their small-bore Kentucky rifles less effective on grizzly bears and bison than they'd been on white-tailed deer and wild turkeys. The Kentucky's long barrel, so graceful in profile, proved awkward to carry on horseback; its slender stock often didn't survive the rigors of life in the saddle. By the late 1700s, rifles on the frontier were getting an overhaul. Iron hardware replaced brass, shorter barrels of bigger bore complemented beefier stocks. The mountain or Tennessee rifle resulted.

Mountain men encountering elk at a distance had to stalk closer to fire their patched round balls.

At the beginning of the nineteenth century, trappers were mining the Rockies for furs. The West yielded great wealth to men willing to brave the perils of the wilderness. General W. H. Ashley, head of the Rocky Mountain Fur Company, successfully promoted the rendezvous as a way to gather furs from trappers in far-flung places. Subsequently, tons of pelts funneled from frontier outposts to St. Louis, Missouri, which soon became a gateway to the West and a hub of resupply. Easterners of various trades came to get their piece of the action. Among them was gunsmith Jacob Hawkins. In 1822 his brother Samuel closed his gunshop in Xenia, Ohio, to join Jake. The two changed their name back to the original Dutch Hawken—a name that would define the rifle of choice for a generation.

In fashioning rifles for trappers and other frontiersmen, the Hawken brothers borrowed heavily from the work of a North Carolinian named Youmans, a preeminent maker of Tennessee rifles. Still made one at a time and thus showing much variation, Hawken rifles typically featured a short, heavy barrel. The half-stock, secured by two keys, was a departure from traditional full-length stocks. The Hawkens preferred maple (in 1845, maple cost $2 per 100 board feet).

Patchboxes, common on Kentucky and Tennessee rifles, were usually omitted on Hawkens. Flint remained the standard mode of ignition until about 1840; the Hawken brothers used Ashmore locks as well as their own. Many Hawken rifles had double-set triggers.

During the short era of the rendezvous, several gunmakers built rifles similar to those turned out by the Hawken shop. The Hawken rifle became, more accurately, the Plains rifle as Henry Lehman, James Henry, George Tryon, and others supplied equally serviceable rifles.

The Hawken's reputation came by way of its accuracy and reach. The typical barrel measured 38 inches. It was 50 caliber, octagonal, and fashioned of soft iron with a slow rifling twist to better stabilize the patched round ball still in common use. Charge weights in Hawken barrels typically ran from 150 to 215 grains, but the rifles were known for their ability to shoot well with a wide range of loads. Hawken barrels proved less susceptible to fouling problems than were the quick-twist, hard-steel barrels of contemporary English rifles built only for conical bullets. The soft bore retained traces of bullet lube. Easier to load, Hawkens delivered remarkable precision at a distance. Francis Parkman told of killing a pronghorn at 204 paces and of watching another hunter drop a bison at nearly 300.

In an article for the *Saturday Evening Post* (February 21, 1920, as cited by Hanson in *The Plains Rifle*), Horace Kephart wrote of finding an unused Hawken rifle in St. Louis. He quickly put it into service and discovered that "it would shoot straight with any powder charge up to a one-to-one load, equal weights of powder and ball. With a round ball of pure lead weighing 217 grains, patched with fine linen so that it fitted tight, and 205 grains of powder it gave very low trajectory and great smashing power, and yet the recoil was no more severe than that of a 45 caliber breech loader charged with seventy grains of powder and a 500-grain service bullet."

Though the demand for new rifles kept them very busy, Jake and Sam Hawken repaired rifles too. On December 26, 1825, the Hawkens billed the U.S. Indian Department, through its agent Richard Graham, $1.25 for "Cutting Barrel & new brich" and 50 cents for "Repairing Rifle." Graham gave the shop more business the following spring, remitting 25 to 87 1/2 cents apiece for lock refurbishing. For "Repairing Lock, bullet molds, ram rod, & hind sight," one bill totaled $2. The Hawkens charged 50 cents for shoeing a horse, 18 cents for fixing spurs. Bartering took care of many bills on the frontier; no doubt the Hawkens were tendered goods and services as well as cash.

Primitive but effective in skilled hands, the Plains rifle was the beefy progeny of the Kentucky.

When the California gold rush started in 1849, a basic Hawken rifle cost $22.50—a substantial price, but one willingly paid by men whose livelihoods (and lives) might hang on one accurate shot. That year, Jake Hawken died of cholera. Sam kept the business afloat, and in 1859 he made his first trek to the Rocky Mountains, where Hawken rifles had become a legend. The journey from Kansas City to Denver took 57 days. After only a week working in nearby mines, he returned to Missouri.

Sam's son, William S. Hawken, became a mountain man and rode with Kit Carson's Mounted Rifles. At age 30, William fought in the Battle of Monterey on September 23, 1847. Badly outnumbered by Mexican troops, General Henderson and a handful of frontiersmen fought to hold a bridge over San Juan Creek. The clash left only 9 of the 43 Texas Rangers ambulatory. William Hawken was among the wounded. He eventually made his way back to Missouri. When Sam traveled to Colorado, he left William in charge of the Hawken shop. During that time, William got this letter:

Evans Landing Nov. 27th 1858
Mr. Wm. Hawkins
    Sir, I have waited with patience for my gun, I am in almost in a hurry 2 weeks was out last Monday I will wait a short time for it and if it don't come I will either go or send. If your are still waiting to make me a good one it is all right. Please send as soon as possible.
    Game is plenty and I have no gun. Yours a friend.
Daniel W. Boon.

William apparently went west shortly after Sam returned. Nothing more was heard of William Hawken until some years later, when a 56-caliber muzzleloader bearing his name was found under a pile of rocks in Querino Canyon, Arizona. The man's fate remains a mystery.

Around 1860, Sam Hawken hired a shop hand. J. P. Gemmer had immigrated to the United States from Germany in 1838. Capable and industrious, he bought the Hawken enterprise in 1862 and kept it open until his death in 1919 at age 92. Gemmer outlived Jim Bridger and Kit Carson and many other frontiersmen who had depended on Hawken rifles. He may have used the "S. Hawken" stamp on some rifles, but he marked most of them "J. P. Gemmer, St. Louis." As the bison went the way of the mountain man and cartridge rifles became popular, Gemmer shifted his production to small-bore and target rifles. Sam Hawken continued to visit his shop in retirement and once built a complete rifle. The Hawken business remained in St. Louis all its life, but the shop location changed several times in later years.

Metallic Cartridge Muscle

Some of my most enjoyable long-range shooting has been done with a Shiloh Model 1874 Quigley Model (Sharps) in .45-110 [at] a life-size metal silhouette of a buffalo at a surveyed 956 yards. Once the Shiloh's tang sight was adjusted properly, it was easy to bounce 520-grain Lyman #457125 bullets off that gong.

—Mike Venturino,
Shooting Buffalo Rifles of the Old West

RIFLES THAT FIRED ALL WEEK

Charging rifles from the muzzle was slow work. The awkward operation was long on movement, which drew an adversary's attention. It rendered a shooter helpless, not only because the barrel was empty but also because it was in his lap or clutched in his hand while the other held a ramrod. Loading from the breech had been a dream long before the advent of the percussion cap. Guns with a hinged breech date to at least 1537, but flint ignition was a poor complement. A seventeenth-century French musket featured a cylindrical breech plug that dropped when the trigger guard was turned. Alas, raising the block into battery sometimes pinched the powder and caused premature detonation. The best example of this type, designed in 1776 by British major Patrick Ferguson, had a threaded breech plug that retracted by rotating the threaded trigger guard. A charge was inserted in the barrel, and the plug spun back into place.

At the close of the eighteenth century, Americans Eli Whitney and Simeon North, working independently, gave a big boost to the development of breech-loading rifles. These inventors came up with machines that manufactured uniform parts. Previously, every gun had to be made individually. Parts could not routinely be taken from one

Single-shot rifles like this Winchester 1885 (here a modern rendition with current ammo) were much more potent than the first lever actions.

rifle and installed on another. Breechloaders made substitutions nearly impossible; the breech seal allowed no play or gap in action parts. After Whitney and North showed how machines could be used to manufacture identical parts, they each won a government contract for guns. Sixteen years later, in 1813, North got the first contract specifying guns with interchangeable components.

Settlers, trappers, and market hunters took full—and shameful—advantage of early breechloaders.

But close-fitting parts did not a breechloader make. Many designs failed. Some functioned with low-powered loads but gave way or stuck under high pressure. The Theiss breechloader of 1804 had a sliding block that moved upward for loading. Using the same basic mechanism, Captain John Harris Hall of Maine designed one of the first successful breechloaders in this country. Hammer, pan, and frizzen all rode on the movable block. The Hall rifle was issued in limited numbers to U.S. soldiers in 1817, six years after its debut. The crude flintlock earned no plaudits among the troops, however, and as war with Mexico threatened to drain arsenals in 1845, factories ramped up to build Harpers Ferry muzzleloaders, which dated to 1803.

Breech-loading was a lot more feasible with cartridges than with loose powder and balls. The first cartridges (assembled in 1586) were made of paper and loaded from the muzzle. Biting or ripping off the base of the cartridge exposed the powder. The case burned to ashes upon firing. Replacing pyrite with a percussion cap did away with the biting and tearing, because the cap's more powerful spark penetrated the thin paper.

Across the Atlantic, Johann Nikolaus von Dreyse was among the first inventors to install a primer in a cartridge. His paper hull clasped a bullet with a pellet of fulminate at its base. A long striker penetrated the paper and powder from the rear to smash the pellet. Roughly

You can still fire Sharps-era breechloaders on the high plains, but the buffalo are gone.

300,000 von Dreyse "needle guns" were built for the Prussian army between 1835 and 1865. Incidentally, the needle gun mentioned by post–Civil War writers was not the European Dreyse but the .50-70 Springfield, which became in 1873 the .45-70 Trapdoor rifle used in the last of the Indian Wars. The long breechblock required a long firing pin.

Stateside, Stephen Taylor patented a hollow-base bullet with an internal powder charge held in place by a perforated heel cap that admitted sparks from an external primer. A year later, in 1848, New York inventor Walter Hunt devised a similar bullet. This one had a cork cap covered with paper. Primer sparks shot through the paper to ignite the charge. To fire this "rocket ball," Hunt developed a repeating rifle with a pillbox mechanism to advance the metallic primers. Its tubular magazine was a brilliant stroke. But the action, operated by a finger lever under the breech, was prone to malfunction. Lacking the money to promote or even improve his "Volitional" repeater, Hunt sold the patent rights to fellow New Yorker and machinist George Arrowsmith. Lewis Jennings, a talented young engineer in Arrowsmith's shop, improved the Hunt rifle. After receiving patents for Jennings's work, Arrowsmith sold the Hunt rifle for $100,000 to railroad magnate and New York hardware merchant Courtland Palmer.

Palmer's financial backing helped gun designers Horace Smith and Daniel Wesson develop a metallic cartridge like that patented in 1846 and 1849 by the Frenchman Flobert. Rather than using a ball atop a primer, as Flobert had, Smith and Wesson modified a rocket ball to include a copper base that held the fulminate priming mix. In 1854 Palmer joined his designers in a limited partnership, putting up $10,000 for tooling in a company that would become known as Smith and Wesson. A year later, a group of 40 New York and New Haven investors bought out Smith, Wesson, and Palmer to form the Volcanic Repeating Arms Company. The investors chose as company director Oliver F. Winchester, a successful shirt merchant. Winchester moved the firm from Norwich to New Haven, Connecticut. Slow sales of Volcanic guns sent the firm into receivership in 1857, but Winchester reorganized after buying all assets for $40,000. The New Haven Arms Company, as it was now called, hired Benjamin Tyler Henry to perfect its rifle.

In 1860 Henry received a patent for a 15-shot repeating rifle chambered for .44 rimfire cartridges. Confederates called the brass-frame Henry "that damned Yankee rifle you loaded on Sunday and fired all week." Though unreliable, underpowered, and prone to leak gas, it was coveted by soldiers because it could be recharged from the shoulder with a flick of the hand.

Meanwhile, as legions of inventors struggled to perfect a repeating rifle, a young machinist named Christian Sharps sought to build a stronger breech-loading single-shot. A New Jersey native, Sharps worked under John Hall at the Harpers Ferry Arsenal. In 1848 he received his first patent, for a rifle with a sliding breechblock. The tight breeching held promise for big-game hunters because it could handle cartridges that would hit hard at very long range.

SHARPS, FOR THE BUFFALO

In a 1930 edition of the *Kansas City Star*, hunter George Reighard explained how he shot bison:

> In 1872 I organized my own outfit and went south from Fort Dodge to shoot buffaloes for their hides. I furnished the team and wagon and did the killing. [My partners] furnished the supplies and the skinning, stretching and cooking. They got half the hides and I got the other half. I had two big .50 Sharps rifles. . . .
>
> We had flour, coffee, sugar, salt, blankets, four 10-gallon kegs for water, a dutch oven, two frying pans, a big tin coffee pot, a camp kettle, bread pan, tin cups and plates but no table knives, forks or spoons. We used our skin-

*ning and ripping knives. . . . Our diet was mostly buffalo
meat, fried, stewed or raw. . . .*

*Usually I went to the top of some rise to spy out the
herd, [then] sneak up to within good ranges. Between 200
and 350 yards was all right. . . . I carried a gun rest made
from a tree crotch, which I would stick into the ground to
rest the gun barrel upon.*

*The time I made my biggest kill I lay on a slight ridge
behind a tuft of weeds 100 yards from a bunch of 1,000
buffaloes. . . . After I had killed about 25 my gun barrel
became hot and began to expand. A bullet from an overheated gun does not go straight, it wobbles, so I put that
gun aside and took the other. By the time that became hot
the other had cooled, but then the powder smoke in front
of me was so thick I could not see through it; there was
not a breath of wind to carry it away, and I had to crawl
backward, dragging my two guns, and work around to
another position on the ridge, from which I killed 54 more.
In 1½ hours I had fired 91 shots, as a count of the empty
shells showed afterwards, and had killed 79 buffaloes, and
we figured that they all lay within an area of about 2 acres
of ground. My right hand and arm were so sore from
working the gun that I was not sorry to see the remaining
buffaloes start off on a brisk run that soon put them
beyond range.*

On that trip, Reighard killed "a few more than 1,000 buffaloes in
one month."

Sharps rifles endured briefly during a time of shameless and insa-
tiable appetite. The last half of the nineteenth century also happened
to be the most productive period in the history of firearms development. Christian Sharps contributed several forgettable rifles before his
company brought out the guns of great reach and power that would
forever be known as "buffalo rifles."

The first patented Sharps model was an 1841 Mississippi rifle with
lock and breech excised. The Sharps mechanism that replaced them
had a vertical sliding block operated by a finger lever that formed the
trigger guard. Dropping the lever dropped the block, exposing the barrel. A Sharps rifle operated as easily as a Hall, but it sealed the barrel
much more effectively.

Christian Sharps designed a powerful breechloader. This modern T/C is just as potent but more compact.

Like many inventors, Christian Sharps knew little about marketing, but he did know that he wanted a U.S. Army contract. So he chose the most direct route, bypassing Chief of Ordnance George Talcott and going right to Secretary of War George W. Crawford. After that, Talcott was in no hurry to give the brash young man an audience. Three months later and almost broke, Sharps secured a $500 loan from businessman Jonathan M. McCalla to "interest an established manufacturer." That effort, too, failed. Then, in February 1849, Sharps met Albert S. Nippes, a gunsmith from Mill Creek, Pennsylvania. Nippes contracted with Sharps to manufacture between 100 and 200 rifles. Costs for tooling were not to exceed $600. The men were to share in the labor, but Sharps did little to help Nippes build guns; instead, he experimented with other rifle designs. Still, less than a year into production, the two men agreed to cofound another gun-building enterprise, and later that summer, Nippes pulled together a company for the manufacture of Sharps rifles. Called Model 1850s, these rifles featured Maynard tape primers instead of the wheel primers of the Model 1849. Fewer than 100 guns were finished.

To pursue his dream of a government contract, Sharps formed his own company shortly after his contract with Nippes expired. Arba Maynard joined him as a partner. Sharps rifles included in the military trials of October 1850 got high praise—even from General Talcott—but no orders came. Scurrying to find other markets, Maynard contracted with New York financier Courtland Palmer for 1,500 guns. But Sharps balked because he had not been consulted, and the partnership was dissolved.

In January 1851 entrepreneur George H. Penfield visited the Nippes offices and recognized the potential of the Sharps action. He offered Christian Sharps a job "making models and making improvements" for $1,500 a year and seven-sixteenths of the profits if Sharps would grant him nine-sixteenths of the patent rights. After clearing the patent mortgage held by Nippes and a claim by Maynard, Penfield bought the remaining Sharps stock for $16,000. All told, Penfield paid $22,853 for the rights to Sharps rifles.

Christian Sharps went to Hartford to look for a factory, but the only one big enough belonged to Sam Colt. He established temporary quarters in a Pearl Street shop while contractor George King built a 10,000-square-foot factory for Sharps and Penfield. Soon thereafter, a flood inundated the factory's lower levels, and King agreed to build them another factory. But before he could, Penfield contracted with Robbins & Lawrence for 5,000 Sharps rifles. Then he scraped up $100,000 to capitalize the Sharps Rifle Manufacturing Company, incorporated October 8, 1851.

Robbins & Lawrence folded in 1856, when the Sharps Rifle Manufacturing Company foreclosed on its mortgage. Up to this time, six guns had been produced under the Sharps name: Models 1849, 1850, 1851, 1852, 1853, and 1855. The last four were "slant-breech" rifles, so called because the breechblock operated at a 112-degree angle to the bore, not perpendicularly, as in earlier guns. There were many variations in triggers, sights, barrels, and stocks. Some military guns even had a coffee mill in the buttstock; mostly, soldiers used it to grind grain. The Sharps plants also produced shotguns. In slant-breech models, even rifles were designated by bore (or gauge—indicating the number of lead balls of that bore size needed to equal 1 pound). The most popular sizes were 60 and 90 bore, or 44 and 36 caliber. In 1858 Richard Lawrence reworked the slant breech to restore a right-angle configuration. His gas plate was superior to the Conant gas ring on earlier actions.

During the late 1850s, Sharps rifles were shipped by abolitionists to Kansas Free Staters to prompt a vote against slavery. A shipment of 100 Sharps carbines was stolen from the river steamer *Arabia* in Lexington, Missouri, but the breechblocks had been taken out and sent along a different route. Another 200 carbines got to John Brown, who, along with 21 fellow insurrectionists, stormed Harpers Ferry Arsenal. In the West, the Sharps rifle became known as "Beecher's Bible" when abolitionist Henry Ward Beecher expressed his belief in the gun as a "truly moral agency" and proclaimed, "You might as well read the Bible to buffaloes as to those fellows who follow Atchison and Stringfellow; but they have a supreme respect for the logic [of] Sharps rifles."

When the Civil War broke out, Sharps employees numbered over 450. They were producing about 30,000 guns annually in a factory driven by a 250-horsepower, single-cylinder Corliss steam engine. Government orders strengthened during the war. The Sharps Model 1859 was followed by New Models 1859, 1863, and 1865. Perhaps most deserving of long-range rifles were Colonel Hiram Berdan's Sharpshooters, selected for their expert marksmanship. But initially these troops were equipped with muzzleloaders. When Berdan asked for better guns, he was sent surplus Colt revolving rifles, which he refused. His troops threatened mutiny if the requested rifles didn't arrive, and they finally got Sharps. Although these lacked the double-set triggers Berdan had ordered, the troops were satisfied. At Gettysburg, 100 sharpshooters and 200 regulars from Maine held Little Round Top against the advance of 30,000 Confederates, firing nearly 10,000 rounds in 20 minutes.

When government contracts dried up after the Civil War, the company courted sportsmen with a New Model 1869 rifle, the first cartridge Sharps with no provision for outside priming. It came in .40-50, .40-70, .44-77, .45-70, and .50-70. Only 650 were built before the Model 1874, announced in 1870, replaced it. The 1874, in its myriad forms, would remain popular for twelve years.

Christian Sharps died of tuberculosis in 1874, leaving a wife, daughter, and son. His Philadelphia factories were shut down, but the Sharps Rifle Manufacturing Company, built on patents Sharps had bargained away to Penfield, continued to seek government contracts. These were slow in coming from a nation at peace. Still, Sharps rifles played a major role in the buffalo slaughter that peaked after the Civil War.

Hugo Borchardt joined Sharps shortly after introduction of the Model 1875 rifle, which incorporated patents by Rollin White and Nelson King. A Long-Range Model 1875 exhibited at the Philadelphia Exposition was bought there for $300 by Colonel John Bodine. It is the only surviving specimen, because no other 1875s were made. But the men who had helped design the rifle—Charles Overbaugh and A. O. Zischang—soon came up with a replacement. The Model 1877 had a leaner, rounder action. Its locks and barrel blanks were imported from Webley of England. Like the Model 1874 Creedmoor that gave Americans their victory over the Irish, it was designed for long shooting. Three grades were listed, priced at $75, $100, and $125. Fewer than 300 Model 1877s were built. Overbaugh fashioned 73 into schuetzen rifles, and Denver dealer J. P. Lower sold 75 cataloged as "special Model 1874s" (these became known as Lower Sharps guns).

Like Nelson King of Winchester fame, who served as plant superintendent at Sharps, Hugo Borchardt took an active part in rifle design. He earned a flat fee of $1,855 for his first rifle, which later became the Sharps Model 1878. The first 300 Borchardt rifles went to the Chinese government in 1877. The action also showed up in a variety of hunting and target guns. Prices ranged from $18 to $125. Barrels were cut with six grooves.

As early as 1875, Sharps had solicited repeating-rifle designs from inventors. Two years later the firm tried to build a magazine rifle on the Swiss Vetterli action. Ordnance trials showed the gun to be trouble prone. In January 1878 Remington designer James Lee came up with a new repeating mechanism; one year later the Lee Arms Company was formed at Sharps's Bridgeport plant. In April 1879 Lee offered to convert government Springfields into magazine rifles. Though this conversion was as affordable as a trapdoor modification, the government

Augusta Wallihan, early Colorado hunter and photographer, favored a Remington-Hepburn rifle.

didn't bite. Lee wound up producing rifles for Remington after building 47 repeaters at Sharps.

Undaunted by its failed bid to market a repeating rifle, the Sharps Rifle Company escalated promotion of its Model 1878, but many shooters still preferred the Model 1874. Strapped for cash and behind on deliveries, the company tried to boost production efficiency. In May 1879 Borchardt sailed to Europe seeking military contracts but secured none. Meanwhile, Sharps was rebarreling guns to make them more appealing. Retailers that ordered guns were given huge markdowns. Carlos Grove & Son of Denver asked for 210 Model 1874s and got 270 at prices of $15 to $17 each. It was the beginning of the end for Sharps.

The last major job done at the Sharps factory was for Joseph Frazier, who in July 1880 sent 1,500 percussion guns for cartridge conversion. By October, the money from that deal was gone. On October 8, only 19 employees recorded work time; no one logged any production hours after that, although the shipping department stayed open until mid-1882. Shortly thereafter, J. W. Coffin of the Davenport Arms Company proposed a loan. He would provide $25,000 to recapitalize if $75,000 could be raised through stock sales. No money came. The Sharps Rifle Company disappeared from Connecticut records in 1905.

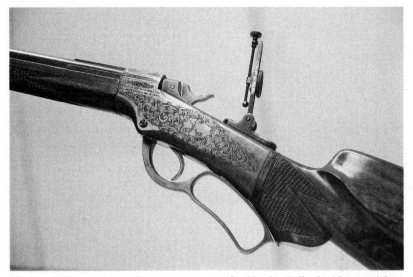

The late 1800s gave rise to long-range target rifles like this Ballard with tang sight.

Sharps also manufactured loading tools and ammunition. The first cartridges were paper. Sharps used the Springfield Armory to make folded-head and bar-primed metallic cases. At one time, Sharps cataloged 14 cases and 50 bullets. Remington and Winchester also supplied ammunition for Sharps. Remington's cartridges are impossible to tell from Sharps ammo fashioned from UMC cases.

The most famous Sharps rifle is the Model 1874, which, if you'd bought one with double-set triggers in 1878, would have cost $44. Replicas can cost 100 times as much now. Shooters have been using modern renditions of the 1874 for years, hunting and in target matches. The movie *Quigley Down Under* introduced the Sharps to many people who had never heard the name. In the movie, star Tom Selleck shoots a bucket at extreme range. Shortly thereafter, the Quigley match emerged in Forsyth, Montana. The bucket-shaped target, 44 inches wide at the top, was placed at 1,000 yards. That's a long shot for a modern, scope-sighted rifle firing high-velocity bullets. And for a blackpowder gun equipped with iron sights and lobbing round-nose bullets at 1,200 to 1,500 feet per second, it's quite a challenge. Still, many shooters hit that bucket with the majority of their shots.

Probably the most celebrated feat involving a Sharps occurred at the frontier town of Adobe Walls in the north Texas panhandle. Renowned Buffalo hunter Billy Dixon was one of just 28 men sleeping

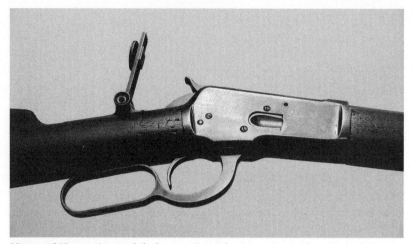

Hunt and Henry pioneered the lever action. John Browning perfected it in the Winchester 1892.

in the tiny settlement early on June 26, 1874. With the rising sun came a fearsome swarm of mounted Comanches, thundering in from the east. The 700 braves, led by Chief Quanah Parker, killed only three whites before the rest of the men barricaded themselves in buildings. Most of them were hunters and well armed. They repulsed the charge with withering rifle fire, but they were badly outnumbered, and many of the Comanches had repeating rifles. The battle wasn't over. Two days later, at least some of the warriors were still lurking just out of range of Adobe Walls. As legend has it, about 15 appeared on a bluff nearly a mile off. Billy Dixon was urged to take a shot with the local saloon owner's 50-caliber 1874 Sharps, which Dixon had used earlier to help drive off the Indians (so when he took aim, it was at least with some familiarity). To everyone's astonishment, the shot caused one of the Indians to fall off his horse. The distance was later surveyed at 1,538 yards. Possible? Surely. Probable? Surely not. But whether or not you believe that Billy Dixon hit a Comanche at more than 1,500 yards with a blackpowder Sharps, you'll have plenty of company.

BROWNING GENIUS; WINCHESTER JACKPOT

One hundred fifty years ago, John Moses Browning was born in frontier Utah. His family hailed from Brushy Fork in Sumner County, Tennessee. There, a generation earlier, Jonathan Browning had accepted a broken flintlock rifle as payment for labor on a nearby homestead. A blacksmith helped him fix it, and 13-year-old Jonathan sold the rifle for

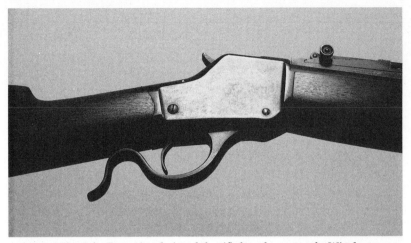

In his twenties, John Browning designed the rifle later known as the Winchester 1885 High Wall.

$4—back to its original owner. By age 19, Jonathan had repaired many guns and could make common parts, but he couldn't drill and rifle barrels, so he walked 30 miles to visit Nashville gun builder Samuel Porter. Porter put him to work, providing in return meals, a berth in a hayloft, and $2 a week. Jonathan later returned to Brushy Fork with a barrel inscribed "Jonathan Browning 1824."

In November 1826 Jonathan turned 21 and married Elizabeth Stalcup. Eight years later, after his father died, Jonathan moved his family 400 miles to Quincy, Illinois. The bustling town on the banks of the Mississippi gave Jonathan plenty of business. By age 35, he'd turned his hand to gun design. The recent invention of the percussion cap had spawned many exciting inventions, among them the revolving cylinder; but boring and indexing required sophisticated equipment. Jonathan adopted a simpler mechanism and called his invention the "slide gun." It featured a rectangular bar that moved from side to side through a slot in the frame. The bar had chamber cavities (usually five), and a thumb lever advanced the bar to line up each chamber in succession. The lever also pushed the bar against the barrel to seal gas. Browning equipped his gun with a trigger guard that served as a mainspring. The hammer lay underneath and swung up to fire.

In 1842 Jonathan and his family moved 43 miles north to Nauvoo, Illinois, a town of 250 that had been founded three years earlier by Joseph Smith and his following of Mormons. Jonathan set up a

John Browning gave western hunters potent lever-action rifles; now scoped bolt guns prevail.

gunshop on the first floor of a two-story brick house. He and others joined the Mormon movement, but there were many people who wanted to obliterate it. On June 25, 1844, Joseph Smith and his brother Hyrum were killed by a mob in Carthage, Illinois. Brigham Young held the Mormons together and planned an exodus for the spring of 1846. But their preparations were cut short by hostile neighbors, who forced them across the river ice in February, months ahead of schedule. Mud, snow, and rain delayed their progress, and exposure claimed several lives. In June the Mormons halted near Kanesville (now Council Bluffs), Iowa. The next month a U.S. Army officer rode into camp to request 500 volunteers to help fight a war with Mexico. This must have seemed ironic to the Mormons, who had pleaded for government protection in Nauvoo. Still, Young mustered volunteers. But when Jonathan Browning stepped forward, Young prevailed on him to stay, to supply guns to other Mormons expected on the trail west. Jonathan opened a shop in Kanesville, building slide guns that held up to 25 shots. These bulky rifles proved effective against Plains Indians, who liked to draw fire and then attack while the settlers were reloading. A Browning gun never seemed to go dry.

Thinned by time and hardship to 143 trekkers, Brigham Young's band of Mormons reached Salt Lake City on July 24, 1847. Five years later, Jonathan Browning and his family settled in Ogden, Utah (named after Hudson's Bay Company explorer Peter Skene Ogden). Jonathan bought a parcel of land and, with the $600 hidden under the floor of one his six wagons, built a house. By this time, Jonathan had eleven children. He would take a second wife in Ogden and father eleven more, one of them John Moses.

In 1862 Jonathan built a tannery, and seven-year-old John Moses rode the horse that plodded in a circle to operate the machinery. But John's mother insisted that he attend school; so he did, until age 15. John was, by all accounts, precocious. As a ten-year-old he built his first gun, a flintlock made from a scrapped musket barrel and a board he had shaped with a hatchet. John fashioned a crude pan and screwed it to the board, which he wired to the barrel. He stuffed the barrel with a heavy charge of powder and rough shot, then heated a batch of coke on the forge. He dumped it into a perforated can and handed that to his young brother Matt. The boys hiked into the sage, Matt swinging the can on a long string to keep air reaching the coke. When they found some dusting prairie chickens, John aimed and Matt stuck a smoldering splinter through the touchhole. John found himself on the ground under dense smoke, but the shot had claimed two birds. When Jonathan Browning heard the tale he said, "Can't you make a better gun than that?" John broke his matchlock into pieces on the forge.

Like his father, John had a natural mechanical bent and spent most of his time working on guns. He was perfectly placed to design and build them. The West was a land of promise, and two railways had just been joined at Promontory Point, only 50 miles from Ogden. Jonathan's shop would soon be his.

In 1878, when John turned 23, he sketched a single-shot action. With no milling machine, he hand-forged the parts, then trimmed them with a file and chisel. A foot-lathe Jonathan had brought by oxcart from Missouri helped with the rest. The finished gun was not only functional but, with massive parts and simple construction, ideally suited to the frontier. John filed for his first patent on May 12, 1879.

In the meantime, Jonathan Browning died, leaving his young protégé as head of the household. Now John *needed* to build and sell guns. Brothers Matt, Ed, Sam, and George assisted with a 25- by 50-foot shop on a 30-foot lot at the edge of Ogden's business district. Intent on turning it into a factory, the Brownings took delivery of power equipment that they didn't know how to install or use. By great good luck, Frank Rushton, an English gunmaker on a tour of the West, wandered in to help. He taught Ed to run the mill, while Sam and George rough-filed receivers. John finished the filing, and Matt made stocks.

John Browning priced his single-shot rifle at $25. The first week after opening a retail counter in a corner of their factory, the Browning brothers sold all the rifles they had made in three months. Buoyed by this success, John ordered material for more rifles, and Matt pressed to expand retail sales. He spent $250 on merchandise (Colt revolvers at that time cost about $30). Unfortunately, the factory was burglarized soon after, and everything of value vanished—including the prototype of John's rifle.

John soon made Matt a partner. Frank Rushton stayed on until his early death. While his brothers repaired customers' guns and built as many as three single-shot rifles a day, John designed new guns. Even before he received a patent for his first rifle, he came up with another dropping-block action. By 1882, John had sketched, then built, a repeater. While waiting for the patent, he went to work on another. In less than a year, in addition to managing a factory, John had designed, patented, and manufactured two repeating rifles.

In 1883 Winchester salesman Andrew McAusland came across a used Browning single-shot rifle and delivered it to Winchester presi-

Browning's fine Winchester 1886 (foreground) *predated by a century the Dakota Longbow, here with a Swarovski range finding scope.*

dent Thomas G. Bennett. At that time, Winchester had a stranglehold on the lever-action rifle market, but its products couldn't handle the popular .45-70 cartridge; this Browning single-shot would. Bennett had never heard of John Browning, but he lost no time traveling to Ogden and what was billed as the biggest gun store between Omaha and the Pacific. He found half a dozen striplings, barely out of their teens, tinkering in a shop smaller than a livery. But Bennett was no fool. He found John and came straight to the point: "How much for your rifle, all rights to it?"

"Ten thousand dollars," said John coolly, as if pawning a used saddle. In 1883 a man could have retired on such a sum. Bennett bought the rifle for $8,000 and paid a $1,000 deposit. Six hours after he had arrived in Ogden, Bennett was on a train for the six-day ride back to New Haven.

During the next month, John Browning pulled out all stops to boost production of his single-shot rifle. After Winchester paid the $7,000 balance, Bennett had to write to Browning to remind him to stop building what was now a Winchester product. John, red-faced, complied. The rifle was featured in Winchester's 1885 catalog and was named for that year. A "high-wall" version, after the original Browning design, had great strength for powerful cartridges; a trim "low-wall" receiver provided easier loading access for smaller rounds.

When Winchester assumed production of John Browning's single-shot in 1883, John immediately turned to a lever-action project that Bennett had suggested. Bennett also bought that rifle, for $50,000—"more money than there was in Ogden," mused John at the time. It would become Winchester's legendary Model 1886. Still, Bennett would not let Browning rest. He asked John to build a lever-action shotgun, but John thought that a pump would sell better. Bennett gave him two years to come up with a lever-action design; John delivered in eight months. The Winchester 1887 is widely considered the first practical repeating shotgun, one of eleven designs John sold to Winchester between October 1884 and September 1886.

In 1887, just after John turned 32 and started a family, he became a missionary. For two years he and a companion traveled through Georgia with the Mormon message. One day he spied in a shop the first Model 1887 Winchester he'd seen. The proprietor remarked as he watched John examine the gun that he seemed to know something about it. "He should!" exclaimed John's companion. "He designed it!"

For four years after returning to Utah in 1889, John Browning worked without pause, garnering 20 patents. "His designs are so simple," said a shop foremen, "that he measures in inches, not thousandths." John built his guns from rough sketches, not blueprints. Winchester money helped the Browning brothers erect a new two-story retail store on Ogden's Main Street. In the back, John whistled as he worked, falling silent whenever a problem appeared. He tested prototypes at home, in wife Rachel's weak, unpracticed hands.

During their 20-year association, Bennett bought 44 of John Browning's patents, apparently for his asking price, but with no royalties. Only 10 were manufactured as Winchester guns. Among the gems was the pump shotgun that Bennett had at first declined. Introduced as Winchester's Model 1893, it later became the Model 1897, a gun that at once swept past all competition and stayed in production for 60 years. Another smash hit was the Model 1890 .22 pump rifle, which John had proposed by mailing sketches to Winchester engineers. Nobody liked the design, but John built the gun anyway, shipping it east with a note: "You said it wouldn't work, but it seems to shoot pretty fair for me."

Bennett, who was Oliver Winchester's son-in-law, voted the stock of Winchester's wife and two daughters and ran the company as he pleased. He often paid for designs he couldn't use, just to keep them from competitors. Browning's genius amazed him. Once, he asked

John for a lever action to replace the Model 1873—something like the 1886 but smaller, for short cartridges. "If you get me a prototype in three months, I'll pay $10,000," said Bennett. "Make it two months, and it's worth $15,000."

John Browning sat silent for a couple of minutes. Then he looked Bennett in the eye and said, "The price is $20,000 if I can deliver it in 30 days. If I'm late, you get it free." Incredulous, Bennett agreed. Within two weeks, John and his brothers had built a prototype for what would become the Winchester Model 92.

Because Browning's rifles were strong, the change from black to smokeless powder was often as easy as switching to barrels of high-tensile steel. The famous Model 1894 originally came only in .32-40 and .38-55. The smokeless .30-30 arrived soon after its debut—no redesign necessary. John found his next challenge at a local shooting match, where he watched grass in front of a prone marksman flattened by the muzzle blast. Why not harness that energy? thought John. At home he strapped an 1873 Winchester to a board, then placed a wooden block a quarter inch from the muzzle. The block's center was drilled to allow passage of the bullet, so any movement of the block had to come from escaping powder gas. At the shot, the block flew violently into the shop wall. Automatic fire was indeed possible.

The Greeks had built machines that launched arrows in quick succession, and multiple-barrel guns dated to the Middle Ages. Dr. R. J. Gatling of Indianapolis had devised a six-barrel, crank-operated repeater just before the Civil War. But no gun John knew about would cycle itself. By November 1890, he'd filed for a patent on an "automatic machine gun." He tried selling it to Colt, perhaps because Colt had built all U.S.-made Gatling guns since 1866. Colt was skeptical, but John's reputation earned him an audience.

The contraption John and Matt lifted out of brown paper in Hartford didn't look impressive, but when John pressed the trigger, 200 rounds chattered through the gun in seconds. The Gatling could be fired faster, but Browning's machine gun needed only one pull of the trigger, not continuous cranking. At just 40 pounds, it weighed half as much as the Gatling. When Colt's president John Hall suggested submitting it for military trials, the Brownings hesitated. These tests called for three minutes of sustained fire—a deck-raking burst, by navy definition. That meant 1,800 rounds of .45-70s, and 1,800 hand-stitched loops in feed belts. John turned to an Ogden tent maker for the belts, then loaded them carefully by hand. Later, back in the Hartford test

Young John Browning and his brothers Matt, Ed, Sam, and George, with help from Frank Rushton, established what they called the biggest gunshop between Omaha and the Pacific.

tunnel, John triggered a prolonged burst that heated the barrel red. The last bullets melted in their passage down the bore, spewing a blue mist. But there was not a single malfunction.

John Browning was the toast of Hartford. He continued his work with automatic guns and by 1910 had designed the Browning water-cooled machine gun. The United States' entry into World War I hurried testing. On test day, John loaded an ammunition belt and pressed the trigger. After he'd fired 20,000 rounds with no malfunction, he immediately rattled off 20,000 more cartridges. The audience stood spellbound as he unpacked a second machine gun, just to show that the first had no special tuning. John held the trigger for 48 minutes and 12 seconds, while his gun roared nonstop.

The Browning automatic rifle (BAR) came next. The BAR provided "walking fire" for infantry. Its cyclic rate of 480 .30-06 rounds per minute could empty the twenty-shot magazine in three seconds. Still, it was a simple mechanism, with just 70 parts. It would shoot its way through World War II and Korea. John got $750,000 from the U.S. government for manufacturing rights to the machine gun, the BAR, and a pistol he designed for Colt: the 1911. He could have sold them privately for $12 million.

In both world wars and Korea, every U.S. machine gun—land, sea, and air—would borrow from a Browning patent. After German field marshal Hermann Göring examined 50-caliber Brownings seized by Rommel in Tobruk, he sighed, "If we'd had these, the Battle of Britain would have turned out differently."

John Moses Browning died in 1926, at age 71, while checking production of his autoloading shotgun on his sixty-first visit to Belgium's FN plant. The military ceremonies that followed honored a man whose genius had garnered 128 patents for 80 distinct firearms. No gun designer has been as prolific. No other has proven so able to fashion, without blueprints, simple parts to perform complex functions. From single-shots to pump- and lever-action rifles to autoloading shotguns and pistols, John M. Browning built guns that broke traditions. His brilliant designs extended the reach and increased the effectiveness of the American shooter.

Stretching the Range in the Twentieth Century

If there's anybody down there who understands these guns better than I do, send him up, and I'll go home.
—John M. Browning, 1918 (insisting that he approve the manufacture of parts he had designed)

CHARLES NEWTON: RIFLES AHEAD OF THEIR TIME

Charles Newton hailed from the nineteenth century but quickly abandoned it for the twentieth. Born in Delavan, New York, on January 8, 1870, Charles worked on his father's farm until finishing school at age 16. He taught school for two years, then applied his quick mind to the study of law. He was admitted to the state bar at age 26, but his passion was not for the courtroom. After a six-year stint in the New York National Guard, Newton devoted his spare time to firearms and to high-performance cartridges using the then-new smokeless powders. His early association with Fred Adolph may have prompted Newton to turn his full attention to designing rifles and cartridges.

An accomplished German riflesmith, Adolph immigrated to the United States in 1908 and established a gun shop in Genoa, New York. By 1914, he had published a catalog listing a variety of sporting rifles, shotguns, and combination guns. Some were no doubt imported; others he built. Adolph distinguished his business by chambering powerful, high-velocity cartridges, among them at least ten designed by Charles Newton. The smallest but perhaps the best known was the

.22 High Power. A 1905 development, it derived from the .25-35 case and drove a 70-grain .228 bullet 2,800 feet per second (fps). The "Imp" built a bigger-than-life reputation on game as formidable as tigers. More realistically, it proved a stellar match for white-tailed deer. It inspired shooters to think of reaching beyond traditional ranges imposed by iron sights and flat-nosed bullets.

In 1912 the talented Newton experimented seriously with the .25-06, calling it the .25 Newton Special. Another of his cartridges, the 7mm Special, foreshadowed the .280 Remington by half a century (as did the 7x64 Brenneke developed across the Atlantic at roughly the same time). Also in 1912, Newton developed for Savage a short rimless .25, the .250-3000. It followed the .22 High Power as a new offering for the Model 99 lever-action rifle. Savage noted in ads that it launched an 87-grain bullet at 3,000 fps—a rocket in those days. Newton himself apparently preferred a 100-grain bullet at 2,800 fps.

The prolific designer came up with a .22 Long Range pistol cartridge by shortening and necking down the .28-30 Stevens. The bullet was the same .228 jacketed spitzer loaded in the .22 High Power. He fashioned his .22 Newton from the 7x57 case, driving a 90-grain bullet at 3,100 fps from a barrel with 1:8 twist. The .22 Special, formed from .30-40 Krag brass, launched a 68-grain bullet at nearly 3,300 fps.

Feeding a passion for single-shot rifles, Charles Newton experimented with big rimmed cases such as the .405 Winchester, necking it down to 7mm and even 25 caliber. He designed .30, 8mm, and .35 Express cartridges from the $3^1/_4$-inch Sharps hull, a .40 Express from the .40-110-$3^1/_4$ Winchester, and even a .45 Express from the .45-125-$3^1/_4$ Winchester. With Fred Adolph, Newton formed the .30 Adolph Express from a rimless case with the capacity of the .404 Jeffery. The rimless .30 Newton had the profile of modern belted .30 short magnums. It delivered more punch than hunters of the day considered appropriate for most North American game. The .35 Newton and various other rimless and rebated cartridges inspired by the .404 case appeared around 1910. The parent hull for many of Newton's later big-bore rounds may have been the 11.2x72 Schuler, a round that postdated World War I. Experimental Newton cartridges included a rimless .280 and .33, neither of which got past token production; nor did the .400, a necked-up .35. The .276, fashioned after an experimental British military cartridge, apparently saw no commercial manufacture.

Perhaps the most significant of Newton's many early cartridges was a 6.5mm-06. Despite its .264 bullets, it appeared as the .256

Newton. Ballistically, it mimicked the .257 Roberts Improved. Newton had two reasons for pursuing an alternative to the .25-06. First, .25-06 chambers cut by gunsmiths of the day varied in dimension. Tight chambers hiked pressures, and Newton did not want to be linked to rifles that fell apart. Second, although no commercial U.S.-made ammunition then featured 6.5mm bullets (and wouldn't until the .264 Winchester Magnum appeared in 1959), Mauser routinely bored and rifled 6.5mm barrels.

Early in his career as a cartridge designer, Newton dreamed of producing his own rifles. In 1914 he formed the Newton Arms Company in Buffalo, New York. While a new factory was under construction there, Newton traveled to Germany to contract for a supply of rifles from the likes of Mauser and J. P. Sauer & Sohn. His intent was to restock these rifles and rebarrel them as the .256 Newton and .30 Adolph Express. In the August 27, 1914, issue of *Arms and the Man* magazine, Newton advertised high-quality Mauser rifles. A concurrent flyer hawked .256 Newton barrels "of the best Krupp steel" with raised, matted ribs and sight slots—for $17. In March 1915 the first Newton rifles appeared in a company catalog. Built on 98 Mauser actions, they wore barrels chambered in .256, .30, and .35 Newton, plus hunting-style stocks designed by Adolph and noted California gunsmith Ludwig Wundhammer (namesake of the "Wundhammer swell" on the grips of many European stocks even now). They came in three grades:

> Grade A: DWM Mauser in .30, 8mm, or .35 Express for $42.50; or in .33 or .40 for $62.50.
> Grade B: DWM Mauser in .256, .30, 8mm, or .35 Express for $55; or in .33 or .40 for $75 (double-set trigger $2.50 extra).
> Grade C: Sauer Mauser with double-set trigger, half-octagon barrel, matted rib in .30, 8mm, or .35 Express for $60; or in .33 or .40 for $80.

Charles Newton's biggest problem in this venture was the war. His timing could hardly have been worse. The first two dozen Mauser rifles were to arrive August 15, 1914, and Germany went to war August 14. Apparently, one shipment of Mausers did arrive at the Buffalo plant before hostilities ended commerce.

When the Great War choked off his promised supply of Mauser rifles, Newton turned to the Marlin Firearms Company for barrels chambered in .256 Newton and threaded for 1903 Springfields. He

Dan O'Connell handloads for the .256 Newton, a cartridge much like the .257 Roberts Improved.

planned to sell them for $12.50 as replacements to hunters who wanted something other than a .30-06. He also contracted for Springfield sporter stocks. But rifles and components were in short supply during the war, and all plants capable of rifle production were fulfilling lucrative government contracts.

Though Charles Newton had to sit on his hands, he didn't stop thinking. By 1916, he'd incorporated desirable features of the Mauser and Springfield designs into a rifle whose only nonoriginal part was the mainspring. He hired lengendary barrel maker Harry Pope to oversee barrel production, and pointed out in the fourteenth Newton catalog that Pope had helped him develop the segmented rifling in Newton barrels. Such rifling comprised five grooves, cut with a tool whose radius was a trifle smaller than that of the bore.

The first of Newton's new rifles went on sale January 1, 1917, and they got favorable press. Once more, though, the timing was wrong. The United States entered the war on April 6, and the government took immediate control of all cartridge production. Although Newton was loading his own ammo, he depended on Remington for cases. Without cases, there was no ammunition—and no market for Newton rifles. Newton scrambled to get the tooling to make cartridge components

Kent "Buzz" Fletcher built this Mauser in Newton-period style and barreled it to .256 Newton.

from scratch, and by January 1918, ammo was coming off the line. But the banks that had carried the firm sent it into receivership, and by the end of the year, the Newton Arms Company was no more. In total, about 2,400 rifles had been produced, and another 1,600 were completed by Bert Holmes, who acquired all the company's assets. Only a quarter of this latter group passed inspection, however; Holmes sold more than 1,000 rifles for $5 each before giving up trying to run the plant himself.

In April 1919 New York machinery dealers Lamberg, Schwartz, and Land formed the Newton Arms Corporation. Their plan was to market as genuine Newtons several binloads of poor-quality rifles they had bought from Bert Holmes. Charles Newton filed suit. Though the case was not heard until June 1920, Newton won on every count. A month later, the Newton Arms Corporation went bankrupt. Charles, meanwhile, had marshaled his assets. On April 19, 1919, he had launched the Chas. Newton Rifle Corporation, with a plan to equip a new factory with surplus tooling from Eddystone Arsenal. He had already cataloged a Mauser with Newton improvements and in Newton chamberings, listing it for $66. He offered .30-06 and .256 Newton

Dan O'Connell, a .25-06 fan, finds a lot to like in the octogenarian .256 Newton (really a .264).

cartridges at $9.50 per 100, .30 Newton rounds for $11 per 100, and .35s for $12 per 100.

Nothing came of the Eddystone deal. The only rifles sold by the Chas. Newton Rifle Corporation were commercial Mausers. They had butterknife bolt handles, double-set triggers, and triple-leaf sights. Some had parabolic rifling, and some had a cloverleaf of muzzle grooves to release gas evenly and prevent bullet tipping. The Newton stocks added appeal, and about 1,000 orders came in. But, Germany's overheated postwar economy could not supply that many rifles under the terms of the contract, and only about 100 arrived in the States.

Ever optimistic, Charles Newton began anew in 1923 with Arthur Dayton and Dayton Evans, two men who had helped him bankroll his 1919 venture. The Buffalo Newton Rifle Corporation was established in Buffalo, New York, but soon moved to New Haven, Connecticut, where the first Buffalo Newton rifles were shipped in 1924. They wore four-groove nickel-steel barrels in .30-06 and four Newton chamberings: .256, .280, .30, and .35. Actions of chrome-vanadium steel boasted interrupted-thread locking lugs. Stocks were of checkered walnut with a quarter-inch castoff. They had a crossbolt behind the magazine well

Charles Newton developed the .250 Savage round for early Model 99s. This rifle still turns up afield.

to absorb recoil, but no recoil lug under the receiver ring. Predictably, many stocks on Buffalo Newton rifles split. The Western Cartridge Company began supplying Newton rounds in 1921.

Money had again become scarce for Newton. After borrowing on his life insurance, he pleaded with Marlin to build his rifles under contract. Marlin's Frank Kenna demurred, despite Newton's insistence that his company was on the brink of success and that, at a rate of 1,000 rifles per month, it could build rifles for $8 each. Buffalo Newtons then retailed for $60.

The Buffalo Newton Rifle Corporation folded in 1929, after producing about 1,500 rifles. With characteristic zeal, Newton applied himself to another action design and came up with the New Newton Straight Pull Rifle. Its two-lug bolt and Springfield cocking piece suggested bolt-action ancestry, but Newton had also borrowed from the straight-pull Lee Navy and Winchester lever-action designs. In fact, Newton renamed the rifle the Leverbolt—no doubt to appeal to the legions of lever-action shooters afield. Again, he asked Frank Kenna for assistance. If Marlin would produce the rifle, said Newton, he'd split the profits down the middle. Kenna, a shrewd businessman, required proof of demand. Newton responded with a flyer that asked sportsmen for a $25 down payment on a new Leverbolt rifle. The remaining $35 would be due when the rifle was delivered. But even this offer failed to bring the necessary 500 orders.

In October, Wall Street collapsed, taking with it Newton's dreams and those of a nation. Charles Newton had nothing left to resurrect. Even his irrepressible spirit could not surmount the Depression. He died at his home in New Haven on March 9, 1932, at the age of 62.

Charles Newton's work with high-performance cartridges set the stage for the post–World War II debut of short-belted magnums. Although the .25-06 round is generally credited to Neidner, it's likely that Newton fired it first. A generation before Roy Weatherby, Newton had big-game bullets clocking well over 3,000 fps. He also developed features for bolt-action rifles that made them easier to operate and better able to bottle the pressures generated by long-range, high-octane cartridges. Hunters familiar with the three-position safety of the Winchester Model 70 may not be aware that Charles Newton put a similar safety on rifles 20 years before the Model 70 appeared. Newton's interrupted-thread locking lugs predated the Weatherby Mark V bolt by 30 years. This lawyer-turned-inventor also designed handloading tools and fashioned a partition-style bullet in 1915. While most jackets were of cupronickel, he employed almost pure copper, like many of today's controlled-expansion bullets.

Alas, Charles Newton's brilliance as an architect of rifles and cartridges, and his perseverance in bringing them to riflemen, earned him few rewards. Luck doesn't always favor the most deserving.[*]

BIRTH OF THE RIFLEMAN'S RIFLE

By the close of the nineteenth century, John Browning had fashioned for Winchester several rifles and shotguns that became hugely popular. The falling out between Browning and Winchester's Thomas Bennett left New Haven on its own. For some time after the Great War, designers there had almost no budget, but that didn't deter engineers in their quest for a successful centerfire bolt rifle. When, after 30 years of trying, they came up with the Model 54 in 1924, the scotch must have flowed. Engineers borrowed the 1903 Springfield's coned breech, the Newton's ejector, and the Mauser's beefy extractor. The stock was patterned after popular Sedgely sporters. A nickel-steel barrel on a cyanide-hardened receiver bottled pressure from a new .270 WCF cartridge, whose 130-grain bullet at 3,000 fps awed hunters used to .30-30s. The Model 54 cost more than a surplus military rifle but less than a Griffin & Howe. Though it never earned the accolades given the earlier Model 94 or the later Model 70, Winchester's Model 54 appeared at a pivotal time. The Springfield had demonstrated the potential of bolt rifles and high-octane cartridges; in the 54, Winchester sold a nimble, lightweight package that shot flat.

The Depression brought Winchester to its knees. In December 1931, after bankruptcy, the venerable firm was acquired by the Western Cartridge Company for $3 million cash and $4.8 million in Western stock. Franklin Olin's son, John, took the reins. In the next decade he would bring 23 new Winchester guns to market.

Western kept the 54 alive, allowing T. C. Johnson and his staff to refine the rifle they had engineered. The Model 54's enduring flaw was a trigger that also served as a bolt stop. Target shooters wanted better. Hunters balked at the high-swing safety, which interfered with low-mounted scopes. On December 29, 1934, Winchester started work on an improved bolt rifle. The Model 70 came to market slowly; indeed, the Model 54 remained in Winchester's catalog until 1941. With people

---

[*] The authoritative book from which much of this information came is titled *Charles Newton, Father of High Velocity,* by Newton rifle enthusiast Bruce Jennings Jr. of Sheridan, Wyoming.

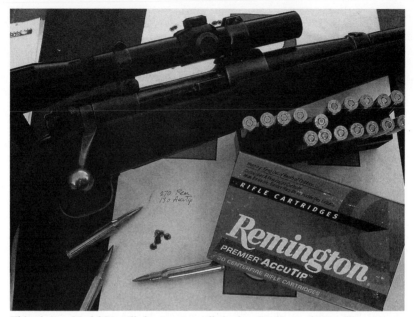

This vintage Model 70 still shoots very well. So does Remington's AccuTip ammunition, introduced six decades later.

still eating in soup kitchens, demand for a new hunting rifle was limited. On January 20, 1936, the first Model 70 receivers got serial numbers, but it wasn't until January 1, 1937, that Winchester announced the official release of 2,238 rifles.

The Model 70's barrel and receiver looked like the Model 54's, but the separate sear permitted trigger adjustment for takeup, weight, and overtravel. The bolt stop was also separate. To eliminate misfires—too common with the 54's speed lock—striker travel on the Model 70 was increased $1/16$ inch. The first Model 70 safety was a tab on top of the bolt shroud; later this would be redesigned as a side-swing tab with a middle detent that blocked the striker while permitting bolt manipulation. Instead of a stamped, fixed magazine cover and guard, the 70 wore a hinged floorplate secured by a spring-loaded plunger in the separate trigger guard.

Model 70 barrels were drop-forged, straightened by hand with a 15-pound hammer, then turned true on a lathe. They were deep-hole-drilled, then straightened again. Bores were then reamed and hook-rifled by a cutter slicing progressively deeper on several passes, one groove at a time. Model 70 receivers were machined from bar stock, each beginning as a 7 1/2-pound chrome-moly billet. After 75 machinings, a finished receiver weighed 19.3 ounces. Spot-hardening the extraction cam behind the bridge preceded a full heat treatment. Each finished receiver spent 24 hours in a 1,200-degree salt bath to test 47C on the Rockwell scale. The test left a dimple in the tang. Most small parts were drop-forged, then machined. The extractor was fashioned from 1095 spring steel.

The Model 70's stocks were roughed by bandsaw from 2-by-36-inch black walnut, then went eight at a time to the duplicator for contouring. Final inletting was done by hand. The first stocks got a nitrocellulose lacquer over stain before checkering. Because the lacquers contained carnauba wax, they produced an oil-like finish. When the war drained supplies of carnauba wax, harder lacquers appeared.

The first Model 70s came in .22 Hornet, .220 Swift, .250-3000 Savage, .257 Roberts, .270 WCF, 7mm Mauser, and .30-06, plus .300 and .375 H&H. All were built on the same magnum-length receiver, which was machined to accommodate cartridges of various lengths; the magazines, bolt stops, and even bolts were modified to fit the cartridge. Between 1941 and 1963, nine more chamberings were added. Model 70s in .300 Savage appeared in limited numbers but were never cataloged. In the 1950s and early 1960s, the rifle was bored for short-belted magnums and rounds based on the .308 Winchester. Eventually, "pre-64" Model 70s would come in 29 basic styles and 48 subconfigurations. The list price in 1937 was $61.25.

Long-range target shooters found the Target and heavier Bull models competitive at any match. To this day, many riflemen consider prewar versions of these paper punchers to be the best bolt-action rifles ever produced for 600- and 1,000-yard shooting. Hunters wanting long reach chose the .300 H&H, the only early Model 70 in a big-game chambering that wore a 26-inch barrel. In 1959 the .264 Magnum was also barreled with a 26-inch tube.

A cartridge with more promise than was ever realized, the .264 "makes a helluva noise and packs a helluva wallop," according to an early magazine ad showing a close-up of the Model 70 muzzle. Called the Westerner in this chambering only, the rifle balanced well and looked good; the long barrel was a fitting complement to a stock that had too much forend for barrels shorter than 24 inches. But Winchester's bid to curry favor among hunters in the Rockies was poorly engineered. Instead of promoting the new .264 Magnum as a combination deer and elk cartridge with great reach, and courting the whitetail

The author fires a custom bolt gun by Hill Country Rifles. It is built on a stainless Model 70 action and chambered in .270 WSM.

The Montana Rifles action is new, but in most respects, this Model 1999 rifle in .257 Roberts is a dead ringer for a Model 70.

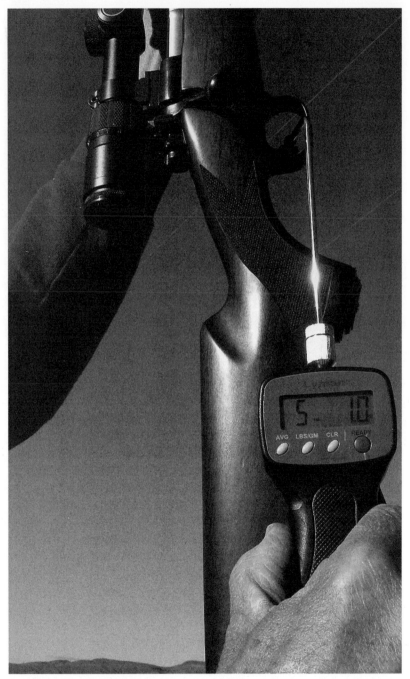

The Model 70 has a sturdy, tunable trigger. Unfortunately, factory rifles now come with very heavy trigger pulls.

This Winchester Model 70 Featherweight is a current model. The stock design is widely admired.

hunter who shot across acres of corn stubble and alfalfa, the ads hawked a varmint-deer cartridge. Loading a 100-grain bullet to a chart speed of 3,700 fps, and a 140 to 3,200, Winchester viewed the round as ideal for woodchucks and coyotes, mule deer and pronghorns. But eastern hunters didn't need so much power to anchor a woodchuck, and they didn't appreciate the .264's noise or recoil. Western hunters wouldn't buy a coyote gun that used costly magnum ammunition and handled like a salmon rod in a pickup cab. Besides, coyotes were mainly incidental game, and they were shot with deer rifles.

On the plains and in the mountains of the West, the .270 was tough competition for any new long-range deer round. When gun scribes wrote that the .264 was essentially a noisy .270 that ate barrels, the cartridge took a bruising. When, three years later, Remington's 7mm Magnum appeared, its fate was sealed. With Winchester's later decision to list factory-loaded 140-grain .264 bullets at 3,030 fps—30 fps below 130-grain .270 velocity—all hope for revival vaporized.

Remington got it right with its 7mm Magnum, a cartridge with essentially the same case as the .264's. There's just .020 difference in bullet diameter: .264 versus .284. But Remington loaded its new

Scoped with a high-power Zeiss, this Model 70 in 7mm Remington Magnum is a fine open-country rifle.

round with 150- and 175-grain softpoints and advertised it as a general-purpose choice for big game, from antelope to elk. This notion played well with hunters who spent lots of time and money chasing big antlers. They didn't own or plan to buy a coyote rifle, but they flocked to see a new cartridge that would shoot harder than a .30-06 and flatter than a .270, yet with little additional recoil. Remington wisely decided to emphasize the 7mm's civility, instead of playing to hunters who equated blast with testosterone. Shooters also liked the Model 700 rifle, which had just replaced the plain 721 and 722. The 700's 24-inch barrel was handier than the 26-inch Westerner's.

Winchester's Model 70 lost some market share to the 700, in part because 70s had become less attractive since the mid-1950s. Poor-quality wood with coarser checkering in reduced patterns and shabby wood-to-metal fit irritated shooters with older Winchesters in their collections. At the same time, factory labor costs were escalating, and the Model 70 had become significantly less profitable. In 1960 company accountants insisted on an overhaul. Engineers identified 50 changes, which were implemented in 1963. Model 70 fans were incensed. The new stock wore crude, pressed checkering; barrel channel gaps yawned wide enough to swallow hamsters. A tiny hook extractor replaced the stout Mauser claw. Machined steel bottom metal was

Charlie Sisk barreled this Model 70 in .450 Marlin and fitted XS sights. The author insisted on a red synthetic stock from High Tech.

supplanted by aluminum, solid action pins were replaced by roll pins, and the bolt stop's coil spring was set aside in favor of music wire. A red cocking indicator stuck out like a tongue from under the bolt shroud. To many shooters, this was no longer the rifleman's rifle. Prices of pre-64 Model 70s rose sharply; new rifles languished on dealers' racks.

Winchester improved the new Model 70 with an antibind bolt in 1966, a classier stock in 1972, and a sleek featherweight profile in 1980. A short-action Model 70 came in 1984. Three years later, Winchester reintroduced the Mauser claw extractor on custom-shop 70s, and three years after that, a Classic version with controlled-round feed entered the line. Current Model 70s are accurate, attractive, and dependable. New Haven accountants still ponder profits, but they've apparently learned that no matter how much money you save in manufacture, you don't make any money if rifles don't sell.

Pre-64 Model 70s in excellent condition command a premium from collectors, and hunters still covet even well-used specimens. Still, recent Model 70s shoot as accurately and are in some ways superior to the first generation of Winchester's famous bolt rifles. Synthetic stocks

Long shots are common in Utah elk country. A Model 70 in .300 WSM shoots flat and hits hard.

make them more durable and less likely to shift point of impact in wet weather. Currently, Winchester lists 15 versions of the Model 70, a dozen of them with a Mauser-style extractor that controls the cartridge from magazine to chamber. Of the 19 chamberings available, the most newsworthy at this writing are the Winchester Short Magnums— .270, 7mm, .300, and .325—and Winchester Super Short Magnums— .223, .243, and .25. These squat, rimless alternatives to the belted

The Remington 700 is the heart of many super-accurate custom rifles, like this one by Dave Smith.

magnums of the 1950s and 1960s offer flat flight from rifles with compact actions.*

REMINGTON: ARTILLERY FOR THE WORKING CLASS

Development of long-range bolt rifles at Remington dates back a century and a half. By the late 1840s, E. Remington & Sons was producing for government arsenals and had acquired the services of designers William Jenks and Fordyce Beals. Manufacturing contracts for the Jenks breech-loading navy carbine went to Remington. In 1846 Lite Remington adapted Eli Whitney's mass production ideas to the manufacture of interchangeable parts for Model 1841 military rifles.

Remington designer Joseph Rider had patented a split-breech carbine late in 1863, contributing to the company's wartime fortunes. It was refined to become the rolling block, a sturdy hunting rifle that would also earn fame on the target range. The first match rifle, a .44-90 shooting 550-grain conical bullets, came off the line in March 1874. On September 26, a favored Irish team shooting muzzleloaders bowed to the Americans and their new Remington and Sharps breechloaders.

---

* In March 2006, U.S. Repeating Arms closed its New Haven manufacturing plant, halting production of the Winchester M70 and M94 rifles and the M1300 shotgun. The closure, which followed a long-term decline in profitability, dismayed M70 enthusiasts. But clones of the M70 exist; many shooters expect a resurrection of the name and the rifle.

KILLED AT ONE SHOT BY MRS. A. G. WALLIHAN, CRAIG, COLO.

A .40-70 Remington-Hepburn killed both these bucks with one bullet. The hunter was Augusta Wallihan, pioneer woman in northwestern Colorado.

Remington Creedmoor rifles posted the highest scores. Any shooter could buy one, complete with windgauge vernier sight, for $108. It was the deluxe version of Remington-Hepburn rifles used on the frontier by the likes of Augusta Wallihan, wife of noted photographer A. G. Wallihan of Colorado. Her .40-70 once killed two mule deer with a single bullet.

Military and commercial orders for rolling blocks came from all over the world. But when the 1873 Winchester appeared, Remington shifted its focus to repeaters. John Keene, a New Jersey inventor, had designed a tube-fed bolt-action magazine rifle bored to .45-70. But the army rejected it in 1881 trials, and Remington made relatively few copies of this, its first bolt rifle, before falling into receivership in 1886.

The company's financial woes during this era were only partly due to the Keene's flagging sales. Remington had diversified beyond reason and, despite the success of its sewing machines, suffered from high overhead and poor investments. Heavy reliance on military contracts left tooling idle in peacetime. Hartley and Graham, a New York firm that also owned giant Union Metallic Cartridge Company, bought E. Remington & Sons. The first military contract after this deal was for the bolt-action Remington-Lee Model 1885 Navy Box Magazine Rifle, invented by James Lee. The first sporting version, a Model 1899, didn't reach the market until Winchester's controlling interest in Remington

(1888 to 1896) ended. Remington-Lee sporters were offered in 7x57, 7.35 Belgium Mauser, .236 Remington, .30-30 Winchester, and .30-40 Krag.

These rifles were dropped in 1909, and 12 years later Remington announced a new bolt-action for hunters. The 30S derived from the 1917 Enfield, which Remington had produced on contract during the Great War. Heavy and expensive, the 30S sold poorly. In 1926 it was replaced by the Model 30 Express, offered not only in .30-06 but also in .25, .30, .32, and .35 Remington—all developed for pump guns. The 30 Express cocked on opening and had a lighter trigger pull. A slim stock and 22-inch barrel reduced its weight to just over 7 pounds. Priced at $45.75, the 30 Express also came in Deluxe and Carbine models. In 1931 the 7x57 was chambered; five years later came the .257 Remington-Roberts. The last 30 Express got serial-stamped in 1940.

The Model 720 High Power Rifle, developed by Oliver Loomis and A. H. Lowe to replace the 30 Express, had a short life. Its 1941 debut, in .30-06, .270, and .257 Roberts, amounted to only 4,000 units before Remington's production shifted to military hardware. In fact, the navy acquired many of the first 720s. Those not issued during World War II were presented, beginning in 1964, as marksmanship trophies by the U.S. Navy and Marine Corps. Remington manufactured many thousands of 1903 and (beginning in 1942) 1903A3 Springfields in a wartime effort that all but canceled the manufacture of sporting guns at the Ilion, New York, plant. Just before adoption of the M1C Garand Sniper rifle, Remington delivered 28,365 Model 1903A4s—the first mass-produced run of U.S. sniper rifles.

Rather than resume manufacture of Model 720 bolt-action rifles at war's end, Remington adopted a new design by engineers Merle "Mike" Walker and Homer Young. Walker, a benchrest shooter, insisted on an accurate rifle; accountants demanded a low price. The Model 721 and short-action 722 appeared early in 1948, with receivers cut from cylindrical tubing. A clip-ring extractor, washer-type recoil lug, stamped bottom metal, and self-contained trigger assembly helped pare costs. The stiff receiver enhanced accuracy. A bolt head shroud added support to the case and security in the event of case rupture. The 721 in .270 and .30-06 sold for $79.95; the 722 in .257 Roberts and .300 Savage cost $5 less. All wore 24-inch barrels. In 1949 the .300 H&H was added to 721 chamberings. A quarter pound heavier than its siblings, it weighed $8^1/2$ pounds with a 26-inch barrel and retailed for $89.95. In 1960 the .280 Remington was offered in the 721; the .264 Winchester Magnum followed a year later. The 722 would eventually

Remington's Model 700 came out in 1962. This .30-06 dates to the mid-1960s, as does its Weaver K-4.

come in .222 Remington (1950), .244 Remington and .308 Winchester (1956), .222 Remington Magnum (1958), and .243 Winchester (1959).

Hunters found the 721/722 functional, if homely. Plain, uncheckedered stocks did not compare well with the checkered walnut of early postwar Model 70 Winchesters. High-grade AC and B versions of both Remington rifles offered cosmetic improvements. These designations were replaced in 1955 with ADL and BDL.

Remington designers Wayne Leek and Charlie Campbell came up with an even better looking rifle in 1958. Called the Model 725, it featured 721/722 receivers but with a hinged floorplate, checkered walnut, hooded front, and adjustable open rear sights. A 22-inch barrel came standard on initial offerings in .270, .280, and .30-06, and also in .244 (1959) and .243 (1960). The .222 (1959) got a 24-inch tube. During 1961 and 1962, Remington's Custom Shop built a Kodiak Model 725. Chambered in .375 and .458 Magnum, it wore a 26-inch barrel and built-in muzzle brake. Just 52 of these 9-pound rifles left the factory. They retailed for $310, about the same price as Winchester's Model 70 African.

Three years before the 725 appeared, Remington had introduced the 40X to replace the expensive Model 37 .22 target rifle. The 40X was a single-shot design but included features from the 721/722. The centerfire version arrived in 1959, barreled to .308. In 1960 Remington added the .222, .222 Magnum, .30-06, and .300 H&H Magnum. Free Rifle variations followed, with 2-ounce and half-ounce triggers.

Remington's most successful bolt-action rifle of the century arrived in 1962. The Model 700 drew heavily from the 721/722 design—in fact, the basic mechanism was the same. Early advertising pointed up the 700's strength: "three rings of steel" (the bolt shroud, chamber wall, and receiver ring) supporting the cartridge head. But the trimmer tang, swept bolt with checkered knob, cast (not stamped) bottom metal, and more appealing stock pulled shooters to the cash registers too. A big assist came from Remington's brand-new 7mm Magnum cartridge, which offered the reach of a .300 H&H Magnum with less recoil. It was one of two magnum rounds listed for the Model 700's initial run. The other, oddly enough, was Winchester's similar but less ably promoted .264. Both these rifles came with 24-inch barrels, as did the .222 and .222 Magnum. A 20-inch barrel was standard for the .243, .270, .280, .308, and .30-06 (all at $114.95). Two action lengths accommodated this wide range of cartridges, which later expanded to include almost every modern hunting round. The list of discontinued Model 700 chamberings is longer than the list of current offerings in many rifles.

Cataloged in ADL and BDL versions, the first 700s had blind magazines and hinged floorplates, respectively. In 1969 Remington jeweled the unblued portion of the bolt and installed a longer rear bolt shroud. A restyled stock wore a buttplate of black plastic instead of anodized alloy. Pressed checkering got its first overhaul in 1969. Cut-checkering machines have since put more attractive, functional grip panels on 700 stocks. The quality of walnut, however, has slipped, because figured wood is now scarce and costly.

Over four decades, myriad versions of the Model 700 have appeared. Here are the milestones:

1965—Model 700C, a special-order high-grade rifle with fancy wood.

1967—Varmint Special, with a 24-inch barrel in .222, .223, .22-250, .243, and 6mm.

1973—Left-hand stock and bolt, in .270, .30-06, and 7mm Remington Magnum.

1978—Classic, with satin-finished, straight-comb stock, hinged floorplate, in .22-250, .243, 6mm, .270, .30-06, and 7mm Magnum. All were gone by 1986. Beginning in 1981, limited-edition Classics came in one chambering per year, for that year only.

The Model 710, a low-priced alternative to the 700, employs a radically different bolt mechanism.

1982—Safety alteration that locked the bolt down with the safety on to prevent accidental opening during carrying. Remington would later revert to the original safety for unloading with the safety on.

1984—Sportsman 78 rifle, a Spartan version of the Model 700, with uncheckered wood and metal and a blind magazine, in .270 and .30-06 (later .243, .308, and .223). The Sportsman 78 was dropped in 1989.

The Model 700 Classic has been offered since 1978, in one chambering a year from 1981 to 2005.

1986—Mountain Rifle, a 6³/₄-pound, walnut-stocked 700 with a slim 22-inch barrel. Chambered first in .270, .280, and .30-06, it came out as a short-action two years later, in .243, .308, and 7mm-08. The .257 Roberts was added in 1991; the .25-06 in 1992.

1987—Kit Guns, finished barreled actions with rough-shaped, inletted wood for do-it-yourselfers. Available in .243, .270, .308, .30-06, and 7mm Magnum, Kit Guns were discontinued in 1989.

1987—Rynite (RS) and fiberglass (FS) stocks—replaced in two years by lighter synthetic stocks.

1987—Left-hand stock and bolt in short-action rifles chambered for the .243 and .308.

1988—Laminated stock on the ADL/LS, first in .30-06; a year later, in .243, .270, and 7mm Magnum.

1992—Stainless Synthetic (SS) version of the BDL, with stainless barrel, receiver, and bolt, blind magazine, in .25-06, .270, .280, and .30-06, 7mm Remington, .300 and .338 Winchester, and .375 H&H Magnums.

1993—European 700 with oil-finished stock in .243, .270, 7-08, .280, .30-06, and 7mm Magnum.

1994—Varmint Synthetic Stainless Fluted (VS SF) with aluminum bedding block per an earlier VS model (1992), but with a heavy fluted barrel. Chamberings: .223, .22-250, .220 Swift, and .308.

The author shot this fine Colorado buck with a Remington 700 Titanium, a 5 1/2-pound rifle.

1994—Sendero Special with graphite composite stock, bedding block, heavy blued barrel (initially 24 inches, then 26). This rifle started out in .25-06, .270, 7mm Remington, and .300 Winchester Magnums.

1994—African Plains Rifle, with laminated straight-comb stock and 26-inch barrel, Custom Shop-built in five magnum calibers: 7mm Remington, .300 Winchester, .300 Weatherby, .338, and .375 H&H.

1994—Alaska Wilderness Rifle, with Kevlar-reinforced stock, stainless metal. This 6 3/4-pound Custom Shop rifle appeared with a 24-inch barrel in five magnum chamberings: 7mm, .300 Winchester, .300 Weatherby, .338, and .375 H&H. The 7mm STW was added in 1998.

1995—DM or Detachable Magazine versions of the BDL and Mountain rifle.

1996—Sendero SF, or stainless fluted, in .25-06, 7mm, and .300 Winchester Magnums (later 7mm STW and .300 Weatherby Magnum).

1996—MLS blackpowder "in-line" rifles on the 700 receiver, .45 and .50 with synthetic stock.

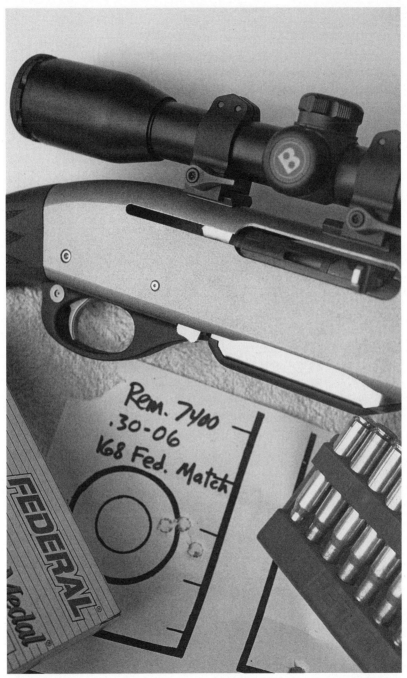

Autoloaders not accurate? This Remington 7400 begs to differ. It evolved from the 740 and 742.

An archetypal modern elk rifle: Remington 700 synthetic stainless, .300 Winchester Magnum, Leupold 3-9x.

1998—VS SF-P, with two ports on the muzzle to reduce jump and deliver an uninterrupted sight picture during recoil of this varmint rifle in .22-250, .220 Swift, and .308.

1998—Youth model with synthetic stock, 13-inch pull, in .243 and 308.

Beginning in 1966, Remington built 700s for military and police forces. Paul Gogol, a Remington engineer and Custom Shop foreman, designed a Marine Corps sniper rifle on a 40X action. Substituting the Model 700 action, Remington built 995 of these .308 M-40 sniper rifles for the Corps over six years. Many saw service in Vietnam. In 1986

Tad Woosley shot this magnificent Oregon ram with a Remington 700 .30-06. Range: 310 yards.

the U.S. Army approved a Model 700 SWS (Sniper Weapon System). It featured a long receiver, Kevlar-reinforced stock, and 24-inch stainless barrel. These rifles were deployed with a bipod and Leupold M3A 10x scope with rangefinding reticle. Remington has also supplied police agencies with a Model 700 Police Rifle in .223 and .308. It's fitted with a Leupold Vari-X III 3.5-10x scope and Harris bipod.

Not all introductions have been inspired. A 700 Etronx that fired specially primed cartridges with a battery-fired electronic impulse sold poorly and was dropped. But the 5 1/4-pound 700 Titanium is both easy to carry and exceedingly accurate. One of the latest chamberings is the 6.8mm SPC, developed jointly with the U.S. Army Marksmanship Training Unit on the .30 Remington case. In 2005 a 700 XCR (Extreme Conditions Rifle) and XR-100 Rangemaster rifle with laminated thumbhole stock joined a low-priced 700 SPS (Special Purpose Synthetic) and a left-hand version of the upscale CDL, just a year old.

Since the Model 700 appeared more than 40 years ago, other bolt rifles have emerged from Ilion, but none has come close to matching the Model 700 in sales. The catalog now lists 15 versions in 29 chamberings from .17 Remington to .375 Ultra Mag. Time-tested popularity, a distinctive profile, archetypal features, unquestioned reliability, and routinely excellent out-of-the-box accuracy describe this classic rifle.

4 Actions, Barrels, and Cartridges

It costs us several times as much to obtain the services of the world's greatest expert in this line as a superintendent, [but] every purchaser of a Newton rifle receives with it a Pope barrel. . . . Heretofore any one wanting a Pope barrel had to pay from $20 to $50 for it.

— Charles Newton, 1916 catalog

DETAILS AT THE BREECH

To talk intelligently about rifles, it's important to distinguish between *rifle* and *cartridge*. The rifle is a detonator and pressure-control device, with sights and a barrel to direct the bullet. The ballistic package belongs to the cartridge. "I shoot a .270" says almost nothing about your rifle; all you've described is the cartridge. You really mean, "My rifle is chambered in .270." Sometimes, numbers aren't enough; for example, there are many .300s. Regardless of chambering, rifle design affects your shooting success, especially at distance.

Identifying a rifle built for long-range target shooting is as easy now as it was in the eighteenth and nineteenth centuries. But the look is not the same. David Tubb, a competitor with many national rifle championships to his credit, uses a modular rifle of his own design. To the uninitiated, it might resemble a ray gun from a science fiction film. It differs a great deal from hunting rifles, because it needn't be lightweight or easily maneuvered in thickets. You don't have to shove target rifles in scabbards or get them into action quickly as you step over a log or shoot them with fingers stiff from cold.

A long-range hunting rifle is not easy to spot in a crowd. Deer rifles with accurate barrels bored for high-octane cartridges feature the same mechanisms as rifles chambered for short-range cartridges or whose barrels deliver only pie-plate precision. Gunsmithing that makes a tackdriver out of an ordinary rifle and adds hundreds of

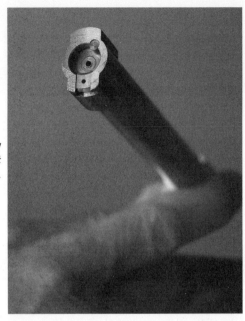

The Dakota Predator's fully enclosed, finely machined bolt face enhances accuracy.

dollars in cost is largely invisible on a hunting rifle. You can't tell if an action has been "trued," so that barrel threads and bolt face are concentric, or if the locking lugs have been lapped for full contact, or if the bolt face is square with the bore axis. You can't see pillar bedding or the alloy extension block that adds spine to a forend. There's no telling at a glance if a barrel is an air-gauged, match-quality tube or one mass-produced and sold to a maker of bargain-priced rifles for $20.

In addition to structural and dimensional refinements, the most accurate rifles have nonstandard parts. Most of these are commercially available and can be retrofitted to popular bolt rifles. David Tubb, for example, sells speed-lock kits for Remington, Ruger, Savage, Weatherby, and Winchester rifles, as well as Mauser 98s. It includes a lightweight alloy striker with a tip of heat-treated 4140 steel, plus a resilient spring made of "the same chrome-silicone alloy used in the manufacture of valve springs for Indy car engines." Those springs endure a million high-temperature compression cycles in one afternoon, so Tubb reasons that a chrome-silicone (CS) firing pin spring will serve a shooter for many years.

The term *speed-lock* dates to the 1920s, possibly earlier. Military rifles of the day were altered by gunsmiths to reduce lock time—the delay between sear release and ignition. Faster firing mechanisms for

A crisp trigger that breaks near 2 pounds is easy to squeeze without moving the rifle.

both target and sporting rifles ensued. Strong springs, lightweight strikers, and short striker travel kept lock times to a minimum. Still, the springs and strikers of modern rifles are supplied with an eye to cost as well as efficiency. In his Superior Shooting Systems catalog, Tubb notes that "flight time of most bullets through the barrel is 1.0 to 1.5 milliseconds, while the lock time of most conventional bolt action rifles varies between 2.6 and 9.0 milliseconds. . . . A SpeedLock Systems firing pin cuts lock time approximately 31 percent. Combined with a SpeedLock CS Spring, lock time is reduced another 8 percent."

That spring is important, insists Tubb. "When a factory Remington 700 firing pin spring has lost half an inch of free length, it has lost over 25 percent of its original power. This amount of set normally occurs in less than one year, even if the rifle is not used. The CS springs we supply are rated for 500,000 compressions with a loss of no more than a quarter inch." Because of its superior resiliency, the CS spring can be made lighter than ordinary springs, so it's faster. Because it's strong for its weight, it can be smaller in diameter, minimizing or eliminating contact (friction) with the bolt body.

Fast lock time means that the rifle releases the bullet before you can ruin the shot. Your body doesn't want to hold the rifle where it was

The success of a hunt can hinge on trigger control. A stiff trigger can move the rifle, causing a miss.

when you decided to pull the trigger. Muscle twitches and pulse have their way. The sight picture you remember when you took the last ounce from the trigger is temporary and can change before the bullet is out of the barrel. The faster the lock time, the less that picture changes during bullet acceleration in the bore. If you think lock time inconsequential, fire a flintlock rifle. Your hold must be solid, and follow-through continued into overtime, or you'll miss. The farther the target, the bigger the miss.

A rifle's trigger can affect intrinsic accuracy. Rough sear release sets up vibrations that disturb the barrel. Inconsistent trigger action imposes another variable. But by far the most egregious problems caused by triggers have to do with field accuracy. In other words, they are difficulties in trigger control.

You don't need an expensive, match-grade trigger to shoot well; exhibition shooters of years gone by made do just fine with inexpensive triggers from off-the-line sporting rifles. But these people shot a lot. They shot more in a month than many hunters these days will shoot in a lifetime. In 1907 Ad Topperwein uncrated 10 Winchester Model 1903 .22 rifles and 50,000 rounds of ammunition at the San Antonio fairgrounds. Shooting at hand-tossed wooden blocks

$2^1/_4$ inches square, he ran out of ammunition and targets in a few days, then was resupplied. Presumably, the lackeys tossing the blocks got a much-needed rest. Ad stepped to the line again and kept firing. He stopped after 72,500 targets—having missed just nine. His longest run without a miss was 14,900 targets. It was reported that Ad required help getting his arms to flex after this feat.

But this record would not go unmatched forever. Half a century later, Remington exhibition shooter Tom Frye collected 100,000 wooden blocks and a team of tossers. He no doubt appreciated the lighter weight of Remington's Nylon 66 .22 autoloader. Using several of these rifles, Frye missed only two of the first 43,725 blocks. He finished with 100,004 out of 100,010. An aged Topperwein wrote to congratulate him.

Given that much practice, you'd develop a measure of trigger control denied most shooters. You'd learn to deal with a heavy trigger, even a rough trigger. A trigger with an inconsistent pull would still be a challenge, but aim and hold honed by 100,000 shots would no doubt cover imperfections in the trigger. The thing to keep in mind is that triggers have not improved over the last century; they've become worse. Fear of litigation following accidental discharges has driven many makers to install rough, heavy triggers. They must pass stringent drop tests, not just resist the accidental brush of a coat sleeve. So the sear as well as the fingerpiece are designed to suffer fools. Unfortunately, they also make accurate shooting difficult. Even Frye and Topperwein would have trouble with some modern triggers. They'd surely wonder why bolt rifles with long-range potential have worse triggers than vintage .22 autoloaders built to bag rabbits at 50 yards.

Some bolt-action triggers have no adjustments. But most do, and if you want to get the most out of your trigger, you'll probably have to change the settings. This may mean tapping the skills of your local gunsmith. If you're uncomfortable with trigger work, that's certainly the best route. You can make a trigger unsafe with improper adjustment. The goal in adjusting a trigger is not to make it supersensitive; rather, it is to afford you better control. You want a smooth, consistent trigger with a breakweight light enough to permit a shot without undue disturbance to the rifle. The trigger should be heavy enough to withstand the pressure of a cold, gloved finger as you prepare to shoot, and secure enough when engaged to hold under the impact of a dropped rifle.

An adjustable trigger typically has three points of adjustment: overtravel, sear engagement, and weight of pull. Overtravel, or the

Weatherby's six-lug Mark V shoots small groups, thanks to solid design and accurate Krieger barrels.

movement of the trigger after it releases the sear, is least important. Some shooters prefer a trigger that gives the sensation of breaking without movement, so they reduce overtravel to a minimum. The problem here is that you can adjust out all trigger movement; the over- travel screw bears against the trigger before it has moved far enough to release the sear. You can detect this right away and correct it by loos- ening the overtravel screw. But temperature changes and even dust and lubricant can change the overtravel setting slightly. If you're within a gnat's eyelash of stopping the trigger short, you may find that your rifle is way too safe at the most inopportune time. I prefer to give triggers enough overtravel to feel. A small amount of trigger move- ment past sear release won't affect the shot if your pull is smooth.

Sear engagement is much more important. A rough feel to the trig- ger pull or long "creep" before sear release indicates that you or a gun- smith should attend to sear engagement. (Military two-stage triggers are designed with a measure of creep before the trigger engages the sear.) Unfortunately, sear contact is impossible to adjust on many rifles without voiding factory warranties, disassembling the trigger, or get- ting out the Arkansas stone. Remington Model 700 sear engagement is

Stocks that fit help you hold the rifle still. This Springfield M1-A has an adjustable comb.

screw-adjustable (although that and the other trigger adjustments on this rifle are shellacked in place to discourage tinkering). Sear engagement on Winchester M70 triggers is not so readily altered; you must hone the sear lip on the trigger. Go too far, and the rifle will not hold cock; try to correct that error, and you change the trigger geometry. Winchester will not sell you another trigger, so think before you act. An aftermarket trigger is often the better solution.

Fortunately, trigger pull weight is easier to adjust. The trigger's fingerpiece bears against a return spring that counters the pressure of your finger. Reduce spring pressure, and you reduce apparent pull. The spring is not all you feel, though. Pressure of the sear against its contacts adds to the resistance. Some triggers, when adjusted so the trigger spring is free, still give you plenty of pull. The problem, of course, is that after the sear releases, there's nothing to return the trigger forward, so you need some tension on the trigger spring. How much depends on the trigger design and on your own preference.

Very lightweight triggers work fine in slow-fire competitive events. My small-bore prone rifle has a trigger that breaks at about 8 ounces. It's heavier than I'd like, but the adjustments won't give me a safe, consistent pull any lighter. Remington markets a 2-ounce trigger on its 40x rifles. During my salad days on the prone circuit, Carl

Long shooting at prairie dogs is more fun if your autoloader cycles. Keep it clean.

Kenyon's triggers were the rage. Beautifully made, they could be adjusted so light that the mere thought of firing would release the striker. One colleague managed to set his to engage positively when the rifle was horizontal but to fire when the muzzle was elevated—no finger on the trigger. A youngster blowing out a birthday candle could have fired that Model 52.

On a hunt, you want a much heavier trigger. You'll be tense, excited. Your fingers may be cold, or you might be wearing gloves. Perhaps you'll have the safety off as you move the last few yards in a stalk, the trigger vulnerable to contact with a twig or the pressure of your finger as you lay it alongside the guard.

My adjustable triggers are set to 2 pounds. That's lighter than many shooters prefer, but I've used target-weight triggers a lot and have a light touch. Three pounds is acceptable; even a 4-pound pull works fine if it's crisp and consistent. But many factory-set bolt-rifle triggers lift more than 5 pounds, which, in my view, is too heavy.

The bigger the gun company and the lower the rifle price, the less likely you are to get a trigger that's usable off the shelf or adjustable to your liking. Expect fine triggers from semi-custom rifle makers such as Ed Brown, who supplies Jewell triggers that break like delicate icicles.

The Tikka trigger is easily adjustable; the magazine is of lightweight polymer and feeds smoothly.

An exception among firms that build more affordable rifles is Savage, whose AccuTrigger gives you a crisp, light pull but is ingeniously designed to withstand accidental blows. Savage CEO Ron Coburn recognized that most triggers were sadly lacking as firing devices. He charged his engineers to come up with an economical trigger that delivered the pull of a more expensive trigger but was absolutely safe in the hands of a neophyte—a tall order. But the result drew applause from the shooting public and has become a standard item on Savage bolt rifles.

Most of the visible features we think of as enhancing accuracy don't affect intrinsic accuracy, but they can help you shoot more accurately. Heavy rifles bounce around less than lightweight rifles do. The inertia of a thick barrel counters the disturbing nudges of wind, muscle tremors, or the pressure of your finger on the trigger. The thick, flat-bottomed forend on rifles designated "varmint," "target," or "tactical" is most useful when you're firing from a rest but has the same jiggle-deadening effect as a heavy barrel if you can get your hand around it in hunting positions.

The problem with rifles that have lots of inertia is that they have lots of inertia. Any burdensome rifle can be a liability on a hunt. Some

Puffing of products no longer stops on the page. This Weatherby was branded after a fine test target.

years ago, while chasing elk, I met a fellow toting a tactical rifle in .338 Lapua. It wore an enormous scope that brought its total weight to 16 pounds. He conceded that it wasn't ideal for hikes into deep canyons but claimed that it shot accurately. And he did shoot an elk. So did another fellow whose 11-pound .300 was a lightweight by comparison. I ended up lugging that rifle out of a canyon for him because the hunter had tired himself out carrying it in. Although both these rifles were intrinsically accurate and bored for cartridges of great reach, they lacked portability. Unlike prairie dogs, elk don't live in towns you can penetrate with a Suburban and a collapsible shooting bench.

Benchrest shooters commonly touch only the trigger to shoot, maintaining that the less contact with the rifle, the less effect on the shot. On the hunt, however, you have to support the rifle with your body. The stock plays an important role. If it fits you—that is, if the rifle wants to point where you're looking—it will give you a sense of control that's all but unconscious. If it doesn't fit, you'll have to fight the rifle onto the target and fight to hold it there. Deficiencies in fit are magnified by distance. A slight rotation of forend or grip as you crush the trigger, varying the pressure of your cheek against an ill-fitting comb, slippage of the butt on your clavicle—all can cause a miss. Shots

Accuracy needn't cost a lot. This Savage tactical rifle in .300 Winchester Magnum shoots tiny groups.

that you call dead center can fly wild if there's an imperfect union between the stock and your body.

Because you'll likely shoot at game from a variety of positions in various types of clothing, the best hunting stock incorporates myriad compromises. Practice can help you master a versatile rifle stock that doesn't fit you perfectly from any position. Exhibition shooters Annie Oakley, Ad Topperwein, Herb Parsons, and Tom Frye shot with blinding speed and great precision using production-line stocks.

One of my favorite long-range rifles doesn't look like one at all—no heavy barrel, no thick stock. It's a 6.5/284 put together by Mel Forbes of New Ultra Light Arms. It weighs about 6 pounds with a 24-inch barrel but will shoot 85-grain bullets into ³/₄-inch groups all day—and different types to the same point of impact. I didn't specify a quick twist in this rifle, so the long, heavy match bullets that competitive shooters favor at 1,000 yards likely wouldn't shine. But what a delightful rifle to carry! Deer and coyotes that gawk from 400 yards had best reconsider.

Come to think of it, few of the rifles I've used to kill game beyond 350 yards look like long-range rifles at a glance. They include

If your rifle has a nonadjustable trigger, replace it. This adjustable Timney fits a 98 Mauser.

Winchester Model 70s in .300 Winchester, .30-06, and .270; a Remington 722 in 6mm; a David Miller Model 70 in .300 Weatherby, and a Magnum Research Sako in .280. I might have sniped a prairie dog that far out with an H-S Precision rifle in .223; it's surely capable. Although I avoid long shots, I like to carry rifles that can make them—rifles accurate enough to explode a grapefruit every time at 300 yards. That level of precision won't satisfy benchrest or 1,000-yard shooters, but it won't let any big-game animal escape, even if the rifle occasionally gets stretched beyond a quarter mile.

GETTING BULLETS TO FLY TRUE
Neither target rifles nor hunting rifles now wear the long, heavy barrels that dominated in the market hunting era. The huge charges of black powder favored by buffalo hunters benefited from barrels longer than those on post–Civil War cavalry carbines. Smoothbore punt gun barrels stretched half the length of the sleek boats that shooters paddled quietly toward resting flocks of waterfowl. Sportsmen after big game and wild fowl also equated reach with barrel length. The advent of smokeless powder during the last decade of the nineteenth century

The author used this Sako to hunt in Austria. Because short barrels are stiff, they vibrate less violently and often print tighter groups than long barrels.

changed barrel requirements. Barrels had to be stronger, to bottle higher pressures. But the only advantages afforded by extra-long rifle barrels were incrementally higher bullet speeds and additional muzzle weight to steady your aim. These days, installing a long barrel to add reach is like putting fat tires on a sedan to make it go fast. A broad footprint boosts traction off the line, but what really makes a car fast is what's under the hood. A rifle's reach has to do mostly with the load. Hitting at a distance can actually be easier with short, heavy (stiff) barrels, because they often deliver the best accuracy.

Modern "fluid steel" barrels surpass barrels manufactured before the advent of smokeless powder with regard to both tensile strength and hardness. Tensile strength is the force required to break a steel rod 1 inch in cross-sectional area by pulling at both ends. Generally, hardening steel increases its tensile strength. But a tensile rating of 100,000 pounds for a rifle barrel is worthless if the steel is so hard that it's brittle. Most makers target a hardness of 25 to 32 on the Rockwell C scale. Heat treating leaves residual stresses in barrels that can be relieved by slow cooling after reheating the blank. Strong barrels are accurate because they retain their dimensional tolerances under the heat and pressure of firing.

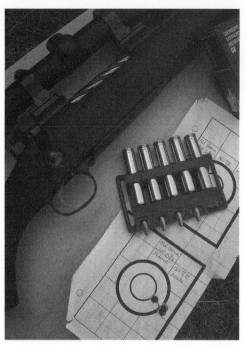

Ed Brown's custom rifles typically shoot well. This .300 Weatherby Magnum is no exception.

Most hunting and military rifles wear chrome-molybdenum barrels. Chrome-moly is the kind of steel used in truck axles and other high-stress components. It takes a traditional blue nicely, so it is preferred for fine custom rifles. It is commonly designated 4140; other four-digit numbers indicate a slightly different alloy. Stainless steel barrels dominate competitive shooting and are gaining favor among hunters. The stainless steel in barrels is not the same as that in cutlery. Barrels of 416 stainless are rust-resistant. Their high chrome content adds hardness (and makes bluing difficult). Sulfur makes it easier to machine. Some shooters claim that stainless lasts longer, making it worth the higher price. Super-accurate barrels can be made from both chrome-moly and stainless steel.

Barrel drilling and reaming haven't changed much over the past century, except for the tooling. Carbide bits and reamers last a long time and deliver superior finish. The deep-hole drill traditionally used to perforate rifle barrels has a stationary bit mounted on a long steel tube with a groove for cooling oil. The barrel rotates around it at up to 5,000 rpm. The hole is commonly drilled .005 inch undersize so a reamer can finish the job, leaving the bore smooth and uniform.

It's hard to beat groups like this, fired with a Dakota Predator in .20 Tactical, with a Nightforce scope.

Central to the accuracy of rifles and pistols (and also shotguns with slug barrels) is the rifling—the spiral grooves and, between them, the lands that impart spin to a bullet. Rifling twist or pitch, or rate of spin, is expressed as the distance a bullet travels while making one complete revolution. A 1:14 twist means that the bullet turns over one time for every 14 inches of forward travel. If all bullets were the same weight and shape and traveled at the same speed, one rate of twist would work for all, but proper rate of twist varies. A patched round ball in a muzzleloader requires a very slow twist, whereas a long bullet in a small-bore rifle cartridge needs a quick twist to stabilize. An appropriate rate of twist might be 1:66 for a round ball in a muzzleloader and 1:32 for a conical bullet in the same rifle. Some muzzleloaders are rifled 1:48 as a compromise. Centerfire rifles designed for long 7mm bullets may have twist rates as short as 1:9.

In 1879 Briton Sir Alfred George Greenhill came up with a formula that works for most bullets most of the time: required twist (in calibers) equals 150 divided by the length of the bullet (in calibers). So if you have a 168-grain 30-caliber bullet 1.35 inches long, you divide 1.35 by .30 to get length in calibers (4.5). Then you divide 150 by 4.5 and get a

Late 19th Century Rifling Types

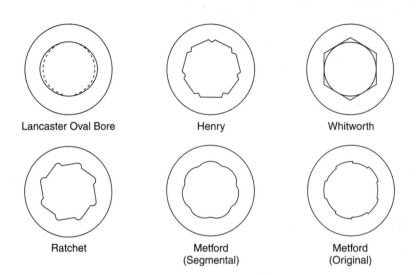

| Lancaster Oval Bore | Henry | Whitworth |
| Ratchet | Metford (Segmental) | Metford (Original) |

fraction over 33 (in calibers). To convert to inches of linear measure, you multiply by .30. The final number is very close to 10, which is a useful rate of spin for most popular .30-caliber hunting cartridges, from the .308 to the .300 Weatherby Magnum. The formula works for most jacketed lead bullets, specific gravity 10.9. Note that bullet length, not weight, is at issue here. A 168-grain boattail spitzer with a long nose might approach the length of a blunt 200-grain bullet.

Rate of twist must sometimes be tailored to the bullet. Barrels for heavy, long-range .223 bullets have a very fast pitch—1:9 to as sharp as 1:7. Such a sharp spin is needed to stabilize 65- to 80-grain bullets, while a 1:12 twist works best for standard 50-grain hunting bullets. Short, frangible bullets fired through a fast-twist barrel can come apart in flight.

Determining how best to spin a bullet took a couple of centuries of work by talented people. In 1854 the British government hired Joseph Whitworth, a bright young ballistician, to try various rifling types and twist rates. Standard twist in military rifles then was 1:78. Whitworth's experiments pointed to a twist of 1:20. Skeptics thought that such a sharp spin would retard the bullet, but a hexagonal bullet of Whitworth's design gave more than twice the penetration of a ball from a slow-twist barrel. His hexagonal bullets flew flat, and at long range

Rifling in Muzzleloaders

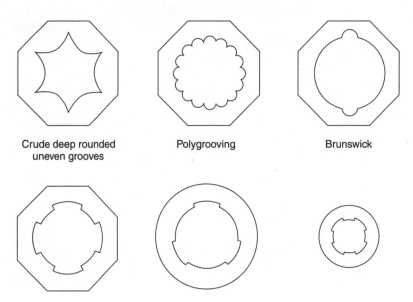

Crude deep rounded
uneven grooves

Polygrooving

Brunswick

Jacobs

Enfield

Modern Enfield

Modern Rifle Types

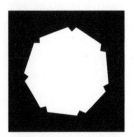

Henry rifling

Lee-Metford rifling

Lee-Enfield rifling

Mannlicher trough-form
rifling

Springfield two-groove
rifling

Springfield four-groove
rifling

Dave Smith draws a bead with a much-modified Ruger 10/22. It wears his composite barrel.

they drilled groups a sixth the size of those shot with ordinary patched balls. Hexagonal bullets, however, were slow to load and expensive. William Greener's narrow-land rifling pitched at 1:30 stabilized small-bore (.40 to .52) bullets out to 2,000 yards. Gunmaker James Purdey built two rifles featuring Greener-style barrels in 1856. He called them "Express Train" rifles because of their power. "Express" became a descriptor of powerful British hunting cartridges.

Breech-loading rifles eliminated the need for bullets that could be loaded from the front. Bullets loaded from the rear could be made harder and longer and cast to full groove diameter. Hard bullets could be stabilized with shallower grooves and thus driven faster. Sharp rifling pitch could be used—even rifling that varied in pitch and depth from breech to muzzle. William Ellis Metford experimented with gain twist, which allowed a bullet easy acceleration from the chamber but increased the rate of spin during barrel time. He used a 34-inch barrel that gave the bullet an exit spin of 1:17 but started it so gradually that the bullet turned over only once before reaching the muzzle. Dan Lilja, who makes barrels for modern rifle cartridges, once employed gain twist. He found that it failed to deliver measurably better accuracy than barrels with a uniform twist rate. But Smith & Wesson has adopted gain twist in its long-range .460 revolver.

A lot of big holes in Dave Smith's muzzle brake make it effective—and loud.

Charles Newton, American inventor and gunmaker, reasoned that since a bullet bears on only one shoulder of a land, the other is unnecessary. His ratchet rifling proved out on the range but failed at market. Marlin, the U.S. gun firm that makes more .22 rimfire rifles than any other manufacturer, uses multiple narrow grooves in its Micro-Groove barrels. They deliver good accuracy, but probably no better than

What throat wear? This group came from a barrel that had fired 1,000 hot .223 WSSM loads.

traditional Metford-style bores with fewer grooves. Metford rifling features wide groove bottoms that are the same radius as the bullet, plus flat-topped, square-shouldered lands. Groove number has varied since World War I, when U.S. soldiers carried two-groove Springfields. Now most rifle and pistol barrels have four to six grooves.

Rifling can be done with a cutter, a button, or a hammer-forging machine. The cutter, developed in Nuremburg in the late fifteenth century, is a hook in a hardened steel cylinder that just fits the barrel blank. The cylinder or cutter box moves through the bore on a rod that pulls the hook against the bore wall, removing about 0.0001 inch of steel with each pass. After indexing to cut every groove, the cutter box is adjusted to deepen the bite for the next pass. Rate of twist hinges on the preset rotation of the cutter box. Rifling a barrel takes about an hour with one cutter. It's a low-stress process, but costly. John Krieger's top-grade barrels are single-point cut. Broaches with multiple hooks in a step-tooth configuration speed the process.

The tungsten-carbide button is much faster. Mounted on the end of a high-tensile rod and rotated by a rifling head set to the desired rate of twist, the button is pushed or pulled through the finished bore by a hydraulic ram, "ironing in" the grooves. A thin-walled barrel is no candidate for a button. To prevent bulging, you must button-rifle the

Vigorous scrubbing, with bore guide in place, keeps metal fouling at bay and maintains accuracy.

tube before turning thick walls down. Dan Lilja's barrels are button-rifled; he says that the smooth interior finish and uniform groove depth give this method an accuracy edge.

A hammer-forging machine pounds the barrel around a mandrel that, like a button, has the rifling in reverse. Because a barrel gets about 30 percent longer in this process, the blank starts short. Stainless barrels can be difficult to hammer-forge because many are very hard. Solution: Substitute 410 for 416 stainless. Hammer forging is fast but leaves considerable radial stress, which is tough to remove.

Although good barrels have been produced with all three rifling methods, makers argue the merits of each. Button proponents even disagree on whether to pull or push—or whether it makes a difference. One requisite applies to all: Cutters and buttons must move smoothly and at a constant pressure through the bore.

Rifling type and bore finish have a lot to do with accuracy. Barrels with shallow grooves generally shoot tighter than those with deep grooves because they distort the bullet less. But shallow-groove barrels don't last as long. Land size is a trade-off too. Narrow lands distort the bullet less and create less drag but also burn away faster. By reducing

Stainless steel barrels are no more accurate than chrome-moly. They resist rust but yield to throat erosion at about the same rate.

the number of lands, a barrel maker can keep them wide while mini-mizing distortion and drag. Rifling configuration will likely remain a topic of heated debate. Two-groove Springfield barrels and Marlin's 16-groove Micro-Groove rifling both deliver fine accuracy.

Rifling must be concentric with the bore, and land corners must be free of irregularities. According to some shooters and barrel makers, uniform roughness in land and groove surfaces may actually be ben-eficial, because a very smooth surface increases friction that can pull jacket material from bullets as effectively as the tool marks in a rough bore. Conventional wisdom is that a uniform surface ripple of 10 to 20 micro-inches delivers the best accuracy. Careful lapping can yield a properly smooth bore. Kenny Jarrett's superaccurate barrels are hand-lapped—a process that takes hours in his shop. But other makers say that lapping isn't necessary, given good rifling technique. A 75-power bore scope helps makers check the finish inside.

Champion high-power shooter David Tubb markets a bore finish-ing kit called FinalFinish. It's an assortment of bullets coated with fine

Keeping a barrel clean extends its life and maintains accuracy, as all benchresters know. A bore guide protects the throat of this Nesika rifle from rod contact.

abrasives. You shoot them in specified order through your barrel to erase the fine machining marks left by the bore drill and rifling device. "The total amount of metal removed by FinalFinish is less than .0003 inches," claims Tubb in his Superior Shooting Systems catalog. The firm, headquartered in Canadian, Texas, also offers a FinalFinish kit for rimfires. Tubb hews to the premise that better accuracy results when the smoother bore resists the accumulation of lead or jacket material. Cleaning is easier and required less frequently. He also recommends the treatment in rifles with throats roughened by erosion, even if the throat has become worn well ahead of the original start of the lands.

Bore uniformity after rifling can be measured with an air gauge, a probe that is moved through the barrel with constant air pressure recording variations from specified dimensions. Shilen's air gauges are sensitive to 50 millionths of an inch. John Krieger recommends that every barrel be trimmed at least an inch at the muzzle when it is fitted to the rifle, because the tooling used in bore finishing can leave a slight flare at the ends. Krieger barrels are lapped to just under 16 micro-inches in the direction of bullet travel. They're held to a tolerance of 0.0005 over nominal groove and bore dimensions, but the dimensions are

This lead-bullet target barrel is hardly one to carry afield. But it's stiff enough to be accurate.

uniform to within 0.0001. Pac-Nor (a button-rifle shop) and H-S Precision (with cut-rifled barrels) specify tolerances of 0.0003 for the bore diameter, and Pac-Nor limits variation in groove diameter to 0.0001.

Experiments to test and improve the inherent accuracy of rifles led, in the mid-nineteenth century, to a sport that has been growing ever since. Benchrest shooting started as a noncompetitive diversion for hobbyists, fueled partly by Joseph Whitworth's "fluid steel," a stronger metal than was available before 1850. Heavy-barreled rifles designed not for battle or hunting but to deliver top accuracy and ballistic performance appeared before the Civil War. For years, their use was limited to the Northeast, where gun factories applied to firearms design what gun enthusiasts learned at the bench. After the 1930s, when benchrest competition bloomed, shooters demanded of their rifles ever higher levels of accuracy. Sharpshooter Mary Louise DeVito fired a 1,000-yard group measuring less than 8 inches, a world record during the Vietnam era. But the competition was just heating up. In August 2003, Kyle Brown put ten shots into 4.23 inches at 1,000 yards.

During the 1990s, several people experimented with sleeved rifle barrels. Steel tubes with very thin walls were coupled with carbon-

Composite barrels have a slender steel core and carbon-fiber jacket. They're big but lightweight.

fiber jackets that added strength without much weight. Sleeved barrels the diameter of varmint-weight steel barrels weighed half as much. One pioneer in this field, Dave Smith of Vancouver, Washington, patented a process for manufacturing composite sleeves. "I used pre-impregnated epoxy resin and unidirectional graphite fibers," he explained. "Almost all the strength is in the fiber. You'll see composite barrels made several ways. I built the liners into the sleeve under high pressure. Freezing the liner and heating the sleeve is another method, but I don't like it because heat and cold induce stress."

Smith's work with rifle barrels resulted in a company, Accurate Composites, in Tualatin, Oregon. In 2003 a Minneapolis firm, Magnum Research, acquired all equipment from that plant, plus three patents for composite barrel manufacture. Smith still experiments with graphite compounds. "They're incredibly strong," he affirms. "Magnum-Lite barrels of my manufacture have been pressure-tested to 129,000 psi, or about twice the pressure you get from a Weatherby magnum cartridge."

His development of rifle barrels fueled Smith's interest in long-range shooting. One day at the local Clark Rifles shooting range, he

The last thing a bullet touches before flight is the crown. It must be perfect for uniform release.

showed me some of his artillery. "I'm not really a competitive shooter," he chuckled, "though I've shot in rifle and pistol matches. Now I get a kick out of breaking eggs at 300 yards." His small-bore gun is a .223 built on a Sako action. It wears one of his own Magnum-Lite barrels, a 29-inch tube with 1:12 twist. Scoped with an 8-25x Leupold Long Range Target (LRT) scope, it has landed five shots inside .33 at 100 yards. "I once put four into .158," he boasted. That load: 27 1/2 grains H335 launching a 52-grain Sierra MatchKing at 3,375 fps.

Another of Smith's rifles is a 7mm STW Rogue (with 35-degree shoulder). It's also based on Sako metal, with a 34-inch, three-groove Magnum-Lite barrel rifled 1:10, topped with an 8-32x Burris scope. "It was built to shoot 120-grain bullets but prefers 168-grain MatchKings," Smith noted. A charge of 78 grains H1000 kicks them downrange at 3,160 fps. Smith once shot a .257 group at 300 yards. Close behind is the .348 cloverleaf punched out by his 6.5/284 Nesika with a 32-inch Magnum-Lite barrel. Like the .223, it wears an 8-25 Leupold LRT sight. "I use Lapua brass, Federal 210 primers, 60 grains of Ramshot Magnum powder, and 140-grain Berger VLD bullets," Smith recites from memory. "The chronograph tells me 3,174 fps."

Long barrels boost velocity, not accuracy. But they do minimize blast. Bipod and scope help you aim.

Most well-known barrel makers now have Web pages, some of which offer barrel-making insights. If you only want to know where to buy good barrels, your search gets easier: Shop Midway USA. This shooter supply outlet has paid attention to the results of benchrest competitions that test barrel accuracy. The logic: To sell shooters the most accurate barrels, stock those that garner the medals. In the 2003 USRA-IR50/50 Nationals, for example, 39 of 87 top competitors used Lilja barrels. Of the 20 best shooters in 10.5-pound centerfire benchrest competition, 16 favored Shilen barrels. Shilen also ranked most popular in the 13.5-pound class. Hart barrels showed up almost as often on the heavy rifles and for decades have been a top choice of small-bore shooters. John Krieger's cut-rifled barrels finished a close third in the latest postings. Douglas appeared on both centerfire and rimfire lists, having served riflemen for half a century at National Match and 1,000-yard events. If marksmen with big stakes in tight groups chose these barrels, reasoned the Midway USA team, hunters and competitors in other target sports would want them.

Of course, these are not the only brands to consider when you're shopping. Some barrels, such as those by Kenny Jarrett and H-S Precision, are less widely distributed but offer superb performance. Not all barrel shops will agree to market through suppliers such as Midway USA, either. Currently, that Missouri catalog store stocks Douglas,

Full-stocked rifles are typically short and carry easily. That forward-barrel contact can affect accuracy.

Krieger, Lilja, and Shilen barrels. Others may join the fold—when the score sheets warrant it. If you own a rifle whose factory barrel shoots well, you're not alone. Even though commercial hunting rifles typically wear inexpensive barrels (one company featured $20 barrels in its flagship bolt gun), you may still get an accurate tube. Take care of it with thorough scrubbing after each shooting session to clean out copper stripped from the bullet jacket. Metal fouling is often the cause when accuracy falls off. Before blaming the barrel, bedding, or ammo, scrub that bore.

SHORT HULLS FOR LONG HITS

Several blackpowder cartridges favored by big-game hunters in the post–Civil War West had hulls over 3 inches long. The .38-90 and .40-110 Winchester come to mind, along with the .45-120 and .50-140 Sharps. The British .450-400 and .500-450 Nitro Express rounds also had $3^1/_4$-inch cases. Brass for the .450 No. 2 was $3^1/_2$ inches long— longer than a loaded .338 Winchester Magnum cartridge.

Ammunition shortened up with the development of smokeless powder. The first successful small-bore military rounds, developed between 1887 and 1891, were all under $2^1/_2$ inches. The 7.65 Belgian

Dakota rifles show traditional elegance. So do Dakota's rimless but potent cartridges.

case measured 2.09 inches, the 7.62 Russian 2.11. The .303 British case was 2.21 inches long, the 7.5x55 Swiss 2.18, and the 8x57 German Mauser 2.24. The .30-40 Krag followed in 1892, its 2.31-inch case much like those of European rounds. The Krag's successor, the .30-06, towered at 2.49 inches.

In those days as now, infantry cartridges also doubled as sporting rounds. But hunters had other options too. In 1895 the .30-30 (case length 2.04 inches) was chambered in the Model 1894 Winchester. This marriage sold a lot of rifles and a lot of ammunition. Then, around 1913, Charles Newton delivered to Savage a new cartridge with a case only 1.91 inches long that would drive a big-game bullet 3,000 fps. The .250-3000 thrived. In 1920 Savage announced an even shorter round in its Model 1899 rifle. The .300 Savage hull measured only 1.87 inches but outperformed the .30-30 by 10 percent.

The .250 and .300 Savages were truly the first compact, high-performance American hunting game rounds. They performed like bigger rounds. Explorer Roy Chapman Andrews used a .250 in the world's wildest places, hunting sheep. The .300 Savage has loaded meat poles wherever deer abound; elk hunters favored it too. I remem-

A short Remington magnum in a Model Seven AWR rifle took this fine buck for Eddie Stevenson.

ber crawling up on a herd of caribou in northern Quebec, a .300 Savage in hand; it was a Model 99 with iron sights. Cold wind brought the sounds of idling hooves and ruminations. Bellying over a granite boil, I closed to 80 yards, then settled the bead high on the ribs of the biggest bull and squeezed. He tried to get up, so I fired again. The antlers, with great scooping bez shovels, were so wide that the 44-inch rifle fell a foot shy of reaching from beam to beam. I wish I could have taken that .300 home, but it belonged to another hunter who had left it to his Inuit guide. No doubt it soon suffered the initiation of the North: salt spray and snow, scarring on canoe gunwales and sleds, plus the ministrations of Inuit gunsmiths skilled in the use of duct tape and brazing rod, and to whom a hammer and a rifle merit equal care.

After World War I, hunters were busy converting Springfields and Enfields for the hunt. The availability of these actions and inexpensive .30-06 ammo had a lot to do with this move away from lever rifles. Sedgley and Griffin & Howe offered lovely sporters, and scopes stretched their effective range. The .300 Savage offered lots of power in a lever action, but bolt guns could handle bigger cases. British shops were getting plenty of orders for bolt guns. Three big cordite cartridges

Steve Comus wrings out a Lazzeroni rifle. The 7.82 (.30) Warbird shoots flat but, predictably, delivers stiff recoil.

developed just before the Great War would influence cartridge development across the Atlantic. In 1910 Jeffery announced a rimless .404 that shot a 300-grain bullet at 2,600 fps. A year later came Rigby's .416, pushing a 410-grain bullet at 2,370 fps. In 1912, Holland & Holland (H&H) trotted out its .375 Magnum, which drove a 270-grain softpoint at 2,650 fps.

The .404, .416, and .375, designed independently, shared no common dimensions. The .404 had a slightly rebated case 2.86 inches long, with a .544 base and .537 rim. The .416 Rigby was rimless, with a .586 base and 2.90-inch overall length. The .375 H&H wore a .532 belt ahead of the extractor groove and .532 rim; case diameter forward of the belt was .512. The belt served as a headspacing device, holding the case head against the bolt face. The steeply tapered 2.85-inch case offered little shoulder when necked to .375; the belt was a more positive stop.

All three big British cartridges required a very long bolt mechanism. Initially, only the Magnum Mausers were long enough to accommodate them. Surplus 1917 Enfields later offered shooters a cheap if ungainly alternative. Winchester's Model 70 handled the .375 and .300 Holland (introduced in the United States in 1925), and the Remington 721 was chambered for the .300. Neither was configured for the bulkier .404 or .416.

Then, in the early 1940s, short magnums appeared in the California shop of a young insurance salesman named Roy Weatherby. He reduced taper on the H&H case to boost capacity and reformed the shoulder. He shortened the case to 2$^1/_2$ inches and necked it down to produce the .257, .270, and 7mm Weatherby Magnums. They'd fit any magazine designed for the .30-06. All you had to do to convert a military action was ream the bolt face from .473 to .532 inside. The full-length .300 and .375 Weatherbys, essentially supercharged Holland rounds, followed. Weatherby built his first rifles on Mauser actions.

The idea of short magnums really caught on with shooters in the late 1950s. Winchester introduced its 2.50-inch .458 Magnum in 1956, following two years later with the .264 and .338. The slightly longer (2.62-inch) .300 Winchester Magnum appeared in 1963. Remington announced its first short belted magnum, a 7mm, in 1962, a couple of years after Sweden gave us the .308 and .358 Norma Magnums.

All these cartridges were cut-down versions of the mother of all magnums, the .375 Holland. But this rush to shorter cases was not the end of full-length magnums. Roy Weatherby used the .416 Rigby case as a model for his belted .378 Magnum in 1953. Five years later he necked the .378 to .460, and in 1989 he fashioned a .416. Remington's ill-fated 8mm Magnum and its more popular offspring, the 7 STW, were based on the .375 H&H. Later came the Remington Ultra Mag series, full-length rounds grafted not from the .375 H&H but from rimless .404 Jeffery cases.

By the 1980s, American shooters were privy to the advantages of rimless hulls: smooth feeding, headspacing on the shoulder. There was less stretch and fewer case separations, it was said, although savvy handloaders knew how to eliminate stretch after the first firing: All you had to do with belted cases was set the resizing die to work the neck only. Chambers cut closer to cartridge dimensions reduced initial stretch. In the magazine and on feed ramps, belted rounds fed as smoothly as rimless ones in rifles of proper dimensions.

Nonetheless, rimless rounds began a comeback in 1992, with Don Allen's Dakota line. The 7mm, .300, .330, and .375 Dakotas are based on the .404 Jeffery. They measure 2.50 to 2.57 inches in length but have more capacity than belted short magnums. For example, the .300 Dakota hull holds 97 grains of water, compared with 89 grains for the .300 H&H. The full-length .300 Weatherby holds 100, the .300 Remington Ultra Mag 110. The Dakota rounds make sense because they maximize the fuel load you can conveniently put into a standard-length

Moose are massive animals, but the Lazzeroni Warbird kills them cleanly at very long range.

action. As this is written, Dakota's latest round is a short .404 with no change in the .423 bullet diameter. There's also a long .416 on the .404 Jeffery case, and a .450 on the .416 Rigby.

During the 1990s, a Tucson entrepreneur named John Lazzeroni developed a potent line of rimless magnums ranging in caliber from .257 to .416. The cases are his own design, but head dimensions run close to the .416 Rigby's. The performance of the 7.82 (.308) Warbird and 8.59 (.338) Titan is similar to that of the .30-378 and .338-378 Weatherbys. Later, Lazzeroni chopped .750 off these cases to come up with a stable of cartridges better adapted to lightweight rifles and easier to control in recoil. The .532 bases for his .243 and .264 short cartridges are identical to those on ordinary belted magnums such as the 7mm Remington (and on Lazzeroni's long .257 Scramjet). Short 7mm, .300, .338, and .416 Lazzeronis have .580-diameter heads, like their longer counterparts. There used to be a .264 and a 7mm with a smaller (.404 Jeffery-size) head. Lazzeroni dropped the .264 but reconfigured the 7mm with .580 brass.

The short Lazzeronis deliver belted magnum ballistics from actions designed around Winchester's .308. Of course, the Lazzeroni hulls are bigger in diameter, so bolt head and magazine must be

From left: .300 H&H,
Lazzeroni's 7.82 Warbird,
and 7.82 Patriot. The Patriot
outsizzles the .300.

opened up. Lazzeroni markets his own commercial ammo but stresses that it is all handloaded. Here's how it performs:

6.17 (.243) Spitfire: 85-grain bullet at 3,618 fps
6.71 (.264) Phantom: 120-grain bullet at 3,312 fps
7.21 (.284) Tomahawk: 140-grain bullet at 3,379 fps
7.82 (.308) Patriot: 180-grain bullet at 3,184 fps
8.59 (.338) Galaxy: 225-grain bullet at 2,968 fps
10.57 (.416) Maverick: 400-grain bullet at 2,454 fps

John Lazzeroni mated his cartridges to rifles of his own design. The L2000SA Mountain Rifle is my favorite. A conservatively styled gun, it features a McMillan action with oversize Sako extractor, three-position safety, and Jewell trigger behind a fluted Schneider cut-rifled barrel. A super-tough, rustproof NP3 electroless nickel finish gives the stainless rifle a platinum hue. The synthetic-stocked Mountain rifle scales about 7 pounds with a 24-inch barrel. Lazzeroni says that the rifle's mild recoil has to do with powder burning more efficiently in the short hull. It concentrates powder closer to the primer, speeding ignition and ensuring that more of the fuel is consumed before the bullet leaves the case. A long case full of slow-burning fuel loses the front of that powder column as ejecta before it is consumed. It's like extra weight on the bullet's tail, increasing recoil. The L2000SA in my rack is chambered to the 8.59 Galaxy, the ballistic twin to Winchester's .338 Magnum, a superior round for long shooting at elk and other tough game.

This and other short, rimless Lazzeroni cartridges came on the leading edge of a wave of stubby cartridges that were much more powerful than they looked. Their origin was, oddly enough, the benchrest circuit. In 1974 accomplished benchrester Lou Palmisano came up with a new cartridge by reshaping the obscure .220 Russian hull. He and fellow shooter Ferris Pindell called this wildcat the .22 PPC; the 6mm PPC followed. Measuring just over an inch from base to 30-degree shoulder, these cartridges were much shorter than common hunting and target rounds of the day. Palmisano bet his scores on the abbreviated powder column, challenging the "triple deuce" (.222 Remington) and 6x47 (a necked-up .222 Magnum). These rounds held most of the records—and the allegiance of top competitors.

Palmisano and Pindell soon proved the PPC in competition. Once the squat little rounds started winning, converts flocked to them. In five years, from 1975 to 1980, the number of PPC rifles used by the top 20 Sporter-class competitors rose from 2 to 15. By 1989 the 20 best scores were all shot with PPCs. Even more impressive, the short cartridges were used by every entrant in the demanding Unlimited class, and 18 of the 20 best marksmen went PPC in Light Varmint and Heavy Varmint categories. Eventually, Sako chambered rifles for PPCs and began manufacturing cases (with small primer pockets) in Finland.

Squat case profiles weren't unknown in hunting circles. Winchester announced the .284 in 1963, a decade before Palmisano's work with the PPC. The .284's fat case had a rebated rim to fit standard bolt faces. Essentially a short-action .280 Remington, the .284 was first chambered in Winchester's Model 88 lever-action and Model 100 autoloading rifles. Savage offered it briefly in the 99. Browning and Ruger also cataloged the chambering, but it's now about as dead as the Ford Pinto— at least in its original form. The .284 worked fine in short actions but better in long ones that allowed you to seat the bullets out. But unlike the .270, whose performance it matched, .284 ammo was hard to find and expensive. The round never hit it big and has since limped along mainly as a parent for wildcats. The 6.5/284 has become popular among 1,000-yard shooters. Norma and Lapua make 6.5/284 cases.

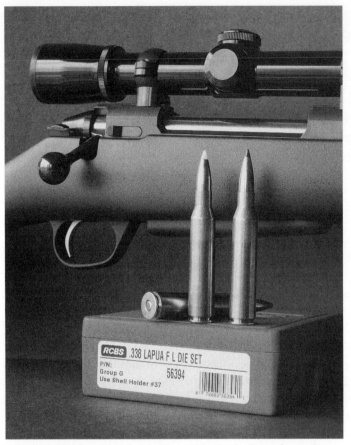

This Sako TRG in .338 Lapua delivers .340 Weatherby performance:
3,000 foot-pounds at 300 yards.

Gunsmiths such as Rick Freudenberg have necked the hull to 30 caliber to duplicate .30-06 performance in a short action.

Remington's first supershort magnums were belted rounds. The .350 and 6.5 Magnums came out in 1965 and 1966, in the 600-series carbines. Neither the squat cartridges nor the ugly carbines sold well. In 1968 Remington changed the carbines, offering the 660 with a 20-inch barrel, $1\frac{1}{2}$ inches longer than on original 600s. Still the market turned a cold shoulder. The dogleg bolt, squarish forend, and crude, pressed checkering had no appeal to riflemen with fresh memories of pre-64 Model 70 Winchesters. And a ventilated rib—what was *that* doing on a rifle?

Remington, Lazzeroni, and Dakota sell full-length rimless magnums in .375 and .416— real muscle.

You can sometimes predict trends in cartridge design by peering over the shoulders of wildcatters. You might say that Don Allen and John Lazzeroni were wildcatters; so too Jim Busha, although his cartridges are not as widely known. Busha developed a line of rounds he called Heavy Express (HE). Formed initially from .348 Winchester brass, the hulls were later minted by MAST of Las Vegas and head-stamped with the HE caliber designation. The .260, .284, and .300 HE measured roughly 2.120 base to mouth, .532 across the base. Web diameter was .545, so HE cases were slightly rebated. Busha's .338, .350, .375, .416, and .450 shared the head and shoulder diameters (.545 and .515) and the 40-degree shoulder of the sub-.33s, in cases 2.250 inches long. The .460 HE had a 45-degree shoulder angle. Body length (1.800, versus 1.700 for the sub-.33s) and overall length were constant for the big-bores, so neck length varied by caliber.

Following their first writeups in the late 1990s, Heavy Express cartridges spawned a new, even shorter line. Busha's .338, .350, .375, .416, and .450 short-action cases measured 2.060—.30-30 length. The 6mm and .257 featured the 2.120 case of the original rounds, but a 28-degree shoulder to smooth feeding.

When I discovered them a few years ago, Busha built rifles in HE chamberings on Ruger 77 Mark II and Winchester 70 Classic actions. Chambers were cut to 0.01 over cartridge length, with 0.110 of freebore.

The author shot this group with a Browning A-Bolt in .270 WSM at 300 yards.

You could also have the people at Heavy Express rechamber your rifle. I worked with two Heavy Express rifles. The .300 threw 150-grain bullets at around 3,200 fps, 165-grain bullets at nearly 3,100 fps, and 180-grain bullets at 3,000 fps—all with powder charges of 67 to 72 grains. The .375 launched 250-grain Swift A-Frames at 2,800 fps and 260-grain Nosler Partitions almost as fast. I got less from 270- and 300-grain Hornadys than was possible (2,400 to 2,600 fps), but as with the .300 HE, heavy bullets require deep seating, which reduces fuel space.

Perhaps remembering the .284 and the Model 600 carbines, Winchester and Remington took long looks before committing to short rimless magnums. The .300 Winchester Short Magnum (WSM) was announced late in 2000. Based on the .404 Jeffery case, the .300 WSM measures just 2.76 inches long, loaded. That's short enough to work in a .308-length action. In comparison, a .300 Winchester Magnum cartridge is 3.31 inches from base to mouth, and a .300 Weatherby is 3.56 inches. Web diameter of WSM cartridges roughly matches belt diameter on traditional short magnums.

The .300 WSM was apparently Browning's idea. According to Travis Hall at Browning's Utah headquarters, company engineers approached Winchester with the idea of an extra-short magnum early in 1999. A joint effort resulted. Despite its squat stature, the .300 WSM carries all the authority of the .300 Winchester Magnum, moving a 180-grain bullet at 2,970 fps. It delivers 3,526 foot-pounds at the muzzle. With a 200-yard zero, it hits 7 inches low at 300 yards, 20 inches low at 400 yards. The first .300 WSM factory loads included a pair in the Winchester Supreme line: a 150-grain Ballistic Silvertip and a 180-grain Fail Safe. The 150 gets away at 3,300 fps. Its sleek form ensures flat flight (16 inches of drop at 400 yards) and high energy retention (1,940 foot-pounds at 400 steps, or 140 more than the Fail Safe). The other charter .300 WSM load was a Super-X with 180-grain Power-Point bullet. It turns up slightly more energy downrange than the Fail Safe, and Super-X ammo is less expensive than Supreme. Only the Supreme cases are nickeled. Now the ammunition choices encompass other bullet types, such as the Nosler AccuBond. The .300 WSM showed up first in the Model 70 Classic Featherweight and soon thereafter in Browning's A-Bolt.

Remington's announcement of .300 and 7mm Short Ultra Mags (SUMs) on the heels of the WSM debut was both surprising and expected: Surprising because they were so close in concept and dimension to the Winchester offerings and came at nearly the same time. Expected because although new cartridges have historically brought little response from competitors, revolutions in cartridge design must either be taken up or rejected. Remington chose to get in the game.

Before it goes to market commercially, any new cartridge must be approved by the Sporting Arms and Ammunition Manufacturers' Institute (SAAMI). Winchester earned SAAMI's stamp while Remington was fleshing out its full-length Ultra Mag series with the 7mm and .375. Big green may have committed a tactical blunder by so doing. Once the .300 WSM had drawn a response, there was little doubt that it had a future. Remington could only counter with a similar but slightly shorter case. The two firms eventually consulted and, with SAAMI, agreed that WSM and SUM cases were different enough in name and dimensions to proceed with both. Winchester was already working on .270 and 7mm WSMS.

Like the Lazzeroni line and the WSM, the .300 and 7mm Short Ultra Mags are fashioned for .308-length actions. Rim diameter for the Lazzeronis is .577, about .043 greater than on the .300 WSM and the

Kevin Howard still hunts along a Colorado rim with a Winchester 70 in .325 WSM.

John Lazzeroni's Model 2000 rifle in 8.59 Galaxy produced these fine groups for the author.

new Remingtons. Larry Barnett at Superior Ammunition in Sturgis, South Dakota, confirmed what my micrometer tells me: The WSM and SUM have near-identical head dimensions. Differences between them and the .404 Jeffery are mostly academic. Winchester's hull is longest to the shoulder but has about the same capacity as the shorter, broader Lazzeroni case. Remington's SUM brass is shorter from base to mouth, to fit the Model Seven rifle. It holds 7.5 percent less powder that you'll get into a Winchester WSM hull. Ballistically, the two are comparable. Winchester claims 2,970 fps from a 24-inch barrel. Remington's .300 SUM with 180-grain Partitions clocks 2,940 fps from the 22-inch barrel of my Model Seven.

Prototype rifles in 7mm SUM and .300 SUM came my way in the form of fetching 6¹/₂-pound Custom-Shop Model Sevens. These were followed by a more affordable Model 700. Remington initially loaded 180-grain Nosler Partitions and 180-grain Ultra Core-Lokt bullets in its .300 SUM ammo, 140-grain and 160-grain Partitions in the 7mm. The performance of these cartridges on big game is hardly novel. We've been driving 160-grain 7mm and 180-grain .30-caliber Partitions at close to 3,000 fps for a long time.

Several loads have become available for each of the Winchester Short Magnums.

I shot what I am sure was the first elk taken with the .300 SUM and the first elk taken with the .270 WSM. To the best of my knowledge, my 8.59 Galaxy was also the first of its kind to down an elk. The rounds fed reliably and killed with authority. I have relied on them in Africa, Australia, and New Zealand. Winchester's latest, the .325 WSM, took a mountain goat for me in Alaska and an elk in Colorado. I haven't sensed any reduction in recoil, comparing the stubby new rounds to traditional belted magnums. Theoretically, squat cartridges go easier on you than their longer, belted counterparts. There's less powder, and faster powder, and more efficient burn.

To the surprise of some gun enthusiasts, Winchester took short a step further with the introduction in 2001 of two Super Short Magnums. The .223 and .243 WSSMs are based on the .300 WSM trimmed from 2.10 to 1.67 inches. A .25 WSM followed. Winchester and Browning scaled M70 and A-Bolt rifle mechanisms to the new rounds.

Although the Super Short cartridges feed reliably, they don't feed as smoothly as traditional cartridges, and saving a few hundredths of an inch in action length hardly justifies a switch from the .22-250 and

Super Short Magnums—.223, .243, and .25—followed the WSM line, in shorter rifle actions.

From left: *.300 Remington Short Ultra Mag, .300 Winchester Magnum, .300 Winchester Short Magnum. Ballistically, they're identical.*

This Ed Brown rifle shoots tight groups with and without a brake, but as is often the case, group centers shift when you install or remove the brake.

.243. Besides, both the Super Short and WSM cartridges mandate a wider magazine box that I find unappealing. Two rounds down instead of three would give you a box of normal width. Pregnant rifle bellies aside, I like the WSM and SUM lines—the rimless, headspace-on-the shoulder design is more efficient and allows for lighter, shorter rifles and quicker bolt throw. None of these advantages compares with the thrill shooters must have had when firing their first smokeless round or first cartridge rifle. The WSM and SUM lines do for today's hunters what the .300 Savage did 80 years ago: They offer great horse-power in a compact package.

SHOOTING FOR SISSIES

Cartridges that shoot big bullets flat and far have a dark side: They make rifles kick. Even if you don't react consciously to heavy recoil, you are likely to start flinching when you expect it, just as you blink when a tree branch swings in front of your face. Flinching moves your rifle, and a miss results.

Sir Isaac Newton described recoil when he figured out that for every action there is an equal and opposite reaction. You can calculate

Part of the appeal of AR-15s is the light recoil of the .223 round, further softened by the gas cycle.

recoil's kinetic energy (KE) with this formula: $KE = MV^2/GC$, where M is the rifle's mass, V is its speed as it moves to the rear, and GC is a gravitational constant for earth: 64.32.

Mass and weight are not the same. Mass is really the measure of an object's inertia, its tendency to remain in a state of motion or stability. The theory of relativity tells us that two objects have equal mass if the same force gives them the same acceleration. If gravity is the force, you can equate mass with weight. That is, weight is a measure of the force with which an object is drawn to earth by gravity. Because rifles respond pretty much the same way to gravity, rifles of the same weight have essentially the same mass.

Rifle velocity figures into recoil the way bullet velocity contributes to kinetic energy. We already know most of the numbers needed to determine rifle velocity (V). The formula is V = bullet weight (grains)/ 7000 x bullet velocity (fps) + powder weight (grains)/7000 x powder gas velocity (fps). Powder and its gas matter because, like the bullet, they are ejecta and cause recoil. You can get powder weight from factory rounds by pulling bullets and weighing charges. Although gas velocity varies, Art Alphin, whose A-Square loading manual has an excellent ballistics section, says that 5,200 fps is a useful average. The 7000 in the formula simply converts grains to pounds so that the units make sense in the end. For a 180-grain bullet fired at 3,000 fps from an $8\frac{1}{2}$-pound .300 WSM, you can calculate recoil this way: 180/7,000 x 3000 + 70 / 7,000 x 5,200 = 8.5 x V. That simplifies to (77.143 + 52)/ 8.5 = 15.19 fps. Then you can calculate recoil using the first formula: KE = MV^2/GC. The result looks like this: 8.5 $(15.19)^2$/64.32 = 30.49 foot-pounds of recoil.

Kinetic energy is not "kick." Felt recoil can differ significantly among rifles with the same amount of recoil in foot-pounds. One reason is that although bullet speed figures into the energy calculation, its contribution to rifle "slap" does not. Slap is what happens during quick recoil. Plainly put, a bullet that exits fast dumps all its energy fast. The rifle seems to slap you instead of shoving you. Pile enough foot-pounds behind that slap, and it becomes a punch. For example: The .45-70 slinging a 405-grain bullet at 1,800 fps from a Ruger Number One (don't try that load in your Springfield!) delivers about the same recoil as a .338 Winchester Magnum thrusting a 225-grain spitzer at 2,800 fps from another Number One. Even calculated recoil speed is similar: about 17 fps. But the .338 is apt to feel more punishing because its bullet leaves faster.

Rumor has it that big-bore British rounds merely push you, while sharp-shouldered magnums belt you, as if cordite somehow made cartridges more genteel. I'm not convinced. There's more than a push to a .600 Nitro or even a .470 in recoil, partly because the short breech sections of doubles put the muzzles closer to your face, and their off-center bullet launch pivots the rifle. It is true that doubles have twice the barrel steel up front, and velocities and breech pressures are low. But bullets that weigh more than an ounce, in front of powder columns as long as a half-smoked cigar, ensure that you'll get quite a jab. Inexperience or faulty locks that set both barrels off in quick succession make recoil more memorable. Also, there's less forehand control with a double. Although you can point surely and quickly, the double's slender forend and slick barrels can't match the checkered forestock of a bolt rifle for grip in absorbing recoil.

It does seem that sharp-shouldered magnum cartridges kick savagely. Combining heavy bullets with high pressures and big charges of powder behind abrupt shoulders can make rifles violent. The .378

A brake is hardly optional on a rifle in .50 BMG. Braked or not, it rattles your dentures.

Weatherby and its derivatives bring on a flinch fast if there's no brake up front. A muzzle brake reduces recoil by reducing jet effect at the muzzle. It bleeds gas pressure through vents instead of letting it erupt suddenly as the bullet clears the muzzle. By siphoning gas, a brake provides opposing surfaces fore and aft of each vent for the gas to push against, so not all the thrust of escaping gas is rearward. Any brake boosts muzzle blast. Noisy rifles are easy to shoot at the bench, where you have ear protection. But you won't wear muffs on the hunt, and shooting through a brake without them can damage your hearing. Big-game guides, who often find themselves beside a hunter at the shot, tend to hate brakes. A brake makes shooting less pleasant from low positions. Prone on dirt, you'll trigger a tornado that leaves dust on your scope lens, in your barrel, and maybe in your eyes. At best, it hangs in the air long enough to obscure your view of the target. Without wind, it may hover there long after the animal and a chance for a second shot are gone. Angling the vents forward helps by directing the blast away from you.

Most brakes now are barrel diameter or slightly larger and come with a cap to protect barrel threads when the brake is off. A .338 Mark

Muzzle brakes mitigate recoil by venting gases to the sides. Expect an increase in blast and noise.

Ported muzzles act like muzzle brakes, but the bullet doesn't contact the inside of the brake.

X Mauser in my rack, stocked and barreled by Intermountain Arms, has a brake that I replace with a knurled cap for hunting. Not all barrels will shoot to the same point of impact with and without a brake. My .338 does, but an Ed Brown rifle in .300 Weatherby throws its bullets 3 inches to 10 o'clock when I remove the brake. (With or without the device, it shoots 3/4-inch groups.) An alternative to the fixed brake is one that you can adjust on the rifle, opening the ports for recoil reduction and closing them to mitigate noise. Savage offers this type of brake on its rifles.

Installing a brake increases the length of your barrel a couple of inches without affecting velocity. If you trim the barrel, it will reduce velocity because there's no bullet contact with the brake, and the gas has little effect on acceleration past the barrel proper.

With or without a brake, a long barrel reduces felt recoil, partly because it delays the jet effect of powder gas at the muzzle, and partly because it thrusts the blast farther from you. It also adds weight to the rifle's front end, counteracting muzzle jump so there's less lift to slam the rifle into your chops.

Another thing that keeps recoil from hurting you is a stock with just enough drop at comb to place your eye behind the sight. A

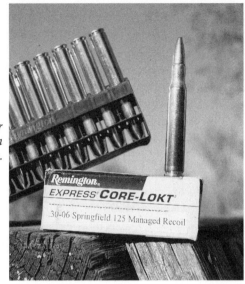

Remington and Federal offer reduced-recoil loads, deadly on big game to 200 yards or so.

gently rounded comb helps too, as does cast-off, the angle of a comb offset to the right. Cast-off is typically an option only on custom rifles. Combs that slope up toward the rear, as on the Weatherby Mark Vs, seem to go easier on shooters than do straight combs. Proper stock pitch (angle of butt to bore) is important too. A soft buttpad of generous length and width slows and spreads recoil. It also protects the buttstock better than does a steel plate.

Heavy rifles offer more inertia to mitigate recoil, and the heavy scopes that are popular now add to that weight. But scopes have inertia of their own that tries to tear them off the rifle during recoil. Ring friction alone can fail to hold a heavy scope on a rifle of violent recoil. The lighter the scope on hard-kicking rifles, the better. Alloy scope tubes are plenty stout and put less stress on rings and mounts.

Once, zeroing a .416 Rigby, I failed to notice a scope working loose. The rings were fastened by screws clamping them on serrated bases. Shoulders on the fronts of the bases kept the rings from sliding forward, but those shoulders also enabled loose rings to bounce back and forth on the bases. And like a gymnast getting a little higher with each jump on a trampoline, the rings would get a slightly longer run each time. When I triggered the last in a series of shots, the scope suddenly flew off the rifle and clobbered me between the eyes. It then somersaulted over my head and landed yards away. The rings had worked free and, after reciprocating a few times, had ended up well behind the shoulder on the front base. That final shot jerked the bases rearward so fast that the rings bounced off the shoulder hard enough to clear the bases.

Shooting positions affect felt recoil. The butts of old lever rifles dig into your shoulder like barbecue forks. But the people who shot them decades earlier held the butts on their upper arms, not tight against their tender necks. They bent their heads over the stocks and let the wood barely touch their cheeks.

It's best to keep head erect and eyes straight ahead when aiming modern rifles, to get the clearest sight picture. But shooters with long necks are at a loss. We can't get full shoulder contact with the butt while holding our head up and keeping our cheek in contact with the stock. So we move the butt up so that little more than the toe bears on our shoulder. All the recoil, then, lands on that small area, and it can make us wince. That is still better than bending over the stock and squinting up under your brow to find a spot of target with a section of reticle. If recoil hurts with the stock placed high enough to keep your head erect, get a recoil pad or a milder cartridge.

Recoil seems most severe in the prone position partly because you are normally shooting at an upward angle, but also because your body has lots of ground contact and can't move easily. This means that you don't act as a shock absorber to help the rifle decelerate; you stop it suddenly. Additionally, you're concentrating recoil on top of your clavicle rather than in front, where pectoral muscles protect it. Shooting sharply uphill from the prone or a low sitting position, you have an even chance of drawing more blood from your skull than from the animal. You'll absorb recoil most comfortably from an offhand or kneeling position. Your body can flex, damping the jolt. The kick can still be memorable, however, and if that memory is vivid, you may find yourself fighting a flinch.

Some years ago I fired a lovely old Jeffery double rifle chambered in .600 Nitro Express. Loading up with 900-grain solids, I knew that this rifle would jump despite its 14 pounds. The recoil drove me back a step, a little dance I remembered from having once shot a Holland rifle in .700 NE. But only my nose hurt. It had been hammered by my thumb. More recently, I got a chance to shoot a blackpowder cartridge rifle launching 1,100-grain bullets 1,500 fps. The concussion under the tin roof of the range seemed to shake the railroad ties supporting it. The muzzle of the 15-pound rifle leaped as if weightless. I staggered back. Blue smoke from 300 grains of spent powder hung thick over awestruck onlookers.

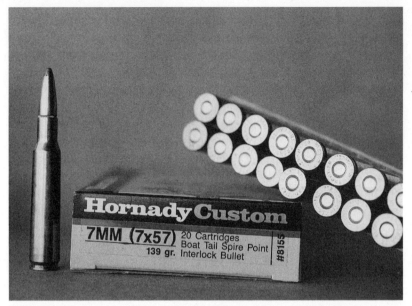

The 7x57, introduced in 1893, marries flat flight and gentle recoil. A fine deer round, it kills elk too.

On a recoil tolerance scale of gun-shy to Godzilla, I'm just a notch above wimp. It's clear to me when I pull a trigger that, save for a thin slice of rubber, all that lies between my clavicle and a small bomb are steel and hardwood. People make hammers out of that stuff. However, because I like to hunt big, tough animals and shoot targets far away, I tolerate the pounding as best I can, trying to control those muscles that tense when they sense I'm taking up the last ounce. It isn't always easy.

Perhaps the most fearsome rifle in my rack is a Mauser in .458. Its stock is proportioned just right for iron sights, and it has that lively feel of an upland bird gun. It doesn't weigh much more than an upland gun either, and that's a liability during recoil. That rifle kicks as fast as lightning on skids. Three shots and my head throbs; my jaw comes out of numb after the fifth, and I start feeling it for cracks. When the sights again settle on paper, I'd almost trade places with it. If this .458 with the hooves of a mule didn't point like a Rizzini and stick 500-grain solids into chestnut-size groups, I would list it in the classifieds.

The worst thing about recoil is that it shuts down practice. Shooters who don't have fun shooting don't shoot enough to get good at it. One way to make shooting on the range more pleasant and keep that

Position affects felt recoil. Prone, your body can't move, and the butt rests on your clavicle. Ouch!

flinch at bay is to use extra padding on your shoulder. A Past Recoil Shield is a convenient and inexpensive item. Folded towels also work well because you can just drape them over your shoulder and shed them between strings on a hot day. You'll also want a soft pad for your elbow on the bench.

You don't need hot loads to hone your marksmanship, or for preliminary zeroing. You may even find that gentle ammunition kills game surprisingly dead. Remington Managed-Recoil and Federal Low Recoil loads for popular deer cartridges offer substantial reductions in kick. Managed-Recoil rounds feature lighter bullets at standard velocities. Low Recoil ammunition pampers you with bullets of ordinary weight driven slower. Both types bring lethal energy to targets as far as 200 yards. In my experience the Remington loads often require no sight change.

If you're concentrating on fundamentals, you'll be less likely to think of recoil, and if you don't think about recoil, it won't make you miss. Does the rifle kick so hard that you can't concentrate? Trade it in, or try milder loads. You can't afford to shoot badly because you anticipate getting hurt. Repeated flinching is flinching well practiced, a routine you don't want your body to learn.

5 Performance by the Numbers

Before I was in business, when I visited Aberdeen Proving Grounds, talking to some of the ballisticians there, finding out how little I knew, they explained . . . that the peak of pressure is immediately in front of the cartridge case.
—Roy Weatherby, in a letter to Grits Gresham, 1980

BALLISTICS, BRIEFLY

Compared with rocks, spears, and arrows, bullets fly very flat. They move so fast that you can't see them, and no doubt the first riflemen considered themselves lethal at great range. Then in 1537, Trataglia, an Italian scientist, wrote a ballistics book. He described the bullet's path as an arc, which was a revelation to some people, who envisioned a bullet flying almost straight until its energy was spent, then dropping abruptly to earth. Trataglia determined that to give a bullet its greatest range, its launch angle would have to approach 45 degrees. Although his conclusion does not hold true for modern ammunition, it was valid for low-velocity projectiles, which are affected more by gravity than by air resistance.

A century after Trataglia studied bullets, Galileo dropped cannonballs from the Leaning Tower of Pisa—a trajectory investigation for the arsenal at Venice. Galileo concluded that because the acceleration of a falling body was a constant, bullet trajectories must be parabolic. But Galileo concurred with Trataglia in assigning 45 degrees as the launch angle for maximum range, because his experiments did not take drag into account. Compared to the acceleration of gravity, drag on a cannonball dropped from a window was inconsequential. Galileo's work was so far ahead of its time that another century passed before anyone else took a substantive step in the field of ballistics.

The sleek bullets Dave Smith loads in his 6.5/284 have a very high ballistic coefficient.

Around 1740, Englishman Benjamin Robins invented a device to measure bullet speed. He called it a ballistic pendulum. The pendulum had a heavy wooden bob of known weight that was brought to rest, hanging vertically. Robins weighed a bullet to be fired, then shot it into the pendulum. By noting the height of the bob's swing, he could calculate impact velocity, because speed (with mass) is a component of momentum. A series of measurements with .75-caliber musket balls yielded speeds of 1,400 and 1,700 fps. People of the day were loath to believe that any projectile could travel that fast. When Robins increased his firing distance, skeptics howled. To account for reduced readings at long range, air resistance had to be 85 times as strong as the force of gravity. This seemed incredible, but of course, it was true.

Another pioneer ballistician was Sir Isaac Newton, who died only 15 years before Robins began his experiments. His laws of mechanics were crucial to the understanding of ballistics, as was his work in calculus. Newton and the German Gottfried Wilhelm von Leibniz developed this branch of mathematics at about the same time. Newton's universal law of gravitation held that the force of gravity varies with altitude. He demonstrated that drag increases with the density of air

Lou Schweibert's weatherproof Ballisticards offer a wealth of information on particular loads.

and the cross-sectional area of a projectile. This brilliant thinker also showed a relationship between drag and the square of the projectile's speed. Because he had no way to measure the speed of musket balls, he couldn't know that drag increases dramatically when projectiles approach the speed of sound (1,120 fps). Accurate measurements of drag eluded scientists until the late 1800s, when inventors came up with chronographs in England and Germany. By this time, conical bullets were in widespread use, and cartridge firearms were supplanting muzzleloaders.

The idea of a "standard" bullet that could be used to develop benchmark values for drag and other ballistic variables came to experimenters in the mid-nineteenth century. The flight characteristics of any bullet could then be computed using a constant factor that defined its relationship with the standard bullet. The concept of a ballistic coefficient followed. Ballistic coefficient (C) defines bullet flight in the following equation: C = drag deceleration of the standard bullet/drag deceleration of the actual bullet. Although this relationship is exactly true only when both bullets are of the same shape and density, it serves well enough when bullets are of similar form. By 1865, ballisticians

Jay Jarrett tacks a target on a 600-yard range. To determine bullet drop for sure, you have to shoot.

worldwide had become engaged in drag calculations with standard bullets. The best-known studies were conducted by Krupp in Germany (1881) and by the Gavre Commission in France (1873–1898). The Gavre Commission's tests were perhaps the most extensive, including velocities up to 6,000 fps plus data from other countries, but atmospheric variations produced inaccuracies in the drag figures. The Krupp studies delivered more reliable results. The Krupp standard bullet was a flat-based conical, 3 calibers long, with a 2-caliber ogive.

Around 1880, an Italian ballistician named Siacci discovered a short alternative to the laborious calculus in determining a bullet's trajectory. He found that by using calculus to plot the path of a standard bullet, he could calculate with simple algebra the path of any other bullet with a known C value. This shortcut proved a real boon to amateur and academic ballistician alike. Shortly thereafter, a Russian colonel named Mayevski developed a mathematical model that illustrated the drag deceleration of this bullet. U.S. Army colonel James Ingalls used Mayevski's work as the basis for his Ingalls tables, first published in 1893 and revised in 1917. The Ingalls tables show the

Leupold offers a scope spool with a tape of ballistics data—for shooters with flagging memories.

ballistic behavior of a standard Krupp bullet—which, it turns out, is quite similar to most modern hunting bullets. Development of the analog computer during the 1940s made ballistics math easier. The digital computer later increased the speed and accuracy of figuring complex trajectories, such as those of bombs dropped at high altitude.

In 1965 Winchester-Western published ballistics tables that grouped small arms bullets into four families, each differing in terms of shape and drag function. G5 drag was for boattail bullets that slipped through the air readily, G6 described flat-base spitzer (pointed) bullets with full metal jackets, GL drag applied to hollow-point bullets, and G1 drag applied to all bullets not described in other categories. All drag functions except the GL had been determined by the U.S. Army Ballistic Research Laboratories at Aberdeen Proving Ground in Maryland. These shapes covered almost all popular hunting bullets. G1 drag closely matches that found in the Ingalls tables. (Incidentally, the "G" descriptor was chosen in honor of the Gavre Commission.)

For accurate bullet flight information, you need actual C values. One way to determine C is with firing tests, comparing the ballistic properties of the test bullet with those of the standard bullet. Another method, developed by Wallace Coxe and Edgar Beurgless at Du Pont in the 1930s, is essentially a matching exercise. The test bullet is

In the hunting field, you think about conditions, not ballistics. Ballistics is homework.

compared with bullet profiles on a chart of various profiles, and when a match is found, the chart provides a number that can be used to calculate C. Although this method has been widely accepted, ballisticians at Sierra Bullets tell me that C values so determined typically vary up to 10 percent from the C values obtained from firing tests. Ballistic coefficients change markedly near the speed of sound.

A caveat: Ballistic coefficients are useful in comparing the flight characteristics of bullets only when those bullets are driven at the same speed. Because drag increases with speed, you can't expect firing tests of the same bullet at different speeds to yield the same C. That said, few shooters have the facilities to conduct firing tests. A simple math formula is an alternative: $C = w/id^2$, where w is the bullet weight in pounds, d is bullet diameter in inches, and i is the form factor.

The higher the C value, the flatter the bullet will fly and the better it will conserve speed and energy. The standard bullet has a C of 1.000. C values for most hunting bullets range from .200 to .600, with midweight spitzers falling in the .300 to .500 range. A flat-nose .45-70 bullet has a C of around .200, as does the standard 170-grain flat-nose .30-30 bullet. A 100-grain .25, 140-grain 7mm, and 165-grain .30 have C values of .350 to .400; adding weight or a tapered heel can boost it to

.450 or so. Only the most streamlined hunting bullets deliver C values near .500.

The effect of C on bullet drop is less than its effect on drag—which, by influencing deceleration rate and flight time, also contributes to drop. Sierra tables show that a bullet with a C of .600 at 3,000 fps drops about 58 inches at 500 yards. A bullet with a C of .400 drops 65 inches when fired at the same speed. That's a relatively small difference, given the 33 percent change in C and 500 yards of bullet travel. The difference in remaining energy mirrors the shift in the point of impact: 2,256 foot-pounds for a bullet with a C of .600, and 1,929 foot-pounds for a bullet with a C of .400. If you trim velocity by 500 fps, to 2,500 fps, the bullet with a C of .600 drops 85 inches, or 27 inches more than it did at a starting velocity of 3,000 fps. The bullet with a C of .400 falls 96 inches, or 31 inches more. The remaining energy is 1,835 and 1,551 foot-pounds, respectively. It seems that a reduction in velocity only half as great (by percentage) as a reduction in C has a greater effect on bullet drop and remaining energy at this distance.

Still, a high C can extend range considerably, even at low velocities. The .300 Whisper, a subsonic round developed on the .221 Fireball case by J. D. Jones for tactical use in suppressed rifles, starts a 200-grain bullet at just over 1,000 fps. But in fast-twist barrels, it delivers fine accuracy out to 200 yards, with less loss of energy (by percentage) than a .300 Winchester Magnum leaks over that yardage. With 165-grain bullets loaded to 1,800 fps, the diminutive Whisper outperforms the .30-30 on deer. The same can be said about the .338 Whisper, based on the 7mm BR. A 300-grain Sierra MatchKing driven 1,050 fps from the 12-inch barrel of a Contender pistol is still lethal and accurate beyond 400 yards.

There are a couple of other things to remember. First, a change in C has a larger effect on remaining energy at high muzzle velocities than at low ones, because as bullets speed up, drag increases as a percentage of the forces impeding bullet flight. Second, a change in C has a greater effect on drop at lower velocities than at high ones, because at low speeds, gravity takes a more active hand than drag in depressing a bullet's arc.

Although drag is commonly assumed to be, like gravity, a single force, it actually comprises several. The sum of drag forces depends on bullet speed, weight, and profile; axial spin; and atmospheric conditions. Jacket texture is also a factor at long range, because skin friction is an important component of drag. There are others: Pressure drag

The .30-378 Weatherby wowed big-game hunters. It's still a best seller; there's no faster .30.

occurs at the bullet's nose. You can feel pressure drag when you hold your hand out the window of a speeding car. The hair on your arm illustrates skin friction as it flattens to the flow of air. A pointed bullet with a long ogive (slope between bullet tip and shank) reduces pressure drag. Supersonic speed (greater than Mach 1.2) shaves it too. Subsonic travel (less than Mach 0.8) increases pressure drag. At the bullet's tail, you'll find pressure drag in reverse; the bullet forms a wake and a vacuum, both of which impede bullet flight. Boattail bullets trim the effect of base drag, but you'll notice the effect only at extreme range.

Wave drag results from the shock waves produced by a bullet traveling through stationary air at a speed greater than the speed of sound. Wave drag occurs only at supersonic velocities.

Yaw sets up drag too. A bullet is in some state of yaw whenever its axis does not coincide exactly with its direction of travel. Air impinging on the bullet's side, even at an oblique angle, adds substantially to overall drag. It occurs at subsonic, transonic, and supersonic speeds.

Precession is the rotation of the bullet's nose about the bullet's axis. It is undesirable but virtually unpreventable. A bullet seldom leaves the muzzle perfectly. Any tipping of the bullet—due to a damaged

This H-S Precision rifle likes Black Hills ammo. The 1:12 twist is right for 50-grain bullets.

muzzle, nicked bullet base, or lack of concentricity in the bullet's jacket—can put the nose into its own orbit around the bullet's axis. Like a top that "goes to sleep" after you give it a hard spin, the bullet may rotate more smoothly, with less precession, after covering some distance. That is why you may get smaller groups (in terms of minutes of angle) at long range. A rifle that shoots 2-inch groups at 100 yards might keep all bullets inside 3 inches at 200 yards. Precession affects yaw drag and can impede penetration.

Drag influences not only a bullet's rate of deceleration but also its stability. A bullet at rest is stable, but once you fire it downrange, it is subject to several forces (including drag) that act to change its intended flight path and attitude. Extreme yaw, however imparted, can cause the bullet to tumble. Axial spin fights yaw, but it must be matched to the bullet's weight, length, and speed. A rate of rifling twist that's too slow to stabilize the bullet can result in tumbling or "keyholing" at the target. Excessive spin increases the bullet's yaw angle, adds to total drag, boosts the deceleration rate, and impairs accuracy at long range. It can also lead to instability as the bullet goes transonic (between Mach 1.2 and .8).

If early marksmen were astonished when ballistic pendulums indicated bullet speeds faster than the speed of sound, many shooters

Warm desert air won't boost pressures noticeably. Hours on a hot dashboard can, so too a hot chamber.

today would be surprised at the spin speed of bullets. A .308 bullet spun one turn in 12 inches at a muzzle velocity of 3,000 fps averages a shade under 2,500 fps over its first 400 yards of travel, which it completes in about half a second. In that half second, the bullet spins 1,500 times. In contrast, an automobile engine pulling you along at 65 miles per hour (mph) might turn at 3,000 revolutions per minute (rpm). That's only 500 rotations per second, or 250 per half second. The bullet is spinning six times faster. Give the rifling a 1:9 twist, and you boost rotational speed by 25 percent, to 3,750 rotations per second. Unlike a bullet's forward speed, which slows under the influence of drag, rotational velocity remains essentially constant.

Bullet upset inside game can affect bullet rotation. Jacket petals spread far to the side add drag to both forward and rotational movement. Petals act as lever arms to tip the bullet, further reducing stability, so the bullet is more easily moved off course. Although protruding petals also cause great tissue damage, in part due to bullet rotation, there's a limited "buzz-saw" effect in bullet wounds. A .270 bullet turning once every 10 inches of travel barely gets through one revolution before exiting the chest of a deer.

VELOCITY VARIABLES

We no longer measure velocity with pendulums but rather with electric eyes that register the passage of a bullet's shadow as the bullet travels a known distance. Chronographs are a century old, but it wasn't that long ago that Texan Dr. Ken Oehler did shooters an enormous service by designing and building the first chronographs meant for consumer use. Before the Oehler instruments, chronographs were found only in the laboratories and shooting tunnels of ammunition companies. They were fixed in place and very expensive. Consequently, shooters had to take the catalog ballistics charts at face value and hope that their handloads were producing the pressures and bullet speeds listed in the loading manuals. Now every serious shooter I know has a chronograph. Some cost less than an ordinary rifle scope.

Portable chronographs have "screens"—electric eyes—set up a short distance apart on a bar or on the electronic box that gives you the velocity reading. The chronograph measures the time between the bullet's passage over the first and second screens. Just as you could drive a car a quarter mile and compute the number of miles per hour your car would travel at that speed, you can time bullet flight for a short distance and extrapolate. Some chronographs allow you to adjust the distance between screens. The greater the distance, the more accurate the reading. A chronograph must be precisely calibrated for the span between screens, or it won't read velocities correctly.

Besides registering bullet speed, a chronograph also tells you the extreme spread (ES)—that is, the range of velocities, slowest to fastest. ES is useful because you want loads that deliver uniform results. High variation in ES often shows up at the target as poor or mediocre accuracy. It's unrealistic to expect all shots to stay within 10 fps of each other, and sometimes a big ES accompanies little groups. Still, ES is best if it's a small figure—for example, under 30 fps for a five-shot group from a powerful hunting round.

The chronograph can also determine standard deviation (SD), a statistical measure that, by all accounts, originated in the late 1890s. American statistician Karl Pearson is generally credited with the formula. Without getting into mathematics (which had me in a headlock from grammar school through my doctorate), SD can be summarized as the positive square root of the variance. Variance is simply the sum of the squares of the deviations from the mean of your chronograph readings, divided by a number that's one less than the number of times you shot. A high SD indicates a lot of spread in your data—that is, a

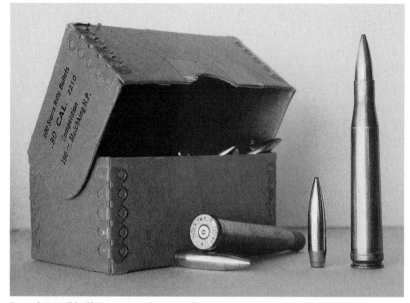

Long boattail bullets retain velocity well and can pass short, light bullets started faster.

great deal of variability among your readings. A low SD means that most of your velocity readings were clustered close to your mean.

With SD, you can construct a bell curve that shows how your velocities grouped around the mean and, for any given speed range, the percentage of shots likely to fall within that range. Once in a while you might get a velocity reading you don't believe—perhaps the chronograph didn't register a bullet's passage accurately, or your load was somehow defective. A rule of thumb is to throw out any reading more than $2^1/_2$ times the SD from the mean.

Bullet velocity is slave to a number of variables, most of which you (and rifle makers and ammo companies) can control. Velocity varies not only with powder type and charge and bullet weight; it is also influenced by chamber and barrel dimensions, throat profile and length, and bore finish. A tight chamber reduces the amount of energy lost to case expansion. So does a tight throat. But a long throat that allows the bullet to move before engaging the rifling and permits long seating of the bullet to increase powder space enables a handloader to load hot. A long throat is generally no boost to accuracy, but on hunting rifles, it's not a liability. Roy Weatherby used long throats and ambitious Norma loads to rev up his cartridges.

The 7mm STW (left) beats the 7mm Remington Magnum ballistically but is less efficient.

Components affect pressures and velocities. Substituting magnum primers for standard caps, for example, elevates pressure. Expect a smaller change in velocity. At full-power levels, increasing pressure kicks velocity up, but not proportionately. Similar changes occur when you substitute cases with smaller powder chambers (thicker walls or webs). Switching bullets may cause no significant change in speed; however, if the new bullet has a long shank, is seated closer to the lands on takeoff, is slightly larger than bore diameter, or has a "sticky" jacket, pressures can rise. Remington's choice of Nosler Partition bullets for the first .300 Ultra Mag loads no doubt disappointed folks at Swift, who were already supplying Partition-style A-Frame bullets to Remington. The rationale: A-Frames had soft jackets, resulting in more bore friction and higher pressures. To get 180-grain bullets to cruise as fast as they wanted them to in the Ultra Mag, Remington engineers had to use Noslers.

Barrel length influences bullet speed because the bullet's exit cuts short the pressure curve that is mainly responsible for the bullet's launch speed. I prefer short barrels when I'm poking around in the brush after whitetails or climbing a steep place for elk or mule deer. Short barrels allow maneuverability; they're faster on target than long barrels, and they weigh less. Increase diameter, and you add stiffness more quickly than with long barrels. The liabilities of carbine-length tubes have to do mainly with muzzle blast and bullet speed. In reality, the velocity issue is not as big as many riflemen assume. Still, it gets a lot of press.

Whereas rimfire rifle barrels can easily be so long that bore friction outlives the powder's thrust, centerfire rifles typically benefit from longer barrels. The smaller the bullet (in diameter) in relation to case capacity, the more length you need. It also stands to reason that the slowest fuels benefit most from long barrels. The pinch of quick-burning powder in a .22 Long Rifle case has spent its energy entirely in 16 inches of barrel. A magnum charge of H4831 behind a heavy bullet warrants a longer tube.

Few shooters have tested the effect of barrel length on velocity. Rifle maker Charlie Sisk lopped barrels to find out. His data are presented below. Loads are not listed because some exceeded practical pressure thresholds. Trials with the .300 Winchester and .340 Weatherby Magnums yielded similar results.

.270 Winchester, 130-grain bullets, H-4350	
Barrel length (inches)	Velocity (fps)
27	3115
26	3093
25	3071
24	3054
23	3035
22	3027

.300 Remington Ultra Mag, 220-grain bullets

Barrel length (inches)	Velocity (fps)	
	H-4895	H-870
27	2740	3107
26	2709	3088
25	2685	3062
24	2663	3046
23	2636	3018
22	2612	2997

Some interesting things are going on here. First, lopping 6 inches off a barrel drains less velocity than many shooters would assume: 114 fps for the .270 Winchester. That's only 18 to 19 fps per inch, and the rate of loss doesn't seem to change much.

Another surprise is the relative performance of fast (H-4895) and slow (H-870) powders in the big .300 Ultra Mag hull. One might have predicted that the slower powder would deliver the worst performance—and the greatest velocity drop per inch—as tube length got down to 22 inches. Not so! The 4895 loads lost 128 fps between barrel lengths of 27 and 22 inches, while the H-870 loads lost only 110 fps.

Load, original barrel length, and case dimensions affect velocities as barrels become shorter. A test conducted by A-Square with a .300

Load data taped to his stock, Skip Dahlstrom homes in on distant caribou. Fast bullets help here.

Winchester Magnum pressure barrel recorded velocities at 1-inch intervals from 28 down to 16 inches. Presented below are some of those
velocities, with loads of 70.5 grains IMR 4350 behind a 150-grain
Nosler Ballistic Tip, and 78.0 grains RL-22 launching a 180-grain Sierra
Spitzer.

Barrel length (inches)	Velocity (fps) 150-grain	Velocity (fps) 180-grain	Velocity loss (fps)
28	3346	3134	150/180
26	3268	3089	78/45
24	3211	3016	57/73
22	3167	2966	44/50
20	3108	2930	59/36
18	3014	2874	94/56
16	2903	2748	111/126

Velocity loss per inch of barrel length varied from a low of 22 fps
to a high of 56 fps for the 150-grain bullet, and 18 to 63 fps for the 180-
grain bullet. Rate of velocity loss increased substantially as the barrel
was chopped to less than 20 inches long. In that case, we're cutting into
the descending pressure curve, before it has flattened out. A lot of pressure is being released to the atmosphere instead of staying in harness
behind the bullet.

Some years ago I ran barrel length comparisons with various loads
in a pair of rifles chambered in 7mm Remington Magnum. At the time,
I thought they were illustrative, but since then, I've been convinced
that some barrels are "fast" and some are "slow," and velocity comparisons are best done in the same tube.

Load	Bullet weight and type	Velocity (fps)	Barrel length (inches)
66 H4831	154 Jensen	2907	24
		3030	26
65 H4831	160 Nosler Partition	2826	24
		2900	26
Federal	160 Nosler Partition	2772	24
		2844	26
Remington	150 Nosler Ballistic Tip	2842	24
		2961	26

Load	Bullet weight and type	Velocity (fps)	Barrel length (inches)
Winchester	160 Silvertip	2709	24
		2873	26
Remington	160 Swift A-Frame	2767	24
		2872	26
Winchester	150 Power-Point	3024	24
		3100	26

How does extra speed play out downrange in terms of energy and trajectory? Say that your .270 spits 130-grain factory-loaded bullets across the screens at 3,000 fps from a 22-inch barrel, and that the same load from a friend's custom rifle with a 25-inch barrel approaches 3,100 fps. Given a common zero of 200 yards, your bullet will hit 0.3 inch higher at 100 yards and 0.6 inch lower at 300 yards. At 400 yards, the difference is 1.7 inches. The short-barreled rifle delivers about 1,800 foot-pounds of energy at 200 steps; the 25-inch barrel delivers 1,920. At 300 yards, the energy difference does not increase; in fact, because the rate of deceleration increases as you boost velocity, downrange velocity and energy figures tend to get closer. At 400 yards, these bullets are hitting within 100 foot-pounds, or 7 percent, of each other.

That's still a bigger number than many shooters want to accept. But foot-pounds are not a reliable measure of killing power, and you seldom need every ounce of punch a cartridge offers. It may well be that the success of your hunt hinges on one fast shot. A barrel that comes to bear quickly can make the difference. If a short, lightweight rifle enables you to investigate one more thicket in a day or climb one more ridge, you may find the biggest buck you've ever seen. Of course, you can trim barrels so far back that velocity loss becomes significant, and blast becomes obnoxious. Rifles that kick violently are much more pleasant to shoot when you add extra weight up front, and more length means less blast. Besides helping to steady a rifle, some forward tilt can help you swing smoothly on running game.

My preferences in barrel length have changed over the years. When I was still young and virile enough to toss alfalfa bales all afternoon or hike 25 mountain miles in a day, I liked the long, elegant looks of bolt rifles with 26-inch barrels. They seemed to balance well, too, being a bit front-heavy like the rimfire target rifles that had helped me learn to shoot. I was impressed by the blazing speed of bullets from the .264 Winchester and .300 Weatherby Magnums. Having the hot gas loose its

Sonoran canyons beg long, heavy bullets, not to kill deer better but to retain speed and fly flat at a distance.

fury so far from my face was comforting, and when firing powerful rifles with shorter tubes, I sometimes caught myself flinching. But hunting with short barrels makes more sense as the hills get steeper. I've come to appreciate the quick response of lighter and shorter rifles. Wand-weight barrels don't seem quite as silly as they once did.

Appropriate length depends partly on application, partly on chambering, partly on barrel weight. Numbers denoting barrel contours vary, so a #2 from one shop won't necessarily match a #2 from another. In my view, most #3 contours work nicely for bore diameters under .30. For bigger bores, I tend to favor #4s, though for a .338 Federal or even a .358 Winchester carbine, a slimmer tube makes sense. Some #4s, like the 25-inch Douglas on a .338-06 in my rack, make the rifle quite heavy.

Cartridge type also matters. The 20-inch barrels on .30-30 carbines are rightly popular. But a 20-inch tube on a .300 Holland wouldn't pass muster because, although the bore is the same, the H&H case is much bigger. Velocity from a carbine-length .300 Holland barely edges that of most .30-06 rifles, and you get a lot more blast. The following barrel lengths would be my picks if I were drawing up specs for a custom rifle:

20 inches: .30-30, .32 Spl., .35 Remington

21 inches: .22 Hornet, .348 Winchester, .358 Winchester, .444 Marlin, .45-70

22 inches: .222, .223, .250 Savage, .300 Savage, .308 Winchester, .450 Marlin

23 inches: .243, .257 Roberts, 7x57, .260 Remington, 7mm-08 Remington, .35 Whelen

24 inches: .22-250, .220 Swift, 6mm Remington, .270 Winchester, .280 Remington, .30-06, .338-06, .358 Norma

25 inches: .25-06 Remington, 7mm Remington, 7mm Weatherby, .300 Winchester, .300 H&H, .308 Norma, .338 Winchester

26 inches: .257 Weatherby, .264 Winchester, 7mm Remington Ultra Mag, .300 Weatherby, .300 Remington Ultra Mag

What about the new short magnums? I'd put them on the same lists as the belted magnums whose performance they match. As for the mightiest of high-velocity cartridges—the .338 Remington Ultra Mag, John Lazzeroni's long .30 and .33, and the .30-378 and .338-378 Weatherbys—choose the longest barrel you can conveniently carry. These behemoths can make a sandbag flinch. The farther the blast from your rosy cheeks, the better. Adding a brake will reduce recoil but boost decibel level. Incidentally, brakes have no ballistic effect on the bullet, so a 26-inch barrel with a brake that extends the length to 28 inches will deliver the same velocity as a 26-inch barrel of the same type without a brake.

As for handgun barrels, the longest you can manage is the top choice ballistically. Even very small bottleneck cases with fast fuels can give you a little more oomph when you add barrel inches. During experiments with the .17 HMR, I chronographed the 17-grain bullets in barrels ranging from 16 to 22 inches. Average speed from the longest bore was 2,545 fps, very nearly matching factory claims. A 16-inch barrel from a Chipmunk rifle delivered 2,459 fps. That's just 86 fps less in a barrel 6 inches shorter! By the old math, that's a drop of about 14 fps per inch.

Fortunately, barrel length is easy to specify on custom-built rifles. Shortening a factory barrel to make a rifle more nimble costs little. A couple of caveats: Make sure that anyone lopping a barrel to your specs is as adept at crowning as at cutting. Within limits, barrel length on sporting rifles has no appreciable effect on accuracy. The crown certainly affects accuracy, and that can determine your effective maximum range.

THROUGH THE TURBID SEA

In my feckless youth, I blazed away at bull's-eyes and big game with great optimism but little effect. I would have done better if I had studied the air.

Atmosphere exerts a huge effect on bullet flight. Air is not a void. Rather, it is like water. It offers substantial resistance. You can feel water's resistance when you swim. A belly flop from a 7-meter board gives you much more appreciation for the impenetrability of water. Shoot into water with a soft-nose bullet, and you'll find it a severe medium, rupturing bullet jackets and flattening cores more effectively than a hit to a big animal's rib cage.

We don't equate air resistance with that of water because a swim stroke done in air is an easy flailing of the arms. But when either air or a body moving through it has any speed, air can become quite a force. Motorcycle riders, sailors, and parachutists can attest to that. Get above the windshield in a convertible cruising at 60 mph, and you'll have some idea of what a bullet encounters when it's moving 88 fps.

A small-bore shooter reads conditions in his spotting scope before risking a record shot.

The author checks the effect of a shot. Clear, still, early-morning air made killing the buck easy.

Shooting prairie dogs is a good way to learn to read and compensate for adverse conditions.

Multiply that by 30, and you've calculated the blast that meets a 180-grain .308 Winchester bullet as it leaves the muzzle. Looking through a high-power target scope as you launch a .22 match bullet down-range, you'll see the path as a hook, its steep trajectory foreshortened in the lens. You might be surprised that the image of the bullet's track, as brief as it is, shows distinctly that a bullet striking center is apparently out of line for a center hit during almost its entire flight. Spin and wind affect its lateral movement as gravity pulls it down.

Thinking of bullets as curveballs thrown by a pitcher can help you put them in the bull's-eye. Long ago my Daisy air gun nailed small targets at ranges to 50 yards. In no part of its flight was a BB traveling even close to straight. But I shot the gun so much that I learned how the little steel orbs reacted to air and gravity. Visions of their lazy arcs ending in the breast feathers of starlings took my mind off arithmetic, to old Miss Bailey's dismay. Come Saturday, the stamped-steel front sight of that Daisy would find some corner of space above and to the side of what I wanted to hit, and in due time, the BB would land there.

Aiming is simply an attempt to arrange a collision. Accurate rifles and optical sights make aiming easier, but watching the hits and misses of slow, crude projectiles can make you a deadly shot. A quarterback and a basketball player, like a pitcher, deliver uncanny consistency with their arms alone. An accomplished archer or fly caster sees what he does wrong, corrects, and eventually improves.

Not being able to see bullets is a handicap to learning. That's why machine guns and antiaircraft cannons are fed to spew tracer bullets at regular intervals. It's enlightening to watch footage of aerial and naval combat shot during World War II. Drag, drift, and deceleration all show up with great clarity in the tracer paths. Gunners trained to shoot at Axis airplanes were often started with BB guns that made trajectory and flight time easy to see close up.

When a bullet leaves the muzzle of your rifle, it starts to drop at an accelerating rate of 32.16 fps per second. One reason few bullets drop 32 feet is that they don't stay aloft for a full second. Another is that we calculate drop not from bore line but from a sight line we manipulate to intersect the bullet's trajectory at two points. The farthest is the zero range, which is significantly below bore line.

While gravity has an obvious effect on bullets at long range, wind can be even more problematic. Wind is gravity on another plane; as the bullet slows, a constant wind has greater effect, just as gravity does on the drop of a decelerating bullet. But unlike gravity, wind does not displace a bullet with accelerating force. And unlike gravity, wind force and direction are not constant. Either or both can vary between rifle and target. In small-bore competition, I've fired through wind that straightened target flags near the target line while midrange flags hung limp and cloth at the target butts was flapping wildly in the other direction. Though a wind change at the muzzle has more effect on impact point than does an equivalent shift downrange, the bullet is more easily moved the farther it gets from the muzzle because there's more time downrange (per unit of distance traveled) for the wind to work its mayhem. So you can't say that a firing-line wind is more important than a downrange wind.

The effect of wind varies not only with its speed and where it intercedes but also with its angle. Full-value wind is a 90-degree crosswind, from 3 or 9 o'clock. It has the greatest influence on the bullet. A wind coming at you or from behind has the least effect. Wind from other points "around the clock" move bullets a little less than a full-value wind of the same speed and interdiction point, depending on the angle. Wind from the right gives a bullet from right-twist rifling a little lift as it moves the point of impact to the left. Wind from the left tends to depress the point of impact. Shooting prone matches, I always shaded low when compensating for a 3 o'clock gust and high when

A companion can be a great help afield, not just for spotting game but also for gauging range and wind.

holding to the left. It was imperative then, as it is when preparing a centerfire rifle for long-range shots at big game, to zero in calm conditions. Wind doesn't always scatter shots; you can drill tight groups in a steady breeze. But they'll land in a different place. For example, if you adjust your sights in a 3 o'clock wind, a let-off that brings dead calm will move your bullets to 4 o'clock.

In the hunting field, you needn't be too concerned about winds of less than 10 mph at ranges of 200 yards or less. At 300 yards, however,

Some shooters avoid breezy days. Smart shooters use them to learn how wind affects bullets.

even a light breeze has a telling effect. Remember that you can over-compensate for wind, just as many hunters miss because they hold high when aiming at game well within point-blank range. A brisk breeze from 7 o'clock may ripple the aspens and bend the prairie grass, but it has relatively little effect on a bullet even at long yardage because of its angle. If that same breeze were coming from 9 o'clock, the situation would be quite different. Just as you learned to hit with a sling-shot or BB gun without the math to tell you about drop and drift—or even an accurate estimate of yardage—you can learn to accurately dope wind without resorting to numbers. Shoot at enough targets (paper, not cans or distant rocks), and you'll soon get a feel for how wind affects a high-speed bullet. If you want the equivalent of a laser rangefinder to help with wind-doping, pick up a pocket anemometer (mine is a Kestrel).

One day, while shooting at prairie dogs with a .223, a couple of friends and I bellied to within 200 yards of a dog town and battled the wind with our 50-grain spitzers. We counted few hits, especially after the 200-yard sod poodles got wise and we were forced to stretch the rifles to 250, then 300 yards. A stiff breeze from 8 o'clock carried bullets from 3 to 6 inches, depending on distance and our timing. Shooting between gusts, we sometimes overcorrected. In spotting for one another, we learned more than if we'd been alone, trying to see bullet

At long range, bullet paths in wind depend not only on a bullet's form but also on its construction.

strikes during recoil. When we moved to another place so that the wind came from 7 o'clock, we saw wind deflection shrink. It confirmed a target-shooting rule: Unless it is very strong, ignore wind from between 11 and 1 o'clock and from 5 to 7 o'clock. A bullet traveling 3,000 fps meets tremendous wind resistance even under still conditions. It generates its own headwind—a 2,000-mph gale. What difference do you think a 20-mph headwind or tailwind would have on this bullet's flight?

Shot distance matters as much as wind speed and angle. A 130-grain .270 bullet launched at 3,000 fps drifts only about 3/4 inch at 100 yards in a 10-mph wind. But at 200 yards, it is 3 inches off course—four times as far as it was at 100. At 300 yards, it drifts 7 inches; at 400 yards, 13 inches. Flight time has a lot to do with this dramatic increase in bullet displacement.

Because it takes a strong wind to blow your bullet out of deer vitals at 100 yards, it's pretty safe to ignore both wind and gravity to your zero range of 200. As with holding over for a long shot, there's a real danger of compensating too much. Beyond 200 steps, you should mind the wind. It's of academic interest that drift quadruples in the second hundred yards; the thing to remember is that it increases with distance, but not at a constant ratio. Drift for a .270 bullet at 500 yards is about 60 percent greater than at 400. A useful rule of thumb is to assume an inch of drift for a 10-mph full-value wind at 100 yards, and double that at 200 yards; triple the 200-yard drift at 300 yards, and double the 300-yard drift at 400 yards. Here's how that works for a 180-grain .30-06 bullet at 2,700 fps:

Distance (yards)	Actual drift (inches)	Rule of thumb drift (inches)
100	0.7	1
200	2.9	2
300	7.0	6
400	12.9	12

In this case, the estimate falls within an inch of actual drift as far as most hunters are concerned when shooting at deer. Nobody I know can hold within an inch at 400 yards under hunting conditions, and few rifles shoot even half that tight. If you're shooting a .30-30 with a flat-nose bullet, the rule of thumb fails beyond 100 yards because the bullet is wind sensitive and decelerating quickly. The rule works well enough for fast spitzers. Out to 300 yards, actual and estimated drifts are close; at 400 yards, a 140-grain bullet from a 7mm Weatherby Magnum hews about 2 inches closer to line of sight than does a .30-06 bullet.

You might think that the problem with the .30-30 bullet has to do with its blunt nose. A bullet the shape of a soup can is not very well adapted for flight. There's a lot of air pressure on the nose, prompting quick deceleration. Because a bullet's form contributes to its ballistic coefficient (C), the .30-30 flat-nose has a low C value. But so do light-weight spitzers, such as 70-grain .243s. A streamlined bullet short for its diameter can be as inefficient, aerodynamically, as a bullet that is longer but has a blunt nose. A 70-grain .243 Nosler has a C of .252; the .30-30's is .268. Wind drift for the .243 bullet at 100, 200, 300, and 400 yards is 1.0, 4.3, 10.3, and 19.7 inches, respectively. That's significantly more deflection than you might expect from most big-game bullets. Velocity is not at issue here. While the .30-30 is sluggish at 2,200 fps, the 70-grain .243s give their dismal performance in wind after leaving the muzzle at 3,400 fps.

When you're shooting in wind, also pay attention to mirage—the visible current of air you can see flowing along railroad tracks on a hot day. It's the reaction of air to a warm surface, and it's the best "windicator" available. Mirage boils straight up when there's no wind, undulates gently ahead of a breeze, then flattens during a pickup in wind speed. Most visible on warm, sunny days, mirage leaves you to your own devices on cold, cloudy, or rainy days. When it's available, I much prefer mirage to wind flags and the ball-bearing vanes competitors bring to rifle matches. Mirage is more sensitive, and it's right there on your target face—you don't have to shift your eye to monitor the flag on a distant stake. Also, mirage can tell you things that flags don't. When it boils, after an extended run from one direction, I don't shoot. First, it's indicating a let-off, which will tug my bullet out of center to the windward direction. Second, a boil often precedes a shift in wind direction or a momentary fishtail. Get caught by that, and your next bullet hole will appear so far out as to make you weep.

Mirage can affect your shot even when the wind is too light to move your bullet off center. On a very hot day, boiling mirage can shift the target image, causing you to aim at a bull's-eye that is not really there. High-power scopes pick this up, but they can't do anything about the problem. You can focus the scope off the target face, but a blurred target is no more conducive to high scores. Experienced shooters in a prone match often focus their spotting scopes just shy of the target, to better pick up mirage. They watch shifting mirage through the spotter; then, when all seems well, they go to the sight, focused sharply on the target. But they don't tarry. Wind can change speed and direction quickly, and the sight might not detect subtle changes. Shooting fast under favorable conditions helps on days of unstable air; if you shoot slowly during calm periods, you'll run out of time. Also, savvy shooters watch the range before a match, to determine prevailing breeze. It's better to zero for that than for a calm that happens just two or three times during a relay.

Beware of the effect of topographic features on air movement. Hills can funnel wind through valleys; rocks and trees can set up whirlpools of air that affect bullets in unpredictable ways. A tall forest may block strong wind, but air moving through the treetops can be raked down to splash and swirl over the ground in all directions. Wind against the face of a mountain bends around it, so that in no place on its slopes will you find calm. The true direction of the incident wind is then of no consequence; what matters is the direction of the wind where you are on the mountain. Thermal drafts are of less import than prevailing winds, but in alpine terrain, they can be quite strong.

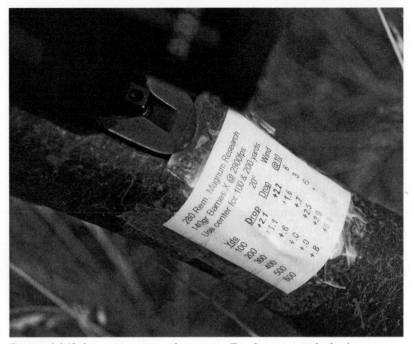

Drop and drift data matter most at long range. Taped to your stock, they're easy to access.

During clear weather, they move uphill during the day and downhill at night, changing at dawn and dusk. If you're shooting repeatedly in a place, whether in competition or at game, it pays to know the wind and mirage patterns there. For example, a rifle range I know in Spokane, Washington, lies along the outer curve of a river that hooks from southwest to northwest. Southwest winds strike the back of the firing line, then angle across the range to the canyon wall that borders the eastern hem of the range. Then they carom back across the target butts in the opposite direction. A gust on your back is a signal to hold fire unless you've got only an ounce left on the trigger, because the mirage at the target frames will soon flatten to the left, and you'll bounce a 9 at 10 o'clock. Firing points near the hill are less affected than those near the river.

The best way to learn to shoot well in the wind is to shoot often in the wind and study its effect on your bullets. You can get a good start as a wind-doper with a ballistics program from Ken Oehler or the people at Sierra Bullets. Punch in the velocity and ballistic coefficient of your bullet, and Oehler's Ballistic Explorer will plot a bullet track for you, showing energy, point-blank range, and wind drift, along with bullet drop. The Sierra program is just as useful. You can even use it to calculate ballistic coefficient from range data.

Computer ballistics programs are no substitute for shooting, but they can help you save ammo by putting you close to center at long range. And they can tell you how conditions you might not experience during practice will affect you on a hunt. Take elevation, for example. The air where you'll be hunting elk in Colorado is considerably thinner than that at the rifle range in Seattle or Baltimore. At normal hunting yardage, when shooting at an animal with vitals the size of a clothes basket, you needn't fret about bullets landing on the fringe. But at long distances, on an elk partially obscured by brush, air density makes a difference. The effect is greatest with flat-nose bullets. According to T. D. Smith, a former fighter pilot who developed long-range shooting aids for small arms, a .30-30 bullet hits about 9 inches higher at 300 yards when fired at 10,000 feet altitude than when fired at sea level. In contrast, a ballistically more efficient 175-grain bullet from a 7mm Remington Magnum strikes less than 3 inches higher in the thinner atmosphere.

Air temperature matters for the same reason that elevation matters: It affects air density. Warm air is thinner than cold air, and your bullet meets less resistance on a warm day—just as an airplane gets less lift in summer's heat. But you won't see much difference in bullet impact due to air temperature. Sierra's ballistics program helped predict the change in point of impact for a 140-grain Ballistic Tip bullet from a 7mm Remington Magnum load offered by Black Hills. With a starting velocity of 3,150 fps, a bullet fired at an air temperature of 59 degrees F should strike 16.9 inches low at 400 yards (with a 200-yard zero). The same bullet fired at 70 degrees hits 16.8 inches low. An industry rule of thumb is to expect a velocity change of 3 fps for every degree. You'd have to travel from the tropics to the Arctic or vice versa to notice any change in bullet impact caused by changes in air temperature, and then only at very long ranges.

Of course, bullet flight is also affected by breech pressure: The higher the pressure, the faster the bullet. A hot day can raise powder temperature, generating higher pressure. A cold day can make powder perform sluggishly. Tests run by Art Alphin (of A-Square) showed that at 40 degrees, a charge of 51 grains RL-15 generated 54,600 pounds per square inch (psi) to push 180-grain Nosler Ballistic Tips 2,675 fps from a .30-06. That rifle and load registered 59,900 psi and 2,739 fps at 120 degrees. The temperature of the ammunition, not the air, made the difference. A cartridge kept in a warm pocket and fired soon after loading on a cold morning will perform as if the chamber temperature were warmer than the ambient temperature. Cartridges left on a hot dashboard can get much warmer than the rifle, building higher pressures than ambient temperature would indicate. Some powders are more temperature sensitive than others, and if you're approaching the safe pressure limit, you may get a dangerous pressure spike with a relatively modest increase in temperature.

Another thing to ignore at normal ranges but to consider at extreme yardage is the Coriolis effect. The earth's rotation causes any projectile to drift slightly right in the Northern Hemisphere, slightly left in the Southern Hemisphere. Get on a merry-go-round moving clockwise and toss a ball to someone else on the merry-go-round, and the ball seems to curve to the left. Of course, only your frame of reference gives you that illusion. Coriolis acceleration for a rifle bullet is described by this equation: $Y = 2wV\sin$ (latitude), where w is the earth's rate of rotation (.0000729 degrees per second) and V is the bullet's average speed in feet per second.

For a bullet moving 2,800 fps at a latitude of 45 degrees north, the Coriolis acceleration comes out to 0.30 fps per second, or roughly 1 percent of the acceleration of gravity. At 350 yards, you'll get about half an inch of displacement. That's not enough to notice, because few hunting rifles shoot half-inch groups at 100 yards, let alone at 350. And I've not yet met a hunter who can hold 1/7 minute of angle in the field.

At very long ranges, the Coriolis effect can be significant. Air force F-16 fighter cannons are not wired for Coriolis correction, T. D. Smith tells me, "but the on-board computer is programmed for a 6-inch correction at 5,000 yards with either the Mark 82 or Mark 84 dive-bomb." Longer bombing ranges bring a higher correction value. If you're shooting at extreme range, figure a 1-inch correction for each second of bullet flight time. It takes a 170-grain flat-nose .30-30 bullet a second to cover 500 yards. The bullets most hunters use for big game these days spend much less time en route to the target.

Big-Game Rounds with Reach

I lift the great ram's ponderous head where he fell after 800-yard shot.
> —George Landreth, photo caption accompanying
> "Greatest Trophy of All," *Outdoor Life*, 1968

DEER AT A DISTANCE

There's no universal definition of a long-range deer cartridge. For me, it's a round that shoots a deer bullet (at least 60 grains) at 2,900 fps or faster, with a 400-yard drop of less than 24 inches given a 200-yard zero. Impact energy of at least 600 foot-pounds is a reasonable minimum. The following chart shows the performance of factory-loaded rounds that meet these long-range criteria. For ballistics data at extended range, consult Sierra's Infinity software (sierrabullets.com).

DEER CARTRIDGES BALLISTICS CHART

Cartridge/Bullet	Range (yards)				
	0	**100**	**200**	**300**	**400**
.22-250 Remington					
Hornady 60 Soft Point					
Velocity (fps)	3600	3195	2826	2485	2169
Energy (ft-lb)	1727	1360	1064	823	627
Arc (inches)		+1.0	0	-5.4	-16.3
Winchester 64 Power-Point					
Velocity (fps)	3500	3086	2708	2360	2038
Energy (ft-lb)	1741	1353	1042	791	590
Arc (inches)		+1.1	0	-5.9	-18.0

HE, high energy; HM, heavy magnum; LM, light magnum.

In coulee country, shots at deer can be long across the flats or short in the draws where deer bed.

Chris Lalik would tell you that almost any flat-shooting cartridge will kill deer if you shoot well.

DEER CARTRIDGES BALLISTICS CHART CONTINUED

Cartridge/Bullet	Range (yards)				
	0	**100**	**200**	**300**	**400**
.220 Swift					
Hornady 60 Hollow Point					
Velocity (fps)	3600	3199	2824	2475	2156
Energy (ft-lb)	1727	1364	1063	816	619
Arc (inches)		+1.0	0	-5.4	-16.3
.223 WSSM					
Winchester 64 Power-Point					
Velocity (fps)	3600	3144	2732	2356	2011
Energy (ft-lb)	1841	1404	1061	789	574
Arc (inches)		+1.0	0	-5.7	-17.7
.243 Winchester					
Black Hills 95 Nosler Ballistic Tip					
Velocity (fps)	2950	2720	2503	2296	2098
Energy (ft-lb)	1836	1561	1321	1112	929
Arc (inches)		+1.6	0	-7.2	-20.9

The .243 Winchester is among the best (and gentlest) long-range rounds for deer and pronghorns.

DEER CARTRIDGES BALLISTICS CHART CONTINUED

Cartridge/Bullet	Range (yards)				
	0	**100**	**200**	**300**	**400**
Federal 85 Sierra GameKing BTHP					
Velocity (fps)	3320	3070	2830	2600	2380
Energy (ft-lb)	2080	1770	1510	1280	1070
Arc (inches)		+1.1	0	-5.5	-16.1
Federal 90 Trophy Bonded					
Velocity (fps)	3100	2850	2610	2380	2160
Energy (ft-lb)	1920	1620	1360	1130	935
Arc (inches)		+1.4	0	-6.1	-19.2
Federal 100 Hi-Shok					
Velocity (fps)	2960	2700	2450	2220	1990
Energy (ft-lb)	1945	1615	1330	1090	880
Arc (inches)		+1.6	0	-7.5	-22.0
Federal 100 Sierra GameKing BTSP					
Velocity (fps)	2960	2760	2570	2380	2210
Energy (ft-lb)	1950	1690	1460	1260	1080
Arc (inches)		+1.5	0	-6.8	-19.8
Federal 100 Nosler Partition					
Velocity (fps)	2960	2730	2510	2300	2100
Energy (ft-lb)	1945	1650	1395	1170	975
Arc (inches)		+1.6	0	-7.1	-20.9
Hornady 100 BTSP					
Velocity (fps)	2960	2728	2508	2299	2099
Energy (ft-lb)	1945	1653	1397	1174	979
Arc (inches)		+1.6	0	-7.2	-21.0
Hornady 100 BTSP LM					
Velocity (fps)	3100	2839	2592	2358	2138
Energy (ft-lb)	2133	1790	1491	1235	1014
Arc (inches)		+1.5	0	-6.8	-19.8
Norma 100 Soft Point					
Velocity (fps)	3018	2748	2493	2252	2020
Energy (ft-lb)	2023	1677	1380	1126	905
Arc (inches)		+1.5	0	-7.1	-21.3

DEER CARTRIDGES BALLISTICS CHART CONTINUED

Cartridge/Bullet	Range (yards)				
	0	**100**	**200**	**300**	**400**
Norma 100 Oryx					
Velocity (fps)	3018	2653	2316	2004	1735
Energy (ft-lb)	2023	1563	1191	892	670
Arc (inches)		+1.7	0	-8.3	-24.5
PMC 80 Pointed Soft Point					
Velocity (fps)	2940	2684	2444	2215	1999
Energy (ft-lb)	1535	1280	1060	871	709
Arc (inches)		+1.7	0	-7.5	-22.1
PMC 85 Barnes XLC					
Velocity (fps)	3250	3022	2805	2598	2401
Energy (ft-lb)	1993	1724	1485	1274	1088
Arc (inches)		+1.6	0	-5.6	-16.3
PMC 85 HP Boattail					
Velocity (fps)	3275	2922	2596	2292	2009
Energy (ft-lb)	2024	1611	1272	991	761
Arc (inches)		+1.3	0	-6.5	-19.7
PMC 100 SP Boattail					
Velocity (fps)	2960	2742	2534	2335	2144
Energy (ft-lb)	1945	1669	1425	1210	1021
Arc (inches)		+1.6	0	-7.0	-20.5
Remington 80 Pointed Soft Point					
Velocity (fps)	3350	2955	2593	2259	1951
Energy (ft-lb)	1993	1551	1194	906	676
Arc (inches)		+2.2	+2.0	-3.5	-15.8
Remington 80 HP Power-Lokt					
Velocity (fps)	3350	2955	2593	2259	1951
Energy (ft-lb)	1993	1551	1194	906	676
Arc (inches)		+2.2	+2.0	-3.5	-15.8
Remington 90 Nosler Ballistic Tip and Scirocco					
Velocity (fps)	3120	2871	2635	2411	2199
Energy (ft-lb)	1946	1647	1388	1162	966
Arc (inches)		+1.4	0	-6.4	-18.8

DEER CARTRIDGES BALLISTICS CHART CONTINUED

Cartridge/Bullet	Range (yards)				
	0	100	200	300	400
Remington 95 AccuTip					
Velocity (fps)	3120	2847	2590	2347	2118
Energy (ft-lb)	2053	1710	1415	1162	946
Arc (inches)		+1.5	0	-6.6	-19.5
Remington 100 PSP Core-Lokt					
Velocity (fps)	2960	2697	2449	2215	1993
Energy (ft-lb)	1945	1615	1332	1089	882
Arc (inches)		+1.6	0	-7.5	-22.1
Remington 100 PSP Boattail					
Velocity (fps)	2960	2720	2492	2275	2069
Energy (ft-lb)	1945	1642	1378	1149	950
Arc (inches)		+2.8	+2.3	-3.8	-16.6
Speer 100 Grand Slam					
Velocity (fps)	2950	2684	2434	2197	1990
Energy (ft-lb)	1932	1600	1315	1072	880
Arc (inches)		+1.7	0	-7.6	-22.4
Winchester 80 Pointed Soft Point					
Velocity (fps)	3350	2955	2593	2259	1951
Energy (ft-lb)	1993	1551	1194	906	676
Arc (inches)		+2.6	+2.1	-3.6	-16.2
Winchester 95 Ballistic Silvertip					
Velocity (fps)	3100	2854	2626	2410	2203
Energy (ft-lb)	2021	1719	1455	1225	1024
Arc (inches)		+1.4	0	-6.4	-18.9
Winchester 100 Power-Point					
Velocity (fps)	2960	2697	2449	2215	1993
Energy (ft-lb)	1945	1615	1332	1089	882
Arc (inches)		+1.9	0	-7.8	-22.6
Winchester 100 Power-Point Plus					
Velocity (fps)	3090	2818	2562	2321	2092
Energy (ft-lb)	2121	1764	1458	1196	972
Arc (inches)		+1.4	0	-6.7	-20.0

DEER CARTRIDGES BALLISTICS CHART CONTINUED

Cartridge/Bullet	Range (yards)				
	0	100	200	300	400
6mm Remington					
Federal 80 Sierra Pro-Hunter					
Velocity (fps)	3470	3060	2690	2350	2040
Energy (ft-lb)	2140	1665	1290	980	735
Arc (inches)		+1.1	0	-5.9	-18.2
Federal 100 Hi-Shok					
Velocity (fps)	3100	2830	2570	2330	2100
Energy (ft-lb)	2135	1775	1470	1205	985
Arc (inches)		+1.4	0	-6.7	-19.8
Federal 100 Nosler Partition					
Velocity (fps)	3100	2860	2640	2420	2220
Energy (ft-lb)	2135	1820	1545	1300	1090
Arc (inches)		+1.4	0	-6.3	-18.7

The author dropped this Montana buck at around 300 yards with a .280 Improved.

DEER CARTRIDGES BALLISTICS CHART CONTINUED

Cartridge/Bullet	Range (yards)				
	0	**100**	**200**	**300**	**400**
Hornady 100 SP Boattail					
Velocity (fps)	3100	2861	2634	2419	2231
Energy (ft-lb)	2134	1818	1541	1300	1088
Arc (inches)		+1.3	0	-6.5	-18.9
Hornady 100 SPBT LM					
Velocity (fps)	3250	2997	2756	2528	2311
Energy (ft-lb)	2345	1995	1687	1418	1186
Arc (inches)		+1.6	0	-6.3	-18.2
Remington 100 PSP Core-Lokt					
Velocity (fps)	3100	2829	2573	2332	2104
Energy (ft-lb)	2133	1777	1470	1207	983
Arc (inches)		+1.4	0	-6.7	-19.8
Remington 100 PSP Boattail					
Velocity (fps)	3100	2852	2617	2394	2183
Energy (ft-lb)	2134	1806	1521	1273	1058
Arc (inches)		+1.4	0	-6.5	-19.1
Winchester 100 Power-Point					
Velocity (fps)	3100	2829	2573	2332	2104
Energy (ft-lb)	2133	1777	1470	1207	983
Arc (inches)		+1.7	0	-7.0	-20.4
.243 WSSM					
Winchester 95 Ballistic Silvertip					
Velocity (fps)	3250	3000	2763	2538	2325
Energy (ft-lb)	2258	1898	1610	1359	1140
Arc (inches)		+1.2	0	-5.7	-16.9
Winchester 100 Power-Point					
Velocity (fps)	3110	2838	2583	2341	2112
Energy (ft-lb)	2147	1789	1481	1217	991
Arc (inches)		+1.4	0	-6.6	-19.7

DEER CARTRIDGES BALLISTICS CHART CONTINUED

Cartridge/Bullet	Range (yards)				
	0	100	200	300	400
.240 Weatherby Mag					
Weatherby 87 Pointed Expanding					
Velocity (fps)	3523	3199	2898	2617	2352
Energy (ft-lb)	2397	1977	1622	1323	1069
Arc (inches)		+2.7	+3.4	0	-8.4
Weatherby 90 Barnes-X					
Velocity (fps)	3500	3222	2962	2717	2484
Energy (ft-lb)	2448	2075	1753	1475	1233
Arc (inches)		+2.6	+3.3	0	-8.0
Weatherby 95 Nosler Ballistic Tip					
Velocity (fps)	3420	3146	2888	2645	2414
Energy (ft-lb)	2467	2087	1759	1475	1229
Arc (inches)		+2.7	+3.5	0	-8.4
Weatherby 100 Pointed Expanding					
Velocity (fps)	3406	3134	2878	2637	2408
Energy (ft-lb)	2576	2180	1839	1544	1287
Arc (inches)		+2.8	+3.5	0	-8.4
Weatherby 100 Partition					
Velocity (fps)	3406	3136	2882	2642	2415
Energy (ft-lb)	2576	2183	1844	1550	1294
Arc (inches)		+2.8	+3.5	0	-8.4
.25-06 Remington					
Black Hills 100 Nosler Ballistic Tip					
Velocity (fps)	3200	2965	2749	2532	2330
Energy (ft-lb)	2273	1952	1671	1424	1208
Arc (inches)		+1.2	0	-5.9	-17.2
Black Hills 100 Barnes XLC					
Velocity (fps)	3200	2980	2771	2572	2382
Energy (ft-lb)	2273	1972	1705	1469	1259
Arc (inches)		+1.2	0	-6.7	-16.8

DEER CARTRIDGES BALLISTICS CHART CONTINUED

Cartridge/Bullet	Range (yards)				
	0	**100**	**200**	**300**	**400**
Federal 100 Barnes XLC					
Velocity (fps)	3210	2970	2750	2540	2330
Energy (ft-lb)	2290	1965	1680	1430	1205
Arc (inches)		+1.2	0	-5.8	-17.0
Federal 100 Nosler Ballistic Tip					
Velocity (fps)	3210	2960	2720	2490	2280
Energy (ft-lb)	2290	1940	1640	1380	1150
Arc (inches)		+1.2	0	-6.0	-17.5
Federal 115 Nosler Partition					
Velocity (fps)	2990	2750	2520	2300	2100
Energy (ft-lb)	2285	1930	1620	1350	1120
Arc (inches)		+1.6	0	-7.0	-20.8
Federal 115 Trophy Bonded					
Velocity (fps)	2990	2740	2500	2270	2050
Energy (ft-lb)	2285	1910	1590	1310	1075
Arc (inches)		+1.6	0	-7.2	-21.1
Federal 117 Sierra Pro-Hunter					
Velocity (fps)	2990	2730	2480	2250	2030
Energy (ft-lb)	2320	1985	1645	1350	1100
Arc (inches)		+1.6	0	-7.2	-21.4
Federal 117 Sierra GameKing BTSP					
Velocity (fps)	2990	2770	2570	2370	2190
Energy (ft-lb)	2320	2000	1715	1465	1240
Arc (inches)		+1.5	0	-6.8	-19.9
Hornady 117 SP Boattail					
Velocity (fps)	2990	2749	2520	2302	2096
Energy (ft-lb)	2322	1962	1649	1377	1141
Arc (inches)		+1.6	0	-7.0	-20.7
Hornady 117 SP Boattail LM					
Velocity (fps)	3110	2855	2613	2384	2168
Energy (ft-lb)	2512	2117	1774	1476	1220
Arc (inches)		+1.8	0	-7.1	-20.3

DEER CARTRIDGES BALLISTICS CHART CONTINUED

Cartridge/Bullet	Range (yards)				
	0	**100**	**200**	**300**	**400**
PMC 100 SPBT					
Velocity (fps)	3200	2925	2650	2395	2145
Energy (ft-lb)	2273	1895	1561	1268	1019
Arc (inches)		+1.3	0	-6.3	-18.6
PMC 117 PSP					
Velocity (fps)	2950	2706	2472	2253	2047
Energy (ft-lb)	2261	1900	1588	1319	1088
Arc (inches)		+1.6	0	-7.3	-21.5
Remington 100 PSP Core-Lokt					
Velocity (fps)	3230	2893	2580	2287	2014
Energy (ft-lb)	2316	1858	1478	1161	901
Arc (inches)		+1.3	0	-6.6	-19.8
Remington 115 Core-Lokt Ultra					
Velocity (fps)	3000	2751	2516	2293	2081
Energy (ft-lb)	2298	1933	1616	1342	1106
Arc (inches)		+1.6	0	-7.1	-20.7
Remington 120 PSP Core-Lokt					
Velocity (fps)	2990	2730	2484	2252	2032
Energy (ft-lb)	2382	1985	1644	1351	1100
Arc (inches)		+1.6	0	-7.2	-21.4
Speer 120 Grand Slam					
Velocity (fps)	3130	2835	2558	2298	2070
Energy (ft-lb)	2610	2141	1743	1407	1140
Arc (inches)		+1.4	0	-6.8	-20.1
Winchester 85 Ballistic Silvertip					
Velocity (fps)	3470	3156	2863	2589	2331
Energy (ft-lb)	2273	1880	1548	1266	1026
Arc (inches)		+1.0	0	-5.2	-15.7
Winchester 90 Positive Expanding Point					
Velocity (fps)	3440	3043	2680	2344	2034
Energy (ft-lb)	2364	1850	1435	1098	827
Arc (inches)		+2.4	+2.0	-3.4	-15.0

DEER CARTRIDGES BALLISTICS CHART CONTINUED

Cartridge/Bullet	Range (yards)				
	0	100	200	300	400
Winchester 110 AccuBond CT					
Velocity (fps)	3100	2870	2651	2442	2243
Energy (ft-lb)	2347	2011	1716	1456	1228
Arc (inches)		+1.4	0	-6.3	-18.5
Winchester 115 Ballistic Silvertip					
Velocity (fps)	3060	2825	2603	2390	2188
Energy (ft-lb)	2391	2038	1729	1459	1223
Arc (inches)		+1.4	0	-6.6	-19.2
Winchester 120 Positive Expanding Point					
Velocity (fps)	2990	2717	2459	2216	1987
Energy (ft-lb)	2382	1967	1612	1309	1053
Arc (inches)		+1.6	0	-7.4	-21.8
.25 Winchester Super Short Mag					
Winchester 85 Ballistic Silvertip					
Velocity (fps)	3470	3156	2863	2589	2331
Energy (ft-lb)	2273	1880	1548	1266	1026
Arc (inches)		+1.0	0	-5.2	-15.7
Winchester 110 AccuBond CT					
Velocity (fps)	3100	2870	2651	2442	2243
Energy (ft-lb)	2347	2011	1716	1456	1228
Arc (inches)		+1.4	0	-6.3	-18.5
Winchester 115 Ballistic Silvertip					
Velocity (fps)	3060	2844	2639	2442	2254
Energy (ft-lb)	2392	2066	1778	1523	1298
Arc (inches)		+1.4	0	-6.4	-18.6
Winchester 120 Positive Expanding Point					
Velocity (fps)	2990	2717	2459	2216	1987
Energy (ft-lb)	2383	1967	1612	1309	1053
Arc (inches)		+1.6	0	-7.4	-21.8

DEER CARTRIDGES BALLISTICS CHART CONTINUED

Cartridge/Bullet	Range (yards)				
	0	**100**	**200**	**300**	**400**
.257 Weatherby Mag					
Federal 115 Nosler Partition					
Velocity (fps)	3150	2900	2660	2440	2220
Energy (ft-lb)	2535	2145	1810	1515	1260
Arc (inches)		+1.3	0	-6.2	-18.4
Federal 115 Trophy Bonded					
Velocity (fps)	3150	2890	2640	2400	2180
Energy (ft-lb)	2535	2125	1775	1470	1210
Arc (inches)		+1.4	0	-6.3	-18.8
Weatherby 87 Pointed Expanding					
Velocity (fps)	3825	3472	3147	2845	2563
Energy (ft-lb)	2826	2328	1913	1563	1269
Arc (inches)		+2.1	+2.8	0	-7.1

There's probably no better long-range deer round than the .25-06. The rifle here: a Weatherby Mark V with a Bushnell Elite scope.

DEER CARTRIDGES BALLISTICS CHART CONTINUED

Cartridge/Bullet	0	100	200	300	400
Weatherby 100 Pointed Expanding					
Velocity (fps)	3602	3298	3016	2750	2500
Energy (ft-lb)	2881	2416	2019	1680	1388
Arc (inches)		+2.4	+3.1	0	-7.7
Weatherby 115 Nosler Ballistic Tip					
Velocity (fps)	3400	3170	2952	2745	2547
Energy (ft-lb)	2952	2566	2226	1924	1656
Arc (inches)		+3.0	+3.5	0	-7.9
Weatherby 115 Barnes X					
Velocity (fps)	3400	3158	2929	2711	2504
Energy (ft-lb)	2952	2546	2190	1877	1601
Arc (inches)		+2.7	+3.4	0	-8.1
Weatherby 117 RN Expanding					
Velocity (fps)	3402	2984	2595	2240	1921
Energy (ft-lb)	3007	2320	1742	1302	956
Arc (inches)		+3.4	+4.31	0	-11.1
Weatherby 120 Nosler Partition					
Velocity (fps)	3305	3046	2801	2570	2350
Energy (ft-lb)	2910	2472	2091	1760	1471
Arc (inches)		+3.0	+3.7	0	-8.9

Range (yards)

DEER CARTRIDGES BALLISTICS CHART CONTINUED

Cartridge/Bullet	Range (yards)				
	0	100	200	300	400
6.53 (.257) Scramjet					
Lazzeroni 85 Nosler Ballistic Tip					
Velocity (fps)	3960	3652	3365	3096	2844
Energy (ft-lb)	2961	2517	2137	1810	1526
Arc (inches)		+1.7	+2.4	0	-6.0
Lazzeroni 100 Nosler Partition					
Velocity (fps)	3740	3465	3208	2965	2735
Energy (ft-lb)	3106	2667	2285	1953	1661
Arc (inches)		+2.1	+2.7	0	-6.7
6.5/284					
Norma 120 Nosler Ballistic Tip					
Velocity (fps)	3117	2890	2674	2469	2290
Energy (ft-lb)	2589	2226	1906	1624	1500
Arc (inches)		+1.3	0	-6.2	-18.0
6.5 Remington Mag					
Remington 120 Core-Lokt PSP					
Velocity (fps)	3210	2905	2621	2353	2102
Energy (ft-lb)	2745	2248	1830	1475	1177
Arc (inches)		+2.7	+2.1	-3.5	-15.5

This Utah bull fell to the author's .308 Remington Model Seven and Hornady Inter-Bond bullets.

Improvements in bullet construction have made lightweight bullets lethal on tough game such as elk.

UPPING THE ANTE: ELK

Elk are tough animals, and three to four times as big as mature northern deer. So it makes sense to use heavier bullets when hunting elk. In my experience, doubling the energy considered minimum for sure kills on deer is a good idea when choosing elk loads. Those listed here don't all meet the 2,900 fps velocity floor of the deer-cartridge category, but they hew pretty closely to its 24-inch drop limit at 400 yards (200-yard zero). You'll find bullet weights are higher—at least 130 grains. And the 400-yard energy for most of these versatile deer/elk cartridges exceeds 1,200 foot-pounds.

ELK CARTRIDGES BALLISTICS CHART

Cartridge/Bullet	Range (yards)				
	0	**100**	**200**	**300**	**400**
6.5/284					
Norma 140 Nosler Partition					
Velocity (fps)	2953	2750	2557	2371	2200
Energy (ft-lb)	2712	2352	2032	1748	1500
Arc (inches)		+1.5	0	-6.8	-19.0

HE, high energy; HM, heavy magnum; LM, light magnum.

ELK CARTRIDGES BALLISTICS CHART CONTINUED

Cartridge/Bullet	Range (yards)				
	0	**100**	**200**	**300**	**400**
.264 Winchester Mag.					
Remington 140 PSP Core-Lokt					
Velocity (fps)	3030	2782	2548	2326	2114
Energy (ft-lb)	2854	2406	2018	1682	1389
Arc (inches)		+1.5	0	-6.9	-20.2
Winchester 140 Power-Point					
Velocity (fps)	3030	2782	2548	2326	2114
Energy (ft-lb)	2854	2406	2018	1682	1389
Arc (inches)		+1.8	0	-7.2	-20.8
.270 Winchester					
Black Hills 130 Nosler Ballistic Tip					
Velocity (fps)	2950	2749	2556	2372	2195
Energy (ft-lb)	2512	2180	1886	1624	1391
Arc (inches)		+1.6	0	-6.9	-20.0
Black Hills 130 Barnes XLC					
Velocity (fps)	2950	2754	2567	2388	2216
Energy (ft-lb)	2512	2190	1902	1646	1417
Arc (inches)		+1.5	0	-6.8	-19.8
Federal 130 Hi-Shok					
Velocity (fps)	3060	2800	2560	2330	2110
Energy (ft-lb)	2700	2265	1890	1565	1285
Arc (inches)		+1.5	0	-6.8	-20.0
Federal 130 Sierra Pro-Hunter					
Velocity (fps)	3060	2830	2600	2390	2190
Energy (ft-lb)	2705	2305	1960	1655	1390
Arc (inches)		+1.4	0	-6.4	-19.0
Federal 130 Sierra GameKing					
Velocity (fps)	3060	2830	2620	2410	2220
Energy (ft-lb)	2700	2320	1980	1680	1420
Arc (inches)		+1.4	0	-6.5	-19.0

ELK CARTRIDGES BALLISTICS CHART CONTINUED

Cartridge/Bullet	Range (yards)				
	0	100	200	300	400
Federal 130 Nosler Ballistic Tip					
Velocity (fps)	3060	2840	2630	2430	2230
Energy (ft-lb)	2700	2325	1990	1700	1440
Arc (inches)		+1.4	0	-6.5	-18.8
Federal 130 Nosler Partition and Solid Base					
Velocity (fps)	3060	2830	2610	2400	2200
Energy (ft-lb)	2705	2310	1965	1665	1400
Arc (inches)		+1.4	0	-6.5	-19.1
Federal 130 Barnes XLC and Triple Shock					
Velocity (fps)	3060	2840	2620	2420	2220
Energy (ft-lb)	2705	2320	1985	1690	1425
Arc (inches)		+1.4	0	-6.4	-18.9
Federal 130 Trophy Bonded					
Velocity (fps)	3060	2810	2570	2340	2130
Energy (ft-lb)	2705	2275	1905	1585	1310
Arc (inches)		+1.5	0	-6.7	-19.8
Federal 140 Trophy Bonded					
Velocity (fps)	2940	2700	2480	2260	2060
Energy (ft-lb)	2685	2270	1905	1590	1315
Arc (inches)		+1.6	0	-7.3	-21.5
Federal 140 Trophy Bonded HE					
Velocity (fps)	3100	2860	2620	2400	2200
Energy (ft-lb)	2990	2535	2140	1795	1500
Arc (inches)		+1.4	0	-6.4	-18.9
Federal 140 Nosler AccuBond					
Velocity (fps)	2950	2760	2580	2400	2230
Energy (ft-lb)	2705	2365	2060	1790	1545
Arc (inches)		+1.5	0	-6.7	-19.6

ELK CARTRIDGES BALLISTICS CHART CONTINUED

Cartridge/Bullet	Range (yards)				
	0	100	200	300	400
Federal 150 Sierra GameKing HE					
Velocity (fps)	3000	2800	2620	2430	2260
Energy (ft-lb)	2995	2615	2275	1975	1700
Arc (inches)		+1.5	0	-6.5	-18.9
Hornady 130 SST (or InterBond)					
Velocity (fps)	3060	2845	2639	2442	2254
Energy (ft-lb)	2700	2335	2009	1721	1467
Arc (inches)		+1.4	0	-6.6	-19.1
Hornady 130 SST LM (or InterBond)					
Velocity (fps)	3215	2998	2790	2590	2400
Energy (ft-lb)	2983	2594	2246	1936	1662
Arc (inches)		+1.2	0	-5.8	-17.0
Hornady 140 SP Boattail					
Velocity (fps)	2940	2747	2562	2385	2214
Energy (ft-lb)	2688	2346	2041	1769	1524
Arc (inches)		+1.6	0	-7.0	-20.2
Hornady 140 SP Boattail LM					
Velocity (fps)	3100	2894	2697	2508	2327
Energy (ft-lb)	2987	2604	2261	1955	1684
Arc (inches)		+1.4	0	-6.3	-18.3
Norma 130 SP					
Velocity (fps)	3140	2862	2601	2354	2110
Energy (ft-lb)	2847	2365	1953	1600	1285
Arc (inches)		+1.3	0	-6.5	-19.4
PMC 130 Barnes X					
Velocity (fps)	2910	2717	2533	2356	2186
Energy (ft-lb)	2444	2131	1852	1602	1379
Arc (inches)		+1.6	0	-7.1	-20.4
PMC 130 SP Boattail					
Velocity (fps)	3050	2830	2620	2421	2229
Energy (ft-lb)	2685	2312	1982	1691	1435
Arc (inches)		+1.5	0	-6.5	-19.0

ELK CARTRIDGES BALLISTICS CHART CONTINUED

Cartridge/Bullet	Range (yards)				
	0	100	200	300	400
PMC 130 Pointed Soft Point					
Velocity (fps)	2950	2691	2447	2217	2001
Energy (ft-lb)	2512	2090	1728	1419	1156
Arc (inches)		+1.6	0	-7.5	-22.1
Remington 130 PSP Core-Lokt					
Velocity (fps)	3060	2776	2510	2259	2022
Energy (ft-lb)	2702	2225	1818	1472	1180
Arc (inches)		+1.5	0	-7.0	-20.9
Remington 130 Bronze Point					
Velocity (fps)	3060	2802	2559	2329	2110
Energy (ft-lb)	2702	2267	1890	1565	1285
Arc (inches)		+1.5	0	-6.8	-20.0
Remington 130 Swift Scirocco					
Velocity (fps)	3060	2838	2677	2425	2232
Energy (ft-lb)	2702	2325	1991	1697	1438
Arc (inches)		+1.4	0	-6.5	-18.8
Remington 130 AccuTip BT					
Velocity (fps)	3060	2845	2639	2442	2254
Energy (ft-lb)	2702	2336	2009	1721	1467
Arc (inches)		+1.4	0	-6.4	-18.6
Remington 140 Swift A-Frame					
Velocity (fps)	2925	2652	2394	2152	1923
Energy (ft-lb)	2659	2186	1782	1439	1150
Arc (inches)		+1.7	0	-7.8	-23.2
Remington 140 PSP Boattail					
Velocity (fps)	2960	2749	2548	2355	2171
Energy (ft-lb)	2723	2349	2018	1724	1465
Arc (inches)		+1.6	0	-6.9	-20.1

ELK CARTRIDGES BALLISTICS CHART CONTINUED

Cartridge/Bullet	Range (yards)				
	0	100	200	300	400
Remington 140 Nosler Ballistic Tip					
Velocity (fps)	2960	2754	2557	2366	2187
Energy (ft-lb)	2724	2358	2032	1743	1487
Arc (inches)		+1.6	0	-6.9	-20.0
Remington 140 PSP C-L Ultra					
Velocity (fps)	2925	2667	2424	2193	1975
Energy (ft-lb)	2659	2211	1826	1495	1212
Arc (inches)		+1.7	0	-7.6	-22.5
Speer 130 Grand Slam					
Velocity (fps)	3050	2774	2514	2269	2030
Energy (ft-lb)	2685	2221	1824	1485	1192
Arc (inches)		+1.5	0	-7.0	-20.9
Winchester 130 Power-Point					
Velocity (fps)	3060	2802	2559	2329	2110
Energy (ft-lb)	2702	2267	1890	1565	1285
Arc (inches)		+1.8	0	-7.1	-20.6
Winchester 130 Power-Point Plus					
Velocity (fps)	3150	2881	2628	2388	2161
Energy (ft-lb)	2865	2396	1993	1646	1348
Arc (inches)		+1.3	0	-6.4	-18.9
Winchester 130 Silvertip					
Velocity (fps)	3060	2776	2510	2259	2022
Energy (ft-lb)	2702	2225	1818	1472	1180
Arc (inches)		+1.8	0	-7.4	-21.6
Winchester 130 Ballistic Silvertip					
Velocity (fps)	3050	2828	2618	2416	2224
Energy (ft-lb)	2685	2309	1978	1685	1428
Arc (inches)		+1.4	0	-6.5	-18.9
Winchester 140 AccuBond					
Velocity (fps)	2950	2751	2560	2378	2203
Energy (ft-lb)	2705	2352	2038	1757	1508
Arc (inches)		+1.6	0	-6.9	-19.9

ELK CARTRIDGES BALLISTICS CHART CONTINUED

Cartridge/Bullet	Range (yards)				
	0	100	200	300	400
Winchester 140 Fail Safe					
Velocity (fps)	2920	2671	2435	2211	1999
Energy (ft-lb)	2651	2218	1843	1519	1242
Arc (inches)		+1.7	0	-7.6	-22.3
Winchester 150 Power-Point Plus					
Velocity (fps)	2950	2679	2425	2184	1957
Energy (ft-lb)	2900	2391	1959	1589	1276
Arc (inches)		+1.7	0	-7.6	-22.6
Winchester 150 Partition Gold					
Velocity (fps)	2930	2693	2468	2254	2051
Energy (ft-lb)	2860	2416	2030	1693	1402
Arc (inches)		+1.7	0	-7.4	-21.6
.270 Winchester Short Mag					
Black Hills 140 AccuBond					
Velocity (fps)	3100	2917	2742	2574	2413
Energy (ft-lb)	2987	2645	2338	2060	1809
Arc (inches)		+1.3	0	-5.9	-17.1
Federal 130 Nosler Ballistic Tip					
Velocity (fps)	3300	3070	2840	2630	2430
Energy (ft-lb)	3145	2710	2335	2000	1705
Arc (inches)		+1.1	0	-5.4	-15.8
Federal 130 Nosler Partition, Nosler Solid Base, and Barnes TS					
Velocity (fps)	3280	3040	2810	2590	2380
Energy (ft-lb)	3105	2665	2275	1935	1635
Arc (inches)		+1.1	0	-5.6	-16.3
Federal 140 Nosler AccuBond					
Velocity (fps)	3200	3000	2810	2630	2450
Energy (ft-lb)	3185	2795	2455	2145	1865
Arc (inches)		+1.2	0	-5.6	-16.2

ELK CARTRIDGES BALLISTICS CHART CONTINUED

Cartridge/Bullet	Range (yards)				
	0	**100**	**200**	**300**	**400**
Federal 140 Trophy Bonded					
Velocity (fps)	3130	2870	2640	2410	2200
Energy (ft-lb)	3035	2570	2160	1810	1500
Arc (inches)		+1.4	0	-6.3	-18.7
Federal 150 Nosler Partition					
Velocity (fps)	3160	2950	2750	2550	2370
Energy (ft-lb)	3325	2895	2515	2175	1870
Arc (inches)		+1.3	0	-5.9	-17.0
Norma 130 Ballistic ST					
Velocity (fps)	3281	3047	2825	2614	2410
Energy (ft-lb)	3108	2681	2305	1973	1675
Arc (inches)		+1.1	0	-5.5	-15.7
Norma 140 Barnes X TS					
Velocity (fps)	3150	2952	2762	2580	2400
Energy (ft-lb)	3085	2709	2372	2070	1790
Arc (inches)		+1.3	0	-5.8	-17.2
Norma 150 Oryx					
Velocity (fps)	3117	2856	2611	2378	2180
Energy (ft-lb)	3237	2718	2271	1884	1590
Arc (inches)		+1.4	0	-6.5	-19.0
Winchester 130 Balistic Silvertip					
Velocity (fps)	3275	3041	2820	2609	2408
Energy (ft-lb)	3096	2669	2295	1964	1673
Arc (inches)		+1.1	0	-5.5	-16.1
Winchester 140 AccuBond					
Velocity (fps)	3200	2989	2789	2597	2413
Energy (ft-lb)	3184	2779	2418	2097	1810
Arc (inches)		+1.2	0	-5.7	-16.5
Winchester 140 Fail Safe					
Velocity (fps)	3125	2865	2619	2386	2165
Energy (ft-lb)	3035	2550	2132	1769	1457
Arc (inches)		+1.4	0	-6.5	-19.0

ELK CARTRIDGES BALLISTICS CHART CONTINUED

Cartridge/Bullet	Range (yards)				
	0	100	200	300	400
Winchester 150 Ballistic Silvertip					
Velocity (fps)	3120	2923	2734	2554	2380
Energy (ft-lb)	3242	2845	2490	2172	1886
Arc (inches)		+1.3	0	-5.9	-17.2
Winchester 150 Power-Point					
Velocity (fps)	3150	2867	2601	2350	2113
Energy (ft-lb)	3304	2737	2252	1839	1487
Arc (inches)		+1.4	0	-6.5	-19.4
.270 Weatherby Mag					
Federal 130 Nosler Partition					
Velocity (fps)	3200	2960	2740	2520	2320
Energy (ft-lb)	2955	2530	2160	1835	1550
Arc (inches)		+1.2	0	-5.9	-17.3
Federal 130 Sierra GameKing BTSP					
Velocity (fps)	3200	2980	2780	2580	2400
Energy (ft-lb)	2955	2570	2230	1925	1655
Arc (inches)		+1.2	0	-5.7	-16.6
Federal 140 Trophy Bonded					
Velocity (fps)	3100	2840	2600	2370	2150
Energy (ft-lb)	2990	2510	2100	1745	1440
Arc (inches)		+1.4	0	-6.6	-19.3
Weatherby 100 Pointed Expanding					
Velocity (fps)	3760	3396	3061	2751	2462
Energy (ft-lb)	3139	2560	2081	1681	1346
Arc (inches)		+2.3	+3.0	0	-7.6
Weatherby 130 Pointed Expanding					
Velocity (fps)	3375	3123	2885	2659	2444
Energy (ft-lb)	3288	2815	2402	2041	1724
Arc (inches)		+2.8	+3.5	0	-8.4

ELK CARTRIDGES BALLISTICS CHART CONTINUED

Cartridge/Bullet	Range (yards)				
	0	**100**	**200**	**300**	**400**
Weatherby 130 Nosler Partition					
Velocity (fps)	3375	3127	2892	2670	2458
Energy (ft-lb)	3288	2822	2415	2058	1744
Arc (inches)		+2.8	+3.5	0	-8.3
Weatherby 140 Nosler Ballistic Tip					
Velocity (fps)	3300	3077	2865	2663	2470
Energy (ft-lb)	3385	2943	2551	2204	1896
Arc (inches)		+2.9	+3.6	0	-8.4
Weatherby 140 Barnes X					
Velocity (fps)	3250	3032	2825	2628	2438
Energy (ft-lb)	3283	2858	2481	2146	1848
Arc (inches)		+3.0	+3.7	0	-8.7
Weatherby 150 Pointed Expanding					
Velocity (fps)	3245	3028	2821	2623	2434
Energy (ft-lb)	3507	3053	2650	2292	1973
Arc (inches)		+3.0	+3.7	0	-8.7
Weatherby 150 Nosler Partition					
Velocity (fps)	3245	3029	2823	2627	2439
Energy (ft-lb)	3507	3055	2655	2298	1981
Arc (inches)		+3.0	+3.7	0	-8.7
7mm-08 Remington					
Federal 140 Trophy Bonded HE					
Velocity (fps)	2950	2660	2390	2140	1900
Energy (ft-lb)	2705	2205	1780	1420	1120
Arc (inches)		+1.7	0	-7.9	-23.2
Hornady 139 SP Boattail LM					
Velocity (fps)	3000	2790	2590	2399	2216
Energy (ft-lb)	2777	2403	2071	1776	1515
Arc (inches)		+1.5	0	-6.7	-19.4

ELK CARTRIDGES BALLISTICS CHART CONTINUED

Cartridge/Bullet	Range (yards)				
	0	100	200	300	400
.280 Remington					
Federal 140 Sierra Pro-Hunter					
Velocity (fps)	2990	2740	2500	2270	2060
Energy (ft-lb)	2770	2325	1940	1605	1320
Arc (inches)		+1.6	0	-7.0	-20.8
Federal 140 Trophy Bonded HE					
Velocity (fps)	3150	2850	2570	2300	2050
Energy (ft-lb)	3085	2520	2050	1650	1310
Arc (inches)		+1.4	0	-6.7	-20.0
Federal 140 Nosler AccuBond Ballistic Tip					
Velocity (fps)	3000	2800	2620	2440	2260
Energy (ft-lb)		2800	2445	2130	1845
Arc (inches)		+1.5	0	-6.5	-18.8
Hornady 139 SPBT LMmoly					
Velocity (fps)	3110	2888	2675	2473	2280
Energy (ft-lb)	2985	2573	2209	1887	1604
Arc (inches)		+1.4	0	-6.5	-18.6
Remington 140 PSP Core-Lokt					
Velocity (fps)	3000	2758	2528	2309	2102
Energy (ft-lb)	2797	2363	1986	1657	1373
Arc (inches)		+1.5	0	-7.0	-20.5
Remington 140 Nosler Ballistic Tip					
Velocity (fps)	3000	2804	2616	2436	2263
Energy (ft-lb)	2799	2445	2128	1848	1593
Arc (inches)		+1.5	0	-6.8	-19.0
Remington 140 AccuTip					
Velocity (fps)	3000	2804	2617	2437	2265
Energy (ft-lb)	2797	2444	2129	1846	1594
Arc (inches)		+1.5	0	-6.8	-19.0

ELK CARTRIDGES BALLISTICS CHART CONTINUED

Cartridge/Bullet	Range (yards)				
	0	**100**	**200**	**300**	**400**
Winchester 140					
Ballistic Silvertip					
Velocity (fps)	3040	2842	2653	2471	2297
Energy (ft-lb)	2872	2511	2187	1898	1640
Arc (inches)		+1.4	0	-6.3	-18.4
Winchester 140 Fail Safe					
Velocity (fps)	3050	2756	2480	2221	1977
Energy (ft-lb)	2893	2362	1913	1533	1216
Arc (inches)		+1.5	0	-7.2	-21.5
7mm Remington Mag					
Black Hills 140 Nosler					
Ballistic Tip					
Velocity (fps)	3150	2950	2758	2575	2399
Energy (ft-lb)	3084	2704	2364	2061	1789
Arc (inches)		+1.3	0	-5.8	-16.9
Black Hills 140					
Barnes XLC					
Velocity (fps)	3150	2958	2776	2599	2430
Energy (ft-lb)	3084	2720	2393	2099	1835
Arc (inches)		+1.2	0	-5.8	-16.7
Black Hills 140					
Nosler AccuB					
Velocity (fps)	3150	2961	2781	2607	2441
Energy (ft-lb)	3084	2725	2480	2113	1851
Arc (inches)		+1.2	0	-5.7	-16.6
Federal 140 Nosler					
Ballistic Tip and AccuBond					
Velocity (fps)	3110	2910	2720	2530	2360
Energy (ft-lb)	3005	2630	2295	1995	1725
Arc (inches)		+1.3	0	-6.0	-17.4
Federal 140 Nosler					
Partition					
Velocity (fps)	3150	2930	2710	2510	2320
Energy (ft-lb)	3085	2660	2290	1960	1670
Arc (inches)		+1.3	0	-6.0	-17.5

ELK CARTRIDGES BALLISTICS CHART CONTINUED

Cartridge/Bullet	Range (yards)				
	0	100	200	300	400
Federal 140 Trophy Bonded					
Velocity (fps)	3150	2910	2680	2460	2250
Energy (ft-lb)	3085	2630	2230	1880	1575
Arc (inches)		+1.3	0	-6.1	-18.1
Federal 150 Hi-Shok					
Velocity (fps)	3110	2830	2570	2320	2090
Energy (ft-lb)	3220	2670	2200	1790	1450
Arc (inches)		+1.4	0	-6.7	-19.9
Federal 150 Sierra GameKing BTSP					
Velocity (fps)	3110	2920	2750	2580	2410
Energy (ft-lb)	3220	2850	2510	2210	1930
Arc (inches)		+1.3	0	-5.9	-17.0
Federal 150 Nosler Ballistic Tip					
Velocity (fps)	3110	2910	2720	2540	2370
Energy (ft-lb)	3220	2825	2470	2150	1865
Arc (inches)		+1.3	0	-6.0	-17.4
Federal 150 Nosler Solid Base					
Velocity (fps)	3100	2890	2690	2500	2310
Energy (ft-lb)	3200	2780	2405	2075	1775
Arc (inches)		+1.3	0	-6.2	-17.8
Federal 160 Barnes XLC					
Velocity (fps)	2940	2760	2580	2410	2240
Energy (ft-lb)	3070	2695	2360	2060	1785
Arc (inches)		+1.5	0	-6.8	-19.6
Federal 160 Sierra Pro-Hunter					
Velocity (fps)	2940	2730	2520	2320	2140
Energy (ft-lb)	3070	2640	2260	1920	1620
Arc (inches)		+1.6	0	-7.1	-20.6
Federal 160 Nosler Partition					
Velocity (fps)	2950	2770	2590	2420	2250
Energy (ft-lb)	3090	2715	2375	2075	1800
Arc (inches)		+1.5	0	-6.7	-19.4

ELK CARTRIDGES BALLISTICS CHART CONTINUED

Cartridge/Bullet	Range (yards)				
	0	**100**	**200**	**300**	**400**
Federal 160 Nosler AccuBond					
Velocity (fps)	2950	2770	2600	2440	2280
Energy (ft-lb)	3090	2730	2405	2110	1845
Arc (inches)		+1.5	0	-6.6	-19.1
Federal 160 Trophy Bonded					
Velocity (fps)	2940	2660	2390	2140	1900
Energy (ft-lb)	3070	2505	2025	1620	1280
Arc (inches)		+1.7	0	-7.9	-23.3
Federal 165 Sierra GameKing BTSP					
Velocity (fps)	2950	2800	2650	2510	2370
Energy (ft-lb)	3190	2865	2570	2300	2050
Arc (inches)		+1.5	0	-6.4	-18.4
Hornady 139 SPBT					
Velocity (fps)	3150	2933	2727	2530	2341
Energy (ft-lb)	3063	2656	2296	1976	1692
Arc (inches)		+1.2	0	-6.1	-17.7
Hornady 139 SST (or InterBond)					
Velocity (fps)	3150	2948	2754	2569	2391
Energy (ft-lb)	3062	2681	2341	2037	1764
Arc (inches)		+1.1	0	-5.7	-16.7
Hornady 139 SST LM (or InterBond)					
Velocity (fps)	3250	3044	2847	2657	2475
Energy (ft-lb)	3259	2860	2501	2178	1890
Arc (inches)		+1.1	0	-5.5	-16.2
Hornady 139 SPBT HMmoly					
Velocity (fps)	3250	3041	2822	2613	2413
Energy (ft-lb)	3300	2854	2458	2106	1797
Arc (inches)		+1.1	0	-5.7	-16.6
Hornady 154 Soft Point					
Velocity (fps)	3035	2814	2604	2404	2212
Energy (ft-lb)	3151	2708	2319	1977	1674
Arc (inches)		+1.3	0	-6.7	-19.3

ELK CARTRIDGES BALLISTICS CHART CONTINUED

Cartridge/Bullet	Range (yards)				
	0	100	200	300	400
Hornady 154 SST (or InterBond)					
Velocity (fps)	3035	2850	2672	2501	2337
Energy (ft-lb)	3149	2777	2441	2139	1867
Arc (inches)		+1.4	0	-6.5	-18.7
Hornady 162 SP Boattail					
Velocity (fps)	2940	2757	2582	2413	2251
Energy (ft-lb)	3110	2735	2399	2095	1823
Arc (inches)		+1.6	0	-6.7	-19.7
Norma 140 Nosler Ballistic Tip					
Velocity (fps)	3150	2936	2732	2537	2350
Energy (ft-lb)	3085	2680	2320	2001	1703
Arc (inches)		+1.2	0	-6.1	-17.8
Norma 140 Barnes X TS					
Velocity (fps)	3117	2912	2716	2529	2355
Energy (ft-lb)	3021	2637	2294	1988	1705
Arc (inches)		+1.3	0	-6.0	-17.7
Norma 150 Scirocco					
Velocity (fps)	3117	2934	2758	2589	2400
Energy (ft-lb)	3237	2869	2535	2234	1970
Arc (inches)		+1.2	0	-5.8	-16.8
Norma 156 Oryx					
Velocity (fps)	2953	2670	2404	2153	1920
Energy (ft-lb)	3021	2470	2002	1607	1260
Arc (inches)		+1.7	0	-7.7	-23.0
Norma 170 Vulkan					
Velocity (fps)	3018	2747	2493	2252	2040
Energy (ft-lb)	3439	2850	2346	1914	1615
Arc (inches)		+1.5	0	-7.8	-21.5
Norma 170 Plastic Point					
Velocity (fps)	3018	2762	2519	2290	2100
Energy (ft-lb)	3439	2880	2394	1980	1710
Arc (inches)		+1.5	0	-7.0	-20.2
PMC 140 Barnes X					
Velocity (fps)	3000	2808	2624	2448	2279
Energy (ft-lb)	2797	2451	2141	1863	1614
Arc (inches)		+1.5	0	-6.6	-18.9

ELK CARTRIDGES BALLISTICS CHART CONTINUED

Cartridge/Bullet	Range (yards)				
	0	100	200	300	400
PMC 140 Pointed Soft Point					
Velocity (fps)	3099	2878	2668	2469	2279
Energy (ft-lb)	2984	2574	2212	1895	1614
Arc (inches)		+1.4	0	-6.2	-18.1
PMC 140 SP Boattail					
Velocity (fps)	3125	2891	2669	2457	2255
Energy (ft-lb)	3035	2597	2213	1877	1580
Arc (inches)		+1.4	0	-6.3	-18.4
Remington 140 PSP Core-Lokt					
Velocity (fps)	3175	2923	2684	2458	2243
Energy (ft-lb)	3133	2655	2240	1878	1564
Arc (inches)		+2.2	+1.9	-3.2	-14.2
Remington 140 PSP Boattail					
Velocity (fps)	3175	2956	2747	2547	2356
Energy (ft-lb)	3133	2715	2345	2017	1726
Arc (inches)		+2.2	+1.6	-3.1	-13.4
Remington 150 AccuTip					
Velocity (fps)	3110	2926	2749	2579	2415
Energy (ft-lb)	3221	2850	2516	2215	1943
Arc (inches)		+1.3	0	-5.9	-17.0
Remington 150 PSP Core-Lokt					
Velocity (fps)	3110	2830	2568	2320	2085
Energy (ft-lb)	3221	2667	2196	1792	1448
Arc (inches)		+1.3	0	-6.6	-20.2
Remington 150 Nosler Ballistic Tip					
Velocity (fps)	3110	2912	2723	2542	2367
Energy (ft-lb)	3222	2825	2470	2152	1867
Arc (inches)		+1.2	0	-5.9	-17.3
Remington 150 Swift Scirocco					
Velocity (fps)	3110	2927	2751	2582	2419
Energy (ft-lb)	3221	2852	2520	2220	1948
Arc (inches)		+1.3	0	-5.9	-17.0

ELK CARTRIDGES BALLISTICS CHART CONTINUED

Cartridge/Bullet	Range (yards)				
	0	**100**	**200**	**300**	**400**
Remington 160 Swift A-Frame					
Velocity (fps)	2900	2659	2430	2212	2006
Energy (ft-lb)	2987	2511	2097	1739	1430
Arc (inches)		+1.7	0	-7.6	-22.4
Remington 160 Nosler Partition					
Velocity (fps)	2950	2752	2563	2381	2207
Energy (ft-lb)	3091	2690	2333	2014	1730
Arc (inches)		+0.6	-1.9	-9.6	-23.6
Speer 145 Grand Slam					
Velocity (fps)	3140	2843	2565	2304	2080
Energy (ft-lb)	3174	2602	2118	1708	1355
Arc (inches)		+1.4	0	-6.7	-19.7
Winchester 140 Fail Safe					
Velocity (fps)	3150	2861	2589	2333	2092
Energy (ft-lb)	3085	2544	2085	1693	1361
Arc (inches)		+1.4	0	-6.6	-19.5
Winchester 140 Ballistic Silvertip					
Velocity (fps)	3100	2889	2687	2494	2310
Energy (ft-lb)	2988	2595	2245	1934	1659
Arc (inches)		+1.3	0	-6.2	-17.9
Winchester 140 AccuBond CT					
Velocity (fps)	3180	2965	2760	2565	2377
Energy (ft-lb)	3143	2733	2368	2044	1756
Arc (inches)		+1.2	0	-5.8	-16.9
Winchester 150 Power-Point					
Velocity (fps)	3090	2812	2551	2304	2071
Energy (ft-lb)	3181	2634	2167	1768	1429
Arc (inches)		+1.5	0	-6.8	-20.2
Winchester 150 Power-Point Plus					
Velocity (fps)	3130	2849	2586	2337	2102
Energy (ft-lb)	3264	2705	2227	1819	1472
Arc (inches)		+1.4	0	-6.6	-19.6

ELK CARTRIDGES BALLISTICS CHART CONTINUED

Cartridge/Bullet	Range (yards)				
	0	**100**	**200**	**300**	**400**
Winchester 150 Ballistic Silvertip					
Velocity (fps)	3100	2903	2714	2533	2359
Energy (ft-lb)	3200	2806	2453	2136	1853
Arc (inches)		+1.3	0	-6.0	-17.5
Winchester 160 AccuBond					
Velocity (fps)	2950	2766	2590	2420	2257
Energy (ft-lb)	3091	2718	2382	2080	1809
Arc (inches)		+1.5	0	-6.7	-19.4
Winchester 160 Partition Gold					
Velocity (fps)	2950	2743	2546	2357	2176
Energy (ft-lb)	3093	2674	2303	1974	1682
Arc (inches)		+1.6	0	-6.9	-20.1
Winchester 160 Fail Safe					
Velocity (fps)	2920	2678	2449	2331	2025
Energy (ft-lb)	3030	2549	2131	1769	1457
Arc (inches)		+1.7	0	-7.5	-22.0

7mm Remington Short Ultra Mag

Cartridge/Bullet	0	100	200	300	400
Remington 140 PSP C-L Ultra					
Velocity (fps)	3175	2934	2707	2490	2283
Energy (ft-lb)	3133	2676	2277	1927	1620
Arc (inches)		+1.3	0	-6.0	-17.7
Remington 150 PSP Core-Lokt					
Velocity (fps)	3110	2828	2563	2313	2077
Energy (ft-lb)	3221	2663	2188	1782	1437
Arc (inches)		+2.5	+2.1	-3.6	-15.8
Remington 160 Partition					
Velocity (fps)	2960	2762	2572	2390	2215
Energy (ft-lb)	3112	2709	2350	2029	1744
Arc (inches)		+2.6	+2.2	-3.6	-15.4
Remington 160 PSP C-L Ultra					
Velocity (fps)	2960	2733	2518	2313	2117
Energy (ft-lb)	3112	2654	2252	1900	1592
Arc (inches)		+2.7	+2.2	-3.7	-16.2

ELK CARTRIDGES BALLISTICS CHART CONTINUED

Cartridge/Bullet	Range (yards)				
	0	100	200	300	400
7mm Winchester Short Mag					
Federal 140 Nosler AccuBond					
Velocity (fps)	3250	3040	2840	2660	2470
Energy (ft-lb)	3285	2875	2515	2190	1900
Arc (inches)		+1.1	0	-5.5	-15.8
Federal 140 Nosler Ballistic Tip					
Velocity (fps)	3310	3100	2900	2700	2520
Energy (ft-lb)	3405	2985	2610	2270	1975
Arc (inches)		+1.1	0	-5.2	-15.2
Federal 150 Nosler Solid Base					
Velocity (fps)	3230	3010	2800	2600	2410
Energy (ft-lb)	3475	3015	2615	2255	1935
Arc (inches)		+1.3	0	-5.6	-16.3
Federal 160 Nosler AccuBond					
Velocity (fps)	3120	2940	2760	2590	2430
Energy (ft-lb)	3460	3065	2710	2390	2095
Arc (inches)		+1.3	0	-5.9	-16.8
Federal 160 Nosler Partition					
Velocity (fps)	3160	2950	2750	2560	2380
Energy (ft-lb)	3545	3095	2690	2335	2015
Arc (inches)		+1.2	0	-5.9	-16.9
Federal 160 Barnes TS					
Velocity (fps)	2990	2780	2590	2400	2220
Energy (ft-lb)	3175	2755	2380	2045	1750
Arc (inches)		+1.5	0	-6.6	-19.4
Federal 160 Trophy Bonded					
Velocity (fps)	3120	2880	2650	2440	2230
Energy (ft-lb)	3460	2945	2500	2105	1765
Arc (inches)		+1.4	0	-6.3	-18.5

ELK CARTRIDGES BALLISTICS CHART CONTINUED

Cartridge/Bullet	Range (yards)				
	0	100	200	300	400
Winchester 140 Ballistic Silvertip					
Velocity (fps)	3225	3008	2801	2603	2414
Energy (ft-lb)	3233	2812	2438	2106	1812
Arc (inches)		+1.2	0	-5.6	-16.4
Winchester 140 AccuBond CT					
Velocity (fps)	3225	3008	2801	2604	2415
Energy (ft-lb)	3233	2812	2439	2107	1812
Arc (inches)		+1.2	0	-5.6	-16.4
Winchester 150 Power-Point					
Velocity (fps)	3200	2915	2648	2396	2157
Energy (ft-lb)	3410	2830	2335	1911	1550
Arc (inches)		+1.3	0	-6.3	-18.6
Winchester 160 AccuBond					
Velocity (fps)	3050	2862	2682	2509	2342
Energy (ft-lb)	3306	2911	2556	2237	1950
Arc (inches)		+1.4	0	-6.2	-17.9
Winchester 160 Fail Safe					
Velocity (fps)	2990	2744	2512	2291	2081
Energy (ft-lb)	3176	2675	2241	1864	1538
Arc (inches)		+1.6	0	-7.1	-20.8

7mm Weatherby Mag

	0	100	200	300	400
Federal 160 Nosler Partition					
Velocity (fps)	3050	2850	2650	2470	2290
Energy (ft-lb)	3305	2880	2505	2165	1865
Arc (inches)		+1.4	0	-6.3	-18.4
Federal 160 Sierra GameKing BTSP					
Velocity (fps)	3050	2880	2710	2560	2400
Energy (ft-lb)	3305	2945	2615	2320	2050
Arc (inches)		+1.4	0	-6.1	-17.4

ELK CARTRIDGES BALLISTICS CHART CONTINUED

Cartridge/Bullet	Range (yards)				
	0	100	200	300	400
Federal 160 Trophy Bonded					
Velocity (fps)	3050	2730	2420	2140	1880
Energy (ft-lb)	3305	2640	2085	1630	1255
Arc (inches)		+1.6	0	-7.6	-22.7
Hornady 154 Soft Point					
Velocity (fps)	3200	2971	2753	2546	2348
Energy (ft-lb)	3501	3017	2592	2216	1885
Arc (inches)		+1.2	0	-5.8	-17.0
Hornady 154 SST (or InterBond)					
Velocity (fps)	3200	3009	2825	2648	2478
Energy (ft-lb)	3501	3096	2729	2398	2100
Arc (inches)		+1.2	0	-5.7	-16.5
Weatherby 139 Pointed Expanding					
Velocity (fps)	3340	3079	2834	2601	2380
Energy (ft-lb)	3443	2926	2478	2088	1748
Arc (inches)		+2.9	+3.6	0	-8.7
Weatherby 140 Nosler Partition					
Velocity (fps)	3303	3069	2847	2636	2434
Energy (ft-lb)	3391	2927	2519	2159	1841
Arc (inches)		+2.9	+3.6	0	-8.5
Weatherby 150 Nosler Ballistic Tip					
Velocity (fps)	3300	3093	2896	2708	2527
Energy (ft-lb)	3627	3187	2793	2442	2127
Arc (inches)		+2.8	+3.5	0	-8.2
Weatherby 150 Barnes X					
Velocity (fps)	3100	2901	2710	2527	2352
Energy (ft-lb)	3200	2802	2446	2127	1842
Arc (inches)		+3.3	+4.0	0	-9.4
Weatherby 154 Pointed Expanding					
Velocity (fps)	3260	3028	2807	2597	2397
Energy (ft-lb)	3634	3134	2694	2307	1964
Arc (inches)		+3.0	+3.7	0	-8.8

ELK CARTRIDGES BALLISTICS CHART CONTINUED

Cartridge/Bullet	Range (yards)				
	0	100	200	300	400
Weatherby 160					
Nosler Partition					
Velocity (fps)	3200	2991	2791	2600	2417
Energy (ft-lb)	3638	3177	2767	2401	2075
Arc (inches)		+3.1	+3.8	0	-8.9
Weatherby 175					
Pointed Expanding					
Velocity (fps)	3070	2861	2662	2471	2288
Energy (ft-lb)	3662	3181	2753	2373	2034
Arc (inches)		+3.5	+4.2	0	-9.9
7mm Dakota					
Dakota 140 Barnes X					
Velocity (fps)	3500	3253	3019	2798	2587
Energy (ft-lb)	3807	3288	2833	2433	2081
Arc (inches)		+2.0	+2.1	-1.5	-9.6
Dakota 160 Barnes X					
Velocity (fps)	3200	3001	2811	2630	2455
Energy (ft-lb)	3637	3200	2808	2456	2140
Arc (inches)		+2.1	+1.9	-2.8	-12.5
7mm STW					
A-Square 140 Nosler					
Ballistic Tip					
Velocity (fps)	3450	3254	3067	2888	2715
Energy (ft-lb)	3700	3291	2924	2592	2292
Arc (inches)		+2.2	+3.0	0	-7.3
A-Square 160 Nosler					
Partition					
Velocity (fps)	3250	3071	2900	2735	2576
Energy (ft-lb)	3752	3351	2987	2657	2357
Arc (inches)		+2.8	+3.5	0	-8.2
A-Square 160 SP Boattail					
Velocity (fps)	3250	3087	2930	2778	2631
Energy (ft-lb)	3752	3385	3049	2741	2460
Arc (inches)		+2.8	+3.4	0	-8.0

ELK CARTRIDGES BALLISTICS CHART CONTINUED

Cartridge/Bullet	Range (yards)				
	0	100	200	300	400
Federal 140 Trophy Bonded					
Velocity (fps)	3330	3080	2850	2630	2420
Energy (ft-lb)	3435	2950	2520	2145	1815
Arc (inches)		+1.1	0	-5.4	-15.8
Federal 150 Trophy Bonded					
Velocity (fps)	3250	3010	2770	2560	2350
Energy (ft-lb)	3520	3010	2565	2175	1830
Arc (inches)		+1.2	0	-5.7	-16.7
Federal 160 Sierra GameKing BTSP					
Velocity (fps)	3200	3020	2850	2670	2530
Energy (ft-lb)	3640	3245	2890	2570	2275
Arc (inches)		+1.1	0	-5.5	-15.7
Remington 140 PSP Core-Lokt					
Velocity (fps)	3325	3064	2818	2585	2364
Energy (ft-lb)	3436	2918	2468	2077	1737
Arc (inches)		+2.0	+1.7	-2.9	-12.8
Remington 140 Swift A-Frame					
Velocity (fps)	3325	3020	2735	2467	2215
Energy (ft-lb)	3436	2834	2324	1892	1525
Arc (inches)		+2.1	+1.8	-3.1	-13.8
Speer 145 Grand Slam					
Velocity (fps)	3300	2992	2775	2435	2200
Energy (ft-lb)	3506	2882	2355	1909	1490
Arc (inches)		+1.2	0	-6.0	-17.8
Winchester 140 Ballistic Silvertip					
Velocity (fps)	3320	3100	2890	2690	2499
Energy (ft-lb)	3427	2982	2597	2250	1941
Arc (inches)		+1.1	0	-5.2	-15.2
Winchester 150 Power-Point					
Velocity (fps)	3250	2957	2683	2424	2181
Energy (ft-lb)	3519	2913	2398	1958	1584
Arc (inches)		+1.2	0	-6.1	-18.1

ELK CARTRIDGES BALLISTICS CHART CONTINUED

Cartridge/Bullet	Range (yards)				
	0	100	200	300	400
Winchester 160 Fail Safe					
Velocity (fps)	3150	2894	2652	2422	2204
Energy (ft-lb)	3526	2976	2499	2085	1727
Arc (inches)		+1.3	0	-6.3	-18.5
7mm Remington Ultra Mag					
Remington 140 PSP Core-Lokt					
Velocity (fps)	3425	3158	2907	2669	2444
Energy (ft-lb)	3646	3099	2626	2214	1856
Arc (inches)		+1.8	+1.6	-2.7	-11.9
Remington 140 Nosler Partition					
Velocity (fps)	3425	3184	2956	2740	2534
Energy (ft-lb)	3646	3151	2715	2333	1995
Arc (inches)		+1.7	+1.6	-2.6	-11.4
Remington 160 Nosler Partition					
Velocity (fps)	3200	2991	2791	2600	2417
Energy (ft-lb)	3637	3177	2767	2401	2075
Arc (inches)		+2.1	+1.8	-3.0	-12.9
7.21 (.284) Firehawk					
Lazzeroni 140 Nosler Partition					
Velocity (fps)	3580	3349	3130	2923	2724
Energy (ft-lb)	3985	3488	3048	2656	2308
Arc (inches)		+2.2	+2.9	0	-7.0
Lazzeroni 160 Swift A-Frame					
Velocity (fps)	3385	3167	2961	2763	2574
Energy (ft-lb)	4072	3565	3115	2713	2354
Arc (inches)		+2.6	+3.3	0	-7.8
.308 Winchester					
Black Hills 165 Nosler Ballistic Tip					
Velocity (fps)	2650	2479	2313	2154	2001
Energy (ft-lb)	2573	2250	1960	1700	1467
Arc (inches)		+2.1	0	-8.6	-24.7

ELK CARTRIDGES BALLISTICS CHART CONTINUED

Cartridge/Bullet	Range (yards)				
	0	**100**	**200**	**300**	**400**
Black Hills 168 Barnes XLC					
Velocity (fps)	2650	2479	2314	2155	2003
Energy (ft-lb)	2619	2291	1996	1732	1496
Arc (inches)		+2.1	0	-8.6	-24.7
Black Hills 180 Nosler AccuBond					
Velocity (fps)	2600	2441	2287	2139	1996
Energy (ft-lb)	2701	2381	2090	1828	1592
Arc (inches)		+2.1	0	-8.8	-25.3
Federal 165 Sierra GameKing BTSP					
Velocity (fps)	2700	2520	2330	2160	1990
Energy (ft-lb)	2670	2310	1990	1700	1450
Arc (inches)		+2.0	0	-8.4	-24.3
Federal 165 Trophy Bonded HE					
Velocity (fps)	2870	2600	2350	2120	1890
Energy (ft-lb)	3020	2485	2030	1640	1310
Arc (inches)		+1.8	0	-8.2	-24.0
Federal 180 Sierra Pro-Hunter					
Velocity (fps)	2620	2410	2200	2010	1820
Energy (ft-lb)	2745	2315	1940	1610	1330
Arc (inches)		+2.3	0	-9.3	-27.1
Federal 180 Nosler Partition					
Velocity (fps)	2620	2430	2240	2060	1890
Energy (ft-lb)	2745	2355	2005	1700	1430
Arc (inches)		+2.2	0	-9.2	-26.5
Federal 180 Nosler Partition HE					
Velocity (fps)	2740	2550	2370	2200	2030
Energy (ft-lb)	3000	2600	2245	1925	1645
Arc (inches)		+1.9	0	-8.2	-23.5
Hornady 150 SP Boattail					
Velocity (fps)	2820	2560	2315	2084	1866
Energy (ft-lb)	2648	2183	1785	1447	1160
Arc (inches)		+2.0	0	-8.5	-25.2

ELK CARTRIDGES BALLISTICS CHART CONTINUED

Cartridge/Bullet	Range (yards)				
	0	100	200	300	400
Hornady 150 SST (or InterBond)					
Velocity (fps)	2820	2593	2378	2174	1984
Energy (ft-lb)	2648	2240	1884	1574	1311
Arc (inches)		+1.9	0	-8.1	-22.9
Hornady 150 SST LM (or InterBond)					
Velocity (fps)	3000	2765	2541	2328	2127
Energy (ft-lb)	2997	2545	2150	1805	1506
Arc (inches)		+1.5	0	-7.1	-20.6
Hornady 150 SP LM					
Velocity (fps)	2980	2703	2442	2195	1964
Energy (ft-lb)	2959	2433	1986	1606	1285
Arc (inches)		+1.6	0	-7.5	-22.2
Hornady 165 SP Boattail					
Velocity (fps)	2700	2496	2301	2115	1937
Energy (ft-lb)	2670	2283	1940	1639	1375
Arc (inches)		+2.0	0	-8.7	-25.2
Hornady 165 SPBT LM					
Velocity (fps)	2870	2658	2456	2283	2078
Energy (ft-lb)	3019	2589	2211	1877	1583
Arc (inches)		+1.7	0	-7.5	-21.8
Hornady 165 SST LM (or InterBond)					
Velocity (fps)	2880	2672	2474	2284	2103
Energy (ft-lb)	3038	2616	2242	1911	1620
Arc (inches)		+1.6	0	-7.3	-21.2
Norma 150 Nosler Ballistic Tip					
Velocity (fps)	2822	2588	2365	2154	1960
Energy (ft-lb)	2653	2231	1864	1545	1256
Arc (inches)		+1.6	0	-7.1	-23.1
Norma 165 TXP Swift A-Frame					
Velocity (fps)	2700	2459	2231	2015	1815
Energy (ft-lb)	2672	2216	1824	1488	1205
Arc (inches)		+2.1	0	-9.1	-26.1

ELK CARTRIDGES BALLISTICS CHART CONTINUED

Cartridge/Bullet	Range (yards)				
	0	**100**	**200**	**300**	**400**
Norma 180 Nosler Partition					
Velocity (fps)	2612	2414	2225	2044	1870
Energy (ft-lb)	2728	2330	1979	1670	1385
Arc (inches)		+2.2	0	-9.3	-26.4
PMC 150 Barnes X					
Velocity (fps)	2700	2504	2316	2135	1964
Energy (ft-lb)	2428	2087	1786	1518	1284
Arc (inches)		+2.0	0	-8.6	-24.7
PMC 150 SP Boattail					
Velocity (fps)	2820	2581	2354	2139	1935
Energy (ft-lb)	2648	2218	1846	1523	1247
Arc (inches)		+1.9	0	-8.2	-24.0
PMC 168 Barnes X					
Velocity (fps)	2600	2425	2256	2095	1940
Energy (ft-lb)	2476	2154	1865	1608	1379
Arc (inches)		+2.2	0	-9.0	-26.0
PMC 168 HP Boattail					
Velocity (fps)	2650	2460	2278	2103	1936
Energy (ft-lb)	2619	2257	1935	1649	1399
Arc (inches)		+2.1	0	-8.8	-25.6
PMC 180 SP Boattail					
Velocity (fps)	2620	2446	2278	2117	1962
Energy (ft-lb)	2743	2391	2074	1790	1538
Arc (inches)		+2.2	0	-8.9	-25.4
Remington 150 PSP C-L Ultra					
Velocity (fps)	2620	2404	2198	2002	1818
Energy (ft-lb)	2743	2309	1930	1601	1320
Arc (inches)		+2.3	0	-9.5	-26.4
Remington 150 Swift Scirocco					
Velocity (fps)	2820	2611	2410	2219	2037
Energy (ft-lb)	2648	2269	1935	1640	1381
Arc (inches)		+1.8	0	-7.8	-22.7

ELK CARTRIDGES BALLISTICS CHART CONTINUED

Cartridge/Bullet	Range (yards)				
	0	100	200	300	400
Remington 165 AccuTip					
Velocity (fps)	2700	2501	2311	2129	1958
Energy (ft-lb)	2670	2292	1957	1861	1401
Arc (inches)		+2.0	0	-8.6	-24.8
Remington 165 PSP Boattail					
Velocity (fps)	2700	2497	2303	2117	1941
Energy (ft-lb)	2670	2284	1942	1642	1379
Arc (inches)		+2.0	0	-8.6	-25.0
Remington 165 Nosler Ballistic Tip					
Velocity (fps)	2700	2613	2333	2161	1996
Energy (ft-lb)	2672	2314	1995	1711	1460
Arc (inches)		+2.0	0	-8.4	-24.3
Remington 165 Swift Scirocco					
Velocity (fps)	2700	2513	2233	2161	1996
Energy (ft-lb)	2670	2313	1994	1711	1459
Arc (inches)		+2.0	0	-8.4	-24.3
Remington 168 HPBT Match					
Velocity (fps)	2680	2493	2314	2143	1979
Energy (ft-lb)	2678	2318	1998	1713	1460
Arc (inches)		+2.1	0	-8.6	-24.7
Remington 180 PSP Core-Lokt					
Velocity (fps)	2620	2393	2178	1974	1782
Energy (ft-lb)	2743	2288	1896	1557	1269
Arc (inches)		+2.3	0	-9.7	-28.3
Remington 180 Nosler Partition					
Velocity (fps)	2620	2436	2259	2089	1927
Energy (ft-lb)	2743	2371	2039	1774	1485
Arc (inches)		+2.2	0	-9.0	-26.0
Speer 165 Grand Slam					
Velocity (fps)	2700	2475	2261	2057	1850
Energy (ft-lb)	2670	2243	1872	1550	1245
Arc (inches)		+2.1	0	-8.9	-25.9

ELK CARTRIDGES BALLISTICS CHART CONTINUED

Cartridge/Bullet	Range (yards)				
	0	100	200	300	400
Speer 180 Grand Slam					
Velocity (fps)	2620	2420	2229	2046	1840
Energy (ft-lb)	2743	2340	1985	1674	1360
Arc (inches)		+2.2	0	-9.2	-26.6
Winchester 150 Partition Gold					
Velocity (fps)	2900	2645	2405	2177	1962
Energy (ft-lb)	2802	2332	1927	1579	1282
Arc (inches)		+1.7	0	-7.8	-22.9
Winchester 150 Ballistic Silvertip					
Velocity (fps)	2810	2601	2401	2211	2028
Energy (ft-lb)	2629	2253	1920	1627	1370
Arc (inches)		+1.8	0	-7.8	-22.8
Winchester 150 Fail Safe					
Velocity (fps)	2820	2533	2263	2010	1775
Energy (ft-lb)	2649	2137	1706	1346	1049
Arc (inches)		+2.0	0	-8.8	-26.2
Winchester 168 Ballistic Silvertip					
Velocity (fps)	2670	2484	2306	2134	1971
Energy (ft-lb)	2659	2301	1983	1699	1449
Arc (inches)		+2.1	0	-8.6	-24.8
Winchester 168 HP Boattail Match					
Velocity (fps)	2680	2485	2297	2118	1948
Energy (ft-lb)	2680	2303	1970	1674	1415
Arc (inches)		+2.1	0	-8.7	-25.1
Winchester 180 Silvertip					
Velocity (fps)	2620	2393	2178	1974	1782
Energy (ft-lb)	2743	2288	1896	1557	1269
Arc (inches)		+2.6	0	-9.9	-28.9

.30-06 Springfield

	0	100	200	300	400
Black Hills 150 Nosler Ballistic Tip					
Velocity (fps)	2900	2702	2512	2331	2157
Energy (ft-lb)	2770	2431	2102	1809	1549
Arc (inches)		+1.6	0	-7.2	-20.7

ELK CARTRIDGES BALLISTICS CHART CONTINUED

Cartridge/Bullet	Range (yards)				
	0	100	200	300	400
Black Hills 165 Nosler Ballistic Tip					
Velocity (fps)	2750	2574	2405	2243	2087
Energy (ft-lb)	2770	2428	2120	1843	1595
Arc (inches)		+1.9	0	-7.9	-22.7
Black Hills 168 BTHP					
Velocity (fps)	2700	2509	2326	2150	1983
Energy (ft-lb)	2719	2348	2018	1725	1466
Arc (inches)		+2.0	0	-8.5	-24.4
Black Hills 180 Nosler AccuB					
Velocity (fps)	2700	2537	2380	2228	2082
Energy (ft-lb)	2913	2572	2264	1984	1733
Arc (inches)		+2.0	0	-8.1	-23.2
Black Hills 180 Barnes XLC					
Velocity (fps)	2650	2490	2336	2187	2044
Energy (ft-lb)	2806	2478	2180	1911	1669
Arc (inches)		+2.1	0	-8.4	-24.2
Federal 150 Sierra Pro-Hunter					
Velocity (fps)	2910	2640	2380	2130	1900
Energy (ft-lb)	2820	2315	1880	1515	1205
Arc (inches)		+1.7	0	-7.9	-23.3
Federal 150 Sierra GameKing BTSP					
Velocity (fps)	2910	2690	2480	2270	2070
Energy (ft-lb)	2820	2420	2040	1710	1430
Arc (inches)		+1.7	0	-7.4	-21.5
Federal 150 Nosler Ballistic Tip					
Velocity (fps)	2910	2700	2490	2300	2110
Energy (ft-lb)	2820	2420	2070	1760	1485
Arc (inches)		+1.6	0	-7.3	-21.1
Federal 165 Sierra Pro-Hunter					
Velocity (fps)	2800	2560	2340	2130	1920
Energy (ft-lb)	2875	2410	2005	1655	1360
Arc (inches)		+1.9	0	-8.3	-24.3

ELK CARTRIDGES BALLISTICS CHART CONTINUED

Cartridge/Bullet	Range (yards)				
	0	**100**	**200**	**300**	**400**
Federal 165 Sierra GameKing BTSP					
Velocity (fps)	2800	2610	2420	2240	2070
Energy (ft-lb)	2870	2490	2150	1840	1580
Arc (inches)		+1.8	0	-7.8	-22.4
Federal 165 Sierra GameKing HE					
Velocity (fps)	3140	2900	2670	2450	2240
Energy (ft-lb)	3610	3075	2610	2200	1845
Arc (inches)		+1.5	0	-6.9	-20.4
Federal 165 Nosler Ballistic Tip					
Velocity (fps)	2800	2610	2430	2250	2080
Energy (ft-lb)	2870	2495	2155	1855	1585
Arc (inches)		+1.8	0	-7.7	-22.3
Federal 165 Trophy Bonded					
Velocity (fps)	2800	2540	2290	2050	1830
Energy (ft-lb)	2870	2360	1915	1545	1230
Arc (inches)		+2.0	0	-8.7	-25.4
Federal 165 Trophy Bonded HE					
Velocity (fps)	3140	2860	2590	2340	2100
Energy (ft-lb)	3610	2990	2460	2010	1625
Arc (inches)		+1.6	0	-7.4	-21.9
Federal 168 Sierra MatchKing BTHP					
Velocity (fps)	2700	2510	2320	2150	1980
Energy (ft-lb)	2720	2350	2010	1720	1460
Arc (inches)		+2.0	0	-8.5	-24.5
Federal 180 Hi-Shok					
Velocity (fps)	2700	2470	2250	2040	1850
Energy (ft-lb)	2915	2435	2025	1665	1360
Arc (inches)		+2.1	0	-9.0	-26.4
Federal 180 Nosler Partition					
Velocity (fps)	2700	2500	2320	2140	1970
Energy (ft-lb)	2915	2510	2150	1830	1550
Arc (inches)		+2.0	0	-8.6	-24.6

ELK CARTRIDGES BALLISTICS CHART CONTINUED

Cartridge/Bullet	Range (yards)				
	0	**100**	**200**	**300**	**400**
Federal 180 Nosler Partition HE					
Velocity (fps)	2880	2690	2500	2320	2150
Energy (ft-lb)	3315	2880	2495	2150	1845
Arc (inches)		+1.7	0	-7.2	-21.0
Federal 180 Sierra GameKing BTSP					
Velocity (fps)	2700	2540	2380	2220	2080
Energy (ft-lb)	2915	2570	2260	1975	1720
Arc (inches)		+1.9	0	-8.1	-23.1
Federal 180 Barnes XLC					
Velocity (fps)	2700	2530	2360	2200	2040
Energy (ft-lb)	2915	2550	2220	1930	1670
Arc (inches)		+2.0	0	-8.3	-23.8
Federal 180 Trophy Bonded					
Velocity (fps)	2700	2460	2220	2000	1800
Energy (ft-lb)	2915	2410	1975	1605	1290
Arc (inches)		+2.2	0	-9.2	-27.0
Federal 180 Trophy Bonded HE					
Velocity (fps)	2880	2630	2380	2160	1940
Energy (ft-lb)	3315	2755	2270	1855	1505
Arc (inches)		+1.8	0	-8.0	-23.3
Hornady 150 SP					
Velocity (fps)	2910	2617	2342	2083	1843
Energy (ft-lb)	2820	2281	1827	1445	1131
Arc (inches)		+2.1	0	-8.5	-25.0
Hornady 150 SP LM					
Velocity (fps)	3100	2815	2548	2295	2058
Energy (ft-lb)	3200	2639	2161	1755	1410
Arc (inches)		+1.4	0	-6.8	-20.3
Hornady 150 SP Boattail					
Velocity (fps)	2910	2683	2467	2262	2066
Energy (ft-lb)	2820	2397	2027	1706	1421
Arc (inches)		+2.0	0	-7.7	-22.2

ELK CARTRIDGES BALLISTICS CHART CONTINUED

Cartridge/Bullet	Range (yards)				
	0	**100**	**200**	**300**	**400**
Hornady 150 SST (or InterBond)					
Velocity (fps)	2910	2802	2599	2405	2219
Energy (ft-lb)	3330	2876	2474	2118	1803
Arc (inches)		+1.5	0	-6.6	-19.3
Hornady 150 SST LM					
Velocity (fps)	3100	2860	2631	2414	2208
Energy (ft-lb)	3200	2724	2306	1941	1624
Arc (inches)		+1.4	0	-6.6	-19.2
Hornady 165 SP Boattail					
Velocity (fps)	2800	2591	2392	2202	2020
Energy (ft-lb)	2873	2460	2097	1777	1495
Arc (inches)		+1.8	0	-8.0	-23.3
Hornady 165 SPBT LM					
Velocity (fps)	3015	2790	2575	2370	2176
Energy (ft-lb)	3330	2850	2428	2058	1734
Arc (inches)		+1.6	0	-7.0	-20.1
Hornady 165 SST (or InterBond)					
Velocity (fps)	2800	2598	2405	2221	2046
Energy (ft-lb)	2872	2473	2119	1808	1534
Arc (inches)		+1.9	0	-8.0	-22.8
Hornady 165 SST LM					
Velocity (fps)	3015	2802	2599	2405	2219
Energy (ft-lb)	3330	2878	2474	2118	1803
Arc (inches)		+1.5	0	-6.5	-19.3
Hornady 168 HPBT Match					
Velocity (fps)	2790	2620	2447	2280	2120
Energy (ft-lb)	2925	2561	2234	1940	1677
Arc (inches)		+1.7	0	-7.7	-22.2
Hornady 180 SP					
Velocity (fps)	2700	2469	2258	2042	1846
Energy (ft-lb)	2913	2436	2023	1666	1362
Arc (inches)		+2.4	0	-9.3	-27.0
Hornady 180 SPBT LM					
Velocity (fps)	2880	2676	2480	2293	2114
Energy (ft-lb)	3316	2862	2459	2102	1786
Arc (inches)		+1.7	0	-7.3	-21.3

ELK CARTRIDGES BALLISTICS CHART CONTINUED

Cartridge/Bullet	Range (yards)				
	0	100	200	300	400
Norma 150 Nosler Ballistic Tip					
Velocity (fps)	2936	2713	2502	2300	2120
Energy (ft-lb)	2872	2453	2085	1762	2092
Arc (inches)		+1.6	0	-7.1	-20.9
Norma 180 Nosler Partition					
Velocity (fps)	2700	2494	2297	2108	1935
Energy (ft-lb)	2914	2486	2108	1777	1515
Arc (inches)		+2.1	0	-8.7	-24.6
Norma 180 Plastic Point					
Velocity (fps)	2700	2455	2222	2003	1800
Energy (ft-lb)	2914	2409	1974	1603	1290
Arc (inches)		+2.1	0	-9.2	-26.0
Norma 180 Vulkan					
Velocity (fps)	2700	2416	2150	1901	1630
Energy (ft-lb)	2914	2334	1848	1445	1230
Arc (inches)		+2.2	0	-9.6	-26.5
Norma 180 TXP Swift A-Frame					
Velocity (fps)	2700	2479	2268	2067	1842
Energy (ft-lb)	2914	2456	2056	1708	1248
Arc (inches)		+2.0	0	-8.8	-25.5
Norma 180 AccuBond					
Velocity (fps)	2674	2499	2331	2169	2010
Energy (ft-lb)	2859	2497	2172	1881	1482
Arc (inches)		+2.0	0	-8.5	-24.7
Norma 200 Vulkan					
Velocity (fps)	2641	2385	2143	1916	1670
Energy (ft-lb)	3098	2527	2040	1631	1170
Arc (inches)		+2.3	0	-9.9	-27.5
PMC 150 X-Bullet					
Velocity (fps)	2750	2552	2361	2179	2005
Energy (ft-lb)	2518	2168	1857	1582	1339
Arc (inches)		+2.0	0	-8.2	-23.7

ELK CARTRIDGES BALLISTICS CHART CONTINUED

Cartridge/Bullet	Range (yards)				
	0	100	200	300	400
PMC 150 Pointed Soft Point					
Velocity (fps)	2773	2542	2322	2113	1916
Energy (ft-lb)	2560	2152	1796	1487	1222
Arc (inches)		+1.9	0	-8.4	-24.6
PMC 150 SP Boattail					
Velocity (fps)	2900	2657	2427	2208	2000
Energy (ft-lb)	2801	2351	1961	1623	1332
Arc (inches)		+1.7	0	-7.7	-22.5
PMC 168 Barnes X					
Velocity (fps)	2750	2569	2395	2228	2067
Energy (ft-lb)	2770	2418	2101	1818	1565
Arc (inches)		+1.9	0	-8.0	-23.0
PMC 180 Barnes X					
Velocity (fps)	2650	2487	2331	2179	2034
Energy (ft-lb)	2806	2472	2171	1898	1652
Arc (inches)		+2.1	0	-8.5	-24.3
PMC 180 Pointed Soft Point					
Velocity (fps)	2650	2430	2221	2024	1839
Energy (ft-lb)	2807	2359	1972	1638	1351
Arc (inches)		+2.2	0	-9.3	-27.0
PMC 180 SP Boattail					
Velocity (fps)	2700	2523	2352	2188	2030
Energy (ft-lb)	2913	2543	2210	1913	1646
Arc (inches)		+2.0	0	-8.3	-23.9
PMC 180 HPBT Match					
Velocity (fps)	2800	2622	2456	2302	2158
Energy (ft-lb)	3133	2747	2411	2118	1861
Arc (inches)		+1.8	0	-7.6	-21.7
Remington 150 AccuTip					
Velocity (fps)	2910	2686	2473	2270	2077
Energy (ft-lb)	2820	2403	2037	1716	1436
Arc (inches)		+1.8	0	-7.4	-21.5
Remington 150 PSP Core-Lokt					
Velocity (fps)	2910	2617	2342	2083	1843
Energy (ft-lb)	2820	2281	1827	1445	1131
Arc (inches)		+1.8	0	-8.2	-24.4

ELK CARTRIDGES BALLISTICS CHART CONTINUED

Cartridge/Bullet	Range (yards)				
	0	100	200	300	400
Remington 150 Bronze Point					
Velocity (fps)	2910	2656	2416	2189	1974
Energy (ft-lb)	2820	2349	1944	1596	1298
Arc (inches)		+1.7	0	-7.7	-22.7
Remington 150 Nosler Ballistic Tip					
Velocity (fps)	2910	2696	2492	2298	2112
Energy (ft-lb)	2821	2422	2070	1769	1485
Arc (inches)		+1.6	0	-7.3	-21.1
Remington 150 Swift Scirocco					
Velocity (fps)	2910	2696	2492	2298	2111
Energy (ft-lb)	2820	2421	2069	1758	1485
Arc (inches)		+1.6	0	-7.3	-21.1
Remington 165 AccuTip					
Velocity (fps)	2800	2597	2403	2217	2039
Energy (ft-lb)	2872	2470	2115	1800	1523
Arc (inches)		+1.8	0	-7.9	-22.8
Remington 165 PSP Core-Lokt					
Velocity (fps)	2800	2534	2283	2047	1825
Energy (ft-lb)	2872	2352	1909	1534	1220
Arc (inches)		+2.0	0	-8.7	-25.9
Remington 165 PSP Boattail					
Velocity (fps)	2800	2592	2394	2204	2023
Energy (ft-lb)	2872	2462	2100	1780	1500
Arc (inches)		+1.8	0	-7.9	-23.0
Remington 165 Nosler Ballistic Tip					
Velocity (fps)	2800	2609	2426	2249	2080
Energy (ft-lb)	2873	2494	2155	1854	1588
Arc (inches)		+1.8	0	-7.7	-22.3
Remington 168 PSP C-L Ultra					
Velocity (fps)	2800	2546	2306	2079	1866
Energy (ft-lb)	2924	2418	1984	1613	1299
Arc (inches)		+1.9	0	-8.5	-25.1

ELK CARTRIDGES BALLISTICS CHART CONTINUED

Cartridge/Bullet	Range (yards)				
	0	100	200	300	400
Remington 180 PSP Core-Lokt					
Velocity (fps)	2700	2469	2250	2042	1846
Energy (ft-lb)	2913	2436	2023	1666	1362
Arc (inches)		+2.1	0	-9.0	-26.3
Remington 180 PSP C-L Ultra					
Velocity (fps)	2700	2480	2270	2070	1882
Energy (ft-lb)	2913	2457	2059	1713	1415
Arc (inches)		+2.1	0	-8.9	-25.8
Remington 180 Bronze Point					
Velocity (fps)	2700	2485	2280	2084	1899
Energy (ft-lb)	2913	2468	2077	1736	1441
Arc (inches)		+2.1	0	-8.8	-25.5

Remington's Titanium Model 700 combines light weight and, in .30-06, a powerful punch.

ELK CARTRIDGES BALLISTICS CHART CONTINUED

Cartridge/Bullet	Range (yards)				
	0	**100**	**200**	**300**	**400**
Remington 180 Swift A-Frame					
Velocity (fps)	2700	2465	2243	2032	1833
Energy (ft-lb)	2913	2429	2010	1650	1343
Arc (inches)		+2.1	0	-9.1	-26.6
Remington 180 Nosler Partition					
Velocity (fps)	2700	2512	2332	2160	1995
Energy (ft-lb)	2913	2522	2174	1864	1590
Arc (inches)		+2.0	0	-8.4	-24.3
Speer 150 Grand Slam					
Velocity (fps)	2975	2669	2383	2114	1840
Energy (ft-lb)	2947	2372	1891	1489	1090
Arc (inches)		+2.0	0	-8.1	-24.1
Speer 165 Grand Slam					
Velocity (fps)	2790	2560	2342	2134	1950
Energy (ft-lb)	2851	2401	2009	1669	1515
Arc (inches)		+1.9	0	-8.3	-24.1
Speer 180 Grand Slam					
Velocity (fps)	2690	2487	2293	2108	1955
Energy (ft-lb)	2892	2472	2101	1775	1538
Arc (inches)		+2.1	0	-8.8	-25.1
Winchester 150 Power-Point Plus					
Velocity (fps)	3050	2685	2352	2043	1760
Energy (ft-lb)	3089	2402	1843	1391	1032
Arc (inches)		+1.7	0	-8.0	-24.3
Winchester 150 Silvertip					
Velocity (fps)	2910	2617	2342	2083	1843
Energy (ft-lb)	2820	2281	1827	1445	1131
Arc (inches)		+2.1	0	-8.5	-25.0
Winchester 150 Partition Gold					
Velocity (fps)	2960	2705	2464	2235	2019
Energy (ft-lb)	2919	2437	2022	1664	1358
Arc (inches)		+1.6	0	-7.4	-21.7

ELK CARTRIDGES BALLISTICS CHART CONTINUED

Cartridge/Bullet	Range (yards)				
	0	**100**	**200**	**300**	**400**
Winchester 150 Ballistic Silvertip					
Velocity (fps)	2900	2687	2483	2289	2103
Energy (ft-lb)	2801	2404	2054	1745	1473
Arc (inches)		+1.7	0	-7.3	-21.2
Winchester 150 Fail Safe					
Velocity (fps)	2920	2625	2349	2089	1848
Energy (ft-lb)	2841	2296	1838	1455	1137
Arc (inches)		+1.8	0	-8.1	-24.3
Winchester 165 Pointed Soft Point					
Velocity (fps)	2800	2573	2357	2151	1956
Energy (ft-lb)	2873	2426	2036	1696	1402
Arc (inches)		+2.2	0	-8.4	-24.4
Winchester 165 Fail Safe					
Velocity (fps)	2800	2540	2295	2063	1846
Energy (ft-lb)	2873	2365	1930	1560	1249
Arc (inches)		+2.0	0	-8.6	-25.3
Winchester 168 Ballistic Silvertip					
Velocity (fps)	2790	2599	2416	2240	2072
Energy (ft-lb)	2903	2520	2177	1872	1601
Arc (inches)		+1.8	0	-7.8	-22.5
Winchester 180 Ballistic Silvertip					
Velocity (fps)	2750	2572	2402	2237	2080
Energy (ft-lb)	3022	2644	2305	2001	1728
Arc (inches)		+1.9	0	-7.9	-22.8
Winchester 180 Power-Point Plus					
Velocity (fps)	2770	2563	2366	2177	1997
Energy (ft-lb)	3068	2627	2237	1894	1594
Arc (inches)		+1.9	0	-8.1	-23.6
Winchester 180 Silvertip					
Velocity (fps)	2700	2469	2250	2042	1846
Energy (ft-lb)	2913	2436	2023	1666	1362
Arc (inches)		+2.4	0	-9.3	-27.0

ELK CARTRIDGES BALLISTICS CHART CONTINUED

Cartridge/Bullet	Range (yards)				
	0	**100**	**200**	**300**	**400**
Winchester 180 AccuBond					
Velocity (fps)	2750	2573	2403	2239	2082
Energy (ft-lb)	3022	2646	2308	2004	1732
Arc (inches)		+1.9	0	-7.9	-22.8
Winchester 180 Partition Gold					
Velocity (fps)	2790	2581	2382	2192	2010
Energy (ft-lb)	3112	2664	2269	1920	1615
Arc (inches)		+1.9	0	-8.0	-23.2
Winchester 180 Fail Safe					
Velocity (fps)	2700	2486	2283	2089	1904
Energy (ft-lb)	2914	2472	2083	1744	1450
Arc (inches)		+2.1	0	-8.7	-25.5
.300 Winchester Mag					
Federal 150 Sierra Pro-Hunter					
Velocity (fps)	3280	3030	2800	2570	2360
Energy (ft-lb)	3570	3055	2600	2205	1860
Arc (inches)		+1.1	0	-5.6	-16.4
Federal 150 Trophy Bonded					
Velocity (fps)	3280	2980	2700	2430	2190
Energy (ft-lb)	3570	2450	2420	1970	1590
Arc (inches)		+1.2	0	-6.0	-17.9
Hornady 150 SP Boattail					
Velocity (fps)	3275	2988	2718	2464	2224
Energy (ft-lb)	3573	2974	2461	2023	1648
Arc (inches)		+1.2	0	-6.0	-17.8
Hornady 150 SST (and InterBond)					
Velocity (fps)	3275	3027	2791	2565	2352
Energy (ft-lb)	3572	3052	2593	2192	1842
Arc (inches)		+1.2	0	-5.8	-17.0
Norma 150 Nosler Ballistic Tip					
Velocity (fps)	3250	3014	2791	2578	2370
Energy (ft-lb)	3519	3027	2595	2215	1875
Arc (inches)		+1.1	0	-5.6	-16.5

ELK CARTRIDGES BALLISTICS CHART CONTINUED

Cartridge/Bullet	Range (yards)				
	0	100	200	300	400
Norma 150 Barnes TS					
Velocity (fps)	3215	2982	2761	2550	2340
Energy (ft-lb)	3444	2962	2539	2167	1830
Arc (inches)		+1.2	0	-5.8	-17.0
PMC 150 Barnes X					
Velocity (fps)	3135	2918	2712	2515	2327
Energy (ft-lb)	3273	2836	2449	2107	1803
Arc (inches)		+1.3	0	-6.1	-17.7
PMC 150 Pointed Soft Point					
Velocity (fps)	3150	2902	2665	2438	2222
Energy (ft-lb)	3304	2804	2364	1979	1644
Arc (inches)		+1.3	0	-6.2	-18.3
PMC 150 SP Boattail					
Velocity (fps)	3250	2987	2739	2504	2281
Energy (ft-lb)	3517	2970	2498	2088	1733
Arc (inches)		+1.2	0	-6.0	-17.4
Remington 150 PSP Core-Lokt					
Velocity (fps)	3290	2951	2636	2342	2068
Energy (ft-lb)	3605	2900	2314	1827	1859
Arc (inches)		+1.6	0	-7.0	-20.2
Remington 150 PSP C-L Ultra					
Velocity (fps)	3290	2967	2666	2384	2120
Energy (ft-lb)	3065	2931	2366	1893	1496
Arc (inches)		+1.2	0	-6.1	-18.4
Winchester 150 Power-Point					
Velocity (fps)	3290	2951	2636	2342	2068
Energy (ft-lb)	3605	2900	2314	1827	1424
Arc (inches)		+2.6	+2.1	-3.5	-15.4
Winchester 150 Fail Safe					
Velocity (fps)	3260	2943	2647	2370	2110
Energy (ft-lb)	3539	2884	2334	1871	1483
Arc (inches)		+1.3	0	-6.2	-18.7

ELK CARTRIDGES BALLISTICS CHART CONTINUED

Cartridge/Bullet	Range (yards)				
	0	**100**	**200**	**300**	**400**
.300 Remington Short Ultra Mag					
Remington 150 PSP C-L Ultra					
Velocity (fps)	3200	2901	2672	2359	2112
Energy (ft-lb)	3410	2803	2290	1854	1485
Arc (inches)		+1.3	0	-6.4	-19.1
.300 Winchester Short Mag					
Federal 150 Nosler Ballistic Tip					
Velocity (fps)	3200	2970	2755	2545	2345
Energy (ft-lb)	3410	2940	2520	2155	1830
Arc (inches)		+1.2	0	-5.8	-17.0
Norma 150 Barnes X TS					
Velocity (fps)	3215	2982	2761	2550	2345
Energy (ft-lb)	3444	2962	2539	2167	1830
Arc (inches)		+1.2	0	-5.7	-17.0

The five most popular elk cartridges, based on the author's surveys. From left: .30-06, 7mm Remington Magnum, .270, .300 Winchester Magnum, .338 Winchester Magnum.

ELK CARTRIDGES BALLISTICS CHART CONTINUED

Cartridge/Bullet	Range (yards)				
	0	100	200	300	400
Winchester 150 Power-Point					
Velocity (fps)	3270	2903	2565	2250	1958
Energy (ft-lb)	3561	2807	2190	1686	1277
Arc (inches)		+1.3	0	-6.6	-20.2
Winchester 150 Ballistic Silvertip					
Velocity (fps)	3300	3061	2834	2619	2414
Energy (ft-lb)	3628	3121	2676	2285	1941
Arc (inches)		+1.1	0	-5.4	-15.9
.300 Weatherby Mag					
Hornady 150 SST (or InterBond)					
Velocity (fps)	3375	3123	2882	2652	2434
Energy (ft-lb)	3793	3248	2766	2343	1973
Arc (inches)		+1.0	0	-5.4	-15.8
Weatherby 150 Pointed Expanding					
Velocity (fps)	3540	3225	2932	2657	2399
Energy (ft-lb)	4173	3462	2862	2351	1916
Arc (inches)		+2.6	+3.3	0	-8.2
Weatherby 150 Nosler Partition					
Velocity (fps)	3540	3263	3004	2759	2528
Energy (ft-lb)	4173	3547	3005	2536	2128
Arc (inches)		+2.5	+3.2	0	-7.7
7.82 (.308) Lazzeroni Warbird					
Lazzeroni 150 Nosler Partition					
Velocity (fps)	3680	3432	3197	2975	2764
Energy (ft-lb)	4512	3923	3406	2949	2546
Arc (inches)		+2.1	+2.7	0	-6.6

Reaching for elk across Montana canyons, Ken Nagel relies on heavy bullets driven fast.

A long shot brought this magnificent bull to bag for Ken Peterson, one of the author's friends.

TIME TO TURBOCHARGE

Setting up to shoot elk at extreme range has become a common tactic for riflemen who hunt where open canyons, mountain basins, and mesas allow long-distance sightings. When long shots are the rule rather than the exception, and when your rifle has the inherent accuracy to hit vitals consistently beyond 300 yards, you're smart to boost horsepower. The cartridges and loads in the following chart start with bullets of at least 165 grains at 2,900 fps or higher. They shoot flat, dropping no more than 24 inches at 400 yards from a 200-yard zero. Heavy bullets deliver more punch at that range than do most popular .270 and 7mm spitzers. Figure 1,600 foot-pounds at the 400-yard mark for these husky .30s and .33s. That's not too much, given the size and tenacity of elk (or Alaskan moose or brown bears or African gemsbok) and the fact that at long range, you're unlikely to get a follow-up shot or reach the stricken animal quickly.

LONG-DISTANCE ELK BALLISTICS CHART

Cartridge/Bullet	Range (yards)				
	0	100	200	300	400
.30-06 Springfield					
Federal 165 Sierra GameKing HE					
Velocity (fps)	3140	2900	2670	2450	2240
Energy (ft-lb)	3610	3075	2610	2200	1845
Arc (inches)		+1.5	0	-6.9	-20.4
Federal 165 Trophy Bonded HE					
Velocity (fps)	3140	2860	2590	2340	2100
Energy (ft-lb)	3610	2990	2460	2010	1625
Arc (inches)		+1.6	0	-7.4	-21.9
Federal 180 Nosler Partition HE					
Velocity (fps)	2880	2690	2500	2320	2150
Energy (ft-lb)	3315	2880	2495	2150	1845
Arc (inches)		+1.7	0	-7.2	-21.0
Federal 180 Trophy Bonded HE					
Velocity (fps)	2880	2630	2380	2160	1940
Energy (ft-lb)	3315	2755	2270	1855	1505
Arc (inches)		+1.8	0	-8.0	-23.3
Hornady 165 SPBT LM					
Velocity (fps)	3015	2790	2575	2370	2176
Energy (ft-lb)	3330	2850	2428	2058	1734
Arc (inches)		+1.6	0	-7.0	-20.1
Hornady 165 SST LM					
Velocity (fps)	3015	2802	2599	2405	2219
Energy (ft-lb)	3330	2878	2474	2118	1803
Arc (inches)		+1.5	0	-6.5	-19.3
Hornady 180 SPBT LM					
Velocity (fps)	2880	2676	2480	2293	2114
Energy (ft-lb)	3316	2862	2459	2102	1786
Arc (inches)		+1.7	0	-7.3	-21.3

HE, high energy; HM, heavy magnum; LM, light magnum.

LONG-DISTANCE ELK BALLISTICS CHART CONTINUED

Cartridge/Bullet	Range (yards)				
	0	100	200	300	400
.300 H&H Mag					
Federal 180 Nosler Partition					
Velocity (fps)	2880	2620	2380	2150	1930
Energy (ft-lb)	3315	2750	2260	1840	1480
Arc (inches)		+1.8	0	-8.0	-23.4
Winchester 180 Fail Safe					
Velocity (fps)	2880	2628	2390	2165	1952
Energy (ft-lb)	3316	2762	2284	1873	1523
Arc (inches)		+1.8	0	-7.9	-23.2
.308 Norma Mag					
Norma 180 TXP Swift A-Frame					
Velocity (fps)	2953	2704	2469	2245	2020
Energy (ft-lb)	3486	2924	2437	2016	1630
Arc (inches)		+1.6	0	-7.3	-21.6
Norma 180 Oryx					
Velocity (fps)	2953	2630	2330	2049	1780
Energy (ft-lb)	3486	2766	2170	1679	1260
Arc (inches)		+1.8	0	-8.2	-24.5
Norma 200 Vulkan					
Velocity (fps)	2903	2624	2361	2114	1890
Energy (ft-lb)	3744	3058	2476	1985	1630
Arc (inches)		+1.8	0	-8.0	-22.5
.300 Winchester Mag					
Black Hills 180 Nosler Ballistic Tip					
Velocity (fps)	3000	2825	2658	2496	2341
Energy (ft-lb)	3598	3190	2623	2490	2189
Arc (inches)		+1.4	0	-6.4	-18.3
Black Hills 180 Barnes X					
Velocity (fps)	2950	2779	2614	2456	2303
Energy (ft-lb)	3478	3086	2731	2410	2119
Arc (inches)		+1.5	0	-6.6	-19.0

LONG-DISTANCE ELK BALLISTICS CHART CONTINUED

Cartridge/Bullet	Range (yards)				
	0	**100**	**200**	**300**	**400**
Black Hills 180 AccuBond					
Velocity (fps)	2950	2777	2612	2452	2298
Energy (ft-lb)	3478	3083	2726	2402	2110
Arc (inches)		+1.5	0	-6.6	-19.0
Federal 180 Sierra Pro-Hunter					
Velocity (fps)	2960	2750	2540	2340	2160
Energy (ft-lb)	3500	3010	2580	2195	1860
Arc (inches)		+1.6	0	-7.0	-20.3
Federal 180 Barnes XLC					
Velocity (fps)	2960	2780	2600	2430	2260
Energy (ft-lb)	3500	3080	2700	2355	2050
Arc (inches)		+1.5	0	-6.6	-19.2

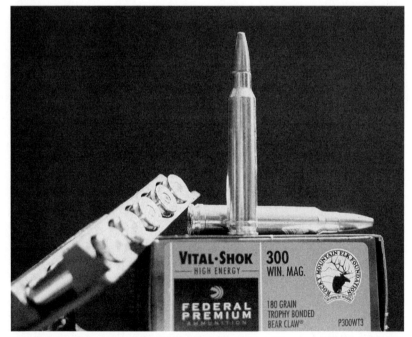

An ideal round for distant elk? Try the .300 Winchester Magnum, 180-grain Trophy Bonded bullets.

LONG-DISTANCE ELK BALLISTICS CHART CONTINUED

Cartridge/Bullet	Range (yards)				
	0	**100**	**200**	**300**	**400**
Federal 180 Trophy Bonded					
Velocity (fps)	2960	2700	2460	2220	2000
Energy (ft-lb)	3500	2915	2410	1975	1605
Arc (inches)		+1.6	0	-7.4	-21.9
Federal 180 Trophy Bonded HE					
Velocity (fps)	3100	2830	2580	2340	2110
Energy (ft-lb)	3840	3205	2660	2190	1790
Arc (inches)		+1.4	0	-6.6	-19.7
Federal 180 Nosler Partition					
Velocity (fps)	2960	2700	2450	2210	1990
Energy (ft-lb)	3500	2905	2395	1955	1585
Arc (inches)		+1.6	0	-7.5	-22.1
Federal 200 Sierra GameKing BTSP					
Velocity (fps)	2830	2680	2530	2380	2240
Energy (ft-lb)	3560	3180	2830	2520	2230
Arc (inches)		+1.7	0	-7.1	-20.4
Federal 200 Nosler Partition HE					
Velocity (fps)	2930	2740	2550	2370	2200
Energy (ft-lb)	3810	3325	2885	2495	2145
Arc (inches)		+1.6	0	-6.9	-20.1
Hornady 165 SP Boattail					
Velocity (fps)	3100	2877	2665	2462	2269
Energy (ft-lb)	3522	3033	2603	2221	1887
Arc (inches)		+1.3	0	-6.5	-18.5
Hornady 165 SST					
Velocity (fps)	3100	2885	2680	2483	2296
Energy (ft-lb)	3520	3049	2630	2259	1930
Arc (inches)		+1.4	0	-6.4	-18.6
Hornady 180 SP Boattail					
Velocity (fps)	2960	2745	2540	2344	2157
Energy (ft-lb)	3501	3011	2578	2196	1859
Arc (inches)		+1.9	0	-7.3	-20.9

LONG-DISTANCE ELK BALLISTICS CHART CONTINUED

Cartridge/Bullet	Range (yards)				
	0	100	200	300	400
Hornady 180 SST					
Velocity (fps)	2960	2764	2575	2395	2222
Energy (ft-lb)	3501	3052	2650	2292	1974
Arc (inches)		+1.6	0	-7.0	-20.1
Hornady 180 SPBT HM					
Velocity (fps)	3100	2879	2668	2467	2275
Energy (ft-lb)	3840	3313	2845	2431	2068
Arc (inches)		+1.4	0	-6.4	-18.7
Hornady 190 SP Boattail					
Velocity (fps)	2900	2711	2529	2355	2187
Energy (ft-lb)	3549	3101	2699	2340	2018
Arc (inches)		+1.6	0	-7.1	-20.4
Norma 165 Scirocco					
Velocity (fps)	3117	2921	2734	2554	2290
Energy (ft-lb)	3561	3127	2738	2390	1930
Arc (inches)		+1.2	0	-5.9	-17.2
Norma 180 Soft Point					
Velocity (fps)	3018	2780	2555	2341	2200
Energy (ft-lb)	3641	3091	2610	2190	1936
Arc (inches)		+1.5	0	-7.0	-20.5
Norma 180 Plastic Point					
Velocity (fps)	3018	2755	2506	2271	2050
Energy (ft-lb)	3641	3034	2512	2062	1680
Arc (inches)		+1.6	0	-7.1	-20.8
Norma 180 TXP **Swift A-Frame**					
Velocity (fps)	2920	2688	2467	2256	2100
Energy (ft-lb)	3409	2888	2432	2035	1765
Arc (inches)		+1.7	0	-7.4	-21.4
Norma 180 AccuBond					
Velocity (fps)	2953	2767	2588	2417	2250
Energy (ft-lb)	3486	3061	2678	2335	2025
Arc (inches)		+1.5	0	-6.7	-19.5
Norma 200 Vulkan					
Velocity (fps)	2887	2609	2347	2100	1860
Energy (ft-lb)	3702	3023	2447	1960	1540
Arc (inches)		+1.8	0	-8.2	-23.4

LONG-DISTANCE ELK BALLISTICS CHART CONTINUED

Cartridge/Bullet	Range (yards)				
	0	100	200	300	400
PMC 180 Barnes X					
Velocity (fps)	2910	2738	2572	2412	2258
Energy (ft-lb)	3384	2995	2644	2325	2037
Arc (inches)		+1.6	0	-6.9	-19.8
PMC 180 SP Boattail					
Velocity (fps)	2900	2714	2536	2365	2200
Energy (ft-lb)	3361	2944	2571	2235	1935
Arc (inches)		+1.6	0	-7.1	-20.3
PMC 180 HPBT Match					
Velocity (fps)	2950	2755	2568	2390	2219
Energy (ft-lb)	3478	3033	2636	2283	1968
Arc (inches)		+1.5	0	-6.8	-19.7
Remington 180 AccuTip					
Velocity (fps)	2960	2764	2577	2397	2224
Energy (ft-lb)	3501	3053	2653	2295	1976
Arc (inches)		+1.5	0	-6.8	-19.6
Remington 180 PSP Core-Lokt					
Velocity (fps)	2960	2745	2540	2344	2157
Energy (ft-lb)	3501	3011	2578	2196	1424
Arc (inches)		+2.2	+1.9	-3.4	-15.0
Remington 180 PSP C-L Ultra					
Velocity (fps)	2960	2727	2505	2294	2093
Energy (ft-lb)	3501	2971	2508	2103	1751
Arc (inches)		+2.7	+2.2	-3.8	-16.4
Remington 180 Nosler Partition					
Velocity (fps)	2960	2725	2503	2291	2089
Energy (ft-lb)	3501	2968	2503	2087	1744
Arc (inches)		+1.6	0	-7.2	-20.9
Remington 180 Nosler Ballistic Tip					
Velocity (fps)	2960	2774	2595	2424	2259
Energy (ft-lb)	3501	3075	2692	2348	2039
Arc (inches)		+1.5	0	-6.7	-19.3

LONG-DISTANCE ELK BALLISTICS CHART CONTINUED

Cartridge/Bullet	Range (yards)				
	0	100	200	300	400
Remington 180 Swift Scirocco					
Velocity (fps)	2960	2774	2595	2424	2259
Energy (ft-lb)	3501	3075	2692	2348	2039
Arc (inches)		+1.5	0	-6.7	-19.3
Remington 190 PSP Boattail					
Velocity (fps)	2885	2691	2506	2327	2156
Energy (ft-lb)	3511	3055	2648	2285	1961
Arc (inches)		+1.6	0	-7.2	-20.8
Remington 200 Swift A-Frame					
Velocity (fps)	2825	2595	2376	2167	1970
Energy (ft-lb)	3544	2989	2506	2086	1722
Arc (inches)		+1.8	0	-8.0	-23.5
Speer 180 Grand Slam					
Velocity (fps)	2950	2735	2530	2334	2160
Energy (ft-lb)	3478	2989	2558	2176	1860
Arc (inches)		+1.6	0	-7.0	-20.5
Speer 200 Grand Slam					
Velocity (fps)	2800	2597	2404	2218	2040
Energy (ft-lb)	3481	2996	2565	2185	1890
Arc (inches)		+1.8	0	-7.9	-22.9
Winchester 180 Power-Point					
Velocity (fps)	2960	2745	2540	2344	2157
Energy (ft-lb)	3501	3011	2578	2196	1859
Arc (inches)		+1.9	0	-7.3	-20.9
Winchester 180 Power-Point Plus					
Velocity (fps)	3070	2846	2633	2430	2236
Energy (ft-lb)	3768	3239	2772	2361	1999
Arc (inches)		+1.4	0	-6.4	-18.7
Winchester 180 Ballistic Silvertip					
Velocity (fps)	2950	2764	2586	2415	2250
Energy (ft-lb)	3478	3054	2673	2331	2023
Arc (inches)		+1.5	0	-6.7	-19.4

LONG-DISTANCE ELK BALLISTICS CHART CONTINUED

Cartridge/Bullet	Range (yards)				
	0	100	200	300	400
Winchester 180 AccuBond					
Velocity (fps)	2950	2765	2588	2417	2253
Energy (ft-lb)	3478	3055	2676	2334	2028
Arc (inches)		+1.5	0	-6.7	-19.4
Winchester 180 Fail Safe					
Velocity (fps)	2960	2732	2514	2307	2110
Energy (ft-lb)	3503	2983	2528	2129	1780
Arc (inches)		+1.6	0	-7.1	-20.7
Winchester 180 Partition Gold					
Velocity (fps)	3070	2859	2657	2464	2280
Energy (ft-lb)	3768	3267	2823	2428	2078
Arc (inches)		+1.4	0	-6.3	-18.3

.300 Remington Short Ultra Mag

	0	100	200	300	400
Remington 165 PSP Core-Lokt					
Velocity (fps)	3075	2792	2527	2276	2040
Energy (ft-lb)	3464	2856	2339	1828	1525
Arc (inches)		+1.5	0	-7.0	-20.7
Remington 180 Partition					
Velocity (fps)	2960	2761	2571	2389	2214
Energy (ft-lb)	3501	3047	2642	2280	1959
Arc (inches)		+1.5	0	-6.8	-19.7
Remington 180 PSP C-L Ultra					
Velocity (fps)	2960	2727	2506	2295	2094
Energy (ft-lb)	3501	2972	2509	2105	1753
Arc (inches)		+1.6	0	-7.1	-20.9

.300 Winchester Short Mag

	0	100	200	300	400
Black Hills 180 AccuBond					
Velocity (fps)	2950	2777	2612	2452	2298
Energy (ft-lb)	3478	3083	2726	2402	2110
Arc (inches)		+1.5	0	-6.6	-19.0
Federal 165 Nosler Partition					
Velocity (fps)	3130	2890	2670	2450	2250
Energy (ft-lb)	3590	3065	2605	2205	1855
Arc (inches)		+1.3	0	-6.2	-18.2

LONG-DISTANCE ELK BALLISTICS CHART CONTINUED

Cartridge/Bullet	Range (yards)				
	0	100	200	300	400
Federal 165 Nosler Solid Base					
Velocity (fps)	3130	2900	2690	2490	2290
Energy (ft-lb)	3590	3090	2650	2265	1920
Arc (inches)		+1.3	0	-6.1	-17.8
Federal 180 Barnes TS and Nosler Solid Base					
Velocity (fps)	2980	2780	2580	2400	2220
Energy (ft-lb)	3550	3085	2670	2300	1970
Arc (inches)		+1.5	0	-6.7	-19.5
Federal 180 Grand Slam					
Velocity (fps)	2970	2740	2530	2320	2130
Energy (ft-lb)	3525	3010	2555	2155	1810
Arc (inches)		+1.5	0	-7.0	-20.5
Federal 180 Trophy Bonded					
Velocity (fps)	2970	2730	2500	2280	2080
Energy (ft-lb)	3525	2975	2500	2085	1725
Arc (inches)		+1.5	0	-7.2	-21.0
Federal 180 Nosler Partition					
Velocity (fps)	2975	2750	2535	2290	2126
Energy (ft-lb)	3540	3025	2570	2175	1825
Arc (inches)		+1.5	0	-7.0	-20.3
Federal 180 Nosler AccuBond					
Velocity (fps)	2960	2780	2610	2440	2280
Energy (ft-lb)	3500	3090	2715	2380	2075
Arc (inches)		+1.5	0	-6.6	-19.0
Norma 180 Nosler Ballistic Tip					
Velocity (fps)	3215	2985	2767	2560	2370
Energy (ft-lb)	3437	2963	2547	2179	2250
Arc (inches)		+1.2	0	-5.7	-16.8
Winchester 165 Fail Safe					
Velocity (fps)	3125	2846	2584	2336	2102
Energy (ft-lb)	3577	2967	2446	1999	1619
Arc (inches)		+1.4	0	-6.6	-19.6

LONG-DISTANCE ELK BALLISTICS CHART CONTINUED

Cartridge/Bullet	Range (yards)				
	0	**100**	**200**	**300**	**400**
Winchester 180 Ballistic Silvertip					
Velocity (fps)	3010	2822	2641	2468	2301
Energy (ft-lb)	3621	3182	2788	2434	2116
Arc (inches)		+1.4	0	-6.4	-18.6
Winchester 180 AccuBond					
Velocity (fps)	3010	2822	2643	2470	2304
Energy (ft-lb)	3622	3185	2792	2439	2121
Arc (inches)		+1.4	0	-6.4	-18.5
Winchester 180 Fail Safe					
Velocity (fps)	2970	2741	2524	2317	2120
Energy (ft-lb)	3526	3005	2547	2147	1797
Arc (inches)		+1.6	0	-7.0	-20.5
Winchester 180 Power-Point					
Velocity (fps)	2970	2755	2549	2353	2166
Energy (ft-lb)	3526	3034	2598	2214	1875
Arc (inches)		+1.5	0	-6.9	-20.1
.300 Weatherby Mag					
Federal 180 Sierra GameKing BTSP					
Velocity (fps)	3190	3010	2830	2660	2490
Energy (ft-lb)	4065	3610	3195	2820	2480
Arc (inches)		+1.2	0	-5.6	-16.0
Federal 180 Trophy Bonded					
Velocity (fps)	3190	2950	2720	2500	2290
Energy (ft-lb)	4065	3475	2955	2500	2105
Arc (inches)		+1.3	0	-5.9	-17.5
Federal 180 Trophy Bonded HE					
Velocity (fps)	3330	3080	2850	2750	2410
Energy (ft-lb)	4430	3795	3235	2750	2320
Arc (inches)		+1.1	0	-5.4	-15.8

LONG-DISTANCE ELK BALLISTICS CHART CONTINUED

Cartridge/Bullet	Range (yards)				
	0	100	200	300	400
Federal 180 Nosler Partition					
Velocity (fps)	3190	2980	2780	2590	2400
Energy (ft-lb)	4055	3540	3080	2670	2305
Arc (inches)		+1.2	0	-5.7	-16.7
Federal 180 Nosler Partition HE					
Velocity (fps)	3330	3110	2810	2710	2520
Energy (ft-lb)	4430	3875	3375	2935	2540
Arc (inches)		+1.0	0	-5.2	-15.1
Federal 200 Trophy Bonded					
Velocity (fps)	2900	2670	2440	2230	2030
Energy (ft-lb)	3735	3150	2645	2200	1820
Arc (inches)		+1.7	0	-7.6	-22.2
Hornady 180 SP					
Velocity (fps)	3120	2891	2673	2466	2268
Energy (ft-lb)	3890	3340	2856	2430	2055
Arc (inches)		+1.3	0	-6.2	-18.1
Hornady 180 SST					
Velocity (fps)	3120	2911	2711	2519	2335
Energy (ft-lb)	3890	3386	2936	2535	2180
Arc (inches)		+1.3	0	-6.2	-18.1
Remington 180 PSP Core-Lokt					
Velocity (fps)	3120	2866	2627	2400	2184
Energy (ft-lb)	3890	3284	2758	2301	1905
Arc (inches)		+2.4	+2.0	-3.4	-14.9
Remington 190 PSP Boattail					
Velocity (fps)	3030	2830	2638	2455	2279
Energy (ft-lb)	3873	3378	2936	2542	2190
Arc (inches)		+1.4	0	-6.4	-18.6
Remington 200 Swift A-Frame					
Velocity (fps)	2925	2690	2467	2254	2052
Energy (ft-lb)	3799	3213	2701	2256	1870
Arc (inches)		+2.8	+2.3	-3.9	-17.0

LONG-DISTANCE ELK BALLISTICS CHART CONTINUED

Cartridge/Bullet	Range (yards)				
	0	**100**	**200**	**300**	**400**
Speer 180 Grand Slam					
Velocity (fps)	3185	2948	2722	2508	2000
Energy (ft-lb)	4054	3472	2962	2514	1600
Arc (inches)		+1.3	0	-5.9	-17.4
Weatherby 165 Pointed Expanding					
Velocity (fps)	3390	3123	2872	2634	2409
Energy (ft-lb)	4210	3573	3021	2542	2126
Arc (inches)		+2.8	+3.5	0	-8.5
Weatherby 165 Nosler Ballistic Tip					
Velocity (fps)	3350	3133	2927	2730	2542
Energy (ft-lb)	4111	3596	3138	2730	2367
Arc (inches)		+2.7	+3.4	0	-8.1
Weatherby 180 Pointed Expanding					
Velocity (fps)	3240	3004	2781	2569	2366
Energy (ft-lb)	4195	3607	3091	2637	2237
Arc (inches)		+3.1	+3.8	0	-9.0
Weatherby 180 Barnes X					
Velocity (fps)	3190	2995	2809	2631	2459
Energy (ft-lb)	4067	3586	3154	2766	2417
Arc (inches)		+3.1	+3.8	0	-8.7
Weatherby 180 Ballistic Tip					
Velocity (fps)	3250	3051	2806	2676	2503
Energy (ft-lb)	4223	3721	3271	2867	2504
Arc (inches)		+2.8	+3.6	0	-8.4
Weatherby 180 Nosler Partition					
Velocity (fps)	3240	3028	2826	2634	2449
Energy (ft-lb)	4195	3665	3193	2772	2396
Arc (inches)		+3.0	+3.7	0	-8.6
Weatherby 200 Nosler Partition					
Velocity (fps)	3060	2860	2668	2485	2308
Energy (ft-lb)	4158	3631	3161	2741	2366
Arc (inches)		+3.5	+4.2	0	-9.8

LONG-DISTANCE ELK BALLISTICS CHART CONTINUED

Cartridge/Bullet	Range (yards)				
	0	**100**	**200**	**300**	**400**
.300 Dakota					
Dakota 165 Barnes X					
Velocity (fps)	3200	2979	2769	2569	2377
Energy (ft-lb)	3751	3251	2809	2417	2070
Arc (inches)		+2.1	+1.8	-3.0	-13.2
Dakota 200 Barnes X					
Velocity (fps)	3000	2824	2656	2493	2336
Energy (ft-lb)	3996	3542	3131	2760	2423
Arc (inches)		+2.2	+1.5	-4.0	-15.2
.300 Remington Ultra Mag					
Federal 180 Trophy Bonded					
Velocity (fps)	3250	3000	2770	2550	2340
Energy (ft-lb)	4220	3605	3065	2590	2180
Arc (inches)		+1.2	0	-5.7	-16.8
Remington 150 Swift Scirocco					
Velocity (fps)	3450	3208	2980	2762	2556
Energy (ft-lb)	3964	3427	2956	2541	2175
Arc (inches)		+1.7	+1.5	-2.6	-11.2
Remington 180 Nosler Partition					
Velocity (fps)	3250	3037	2834	2640	2454
Energy (ft-lb)	4221	3686	3201	2786	2407
Arc (inches)		+2.4	+1.8	-3.0	-12.7
Remington 180 Swift Scirocco					
Velocity (fps)	3250	3048	2856	2672	2495
Energy (ft-lb)	4221	3714	3260	2853	2487
Arc (inches)		+2.0	+1.7	-2.8	-12.3
Remington 180 PSP Core-Lokt					
Velocity (fps)	3250	2988	2742	2508	2287
Energy (ft-lb)	3517	2974	2503	2095	1741
Arc (inches)		+2.1	+1.8	-3.1	-13.6

LONG-DISTANCE ELK BALLISTICS CHART CONTINUED

Cartridge/Bullet	Range (yards)				
	0	**100**	**200**	**300**	**400**
Remington 200 Nosler Partition					
Velocity (fps)	3025	2826	2636	2454	2279
Energy (ft-lb)	4063	3547	3086	2673	2308
Arc (inches)		+2.4	+2.0	-3.4	-14.6
.30-378 Weatherby Mag					
Weatherby 165 Nosler Ballistic Tip					
Velocity (fps)	3500	3275	3062	2859	2665
Energy (ft-lb)	4488	3930	3435	2995	2603
Arc (inches)		+2.4	+3.0	0	-7.4
Weatherby 180 Nosler Ballistic Tip					
Velocity (fps)	3420	3213	3015	2826	2645
Energy (ft-lb)	4676	4126	3634	3193	2797
Arc (inches)		+2.5	+3.1	0	-7.5
Weatherby 180 Barnes X					
Velocity (fps)	3450	3243	3046	2858	2678
Energy (ft-lb)	4757	4204	3709	3264	2865
Arc (inches)		+2.4	+3.1	0	-7.4
Weatherby 200 Nosler Partition					
Velocity (fps)	3160	2955	2759	2572	2392
Energy (ft-lb)	4434	3877	3381	2938	2541
Arc (inches)		+3.2	+3.9	0	-9.1
7.82 (.308) Lazzeroni Warbird					
Lazzeroni 180 Nosler Partition					
Velocity (fps)	3425	3220	3026	2839	2661
Energy (ft-lb)	4689	4147	3661	3224	2831
Arc (inches)		+2.5	+3.2	0	-7.5
Lazzeroni 200 Swift A-Frame					
Velocity (fps)	3290	3105	2928	2758	2594
Energy (ft-lb)	4808	4283	3808	3378	2988
Arc (inches)		+2.7	+3.4	0	-7.9

LONG-DISTANCE ELK BALLISTICS CHART CONTINUED

Cartridge/Bullet	Range (yards)				
	0	100	200	300	400
.325 Winchester Short Mag					
Winchester 180 Ballistic ST					
Velocity (fps)	3060	2841	2632	2432	2242
Energy (ft-lb)	3743	3226	2769	2365	2009
Arc (inches)		+1.4	0	-6.4	-18.7
Winchester 200 AccuBond CT					
Velocity (fps)	2950	2753	2565	2384	2210
Energy (ft-lb)	3866	3367	2922	2524	2170
Arc (inches)		+1.5	0	-6.8	-19.8
8mm Remington Mag					
Remington 200 Swift A-Frame					
Velocity (fps)	2900	2623	2361	2115	1885
Energy (ft-lb)	3734	3054	2476	1987	1577
Arc (inches)		+1.8	0	-8.0	-23.9
.338 Winchester Mag					
Federal 225 Trophy Bonded HE					
Velocity (fps)	2940	2690	2450	2230	2010
Energy (ft-lb)	4320	3610	3000	2475	2025
Arc (inches)		+1.7	0	-7.5	-22.0
Hornady 225 Soft Point HM					
Velocity (fps)	2920	2678	2449	2232	2027
Energy (ft-lb)	4259	3583	2996	2489	2053
Arc (inches)		+1.8	0	-7.6	-22.0
Remington 200 Nosler Ballistic Tip					
Velocity (fps)	2950	2724	2509	2303	2108
Energy (ft-lb)	3866	3295	2795	2357	1973
Arc (inches)		+1.6	0	-7.1	-20.8
Remington 210 Nosler Partition					
Velocity (fps)	2830	2602	2385	2179	1983
Energy (ft-lb)	3734	3157	2653	2214	1834
Arc (inches)		+1.8	0	-7.9	-23.2

LONG-DISTANCE ELK BALLISTICS CHART CONTINUED

Cartridge/Bullet	Range (yards)				
	0	100	200	300	400
Winchester 200 Ballistic Silvertip					
Velocity (fps)	2950	2724	2509	2303	2108
Energy (ft-lb)	3864	3294	2794	2355	1972
Arc (inches)		+1.6	0	-7.1	-20.8
.340 Weatherby Mag					
Federal 225 Trophy Bonded					
Velocity (fps)	3100	2840	2600	2370	2150
Energy (ft-lb)	4800	4035	3375	2800	2310
Arc (inches)		+1.4	0	-6.5	-19.4
Weatherby 200 Pointed Expanding					
Velocity (fps)	3221	2946	2688	2444	2213
Energy (ft-lb)	4607	3854	3208	2652	2174
Arc (inches)		+3.3	+4.0	0	-9.9
Weatherby 200 Nosler Ballistic Tip					
Velocity (fps)	3221	2980	2753	2536	2329
Energy (ft-lb)	4607	3944	3364	2856	2409
Arc (inches)		+3.1	+3.9	0	-9.2
Weatherby 210 Nosler Partition					
Velocity (fps)	3211	2963	2728	2505	2293
Energy (ft-lb)	4807	4093	3470	2927	2452
Arc (inches)		+3.2	+3.9	0	-9.5
Weatherby 225 Pointed Expanding					
Velocity (fps)	3066	2824	2595	2377	2170
Energy (ft-lb)	4696	3984	3364	2822	2352
Arc (inches)		+3.6	+4.4	0	-10.7
Weatherby 225 Barnes X					
Velocity (fps)	3001	2804	2615	2434	2260
Energy (ft-lb)	4499	3927	3416	2959	2551
Arc (inches)		+3.6	+4.3	0	-10.3
Weatherby 250 Pointed Expanding					
Velocity (fps)	2963	2745	2537	2338	2149
Energy (ft-lb)	4873	4182	3572	3035	2563
Arc (inches)		+3.9	+4.6	0	-11.1

LONG-DISTANCE ELK BALLISTICS CHART CONTINUED

Cartridge/Bullet	Range (yards)				
	0	100	200	300	400
Weatherby 250 Nosler Partition					
Velocity (fps)	2941	2743	2553	2371	2197
Energy (ft-lb)	4801	4176	3618	3120	2678
Arc (inches)		+3.9	+4.6	0	-10.9
.330 Dakota					
Dakota 200 Barnes X					
Velocity (fps)	3200	2971	2754	2548	2350
Energy (ft-lb)	4547	3920	3369	2882	2452
Arc (inches)		+2.1	+1.8	-3.1	-13.4
Dakota 250 Barnes X					
Velocity (fps)	2900	2719	2545	2378	2217
Energy (ft-lb)	4668	4103	3595	3138	2727
Arc (inches)		+2.3	+1.3	-5.0	-17.5
.338 Remington Ultra Mag					
Federal 210 Nosler Partition					
Velocity (fps)	3025	2800	2585	2385	2190
Energy (ft-lb)	4270	3655	3120	2645	2230
Arc (inches)		+1.5	0	-6.7	-19.5
Federal 250 Trophy Bonded					
Velocity (fps)	2860	2630	2420	2210	2020
Energy (ft-lb)	4540	3850	3245	2715	2260
Arc (inches)		+0.8	0	-7.7	-22.6
Remington 250 Swift A-Frame					
Velocity (fps)	2860	2645	2440	2244	2057
Energy (ft-lb)	4540	3882	3303	2794	2347
Arc (inches)		+1.7	0	-7.6	-22.1
Remington 250 PSP Core-Lokt					
Velocity (fps)	2860	2647	2443	2249	2064
Energy (ft-lb)	4540	3888	3314	2807	2363
Arc (inches)		+1.7	0	-7.6	-22.0

LONG-DISTANCE ELK BALLISTICS CHART CONTINUED

Cartridge/Bullet	Range (yards)				
	0	**100**	**200**	**300**	**400**
.338-378 Weatherby Mag					
Weatherby 200 Nosler Ballistic Tip					
Velocity (fps)	3350	3102	2868	2646	2434
Energy (ft-lb)	4983	4273	3652	3109	2631
Arc (inches)		0	+2.8	+3.5	0
Weatherby 225 Barnes X					
Velocity (fps)	3180	2974	2778	2591	2410
Energy (ft-lb)	5052	4420	3856	3353	2902
Arc (inches)		0	+3.1	+3.8	0
Weatherby 250 Nosler Partition					
Velocity (fps)	3060	2856	2662	2475	2297
Energy (ft-lb)	5197	4528	3933	3401	2927
Arc (inches)		0	+3.5	+4.2	0
8.59 (.338) Titan					
Lazzeroni 200 Nosler Ballistic Tip					
Velocity (fps)	3430	3211	3002	2803	2613
Energy (ft-lb)	5226	4579	4004	3491	3033
Arc (inches)		+2.5	+3.2	0	-7.6
Lazzeroni 225 Nosler Partition					
Velocity (fps)	3235	3031	2836	2650	2471
Energy (ft-lb)	5229	4591	4021	3510	3052
Arc (inches)		+3.0	+3.6	0	-8.6
Lazzeroni 250 Swift A-Frame					
Velocity (fps)	3100	2908	2725	2549	2379
Energy (ft-lb)	5336	4697	4123	3607	3143
Arc (inches)		+3.3	+4.0	0	-9.3

There's a big difference in energy values between the .243 and the .338 Ultra Mag, though the arc values are close. Killing power has little to do with trajectory, but both are affected by velocity. Flat arc and high energy values in foot-pounds result when bullets travel fast. High ballistic coefficients buoy energy at long range and keep the bullet's arc from sagging steeply. Because velocity is squared in calculations of foot-pounds, lightweight bullets outscore slower, heavier bullets that might deal an equally lethal blow. So while killing power is enhanced by increasing bullet speed and bullet weight, the relative contribution of each has long been argued.

Killing effect is also influenced a great deal by bullet design. Animals of light skin and frame can be taken most suddenly with bullets that expand fully and even fragment as they reach the shallow vitals. Bigger game with thick hides and heavy bones and muscles can survive hits with frangible bullets that don't reach the vitals. So-called controlled-expansion bullets (a misnomer, because all expanding bullets are engineered to upset in a predictable way) feature thick jackets, core-jacket bonding, internal dams and other features to ensure deep penetration in big animals. These devices do not delay upset; all bullets start to expand on impact. A bullet's nose endures by far its greatest stress at the point of collision. Entering the animal, its deceleration rate increases, as does pressure around the jacket. If a bullet doesn't initiate expansion at contact, it likely won't expand at all—although bone strikes inside the animal can break a bullet apart or change its direction following a less violent reaction to initial contact.

Distance drains velocity, so at long range, bullets do not expand as violently as they do closer to the rifle. Penetration at long range can thus be greater than up close, despite the velocity loss. If a bullet's nose does not mushroom fully, there's less frontal resistance. The shank's inertia keeps the bullet moving forward. A high-speed collision at short yardage puts maximum stress on the bullet, ensuring as complete a deformation as the bullet's construction will allow. A big frontal area and a short shank impede penetration; fragmentation scuttles it and can throw the main bullet remnant off course.

Accuracy, not foot-pounds of payload, is the crucial factor in long-range shooting. Unless you hit an animal in the right place, you won't kill it. If a hard-kicking rifle causes you to flinch, you're better off using a gentler cartridge. Ranges at which bullet energy drops below reasonable levels, or at which there's too little speed to initiate expansion, are typically greater than distances at which hunters can place bullets precisely.

One well-placed .300 Winchester bullet from a far-away ridge dropped this long-tined five-point.

John Nosler, here with his pet .280, still enjoys shooting fifty years after crafting the Partition bullet.

BIG-GAME BULLETS

A patched round ball can be extremely accurate. But no matter how carefully rifled the barrel or how fastidious the rifleman who loads it, a ball is ballistically inefficient. Following the Civil War, hunters shifted to conical bullets because they "carried up" better at long range and penetrated better at all ranges. Long bullets have the highest sectional density (ratio of bullet weight to cross-sectional area), but because they are heavy and generate lots of friction as they race down the bore, long bullets cannot be driven as fast as shorter bullets.

In the late 1870s, Sharps listed bullet weights of 293 to 550 grains for the .45-70. When smokeless rounds supplanted blackpowder cartridges in military service a couple of decades later, hunting and military rounds were given long bullets, heavy for the bore: 162 grains in 6.5x52 Carcano, 173 grains in 7x57 Mauser, 215 grains in .303 British. These bullets trundled along at less than 2,300 fps but were considered fast in their day.

The 7.9x57 cartridge, designed for Germany's Gewehr 88 infantry rifle, arrived two years after the French had pioneered the military use of smokeless powder with their 8mm Lebel. Like the infantry rounds that followed it, the 7.9x57 featured a heavy round-nose bullet. In 1898 the modified Mannlicher action of the 1888 rifle was replaced by a new, much stronger mechanism: Paul Mauser's Model 1898. The cartridge remained unaltered until 1905, when German engineers came up with a lighter bullet at higher velocity. They changed the bore diameter from .318 to .323 (8mm) and replaced the blunt 226-grain bullet with a pointed 154-grain spitzer. Muzzle velocity jumped from 2,090 to 2,880 fps. Both the 7.9x57 and the later 8x57 have been called 8mm Mauser cartridges, so letter designations were added to distinguish them. The early .318 round carries a J suffix for "infanterie" (J and I are interchangeable in German); .323 ammunition with spitzer bullets has an S suffix.

Stateside, the evolution of high-velocity, long-range bullets paralleled ordnance changes in Germany. The .30-03 launched a 220-grain round-nose bullet at 2,300 fps, the .30-06 a 150-grain bullet at 2,700 fps. Our first soft-nose hunting bullets were long and blunt, just like the bullets that had bloodied battlefields in France. Hunting ammo featured high-speed spitzers only after armies had proved them. In those days, the challenges posed by fast bullets had to do mainly with the heat generated by high-energy smokeless powder and increased bore friction. Pure lead would melt into the rifling if driven at speeds much over 1,200 fps. Adding up to 10 percent tin increased hardness and reduced leading. An alloy of 90 percent lead, 5 percent tin, and 5 percent antimony stood up to even more heat, but velocities still had to be kept under 1,500 fps for acceptable accuracy.

By 1900, English shooters were using gas checks to protect bullet bases from powder gas. Introduced in the United States five years later by the Ideal Manufacturing Company, gas checks are brass or copper cups crimped onto the bullet from the rear. Half-jackets are similar but extend most of the way up the bullet's sides to keep lead from touching the rifling. A gas check lets you wring 2,000 fps from most bullets without compromising accuracy. Half-jackets are good for 2,200 fps or so. At higher speeds, jacketed bullets are necessary. The first of these came along in the 1890s. Steel jackets coated with cupronickel kept cores from melting and eliminated leading bores at .30-40 Krag velocities, but they produced metal fouling in .30-06 barrels. Plating bullets with tin seemed to help, but tin was dropped when soldiers found that it sometimes "cold-soldered" to case mouths and sent pressures soaring. Incorporating tin in the jacket made more sense. Western Cartridge Company soon announced its Lubaloy bullet, with a jacket of 90 percent copper, 8 percent zinc, and 2 percent tin. Later, the tin was dropped from most jacket alloys altogether. Now most bullet jackets are of gilding metal, commonly 95 percent copper and 5 percent zinc. Nosler's first Partition bullets had 90-10 jackets.

A jacketed bullet's core is mainly lead. Some cores are advertised as pure lead, but even the purest have traces of copper, zinc, nickel, aluminum, and arsenic. Most cores contain a little antimony to make them harder; 2.5 percent is the usual dose. A little antimony makes a big difference, so 6 percent is about as high a proportion as you'll see. Sierra offers three degrees of hardness in its rifle bullets, with antimony proportions of 1.5, 3, and 6 percent. A hard core stands heat best but fragments more readily on impact. Unalloyed lead cores hold together well but deform like dough, so they must wear heavy jackets to control expansion.

Most bullet cores are cut from lead wire or extruded from bar stock. Annealing prevents dimensional changes during forming. Inserted as cold plugs into the gilding metal cups that will become their jackets, bullets pass through a shaping die that also mates core and jacket. A cannelure (crimping groove) may follow.

Increasing velocity has prompted changes in internal design. The first jacketed softpoint bullets were round-nosed, with lots of lead exposed in front so they'd open readily. When Charles Newton developed his line of powerful sporting cartridges just before World War I, he found that traditional round-nose bullets went to pieces when driven into big game at velocities exceeding 2,700 fps. Pointed soft-nose bullets sometimes sailed through an animal without opening; sometimes they ruptured, then fragmented. In 1914 Newton was marketing a spitzer with a wire nose insert to control expansion. He wrote: "A copper wire is embedded in the center of the bullet point, and . . . protects the point against every deformation except upsetting." Newton's bullets also featured paper insulation between jacket and core to keep the core from melting during barrel passage. Newton discovered core melt by drilling a hole in bullet jackets and firing into white cardboard at 20 feet. A smear of melted lead on the cardboard resulted. After wrapping the cores in thin paper, he repeated the test and found no smears.

Major ammunition companies have historically gone to great lengths to court hunters. Winchester's early Precision Point had a cone of jacket material covering the bullet tip and inserted at three points under the jacket proper. Three windows of lead exposed at the juncture of cone and jacket initiated expansion. Not to be outdone, Peters developed the Protected Point. A cone point capped a flat-topped lead core whose front third was wrapped in a "driving band" under the jacket. On impact, the front of the bullet pushed back as it opened, forcing the driving band down. The band controlled the core's expansion. A Protected Point bullet required 3 hours and 51 operations to make. Winchester later brought out a similar but less expensive bullet minus the driving band: the Silvertip.

Remington's first answer to bullet deformation was the Bronze Point, a streamlined hollowpoint with a peg in the hole. The peg's front half was a bronze cone that formed the bullet tip. Impact forced the peg back into the bullet core. At high speeds, upset was violent. Remington's best-selling bullet, the Core-Lokt, is a modern inner-belted softpoint that expands readily but holds up well in game as big as elk.

Hollowpoint bullets are commonly thought to be suitable only for light game. But before World War II, the Western Tool and Copper Works made a hollowpoint with a tiny cavity that proved deadly on elk-size animals, even when driven by cartridges such as the .30 Newton and .300 H&H Magnum. DWM offered a "strong-jacket" bullet with a long, narrow nose cavity lined with copper tubing and capped. Expansion of hollowpoint bullets depends on cavity dimensions and the design and materials of jacket and core.

Popular among hunters these days is the polymer-tipped spitzer. Though the front 0.10 inch of nose has little effect on trajectory, these sleek, sharply pointed spitzers have lots of eye appeal and do indeed fly flat. Nosler's Ballistic Tip has a lot of fans, most of whom enthuse over its extraordinary accuracy. Hornady's SST and the Remington AccuTip are similar in shape and performance. These bullets deliver an explosive strike and kill deer-size game quickly. Heavier jackets on .33-caliber Ballistic Tips make them suitable for elk. Bonding of core to jacket makes the polymer-tipped Swift Scirocco an excellent choice for heavy game. A pointed plastic tip on Hornady bullets for the .30-30 is softer by design so that it can safely rest in tube magazines against primers of cartridges in front. In Hornady ammunition (loaded stiff), it flies and hits like a .300 Savage.

It didn't take bullet companies long to adapt the polymer tip to bullets that have historically struggled at long range. Muzzle-loading bullets and shotgun slugs, by virtue of their large diameters and low starting speeds, drop fast. Round noses set up high air resistance that increases the already substantial drag on the big lead shanks. Replacing soft-lead, full-diameter bullets with jacketed subdiameter bullets flattened trajectories.

First, of course, came the sabot (pronounced SAY-bo). This device is a bore-diameter sleeve that holds the primary projectile in its trip down the barrel. The sleeve engages the rifling and imparts spin to the slug or bullet in its bosom. Sometime after exit, wind resistance strips the sleeve from the projectile, which continues on to the target. Because it is of smaller diameter (typically .45 in a 50-caliber bore), a sabot bullet can be made longer to equal the weight of a full-diameter bullet. A long bullet has a higher sectional density than a short one of the same weight.

Because in muzzleloading rifles a sabot takes the rifling, you can load a jacketed bullet. In shotguns, a sabot absolves the slug of having to seal gas or conform to the choke's squeeze. There's no reason, when loading a saboted bullet, to give it a blunt nose. So Hornady and Barnes and BPI have developed pointed, poly-tipped bullets for muzzleloaders and shotguns. These not only fly flatter than traditional balls and conical lead bullets and slugs; they also shoot more accurately in rifled bores.

"Our SST bullets for shotguns are as uniform in weight and shape as our rifle bullets," says Hornady's Steve Johnson. "Our 12-gauge load kicks it out at 2,050 fps." It's still moving at 1,700 fps at 100 yards, and it gets to 200 yards clocking 1,400 fps. Muzzle energy is 2,330 foot-pounds—a hard-hitting ton. But what's truly noteworthy is that the SST slug brings nearly 1,100 foot-pounds to 200 yards. And it shoots flat enough that if you zero 3 inches high at 100 yards, you'll hit just $4^1/2$ inches low at 200 yards. At 250 yards, the slug drops about 15 inches but still carries 900 foot-pounds of punch. If your shotgun wears a scope and you've practiced out to 250 yards, killing deer at that range should be easy enough, given favorable conditions. Groups from the SST slug and kin run much tighter than those from smoothbore guns shooting Foster or Brenneke slugs. In fact, many of these saboted slugs shoot as well as ordinary rifle bullets to 200 yards.

Dudley McGarity, who runs Black Powder Products, Inc., is enthusiastic about its Power Belt bullets, full-diameter muzzle-loading bullets with plastic driving bands and base cup. They too feature polymer tips. Not long after they were introduced, they became the most popular muzzle-loading bullet on the market. "Saboted bullets work fine," says McGarity. "But Power Belts typically turn in superior accuracy. And you get the bonus of a full-diameter impact on big game." The great weight of Power Belts puts a lid on muzzle velocity, but their sharp polymer tips and sleek ogives enable them to "carry up" well at long range. Momentum can be as deadly as high speed. Indeed, many black-powder shooters after tough game prefer it.

Power Belt bullets and Triple Seven pellets make muzzleloaders fast to load and extend their reach.

One visible asset of polymer-tipped bullets in rifles and shotguns is their sleek, smooth tip profile and that tip's resistance to deformation. Ordinary jacketed bullets have a nose of exposed lead, which can get battered against the front of the magazine during recoil or even deformed on the feed ramp. Opinions vary as to the effect of a mashed tip on accuracy. Ace rifleman David Tubb, who at this writing has won a record eleven Camp Perry High Power championships, has found that battered bullet noses do affect group sizes. His company, Superior Shooting Systems, markets a Ballistic Meplat Uniformer (BMU) to ensure perfect nose profiles (the meplat is the end diameter of the nose). The BMU tool turns just the tip to create a form that reduces the ballistic coefficient very slightly. But it also trims group sizes at long range. Tubb indicates that 300-yard machine-rest testing of Federal Match .308 showed a minimum decrease in group size of 15 percent for treated bullets (average of ten groups, ten shots each). The tool also ensures a uniform ogive, the arch of the bullet's nose between tip and shank. Competitive riflemen note that at 1,000 yards, the change in ballistic coefficient amounts to roughly $1/4$ minute of additional drift. At hunting ranges, you'll notice no change in drift or drop.

Hunters may also fail to notice any change in accuracy. The truth is that small changes in the profiles or uniformity of bullet tips have

Dudley McGarity and Chad Shearer admire Dudley's big bear, taken with a Power Belt bullet.

scant effect on group sizes of ordinary rifles. You must have a tight-shooting rifle to detect another inch of drift at 400 yards. And you must be obsessed with accuracy to think that on a big-game hunt such a difference would matter. To find out how badly I could mutilate a bullet without losing practical hunting accuracy, I once snipped the front third off several 265-grain .338 bullets. I didn't measure or weigh them to ensure uniform amputation, and the cutting pliers actually smashed the bullets out of round. I had to squeeze them in a vise to seat them in .338 Winchester cases. Expecting to miss the paper entirely, I took the ragged-looking loads to the range. They printed 3-inch groups, just a little bigger than I got with undamaged bullets!

These days, I don't fret about deformed noses on hunting bullets. Bases are another story, however. Even a slight ding or groove on a bullet's base edge can allow the powder gas to tip the bullet on exit, ruining accuracy. Your standards and the intrinsic accuracy of your rifle will determine whether you'll benefit from use of the BMU tool or from weighing bullets or running them through a concentricity gauge.

The booming market in high-velocity rifle cartridges has tested the ability of engineers to develop bullets that will retain their integrity

Rifled slug barrels and sabot slugs, coupled with scopes, extend the reach of shotgun deer hunters.

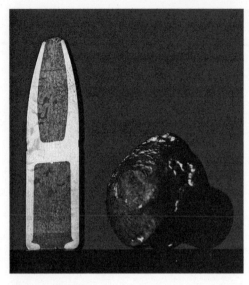

The Swift A-Frame uses the divided-core principle of Nosler's Partition, but with a bonded front.

during violent impact with heavy animals up close, then penetrate thick bones and muscles. At the same time, these bullets must open readily on deer at long range, after velocity has dropped off. Core-jacket separation has been the most nettlesome problem. Bonding has become the most common solution, though methods vary, and the processes are closely guarded secrets. Speer says that its Hot-Core process gives a tight bond because the lead snuggles up tighter to the jacket than with cold-forming, but it is careful not to claim bonding. Corbin, the well-known supplier of bullet-making equipment for hobbyists, points out that with its gear you can make your own chemically bonded bullets, along with partitioned bullets and those with several telescoping jackets. Corbin's swaging machinery has apparently helped launch more than 200 bullet businesses.

Trophy Bonded bullets, designed by the late Jack Carter (then bought by Federal Cartridge), followed the thick-jacketed Bitterroot Bonded Core bullets that first served elk hunters in northern Idaho. A herd of bonded-core bullets came on the heels of Swift's A-Frame, whose internal dam of jacket material and two-piece core mirrored the European H-Mantle and the Partition developed by John Nosler in 1947. Swift's bonded, polymer-tipped Scirocco has been succeeded by similar offerings from Hornady (InterBond) and Nosler (AccuBond). Remington's Core-Lokt Ultra has the profile of the pointed Core-Lokt but is bonded to boost weight retention and penetration. All bonded

Factory loads now feature controlled-expansion bullets that were once available only to handloaders.

bullets cost more than ordinary softpoints. Most shoot accurately enough, though they are not match bullets. Nosler's Partition and Partition Gold, with the Barnes Traditional and X-Bullets, deliver deep penetration without bonding. Small shops such as Lost River Technologies and overseas firms such as Woodleigh have shouldered in among the big names for a slice of the market

As important as a bullet's internal design are its shape and weight. The high sectional density of long bullets helps them penetrate. It also contributes to a high ballistic coefficient, which flattens trajectory. But there are practical limits to bullet length. Long bullets require a fast rifling twist for the best accuracy, and they must often be seated deep to accommodate magazine boxes and throats. Deep seating may limit performance as it reduces powder capacity. You can go shorter without going lighter if you choose a blunt bullet; however, in doing so, you'll reduce the ballistic coefficient (by as much as 30 percent). That won't matter if you shoot close, but a round bullet nose means steep bullet drop and quick loss of energy downrange.

A commonsense way to choose a big-game bullet for long shooting is to start near the midpoint in bullet weights for the bore and

Handloading is especially useful if you shoot a cartridge with a token number of factory loads.

consider only spitzer or semi-spitzer bullets. If you have a .25-06, try 100-grain bullets. I'd pick 130s in a .270, 140s in a 7mm. If you shoot a .308 Winchester, try 150- and 165-grain bullets. A 180-grain spitzer will give better penetration, all things being equal, and its high ballistic coefficient will help it catch and pass lighter bullets at long range. But bullets heavier than 165 grains aren't needed for the game you would ordinarily tackle with a .308, and the 165's velocity between 100 and 250 yards will probably prove more useful (because it means flatter trajectory) than additional bullet weight. The 180s excel in the .30-06 and .30 magnums. Should you favor a 6mm, midweight bullets can be too light and fragile for big game; look to the 95-grain Nosler Partition and the various 100-grain softpoints. Conversely, if you're toting a .338, you may want to shade on the light side of midweight to keep bullet arc flat and recoil manageable. Here's an overview of rifle bullets that are popular with deer hunters:

Federal Hi-Shok. The standard bullet for Federal's Classic line, Hi-Shok was available in round-nose, flat-nose, and spitzer form. Unremarkable in design, it was replaced in 2004 by Vital-Shok.

Polymer tips, as on this Hornady SST bullet, are renowned for accuracy and have become increasingly popular.

Federal Vital-Shok. Federal's parent company ATK used the jacket technology of Speer Gold Dot bullets to augment its line of name-brand controlled-expansion bullets with its own affordable soft-point.

Hornady Interlock. Derived from the company's flagship Spire Point, the Interlock features inner jacket belting to secure the core during upset. Round-nose versions also show fine accuracy and reliable upset.

Hornady SST. The answer to Nosler's Ballistic Tip, this red-nosed polymer-tipped bullet has become more prominent in the Hornady line than traditional soft-nose spitzers. It is very accurate.

Remington AccuTip. Designed to compete with other polymer-tipped bullets, this offering is built to Remington specs under contract. It's available in Remington loaded ammo from .243 to .300 Magnum.

Remington Core-Lokt. In both round-nose and pointed form, this veteran may have killed more big game than any other softpoint. An internal lip holds the core in place and delivers 50 to 70 percent weight retention.

Sierra GameKing. Renowned for superior accuracy and flat flight, Sierra boattail hollowpoints open violently. Expect lightning kills on deer. The 250-grain .338 and the 300-grain .375 have thick jackets.

Speer Hot-Cor. Soft-nose construction and a sleek profile make Speer Hot-Cors ideal for long shots at deer-size game. You'll find weights not available elsewhere, such as .366 spitzers for a 9.3mm rifle.

Winchester Power-Point. This forty-year-old softpoint is an archetype with no special features, except for nose notches on its tapered jacket. These ensure violent but predictable upset, with off-side penetration on deer-size game.

Winchester Silvertip. For years, this was the company's heavy-game bullet, but the Silvertip got a more fragile nose cap in the 1960s. This bullet now opens more violently, even more so than the Power-Point.

The following bullets are built specifically for tough game:

Alaska Kodiak: This bonded-core bullet delivers double-diameter upset, with superior weight retention. Jackets are of drawn gilding metal, not pure copper.

Barnes X: A solid copper hollowpoint, this bullet is long for its weight. Weight retention of 95 percent or more means that you can get penetration with lighter weights and higher starting speeds.

Hornady InterBond: This bonded, polymer-tipped bullet has an inner-belted jacket to help control upset, which is relatively violent. A sleek ogive gives it a flat trajectory.

Lapua Mega: The copper jacket of this bullet has a wide inner belt to hold the core to the jacket. Mega is available in Lapua ammunition. Its round-nose profile is consistent with European tradition.

Norma Oryx: This bullet typically expands to double diameter before peeling back; the bonded core prevents separation and yields a retained weight higher than 90 percent.

Norma TXP: A partitioned core of pure lead is Nosler-like in cross section. The front end is cold-soldered to the jacket. Like Oryx, it has a "protected point" meplat. It's really a Swift A-Frame renamed.

Nosler AccuBond: To stay competitive in a market enamored of polymer-tipped bullets (which Nosler itself popularized), the company now offers this bullet, a bonded version of its Ballistic Tip.

Nosler Partition: Developed in 1947 by John Nosler, this classic bullet with a two-piece core has a dam that stops expansion and guarantees penetration by the heel. Loss of the nose is common in tough game, but most fragmenting occurs in the vitals, with deadly effect.

Waterbuck! This shot may be your only one; bullet upset counts as much as accuracy.

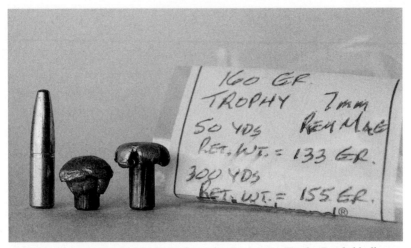

Broad mushrooms and high retained weight characterize Trophy Bonded bullets.

Remington Core-Lokt Ultra: The Ultra has a bonded core to endure close-range impact from Ultra Mag rounds. Its jacket is 20 percent heavier than Core-Lokt's, and the belt is 50 percent thicker. Weight retention: 80 to 90 percent.

Speer Grand Slam: A flat meplat atop a long, sleek ogive and a cannelure groove distinguish this bullet. The thick rear jacket arrests expansion. I've had it come apart in elk shoulders.

Swift A-Frame: Developed by Lee Reed on the Nosler Partition design, this bullet has a bonded front end that gives it better weight retention. Expect a wide, deep wound channel and picturebook upset.

Swift Scirocco: This sleek polymer-tipped bullet has great flight characteristics, but the bonded core and thick jacket hold it together in tough game. I've shot it through 6-inch spruce trees.

Trophy Bonded Bear Claw: Developed by Jack Carter and now loaded by Federal, this bonded softpoint is among my favorites because it mushrooms broadly but doesn't fragment. It is not as streamlined as some bullets.

Winchester Fail Safe: This black oxide-coated bullet has a lead core capped by a steel insert in the heel, and a solid copper front with a hollow nose. It flies flat, penetrates deep. Weight retention is 95+ percent.

Winchester Partition Gold: Based on the Nosler Partition, this bullet has a longer shank section to boost weight retention, and a steel cap at the rear of the dam to control bulging there at impact.

The author shot this bull up close. Elk bullets must hold together under high-speed impact.

Woodleigh Weldcore: Made in Australia and distributed in the United States by Huntington's in Oroville, California, Weldcores come in many diameters and heavy weights. Expect at least 90 percent weight retention.

Loading Up

In 1946, I was shooting a Model 70 Winchester, chambered for a .300 H&H Magnum, using 180-grain bullets. I loved the way this rifle would shoot at long range. . . . The problem was that the bullets expanded too much on heavy game.
—John Nosler, developer of the Partition bullet

REACHING FAR WITH THE .30-06 AND .270

Professional hunters in Africa have told me that they'd prefer to see clients show up with a .30-06 than a .300 Magnum. A .30-06 bullet sent through the forward ribs kills big animals quickly, and shooters are better able to place shots if they aren't cowed by recoil. The '06 has plenty of reach for open country. On a safari in 1911, author Stewart Edward White wrote about killing kongoni at 566 and 638 paces to test his Springfield with military spitzer bullets. His bag on that trip: 185 animals, almost all taken with the '06.

The .30-06 dates to 1900, when U.S. ordnance engineers at Springfield Armory also began work on a battle rifle to shoot it. The .30-40 Krag was then the official U.S. military round, a veteran of the Spanish-American War. But Paul Mauser's bolt rifles were in some ways superior to the Krag-Jorgensen, which was also a costly rifle to build. And rimless cartridges had the brightest future.

A prototype rifle appeared in 1901, and just two years later the Model 1903 Springfield was in production. Its 30-caliber rimless cartridge headspaced on the shoulder, like the 8x57 Mauser. The .30-03 was longer than both the 8x57 and the Krag. Powder capacity and operating pressure exceeded the Krag's. The .30-03's 220-grain bullet at 2,300 fps was a ballistic match for the Mauser's 236-grain bullet at 2,125 fps.

The .30-06 has manageable recoil, making it easy for slightly built shooters to use effectively.

Eager to extend the reach of the 8mm, Germany fielded a new load a year after the .30-03 showed up. A 154-grain spitzer at 2,800 fps shot flatter than other infantry bullets of the day. The Americans were obliged to follow and introduced the Ball Cartridge, Caliber .30, Model 1906. It drove a 150-grain bullet 2,700 fps, increasing range. The case could have been left unchanged, but someone decided to shorten it .07, to .494. Consequently, all .30-03 chambers were a tad long for the new round. Soon, all .30-03 rifles were recalled and rechambered to .30-06.

Initially, .30-06 bullets were jacketed with an alloy of 85 percent copper and 15 percent nickel. This recipe had worked in the Krag, but the jackets softened at .30-06 speeds, and severe bore fouling resulted. When tin plating didn't help, the army tried a bullet jacket of zinc and copper in 5-95 or 10-90 proportions. This reduced fouling. These alloys became known as gilding metal, which is still used in sporting ammunition.

The first 150-grain .30-06 bullet was faster than most loads riflemen had encountered, on or off the battlefield. Optimism got the best of military ballisticians, who gave it a maximum range of 4,700

Western hunters still find the .30-06 a do-it-all pick for pronghorns, deer, bears, and elk.

The author dropped this big Alaska-Yukon moose with one shot from a Springfield 03 in .30-06.

The .30-06 had its genesis in uniform. In the M-1 Garand, it brought the United States through World War II.

yards. But troops in World War I found that the effective limit was nearer 3,400 yards. To increase reach, the army again changed the load, to a 173-grain spitzer with a 7-caliber ogive and 9-degree boattail. Muzzle velocity was trimmed to 2,647 fps—a minor concession, given the substantial increases in sectional density and ballistic coefficient. Introduced in 1925, the M-1 round extended maximum range to 5,500 yards—at least, that was the official estimate. Although this claim bordered on fantasy, the development of a 30-caliber load with a 3-mile reach had to affect morale on both sides of the trenches.

Oddly enough, the army saw fit to change bullets again—reportedly because the Garand rifle didn't function well with long boattails and because soldiers objected to the recoil of the 173-grain load. In 1939 the heavy bullet gave way to a 152-grain replacement at 2,805 fps. With the M-2 .30-06 cartridge, the United States fought World War II. Surplus military '06 ammo later sold cheaply, but corrosive primers deposited salts in the rifle bores, causing rust. Remington developed noncorrosive Kleanbore priming in 1927, and by 1930, noncorrosive priming was standard in sporting rounds. Military cartridges, however, had the corrosive FA 70 primers as late as 1952. Since the Korean War, the only domestic .30-06 fodder with harmful

Accurate, versatile, and available in most rifles, the .30-06 remains the all-around rifle cartridge.

priming was a run of Western Match cartridges with corrosive, mercuric 8$^{1}/_{2}$ G caps.

Its service record and a wash of surplus rifles following World War I helped the .30-06 overtake the .30-30 as America's favorite big-game cartridge. The shift away from lever mechanisms to bolt rifles that bottled higher pressures and accommodated optical sights only accelerated the rise of the .30-06. Its debut in the Winchester Model 54 and Remington 30S rifles, and later in the Models 70 and 721, gave the American hunter more reasons to own an '06. Myriad loads from ammunition companies, with bullets from 150 to 220 grains in weight, made it the most versatile big-game round on the planet. High-octane ammo in the Hornady and Federal lines brought the .30-06 within a ballistic sigh of the .300 H&H Magnum. Now this old warhorse is chambered as often as any sporting cartridge worldwide—despite a growing market in more powerful rounds. Here's how the .30-06 compares with a couple of popular belted magnums, with regard to factory-listed velocity and energy. Data are for Winchester's 160- and 165-grain Silvertip Boattails and 180-grain Fail Safes.

Cartridge, Bullet weight (grains)	Muzzle	100 yards	200 yards	300 yards	400 yards
.30-06, 165					
Velocity (fps)	2800	2597	2402	2216	2038
Energy (ft-lb)	2873	2421	2114	1719	1522
7mm Remington Mag, 160					
Velocity (fps)	2950	2745	2550	2363	2184
Energy (ft-lb)	3093	2697	2311	1984	1694
.30-06, 180					
Velocity (fps)	2700	2486	2283	2089	1904
Energy (ft-lb)	2914	2472	2083	1744	1450
.300 Winchester Mag, 180					
Velocity (fps)	2960	2732	2514	2307	2110
Energy (ft-lb)	3503	2983	2528	2129	1780

The 7mm Remington Magnum has a slight edge on the .30-06. At 400 yards, Winchester's .300 delivers the energy that an '06 carries only to about 300 yards. Differences in drop are less notable, however: Given a 200-yard zero, the 7mm Magnum bullet sags 7.2 and 20.6 inches at 300 and 400 steps, respectively, compared with 8.2 and 23.4 inches for the 165-grain .30-06 bullet. At 300 yards, the 180-grain bullet from the .300 Magnum dips 7.1 inches, while the same bullet from a .30-06 falls 8.7 inches. At 400 paces, the .300 rules: 20.7 versus 25.5 inches of drop. To at least 300 yards, you can hold the same with a .30-06 as with popular magnums. Fans of the '06 have already found that with 175-grain bullets, the 7mm Remington Magnum actually delivers less speed and energy than a 180-grain .30-06 bullet in Hornady Light Magnum and Federal High Energy loads.

Most hunters who give the .30-06 a chance stay with it. I once guided a fellow who had served as a sniper in Vietnam and was used to shooting at extreme range. He might have chosen a super-magnum for long shots at elk. His preference for a .30-06 might have surprised some hunters, but it didn't surprise me. At 500 yards, a 180-grain spitzer from the '06 delivers as much energy as a .30-30 bullet at 150 yards.

Far and away the most popular bullet weight for the '06 is 180 grains. It's a logical pick, with enough speed for flat midrange flight and enough sectional density to penetrate tough game on oblique shots. Ballistic coefficients in the middle .400s offer high retained energy and minimal bullet drop at long range. Runners-up would be 165-grain and 200-grain bullets. Bullets with bonded cores or captive heels don't need a lot of starting weight to ensure deep penetration, so a 165-grain bullet is no longer on the light side for elk and moose. In my view, the 150-grain bullet is better matched to smaller cases. Here's why: A factory-loaded 180-grain Remington Core-Lokt strikes 1 inch above sight line at 50 yards. It hits 2.4 inches high at 100 steps and 2 inches high at 150 steps. It drops 3.7 inches at 250 yards, 9.3 inches at 300, and 27 inches at 400. The arc from a factory-loaded 150-grain Core-Lokt is essentially the same: +.8 at 50, +2.1 at 100, +1.8 at 150, -3.3 at 250, -8.5 at 300, and -25 at 400. A minute-of-angle rifle spreads its bullets across 3 inches of target at 300 yards, 4 inches at 400. So differences in the point of impact between 150- and 180-grain .30-06 bullets at the longest practical hunting ranges and with very accurate rifles lie within half the extreme spread of a machine-rest group. Add wind, shooter wobbles, and aiming error, and you get groups big enough to obliterate any difference in point of impact due to weight. Although 150-grain bullets leave the muzzle at 2,910 fps rather than 2,700, the 180s carry a 20 percent weight advantage at all ranges. They deliver more killing energy and, all else being equal, deeper penetration.

The same logic favors 200-grain bullets. A 200-grain Nosler Partition can be driven at 2,650 fps from the .30-06. Given that velocity and a ballistic coefficient of .480, it crosses the 200-yard line at nearly 2,300 fps and reaches 300 yards still clocking over 2,100 fps. With 2,330 foot-pounds of energy at 200 steps and an even ton at 300, it is a top choice for game that you pack out one quarter at a time. Standard rifling twist for the .30-06 is 1:10, sharp enough to stabilize bullets up to 220 grains.

Long ago I lay down on a cold rock high on a mountain and tried to steady the crosswire of my scope on a deer standing in the canyon shadows far below. It was a long shot. I held left for the soft north breeze, but not enough. The second bullet also missed. I hit that buck in the heart with my third shot by holding 2 feet high and almost that far into the wind. Because this buck was too far off for a first-round kill, I wouldn't take the shot now. But my .30-06 had plenty of reach and punch—I only had to correctly estimate range and drift and trigger the shot carefully.

AccuBond bullets make this Hill Country Rifles .270 a lethal elk gun at long and short range.

One of the biggest elk I've ever killed fell to an '06, as did a high-country mule deer with six points on a side. My rack holds five .30-06 rifles now, and I've sold several I'd like to buy back. The .30-06 may or may not be among your favorites, but you won't find a more versatile cartridge.

You might also say that about the .270, which by some measures is the most successful long-range big-game cartridge old enough to matter. To argue that the .270 isn't a crackerjack deer cartridge is like saying that Bugattis don't drive well or that Grandma's cinnamon rolls need more sugar. In elk camps, though, the .270 generates some debate. The fact that it has killed lots of elk is beside the point, because it's been chambered in nearly every bolt-action sporting rifle made in the last 80 years.

At first blush, the .270, introduced in 1925 in Winchester's new Model 54 rifle, seemed to be a necked-down .30-06. The .270 is slightly longer in the neck, but lots of .270 cases have been formed from '06 brass simply by running it through a .270 die. An almost instant success, the .270 was originally loaded with 130-grain bullets clocking 3,140 fps at the muzzle. Three hundred yards out, they still

Across Canadian grain fields, nothing beats a .270 for shooting deer.

clipped along at 2,320 fps. In 1933 a l50-grain factory load appeared, followed in 1937 by a lightly jacketed l00-grain spitzer.

The first 150-grain bullets were produced not for elk but for deer. Apparently, some hunters thought that the fast-stepping 130-grain bullets were destroying too much meat, and they wanted a more sedate load. Meat destruction may have been a valid complaint, as many bullet jackets could not control expansion, resulting in premature jacket rupture. Sometimes the bullets fragmented on impact. Slow, heavy bullets appeared to be the answer, so Winchester throttled its 150-grain load to 2,675 fps. Nobody bought these cartridges. Back at 2,900 fps, modern 150-grain factory loadings sell—and perform—much better.

The first .270, Winchester's 54, was conceived in 1922 on a 1903 Springfield receiver. While the Springfield's coned breech was retained, the 54's bolt, extractor, and safety hailed from the Model 98 Mauser. The 54 easily bottled the 52,000 psi generated by .270 factory loads. Barrels for the 54 were initially of nickel steel, as were the cyanide-hardened receivers. When chrome-molybdenum steel was developed in the 1930s, it replaced nickel steel in most gun applications. The 54's stock reflected a design made popular by R. F. Sedgely on Springfield sporting rifles. A slender schnabel forend and shotgun-style butt gave the gun great handling qualities, although a low, sharp comb made scope use uncomfortable.

By 1931 Winchester was in receivership, a victim of the Depression. On December 22, 1931, the firm was acquired by the Western Cartridge Company, which retained the Model 54 and within a year improved it by adding a speed-lock. Eventually, the 54 would appear in 10 styles and 10 chamberings. The last Model 54 was assembled in 1941, but of the 52,029 rifles serialed, 49,009 were made before 1936. Winchester had already been planning the demise of the Model 54 when it had authorized the development of another bolt action—the Model 70. When finally put out to pasture, the Model 54 not only had become a successful rifle in its time but also had launched one of the most successful cartridges of all time.

When Jack O'Connor adopted the .270 as his favorite hunting round, he used it to shoot everything from javelina to Alaska Yukon moose. His experiences spanned 40 years, and one year he fired 10,000 .270 test rounds. O'Connor preferred the 130-grain bullet to heavier ones, claiming velocities of 3,130 and 3,210 fps from two Model 70 Featherweight rifles with 22-inch barrels. His load of 62 grains of #4831 in Winchester-Western cases (with CCI Magnum primer) was about all a .270 hull could hold. He also wrote of a Nosler 150-grain Partition bullet with 58.5 grains of 4831, and a 160-grain Barnes with 56 grains of 4831or 52 grains of 4350.

One of the things that has kept the .270 popular is its stiff factory loadings. It was never downloaded to protect weak rifles, as was the 7x57 Mauser. Save for that brief early run of 150-grain bullets to reduce venison damage (and current Federal Low Recoil and Remington Managed-Recoil ammunition), factory .270 rounds have consistently been loaded with pressures above 50,000 psi. The .270 reaches far, kills better than the charts suggest, generally delivers fine accuracy, is easy on bores and brass, and slaps the shooter with only 17 1/2 foot-pounds of recoil in a 7 1/2-pound rifle.

Oddly, only a couple of other .270s have achieved commercial success. In 1943 Roy Weatherby's .270 Magnum became the first of his high-velocity belted rounds. Current loads from Norma push 130-grain bullets at 3,375 fps, 140s at 3,300, and 150s at 3,245. The .270 Winchester Short Magnum that came along in 2001 approaches this

The .270 not an elk round? This great bull fell to one 140-grain Hornady at 190 yards.

performance and has already become quite popular among hunters. The 6.8mm SPC, a cartridge developed by Remington in conjunction with U.S. military units as a tactical round, is available with hunting bullets too. At this writing, its future is uncertain, but I like it as a midrange deer round.

Although almost every convenient alteration imaginable has been made to the .30-06 case, wildcatters have not come up with many .270-bore variants. In the late 1940s Bliss Titus developed a cartridge now known as the .270 Titus Savage (Roy Triplett, Charles Evans, and F. R. Krause have also been credited with designing the case). It derived from a .300 Savage, with the shoulder set back a bit to give an ideal neck length of .270 atop a 28-degree slant. Although it would have worked fine in Savage's Model 99 rifle, the company chose not to adopt it. At that time, after four years of war, ammunition makers were still trying to catch up with domestic demand, and they didn't feel a need for new cartridges. By the early 1950s, when new rounds again made sense, the .308 Winchester had appeared. It delivered more power than the .300 Savage and shot as flat as the Titus.

During the late 1950s, Idaho rifle maker and cartridge designer Rocky Gibbs offered seven wildcats based on the .30-06 case with the shoulder moved forward. He loaded them hot and brooked no modesty in his descriptions. The .270 Gibbs was said to launch a 130-grain bullet at 3,430 fps with 63 grains IMR 4350. This load deserves a cautious approach.

A more efficient .270 is P. O. Ackley's .270/257 Improved, on the 7x57 case. Slightly shorter than the .270 Winchester, this cartridge can all but duplicate its performance. A favorite of mine is the .270 Redding, a short-action round based on the .308 case. It has a 30-degree shoulder and slightly less body taper. Velocities from my rifle, a Remington 78 with a 25-inch barrel, run about 100 fps below those of a .270 Winchester.

Hunters who use magnums because they shoot flatter than cartridges with the capacity of the .30-06 aren't gaining much. The .30-06 and .270 shoot almost as flat as their magnum counterparts. So do the .280 Remington, .35 Whelen, and wildcat .338-06, legitimized in Weatherby's lightweight six-lug Mark V rifle. Consider the following differences in bullet drop at 300 and 400 yards, given a 200-yard zero:

Cartridge, Bullet, Velocity (fps)	300-yard drop (inches)	400-yard drop (inches)
.270 Winchester, 130-grain bullet @ 3100	6.3	18.5
.270 Weatherby Magnum, 130-grain bullet @ 3300	5.5	16.0
.280 Remington, 150-grain bullet @ 3000	6.6	19.3
7mm Remington Magnum, 150-grain bullet @ 3200	5.8	16.7
.30-06, 180-grain bullet @ 2700	8.5	24.4
.300 Winchester Magnum, 180-grain bullet @ 3000	6.5	19.1
.338-06, 225-grain bullet @ 2600	9.3	26.7
.338 Winchester Magnum, 225-grain bullet @ 2900	7.2	21.0
.35 Whelen, 250-grain bullet @ 2500	10.1	29.4
.358 Norma Magnum, 250-grain bullet @ 2700	8.6	24.8

The 300-yard disparities of 1 to 2 inches are negligible. Unless you're an exceptional marksman, you can't hold within 2 inches at 300 yards from hunting positions. Even at 400 steps, the .270 and 7mm magnums show insignificant advantage. Bigger bores increase the spread, but 5 inches is still a mighty small difference. Remember, too, that 400 honest yards is a very long shot.

THE 6MMS

We think of 6mm (.243) cartridges as modern; however, the first of them appeared in the 1895 Lee straight-pull bolt rifle. Also called the .236 Navy, the 6mm Lee Navy was a semi-rimmed round chambered in about 15,000 military rifles. Its 112-grain bullet shuffled along at only 2,560 fps but could have been driven much faster had modern powders been available. The bullet was long, prompting a rifling

Rick Freudenberg built this .30-06 on a Model 70 action, installing a Lilja three-groove barrel.

twist of 1:7 $^1/_2$. The 6mm Lee Navy died in 1935. Shortly thereafter, the .220 Swift was born of the same case.

Not until 1955 would American factories again produce 6mm ammunition. But in the early 1920s, Holland & Holland gave British shooters two new cartridges: the .240 Flanged Nitro Express and the .240 Belted Nitro Express (.240 Apex). The first was a rimmed case, the second a rimless belted. Both were loaded with 100-grain .245 bullets, the belted version to 3,000 fps for bolt-action rifles, and the rimmed cartridge to 2,900 fps for doubles. In 1921 Purdey introduced its .246 Flanged cartridge with 100-grain .253 bullets at 2,950 fps; in 1923 the .242 Vickers Rimless Nitro Express appeared, pushing 100-grain .249 bullets 2,800 fps. (The designation "Express" is a Purdey creation, dating to 1856. Originally it was "Express Train," denoting extra power, but the second word was later dropped. In its day, "Express" meant what "Magnum" would come to mean to American shooters. Both terms were marketing tools, not technical descriptors.)

In Europe, Germans Halbe and Gerlich kept the 6mm bore alive with rimmed and rimless cases for the .244 Halger. Basically a 6.5x57

Coyote hunters favor 6mms for long shots down windy senderos.

case, it was a modern shape for the 1920s. Evidently, however, it did not reach claimed velocities. In 1955 Holland & Holland came along with the biggest six of all: the .244 H&H Belted Rimless Magnum. A .375 case necked down, this bottle-size brass was originally stuffed with cordite but came close to its sizzling potential only with the slowest of progressive powders. Even with fuels such as the later H-570, however, 3,500 fps with 100-grain bullets proved elusive.

When the Lee Navy cartridge faded, no 6mms came along to replace it. But shortly after World War II, wildcatters got busy. One of their first creations was the 6mm International, based on the .250 Savage case. In the Donaldson version, with its 30-degree shoulder, or in the later long-necked Remington configuration, it remains a useful cartridge. Also noteworthy was the Page Pooper, developed by writer Warren Page and Remington's Mike Walker. A .308 case necked down, this 6mm became the forerunner of Winchester's .243. The name was a mimicry of the .25 Souper that wasn't supposed to be taken seriously. Later, Walker also worked on the 6x47, a .222 Magnum case necked up to .243. It has since been overtaken by the 6x45 on the ubiquitous .223 case. Both have their biggest following among

The author used a 6mm and Federal 100-grain ammo to take this fine Coues deer at 200 yards.

benchrest shooters, who subsequently drifted to the 6mm BRs by Remington and Norma and the 6mm PPC, courtesy of Lou Palmisano and Ferris Pindell.

Among the most enduring of postwar wildcats was Fred Huntington's .243 Rockchucker. Based on the .257 Roberts case, this round became the prototype for Remington's similar 6mm. At his reloading-tool firm of RCBS (Rockchuck Bullet Swage), Huntington also developed a .243 RCBS on the .308 case. Wildcats on the .30-30, .303 British, .30-40 Krag, and .30-06 followed. The 6mm Arch uses the 6.5x55 Swedish Mauser hull. It and a sibling on the 6.5x54 Mannlicher-Schoenauer are close to the .243 Winchester in case capacity and ballistic performance. Mashburn's .240 Falcon derives from a shortened .270 case and approximates the 6mm Remington in size. A friend of mine has a .243 Improved, with the 40-degree Ackley shoulder. It is a fast-looking cartridge but doesn't do much better than a standard .243 over the chronograph screens. That's largely because the standard case has about as much room as you can use efficiently behind a 6mm bore.

Though based on the 7x57 case, the 6mm Remington fits in short rifle actions like this M600 Remington, altered and stocked by Patrick Holehan.

*Popular 6mms and .25s. From left: .243, 6mm, .240 Weatherby, .250 Savage, .257
Roberts, .25-06, .257 Weatherby. All are fine deer rounds with long histories.*

Winchester unveiled its .243 and Remington its .244 in 1955. The
.243 was simply the still-new .308 case necked down to accept .243
bullets. Remington's round was the .257 Roberts case choked to .243
and given a sharper 26-degree shoulder. Winchester's hull offered
slightly less capacity, so the Remington had a slight ballistic edge. But
the .244's parent case derived from the 7x57 Mauser, a cartridge
designed not for a modern short-action bolt rifle but for Paul
Mauser's Model 1893. Postwar mechanisms engineered for the .308
Winchester and its offspring, all with 51mm cases, could accommodate the longer Mauser derivatives only if the bullets were seated
deep. So the effective powder capacity of the .244 in short actions was
less than what it provided in long actions. At first, the 6mm appeared
to beat the .243 ballistically by quite a margin. Part of the reason was
that .243 factory loads were often chronographed in 22-inch barrels,
not the 26-inch barrels used for 6mm testing. Also, some of the early
Winchester cartridges were loaded to 47,900 psi, versus 51,100 psi for
Remington's 6mm rounds. When both cartridges were handloaded
with IMR 4350 to 50,000 psi with 100-grain bullets, both generated
about 3,100 fps from a short action and a 26-inch barrel.

Early factory loads fitted the .243 with 80- and 100-grain bullets and the .244 with 75- and 90-grain bullets. Rifles chambered for the .243 had a 1:10 twist, compared with 1:12 for the .244. The two spins reflected differences in company philosophy: Winchester intended its new round as a varmint big-game cartridge, while Remington considered the .244 primarily a wind-bucking panacea for woodchuck, fox, and coyote hunters. Word got out that the 1:12 twist wouldn't stabilize the 100-grain bullets hunters preferred for deer. The .243 rocketed to fame, while the .244 fell off its launch pad.

I owned an early Remington .244—a 722 bolt rifle that shot as tightly with 100-grain bullets as with lighter ones. Bullet shape and length, not just weight, determine how bullets will stabilize with any given twist. Round-nose bullets, shorter than spitzers, generally stabilize more easily. High velocity helps bullets stabilize too. Although Winchester's rifles were more appropriately rifled for heavy bullets than the Remingtons in .244, some 1:12 barrels shot a variety of bullets well. Besides the 722, Remington marketed its slide-action 760 and, for a time, its 742 autoloader in .244.

In 1963 Remington introduced a new round: the 6mm. Factory loaded with 80-, 90-, and 100-grain bullets, it supplanted the .244. The two cases are identical and can be interchanged. The new name was a marketing ploy and coincided with a change to a 1:9 twist in Remington 24-caliber barrels. Winchester's round had a head start by this time, and a daunting reputation. Still, the 6mm Remington has become popular.

The only other factory-loaded 6mm suitable for long shooting at big game is the .240 Weatherby Magnum, introduced in 1968. Loaded to equal pressures from barrels of the same length, it shades the .243 Winchester and 6mm Remington by about 200 fps. The belted .240, with its .30-06-size head, is neither parent nor offspring of any other case. It is chambered only in Weatherby Mark V rifles.

Because of their light recoil, 6mm cartridges have often been recommended for beginning shooters and women. Such stereotyping is narrow-minded if not egotistical, implying that only experienced shooters and men can handle bigger rounds. The truth is that almost everyone shoots better with a rifle that doesn't kick viciously. While the first round out of a .30 Magnum might seem manageable, the end of a 40-shot chronograph session has me sweating. With a .243, I'm free to think about shooting fundamentals and the wind.

Lighter recoil means that you can carry a lighter rifle. A 7-pound .243 shooting a 100-grain bullet bumps you with only 11.5 foot-

The 6mm BR has had little exposure outside the benchrest circuit but would kill deer handily.

pounds of recoil. That's about half the recoil of a 7-pound .280 Remington launching 160-grain softpoints, and about a third the thump of a .300 Winchester Magnum with 180s. A 7-pound .340 Weatherby Magnum booting 250-grain bullets hits you with four times the recoil of a .243—no fun at the bench.

Lightweight rifles and powder-puff recoil aside, how lethal are the 6mms? Well aimed, the 6mms can kill big animals. One hunter reported downing a grizzly and a polar bear with his .243! That's probably stretching the point, but the record on lighter game is indeed rosy. After the .243 had been afield a season, a survey recorded 83 kills, most of which were whitetails and mule deer at ranges averaging 140 yards. Of the 83 animals taken, 60 fell right away to one shot; 13 moved off but dropped within 200 yards; only 6 had to be trailed. Another survey recorded mule deer, pronghorns, and black bears smacked with the .243 at ranges to 500 yards. None moved from where they were hit, and only a few required a finishing shot.

You might expect good results, given the civil dispositions of these 6mms. Also, they're flat-shooting cartridges, minimizing errors in range estimation. Finally, the surveys no doubt included experienced hunters—gun writers and perhaps guides who would provide

This 600-yard group from Kenny Jarrett's high-velocity .243 Catbird is just a hand's width across.

A Ballistic Tip bullet from a .243 Winchester Super Short Magnum downed this Texas deer.

Neck down a .270 case to .243, and you have Kenny Jarrett's Catbird. It shoots well in his rifles.

a lot of survey information but who also might deliver better-than-average shot placement.

Although hunting-class 6mms generate plenty of foot-pounds of energy, most of that is due to bullet speed. In comparisons using Elmer Keith's pounds-feet measure of energy (in which velocity is not squared, so bullet weight gets more credit), no 24-caliber bullet fares well. Lightning killers on deer-size game, the 6mms do not deliver the killing effect on tough game that traditional energy charts (in foot-pounds) suggest. For example, a 180-grain .30-06 bullet at 2,700 fps generates 2,910 foot-pounds. A factory-loaded 100-grain bullet launched at 3,070 fps from a .243 delivers 2,090 foot-pounds. A much lighter and only slightly faster bullet, it turns up 72 percent of the '06's energy. The 180-grain bullet's killing effect on tough game is greater, the result of not only a larger, heavier bullet but also a jacket designed for game typically shot with .30-bore rifles.

Now let's calculate pounds-feet: bullet weight (grains)/7,000 × velocity (fps). The .30-06 yields 69.4 pounds-feet; the .243 yields not quite 43.9, or only 63 percent of the standard. In animals such as elk, with thick hide and hair, heavy bones, and great muscles, bullet

Mule deer hunters often use bigger bullets, but 100-grain 6mms are adequate even at long range.

weight and size matter as much as velocity. Although pounds-feet is arguably no more valid than foot-pounds as an index of killing power, it helps complete a picture skewed by squaring velocity in the calculation of foot-pounds.

Weatherby's .240 delivers much more punch than the .243. At 300 yards, its 100-grain bullet drops only 5 inches from a 200-yard zero and retains 1,660 foot-pounds of energy—as much as a 180-grain .30-06 spitzer. While the .240 Weatherby's launch velocity of 3,350 fps extends the effective range on rib-cage shots, it is no better than the .243 Winchester or 6mm Remington close up. In fact, the higher velocity puts more strain on the bullet, promoting fragmentation. Velocity means energy on paper, but retained bullet weight is crucial for deep penetration. Regardless of their case capacity, the sixes have no bullet weight or diameter to spare. It's good to remember that the .243 Winchester at 300 yards just matches the muscle of the old .25-35 at 100.

On a shelf above my desk is a little piece of cardboard with a $^3/_4$-inch cluster of .243 bullet holes. It's delightful to shoot a rifle that funnels bullets to the same spot, spitting them out with soft recoil and a thin, almost apologetic report. In contrast, .30 and .33 Magnums

This Montana/Serengeti rifle in .257 Roberts groups tightly with Hornady ammunition.

thrust their payloads downrange with a boom and the jab of a flying sewer pipe. Precise shot placement is easier with the gentle sixes. But for elk-size animals in cover as well as at long range across windy canyons, you want heavier bullets than will fit in a .243 bore.

QUARTER-BORES

Once upon a time, a rifle's range and power could be assessed by the size of the hole in the barrel. A big ball had more weight and energy than a little ball. Conical bullets made any rifle more efficient, but black powder imposed a ceiling on velocities, regardless of the bore size or bullet type. The first cartridges had the same lid—the .44 Henry drove a 200-grain bullet at only 1,150 fps.

During the 1870s, rifle cartridges got longer and took on a bottle shape. Solid-head centerfire cases helped contain higher pressures. When smokeless powder came along, gun designers further restricted bore size. Stronger metals and mechanisms, along with powders whose pressure curves could be manipulated by varying the size, shape, and coating of the grains, made small-bore, high-velocity cartridges practical.

The author is fond of this lightweight 6.5/284 by Melvin Forbes of New Ultra Light Arms. It wears a 6x Sightron scope.

Our first high-velocity 25-caliber cartridge arrived soon after the first automobile. Charles Newton's .250, circa 1912, fired a 100-grain bullet at around 2,800 fps. But when Savage adopted it in 1915, the company chose an 87-grain bullet to advertise higher velocity. This round, based on a shortened .30-06 case, became the .250-3000. The .250 Savage is still with us, half its name deleted because 3,000 fps is ho-hum these days. Not the first .25 designed for smokeless powder (the .25-35 has that honor), the .250 confirms what Newton's earlier .22 High Power had already shown: that small-diameter, high-speed bullets not only fly flat; they also hit with a level of authority far out of proportion to their size.

Since then, hunters have argued over the relative merits of high velocity and bullet weight in big-game cartridges. How fast and how heavy a bullet has to be depends on what you're hunting and what kind of shots you expect. An 87-grain .250 Savage bullet is a lightning-like killer on deer shot through the slats at ranges up to 250 yards or so. It's less than ideal at long range or with raking shots close up. But what if a quarter-bore had more case capacity? Ned Roberts found out 70 years ago by necking down the 7x57 Mauser case to form the wildcat .25 Roberts. It was a cooperative venture with A. O. Neidner

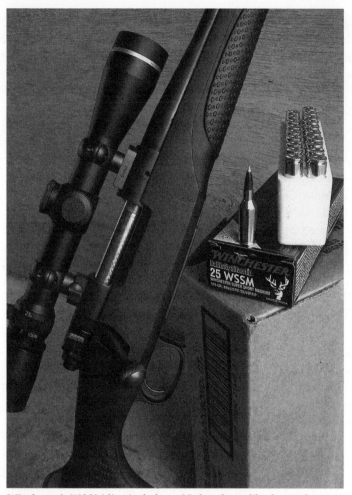

Winchester's WSSM line includes a .25 that shoots like the much longer .25-06.

and F. J. Sage, who agreed that a case the size of the .30-40 Krag would be just right to fashion into a .25. But Roberts chose instead the 7x57 because it combined the capacity of the Krag with the modern rimless design of its successor, the .30-06. During the late 1920s he experimented with chambers, groove dimensions, and rifling twists. Townsend Whelen advised him to keep the shoulder at 15 degrees to hold down pressures. He also trimmed the brass $^1/_{16}$ inch after sizing.

By 1930, Griffin & Howe had become interested in Roberts's .25 wildcat and started making rifles for it. Late in 1932, Mr. Griffin decided that trimming was unnecessary. Roberts agreed, and chambers were lengthened. In 1934 Remington adopted the round as the .257 Roberts, acceding to Captain E. C. Crossman, who suggested using the groove diameter in the name to distinguish it from other .25-caliber cartridges. Before starting commercial production, Remington moved the shoulder forward a little and increased its angle to 20 degrees. Remington chambered its Model 30 for the cartridge, then the 722 and 760. Winchester listed it in the Model 54 and, later, the 70.

Captain Crossman referred to the Roberts as a "super 250." At 300 yards, its 87-grain bullet penetrated $1/8$-inch steel plate that was only dented by the same bullet from a .250-3000. He preferred the 100-grain bullet, finding the 87-grain too light for big game. Crossman said that the 117-grain bullet (a round-nose at an uninspiring 2,650 fps) drove deeper than necessary in deer and dropped 4 inches more than 100-grain spitzers at 200 yards.

Whelen considered the .257 Roberts adequate for deer, black bears, and caribou. Jack O'Connor rated it high on his list of wind-bucking varmint rounds and thought it a fine choice for mule deer and bighorn sheep. Warren Page worked extensively with the .257, finding, as did others, that the round was somewhat hampered by its 2.75-inch overall length—not long enough to hold .30-06-size powder charges, but too long for a short action unless bullets were seated deep.

The first .257 Roberts loads (engineered to keep pressures under 48,000 psi) were hardly meatier than those of the .250 Savage. Magazine alterations enabled shooters to use longer, stronger handloads, but standard throats would snag those bullets. Experimenters who lengthened throats when they revamped magazine boxes found the Roberts surprisingly potent. Their load data are not transferable to unaltered guns.

With about 7 foot-pounds of recoil in rifles of average weight, the Roberts is gentler in the hand than a .30-30 carbine. That pleasant disposition prompted Jack O'Connor to predict at the close of World War II that within five years the .257 Roberts would be one of the three most popular chamberings in bolt-action rifles. He was wrong. The Roberts slipped partly because its first light bullets didn't shoot well enough to satisfy serious varmint hunters, and blunt big-game bullets lost enthusiasm too quickly. By the early 1950s, when Winchester-

A Legacy Mauser action, E. R. Shaw barrel, and Boyd's stock will become a new .264 Magnum, a twin to the anuthor's .270 Weatherby Magnum that boasts the same components and shoots very well.

Western announced a good thin-skinned 87-grain varmint bullet and Remington a 100-grain pointed Core-Lokt, sketchy bullet performance had soured some shooters on this round. Others were disappointed that velocities had been pulled back on factory loads—from 3,000 to 2,900 fps for 100-grain bullets. The first .257 fuel, IMR 3031, proved too fast, and pressures dictated retreat. Du Pont 4320 and 4350 came a few years too late. In 1955 the .243 Winchester charged out to capture much of the market previously held by the Roberts.

These days, the .257 has more to offer, with Federal loading 120-grain Nosler Partitions to 2,780 fps. Hornady lists its polymer-tipped Interlock at the same velocity and catalogs a Light Magnum .257 Roberts with a 117 SST at a scorching 2,940 fps. At 400 yards, this load is still clocking over 2,000 fps and delivers nearly 1,100 foot-pounds of energy—on par with standard loads for a .25-06.

Before the .257 Roberts came along, several prominent shooters were experimenting with even bigger .25s. In 1913 the .256 Newton drove a 129-grain bullet at 2,760 fps. This round was not, however, a true .25; its bullet miked .264, or 6.5mm. Case length was 2.457 inches,

The author fires offhand with his Sisk rifle in .25 Souper, a necked-up .243 that crowds the .25-06.

slightly shorter than that of the .30-06. Head and rim diameters were essentially the same. With modern powders, handloaders can make the .256 Newton act like the .25-06, driving 100-grain bullets at over 3,200 fps. (Four decades after Newon's experiments with this round, Kent "Buzz" Fletcher, a Colorado gunsmith, barreled a 98 Mauser in .256 Newton, installing a slim, full-length stock checkered with a Len Brownell pattern. Equipped with an aperture sight and a QD scope mount, the Still-Hunter performed well in my handloading trials and has a lot in common with rifles that Charles Newton planned to sell. But Newton's .256 cartridge has been dead longer than the kaiser.)

A less ambitious cartridge that has outlived the .256 is the 6.5x55 Swedish Mauser, a military round adopted in 1894 for use in the Swedish Mauser and Norwegian Krag-Jorgensen rifles. At 2.165 inches, its case is significantly shorter than the Newton's. Its head and rim both measure .476; however, the slightly larger diameter does not prevent its use in bolt faces made for .30-06-class cartridges. Case capacity matches that of the .257 Roberts. Although the 6.5x55 gained a good reputation on big game with long, blunt 156-grain bullets at 2,070 fps, modern loads commonly feature 139- and 140-grain bullets at around 2,500. The most potent factory loading by far is Federal's Premium, with a 140-grain Nosler Partition at 2,850 fps.

Except for Newton, America's post–World War I experimenters had little to do with 6.5mm rounds, concentrating instead on the .25s. In 1920 A. O. Neidner necked down the .30-06 case to form the wildcat .25 Neidner. This was after Neidner and F. W. Mann had engineered the .25 Krag from the .30-40 case rejected by Roberts. Several versions of the .25-06 followed: .25 High Power, .25 Whelen High Power, G&H .25 High Power Special. When Remington began loading the .257 Roberts commercially, interest in Neidner's wildcat round waned. Ironically, Roberts had help from Neidner in developing the .257. Neidner had rejected Newton's .256 at least partly because its 123- and 129-grain bullets were best on big game, and Neidner wanted to launch lighter bullets at velocities useful to fox and woodchuck hunters.

Not until 1969 did the .25-06 have a commercial home. Remington adopted this popular wildcat in its original Neidner form (a 17.5-degree shoulder) and gave a 120-grain bullet 2,990 fps—roughly the same speed as that of the 87-grain .250 Savage bullet. Now a plethora of loads makes the .25-06 one of the most versatile of the long-range big-game cartridges. One of my hunting partners, Dan O'Connell, favors 100-grain Hornadys in his Remington 700 Classic rifles. He handloads them to the chart velocity of 3,210 fps and uses them on game as big as elk. That load has taken 20 elk without costing Dan a cripple. New 110-grain bullets by Nosler bridge the nettlesome gap between the 100-grain spitzers that show lots of hustle and the traditional 117- and 120-grain bullets that must be throttled to around 3,000 fps in the quarter-inch bore. Hornady lists the hottest factory load: a Light Magnum that kicks a 117-grain BTSP downrange at 3,110 fps. That bullet carries 1,000 foot-pounds to 500 yards, where it's still traveling 2,000 fps.

The brawniest .25 is Weatherby's .257 Magnum. Appearing in 1944, a year before Roy Weatherby started his gun business, it springs from the same case as Weatherby's more versatile .270 and 7mm Magnums. The .257 Weatherby has been commercially loaded since 1948, and with Norma components since 1951. With few exceptions, only Weatherby rifles have been chambered for this proprietary round, so its popularity has been limited. Maximum working pressure is a relatively high 55,100 psi. There's nothing efficient about this .25, with its huge case and little bullet, but efficiency is not its claim. Swallowing

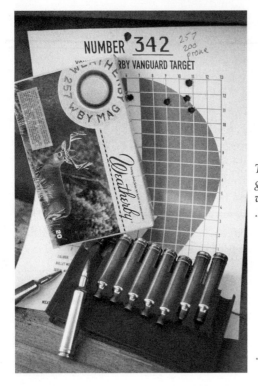

The author fired this five-shot group prone at 200 yards with factory ammo and a .257 Weatherby.

more than 75 grains of slow powder, it can spit a 117-grain bullet downrange at 3,300 fps, generating 2,824 foot-pounds of muzzle energy. That bullet crosses the 200-yard line still cooking along at 2,770 fps—about the same speed you get from the best .257 Roberts loads at the muzzle. Its 300-yard punch is 1,650 foot-pounds—100 more than that of a 130-grain .270 bullet. The .257 Weatherby has been used on big animals, including Cape buffalo. It is most appropriate where long yardage, not heavy bone, marks the challenge.

The field of high-performance .25s was, arguably, full enough with the .25-06 Remington and the .257 Weatherby Magnum, but Winchester thought differently. Following the success of its Short Magnum line, introduced in the late 1990s, it engineered the Super Short Magnums: a .223 and .243 that used an even shorter case. The .270, 7mm, and .300 were designed for .308-length rifle actions; the magazine boxes and bolt faces opened to take hulls so big in diameter that case capacities (and performance) matched that of belted magnums. But the Winchester Short Magnums had more capacity than

An old military round, the 6.5x55 is an excellent pick for deer. The author has also used it on elk.

was needed in smaller bores. The Super Shorts committed Winchester and Browning to the manufacture of subcompact rifle actions—and at least one more cartridge. The .25 Winchester Super Short Magnum appeared in 2002. It launches an 85-grain bullet at 3,470 fps, 110- and 115-grain spitzers near 3,100 fps. A Super-X 120-grain load clocks 2,990 fps, the same as a .25-06.

Standard rate of twist for the .25s is 1:10. This is enough to stabilize the longest 120-grain bullets, given reasonable velocities. Some .250 Savage rifles have been given twists as slow as 1:14, inadequate for long spitzer bullets. And a few early Weatherby rifles in .257 Magnum featured a 1:12 spin.

A decade before the .25-06 got commercial life at Remington, American shooters had another chance at a new 6.5mm cartridge. Winchester's .264 Magnum, chambered in the Model 70 beginning in 1959, had the case capacity of Weatherby's .257, with a bullet .007 bigger. Like the .458 and .338 Magnums that preceded it in 1956 and 1958, the .264 was based on the .375 H&H case shortened to 2.50 inches. The 25-degree shoulder was common to other belted magnums. The .264 made its debut in a 26-inch-barrel Model 70 that Winchester dubbed

Beaten at market by the similar 7mm Remington Magnum, Winchester's .264 has "long legs."

the Westerner. Initially, catalogs listed 140-grain Power-Point bullets at 3,200 fps and 100-grain softpoints at 3,700 fps. These figures were later revised down, but it is no trick to handload to the original .264 performance.

The .264's problem was that, while Jack O'Connor trumpeted the virtues of the .270 and Warren Page touted 7mm wildcats, nobody with a pulpit had much good to say about a belted 6.5. Soon after its introduction, the .264 was criticized for its muzzle blast and a tendency to eat throats. Both barbs were justified, but the blast from 24-inch-barrel 7mm Magnums, which later sold like hotcakes, was equally unnerving. The throat in any rifle that chambers big cases and delivers scorching bullet speeds gets a pounding—no more so from a hot 6.5.

Another of the .264's shortcomings was limited bullet selection. Because 6.5mm cartridges had long struggled for acceptance Stateside, .264 bullets did not abound. Oddly, shooters hadn't found component choice a problem with the .270 Winchester. But when the .270 was getting traction, shooters hadn't been spoiled by broad selections of bullets in other diameters, and handloading hadn't reached the popularity it enjoyed in the 1950s. In addition to the lack of .264 bullet availability, tradition had it that elk required heavier missiles than the 140-grain spitzers at the top of the 6.5mm weight range. The kinetic energy of original factory-loaded 140-grain .264 Magnum softpoints matched that of 175-grain bullets in 7mm Magnum ammo—and exceeded what elk hunters were getting with 130-grain .270 bullets, which still knocked off elk with monotonous regularity. But, hunters asked, if the case had such great capacity, why wasn't some of that extra fuel put to use behind heavier bullets? Winchester's marketing team didn't field that question.

Unlike Remington, which hawked the 7mm Magnum as a cartridge for all-around western hunting, including elk, Winchester implied that its .264 magnum was the ultimate deer round, with lighter bullets for coyotes and lesser game. But hunters didn't want a fire-breathing magnum to knock off coyotes; they wanted a rifle that would put the skids under elk at long range. Remington obliged, cleverly noting that the 7mm was more civil in recoil than a .30 Magnum, although it hit harder than a .30-06. Winchester could have played this card. Instead, it *emphasized* the .264's violence. One of the first published jingles, below an end-on view of the muzzle, was: "It makes a helluva noise and packs a helluva wallop."

I can't say when the 100-grain load was dropped, but nobody mourned it. In the .264 rifles I've owned, it never shot as accurately as 140-grain bullets. Now Winchester and Remington offer only 140-grain factory loads (Power-Points and Core-Lokts). Listed velocity is an anemic 3,030 fps—30 fps slower than standard gate speed for a 130-grain .270 bullet. At 400 yards, the two are neck and neck. Polymer-tipped bullets such as the Swift Scirocco and Remington AccuTip afford the .270 a 150 fps edge at 400 yards. A 140-grain Light Magnum load from Hornady gives the .270 a 230 fps advantage and 325 more foot-pounds of punch.

So why buy a .264? Few hunters have found a reason. Still, my handloading shows that this cartridge can easily outperform the .270 and, with bullets up to 140 grains, will beat the 7mm Magnum downrange. Bullet selection has improved lately. At this writing, Barnes lists five 6.5mm bullets, Berger one, Hornady eight, Lapua seven, Norma one, Nosler six, Remington two, Sierra nine, Speer five, Swift two, and Woodleigh one—this according to Midway USA, which carries them all. You need only one good load.

Although the .264's 140-grain bullet is closer in diameter to .257 than .277, it more nearly matches .277 bullets in weight. Its sectional

The 6.5/284 gets plaudits from long-range target shooters and is catching on with hunters.

density of .287 beats that of both 120-grain .257 and 150-grain .270 bullets.

Remington's answer to the .264 was the 6.5 Remington Magnum, introduced in 1966 for the firm's Model 600 carbine. Based on the .350 Remington Magnum case, which had appeared a year earlier, this 6.5 has the same belted head as the .264 Winchester Magnum. Its case is shorter: 2.17 inches instead of 2.50. Factory-loaded ammunition gives 120-grain bullets an advertised 3,210 fps. The 18 1/2-inch barrel of the Model 600 was poorly suited to this small-bore magnum, and the 20-inch tube of the later 660 offered scant improvement. Remington's 700 and 40-X rifles wore barrels long enough to show the round's potential, and for a time, Ruger offered this 6.5 in its Model 77. But now no factory rifles are chambered in 6.5 Remington Magnum, and 6.5 Magnum ammunition was discontinued until 2005, when a 120-grain load at 3,210 fps was listed again.

Probably the most newsworthy long-range cartridge in the .257-.264 class is the 6.5mm-284. It is based on Winchester's .284, a short-

Northern Rockies deer country: just where a .25-06 belongs, with 110-grain Nosler Ballistic Tips.

Dave Smith admires his long-range 6.5/284. He shoots eggs with it at 300 yards in matches, a definitive accuracy test.

action, rebated-rim round trotted out in 1963 to deliver .270 ballistic performance in the company's Model 88 lever-action and Model 100 autoloader. Competitive riflemen shooting at 1,000 yards have found that necking the .284 to .264 and capping it with long, sleek 140-grain bullets can help boost scores. The short case means a short powder column and consistent burn. It also permits use of a short, stiff receiver. A selection of match-grade VLD (very low drag) 6.5mm bullets as heavy as 155 grains has followed the growing interest in this round. So has the manufacture of 6.5/284 brass by Hornady, Lapua, and Norma. My own 6.5/284 rifle is by Ultra Light Arms.

Rifling twists of 1:9 are standard for .264 Winchester and 6.5 Remington Magnum rifles. The 6.5x55 Swedish Mauser has a 1:8 twist. Target barrels bored to 6.5/284 are best rifled to suit the bullet of choice. Long-nosed target bullets require a steeper pitch than do most hunting bullets.

MODESTY GOES BALLISTIC: THE 6.8 SPC

I live in a small rural town that has yet to get its first stoplight. A day's ride upriver on horseback puts you in another small town where it is still illegal *not* to own a gun. You'll find plenty of shooters

Despite its modest size, the 6.8 SPC has reach. The author's first round at 600 yards with a Remington 700 drilled an X.

in these parts, but not a lot of new-fangled guns. These are salt-of-the-earth people, scraping by in a beautiful place that has been throttled economically by low apple prices and logging moratoriums. They shoot ordinary rifles and cartridges. The latest short magnums seem oddly redundant to hunters who've not yet bought into belted magnums and whose trail-worn .270s have knocked the stuffing out of big game since Truman beat Dewey.

Sharing local disdain for hard-kicking rifles, I was delighted as this book was progressing to encounter a new long-range cartridge with more manners than machismo. Oddly enough, the 6.8 SPC (Special Purpose Cartridge) dates to 1906, the birth year of our most feted military cartridge, the .30-06. The 6.8 derives from the .30 Remington, a rimless .30-30 fashioned for the Remington Model 8 autoloading rifle, which was new that year. Also available in .25, .32, and .35, the Model 8 was replaced by the Model 81 in 1936. It lasted until 1950. The sleek Model 740 appeared in 1955 in .30-06 and .308, a Winchester round that began life as the military T-65. In comparison, Remington's .25, .30, and .32 seemed woefully underpowered. They had served ably in the square-backed Model 8 and in the slide-action Model 14, introduced in 1912. But only the .35 hung on in both the improved 141 (1936) and the

Based on the compact .30 Remington case, the 6.8 SPC fires 115-grain bullets gently.

postwar 760. Marlin's 336 lever rifle kept the .35 alive long after its siblings had vanished, although the .30 prospered between the wars. In Washington State, it made a list of most popular elk rounds, circa 1939.

At .421, the rim diameter of the .30 Remington is the same as that of the .25, .30, and .32 but smaller than that of the .35's .460 rim. The .308 and .30-06 measure .470 across the base. This dimension matters because in its quest for a new twenty-first-century infantry round, the army focused on cases that would function in M-4 and M-16 mechanisms. Opening the bolt face from .375 (the diameter of the .223 or 5.56 NATO rim) to accommodate larger hulls was necessary, given the other requisites: more power up close, and flat flight for easy torso hits to 500 meters, where the new round would also deliver lethal energy. You could hardly add muscle to the M-16 without increasing case capacity and bullet weight. Changing the bolt throw, magazine length, or receiver dimensions would not pass muster. There were no .308-based cartridges. Even the .30 Remington needed body work. The hull was pruned from 2.05 inches to 1.69 (43mm), .07 shy of a .223 case. Both the .223 and 6.8 SPC mike 2.26 inches loaded, albeit the 6.8 holds 17 percent more fuel.

At 200 yards, this Model 700 prototype in 6.8 SPC showed promise. Shooting was fun, with no kick.

The 6.8 SPC project began quietly, with the U.S. Army Marksmanship Unit and Fifth Special Forces Group exploring case and bullet options. Fitting the hull to the M-16 mechanism, the design crew fashioned a 23-degree shoulder and reduced the neck diameter from 7.62 to 6.8mm (inside), the same as Winchester's .270. The finished body measures 1.295 inches long, the neck .290.

The bullet had to be lighter than the 130-grain spitzers standard for a .270, which would have been too long for the magazine and available powder space and too heavy to reach intended speeds. Hornady came forth with a 115-grain OTM (open-tip match) bullet, loaded to 2,800 fps. It delivers a ton of muzzle energy and holds up well downrange, clocking 2,535, 2,285, 2,049, and 1,828 fps at 100, 200, 300, and 400 yards, respectively. At 100 yards it unloads 1,640 foot-pounds, 78 percent more energy than a 55-grain .223 bullet. At 300 yards, it still carries more than 1,000 foot-pounds—about the same as a 100-grain bullet from a .243 and 400 foot-pounds more than 125-grain hardball ammo from the 7.62x39. With a 200-yard zero, the 6.8mm SPC bullet drops 9 inches at 300 yards, 26 inches at 400 yards, and 53 inches at 500 yards. Ballistically, it's a near match for

.257 Roberts ammunition loaded with 117-grain spitzers at 2,780 fps. Here's a summary comparison:

Bullet	Muzzle	100 yards	200 yards	300 yards	400 yards
6.8mm SPC, 115 OTM (Remington)					
Velocity (fps)	2800	2535	2285	2049	1828
Energy (ft-lb)	2002	1641	1333	1072	853
Arc (inches)		+2	0	-9	-26
.257 Roberts, 117 SPBT (Hornady)					
Velocity (fps)	2780	2550	2331	2122	1925
Energy (ft-lb)	2007	1689	1411	1170	963
Arc (inches)		+2	0	-8	-24
.250 Savage, 100 PSP (Remington)					
Velocity (fps)	2820	2504	2210	1936	1684
Energy (ft-lb)	1765	1392	1084	832	630
Arc (inches)		+2	0	-9	-28
.243 Winchester, 100 PP (Winchester)					
Velocity (fps)	2960	2697	2449	2215	1993
Energy (ft-lb)	1945	1615	1332	1089	882
Arc (inches)		+2	0	-8	-23

Compared with traditional deer loads with round-nose bullets, the 6.8 shows its long-range edge:

Bullet	Muzzle	100 yards	200 yards	300 yards	400 yards
.257 Roberts, 117 SPCL (Remington)					
Velocity (fps)	2650	2291	1961	1663	1404
Energy (ft-lb)	1824	1363	999	718	512
Arc (inches)		+3	0	-12	-36

Bullet	Muzzle	100 yards	200 yards	300 yards	400 yards
7-30 Waters, 120 Sierra GK (Federal)					
Velocity (fps)	2700	2300	1930	1600	1330
Energy (ft-lb)	1940	1405	990	685	470
Arc (inches)		+3	0	-12	-38
.30-30 Winchester, 150 PP (Winchester)					
Velocity (fps)	2390	2018	1684	1398	1177
Energy (ft-lb)	1902	1356	944	651	461
Arc (inches)		+3	0	-17	-53

Remington engineers who joined the military design team in 2001 had no mandate to develop the 6.8 SPC as a hunting round. But given American shooters' appetite for new cartridges and a sporting press always clamoring for new products, it was soon clear that the bullet selection would grow—and that Big Green would chamber the round in hunting rifles. Soon the original Hornady OTM bullet was joined by a Sierra MatchKing, a metal case spitzer, and a pointed Core-Lokt Ultra in Remington loads. All these bullets weigh 115 grains. At this writing, a heavier bullet seems a probability.

Several rifles are now bored for the 6.8mm SPC, including a favorite of mine, Remington's Model Seven AWR (Alaska Wilderness Rifle). This lightweight is finely balanced and wears a beautifully shaped composite stock. It is lithe and fast to shoulder, with a properly open-grip straight comb. The only fly is a front swivel stud too far to the rear for easy sling use. The Model Seven's smooth, dependable action and adjustable trigger offset such minor flaws.

The first 6.8mm SPC rifle that came my way was a Remington 700 with a Leupold 6.5-20x scope. I had yet to shoot it when, with the summer afternoon quickly slipping by, I spun the elevation dial dozens of clicks to move the sight from a 200-yard zero out to 600. I'd have been satisfied to put the first shot on paper, which high-power shooters know is the size of a small garage door. (A third of a mile distant, it appears more like a postage stamp.) I radioed to my friend in the pits that the line was hot, then settled into a tight sling, prone. Bang! Not much recoil. A wind gusting from 2 o'clock would have its way with a bullet this light at long range. If Joe couldn't find a hole, how would I adjust?

The 6.8 SPC was offered first to sportsmen in Model Seven and Model 700 rifles. This one wears a Bushnell Elite scope.

The target didn't stay long in the pits. When it arose, there was a white marker on the X-ring. With no further sight adjustments, I squeezed off nine more shots. Only two leaked into the 9 ring. A rifle that hits at long range in difficult conditions but pampers your shoulder and eardrums is easy to love. I'm afraid my assessment of the 6.8mm Remingon SPC was colored by that afternoon on the 600-yard line. Nonetheless, I was keen to confirm my prediction that this would be a dandy deer cartridge.

My chance came in the Southeast, where multiple tags encourage whitetail hunters to keep robust deer populations in check. When I climbed into a treestand on what would be my only afternoon afield, the instructions were to shoot does or, if one came by, a mature buck. I didn't have long to wait. A button buck slipped silently into an open strip 160 yards through the pines. Seconds later, another young deer appeared, then a big doe. I slid the cross-wire of the Kahles scope onto the doe's shoulder and pressed the trigger. The Model Seven bounced. The doe dropped, kicked convulsively a couple of times, and then lay still.

A month later, I would take a second deer with the 6.8 SPC in a Thompson/Center (T/C) pistol. The doe was quartering to me when I unleased a 115-grain Core-Lokt. She dashed off into the darkening

Thompson/Center chambers its Contender G2 in 6.8 SPC. The author shot deer with this one.

Kentucky woods. Sure of a hit, I trailed the animal on a carpet of hardwood leaves, but I soon lost the track. There'd been no blood, but deer on the sprint often cover many yards before leaking. I circled the last place I'd seen her, eventually breaking out my flashlight to illuminate the leaves. No luck. Then I tried a trick I've found useful before: letting my feet find the way of least resistance. Beyond the first couple of bounds, deer take the easiest path, established or not. You can do the same thing if you subordinate your mind and let your legs lead. Shortly after my second start, a drop of red winked at me from an oak leaf. A few minutes later, I was standing at the carcass. The bullet had angled to the off-flank, retaining just over half its weight.

The 6.8mm Remington SPC had already shown itself to be an exceptional performer in that T/C pistol. On the 100-yard range from a rest, it landed three bullets in a $^3/_4$-inch group. The cartridge is a stellar pick for an extra barrel in your T/C Contender rifle or pistol, and a fine excuse to buy a G2 if you don't own one. It is gentler in recoil than a .243 or a .257; you get 30 percent less kick than from a .30-30. But the 6.8 SPC has more reach than any pistoleer will need. I've taken game with handguns to around 100 yards. If you're steadier on the rest, perhaps you can double that range. I've never seen

The 6.8 SPC has shot well with Open Tip Match and Core-Lokt Ultra bullets, both 115 grains.

anyone who can hit consistently with pistols at ranges much beyond 200 yards. It isn't that the guns aren't accurate—a T/C will outshoot many bolt rifles. The problem is that you can't keep the handgun still as you apply pressure to the trigger. Even if you're the exception, the 6.8mm Remington SPC will give you all the reach you need.

In rifles, the SPC's low recoil level, coupled with the punch and range of a .243, makes it an ideal choice for youngsters and those of us who have come to favor gentle guns. You can buy or build a very lightweight 6.8 without a brake. The modest case capacity means that you won't need a long barrel to accelerate bullets.

The factory ammunition I've tried has shot accurately and at close to the listed velocity. Bullet selection is limited, but that's because the 6.8mm SPC has a small case and medium-size bore. Bullets heavier than 115 grains have to be seated deeper to fit the compact M-16 magazine. More weight and less fuel space mean lower velocities. Reduce bullet weight to increase speed, and you trim the already modest sectional density. Ballistic coefficient drops, and deceleration rate increases. Long-range performance suffers.

It's unlikely that the 6.8mm SPC will enjoy the popularity of the .243. Partly that's because the .243 already has a strong following, and partly it's because the 6.8 doesn't share a .470 head with the .308 clan of big-game rounds. Barreling to Remington's new round isn't just a matter of screwing a new barrel on a short-action bolt gun. The bolt face must be sized to fit the .421 rim. By all other measures, the 6.8 has the marks of a cartridge doomed to ratings below those it deserves. It is not a magnum. It is less powerful than the most popular deer cartridges. It shoots a relatively lightweight bullet at under 3,000 fps. So why would shooters on the Okanogan River—or anywhere—buy a rifle in 6.8? Because better bullet placement means more lethal hits, and this round is easy to shoot well. As for power, calling the 6.8 a marginal deer cartridge is like saying the .30-06 is iffy for elk. You can buy more power, but in my view, it's entirely unnecessary. Trainloads of deer have fallen to the likes of the .25-35, whose flat-nose bullet generates 350 foot-pounds less moxie than the 6.8mm SPC at the muzzle, and increasingly less downrange. The .30 Remington matches the 6.8 at the muzzle but loses energy faster. Inuit hunters take caribou by the score with centerfire .22s that don't approach the 6.8 in killing power.

Shoot it, and you will like the 6.8mm Remington SPC. It's as beguiling as an ordinance mandating that every citizen own a gun.

7MM MOXIE

Not all numbers become icons, but shooters have given special status to 7. The 7mm or .284-diameter bullet has seduced shooters for some time. Why? you might ask. After all, rifles and cartridges fashioned to shoot 7mm bullets could just as well have been made for shanks miking .278 or .290.

There is little black-powder history for 7mms. The .28-30-120 Stevens, a straight, rimmed case, appeared around 1900. Developed by C. H. Herrick, it was chambered by the J. Stevens Arms and Tool Co. in 44 and 44½ single-shot target rifles. Renowned barrel maker Harry Pope liked it and fitted barrels in .28-30 to other actions. But by 1918, Remington had dropped the round.

Modern 7mms got their start in the Spanish army, which in 1893 adopted a rifle designed by Peter Paul and Wilhelm Mauser. It chambered a bottleneck case 57mm long, clenching a bullet 7mm in diameter. The 93 Mauser and its smokeless 7x57 round became hugely popular, filling arsenals the world over. None of the later Mauser

The 7mm-08 and 7mm Remington Magnum are the most versatile and popular 7mms in the United States now.

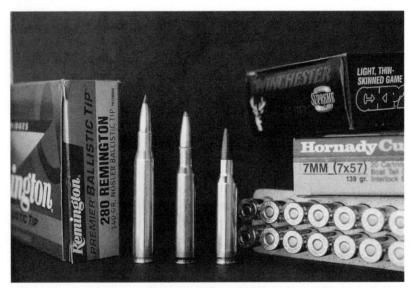

The 7x57 (center) is too long for short actions and ballistically inferior to the .280, but it's a classic round.

rounds have made the jump from battlefield to sporting field as successfully as has the 7x57. The best gunmakers have built rifles for it, and the world's most famous hunters still praise it. Ivory hunter W. D. M. "Karamojo" Bell fired 173-grain solids (at 2,300 fps) from his 7x57 to topple elephants. Stateside, between the wars, it proved deadly on all manner of thin-skinned game, shooting lighter bullets almost as flat as the .270 and more gently than the .30-06. The 7x57 suffered for a time because it was loaded to pressures easily bottled by early Mausers, while its competition cooked up 50,000 psi. Some factory loads now do a lot better (Hornady's Light Magnum kicks a 139-grain bullet downrange at 2,830 fps, 150 fps faster than standard loads). For decades, handloaders have shoveled the coal to 7x57 ammo.

But not all the early 7mms were as successful as the 7x57. In turn-of-the-century England, F. W. Jones designed a cartridge for Sir Charles Ross and ammunition giant Eley. First chambered in Canadian Ross straight-pull military rifles, the .280 Ross kicked 160-grain bullets along at 2,900 fps. But the Ross rifle could be assembled to fire without lockup, endangering shooters. Also, bullets of the day weren't built for high-speed impact. Hunters used the Ross in Africa on game as tough as lions. Some hunters died.

In 1907 English gunmaker John Rigby introduced the .275 Rimless in his magazine rifles. It used a .284 bullet and hewed close in dimensions to the 7x57. The original 140-grain spitzer was replaced by a semi-pointed 140 after World War I. The apparent reason: Rigby's managing director had been struck in the head by an 8mm German spitzer during the war, and the bullet bounced off, badly shaking his faith in pointed bullets. The .275 spawned a rimmed version for double rifles in 1927. Conservatively loaded, the rimmed round mirrored the 7mm Rimmed H&H Magnum and Lancaster's .280 Flanged Nitro-Express. The .280 Rimless Jeffery set the bar higher in 1915, pushing a 140-grain bullet 3,000 fps.

Meanwhile, the United States was teething on 30-caliber rounds, and a new 7mm had appeared in Europe. Germany's gun genius Wilhelm Brenneke designed the 7x64 in 1917. A ballistic twin to the Ross, the 7x64 (with the rimmed 7x65) looked and performed a lot like the .280 Remington, which came 40 years later.

During the 1920s and 1930s, wildcatters concocted several 7mms on the belted .300 Holland case and on Charles Newton's big rimless .30. Western Cartridge Company produced, briefly, John Dubiel's .276. The .280 Dubiel, with a .288 bullet, delivered stellar performance

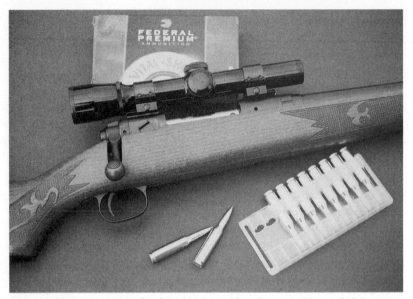

The author's Savage 111 is chambered in 7mm-08 and wears a Weaver K-2.5 scope.

from its full-length .300 H&H hull. Although Newton's .280 failed, P. O. Ackley hawked a .276 Short Magnum. A. E. Mashburn fashioned a sharp-shouldered 7mm from the long Holland case, and *Field & Stream* gun editor Warren Page killed a lot of game with it. Charlie O'Neil, Elmer Keith, and Don Hopkins followed with the .285 OKH.

Holland & Holland's .275 Belted Rimless Magnum Nitro cartridge, a shortened, reshaped .375 H&H, appeared in 1912, with a rimmed version for double rifles. Factory-loaded to bland levels, the .275 Rimless Magnum rewarded handloaders. It was sold by Western Cartridge in the United States until 1939.

In 1944 Roy Weatherby added a 7mm to his .270 and .257 wildcats on the shortened Holland hull. This hot seven never became as popular as the full-length .300 Weatherby Magnum, but it shot as flat, with less recoil. You can get as much speed from a 160-grain bullet as from a 180 in the larger .30—about 3,200 fps. Luckily for Remington, Weatherby kept a short proprietary leash, and no commercial rifles were chambered for the 7mm Weatherby Magnum for 20 years. The 1962 debut of Remington's Model 700 rifle was all the livelier because its chamberings included the new 7mm Remington Magnum. As capacious as the 7mm Weatherby, it was tamed to SAAMI pressures.

Remington's 7mm Ultra Mag is very fast and put the skids under the firm's 7mm STW. It did not appreciably affect sales of the 7mm Magnum.

The 7mm Remington Magnum achieved almost instant success, mainly because it was smartly advertised. Wyoming outfitter Les Bowman had pointed out to Remington the need for a cartridge that shot as flat as a .270 but carried more punch, one that developed no more recoil than a .30-06 but reached farther. It would fit standard-length actions, as had the .458, .338, and .264 Winchester Magnums already on the market. The ideal cartridge would be a peppy 7mm that hunters could use for deer, elk, and pronghorns. So that's how Remington promoted its new round, and hunters bought it.

Three years earlier, Winchester's .264 Winchester Magnum had endured a lukewarm welcome, partly because its 140-grain bullet was not what elk hunters wanted. With a same-size case and a bullet just .020 smaller than the 7mm Remington Magnum's, the .264 languished. So did the .280 Remington, which could not budge the .270's share of the market. The 7x61 Sharpe & Hart, a belted magnum chambered in Schultz & Larsen rifles in 1953, never had a major firearms or ammunition company behind it.

In my surveys of elk hunters in the early 1990s, the 7mm Remington Magnum rivaled the .30-06 in popularity, well ahead of other cartridges. Considering that the '06 appeared in sporting rifles 50 years

Winchester's Greg Kostick took this Australian buffalo with a 7mm WSM—power aplenty!

before the first 7mm Remington Magnum, and that many thousands of .30-06 military rifles were surplused to hunters (with millions of rounds of .30-06 ammo), hunter response to the belted seven has been electric. Remington's star 7mm remains a favorite in the West but has also shown up all over the world.

The 7mm STW (Shooting Times Westerner) popped up in the 1980s. A super-seven on full-length 8mm Remington Magnum brass, it was pioneered by gun writer Layne Simpson. At 3,325 fps, its 140-grain bullet flies 150 fps faster than the Remington Magnum's. The difference narrows downrange, because the faster a bullet, the greater its drag. At 500 yards, the STW is only about 110 fps ahead of the 7mm Magnum.

But the STW is not the last word in speed. Remington's rimless, full-length 7mm Ultra Mag and the 7mm Dakota (on a shortened .404 Jeffery case) have upstaged it by 100 fps. John Lazzeroni's Firebird offers even more horsepower. Perhaps more practical are the newer 7mm Winchester Short Magnum and Remington Short-Action Ultra Mag rounds, duplicating 7mm Remington Magnum performance in stubby, rimless cases. The short Lazzeroni Tomahawk outperforms all three.

Though it predated and outperformed Remington's, the Weatherby 7mm Magnum is less popular.

I prefer even less noise and recoil from sevens such as the .284 Winchester, designed in 1963 to give that company's Model 88 lever-action and Model 100 autoloading rifles the reach of a bolt-action .270. The .284's rebated case holds about as much fuel as a .270 or a .280. Melvin Forbes, whose Ultra Light bolt rifles feature 3-inch magazines, has chambered a lot of barrels in .284. Savage cataloged the Model 99 in .284, and Browning the A-Bolt and BLR.

In 1980 an unlikely 7mm appeared, named after gun writer Ken Waters. The 7-30 Waters was first chambered in Winchester 94XTR rifles. It has a shorter neck, sharper shoulder, and more case capacity than its .30-30 parent and was advertised to launch a 120-grain bullet at 2,700 fps. Three years later, Remington announced the 7mm-08, a .308 necked down. This remains an eminently practical design, adaptable to any short-action rifle that handles the .308 and .243. Its 140-grain bullet at 2,860 fps edges the 7x57 by 200 fps, although the Mauser cartridge is 0.2 inch longer. I've shot game as big as elk with the 7mm-08 and consider it one of the most versatile of North American big-game rounds. It is also pleasant to shoot.

Some hunters talk about 7mm cartridges as if their bullets have some innate advantage over bullets .277 or .308 in diameter. Not so. It is true that popular 7mm bullets include a few with extraordinarily high ballistic coefficients. Hornady makes a 162-grain 7mm boattail bullet with a ballistic coefficient of .534. The firm's 190-grain .308 Match bullet registers .530.

I've heard that the 7mm Remington Magnum kills better than the charts indicate it should. Those animals I've seen shot, however, reacted to the hits about as they'd react to hits with other bullets. I once got a letter from a reader castigating me for writing that the .30-06 was essentially the equal of the 7mm Remington Magnum. With 150-grain bullets of equal weight, the 7mm wins, but the '06 with a 180-grain bullet hits like a factory-loaded 175-grain bullet from the Magnum. Pick Hornady's Light Magnum .30-06 load, which launches a 180 at 2,900 fps, and the Magnum loses in both the velocity category (2,860 fps) and on the energy scorecard (3,361 foot-pounds for the '06, versus 3,178 for the 7mm). In fact, no 7mm Remington Magnum factory load equals Hornady's most potent .30-06 or Federal's 180-grain '06 High Energy loads.

There is a huge selection of 7mm cartridges and bullets. But you don't need a high-octane seven to kill big game, nor a smorgasbord of bullets to shoot. The 7mm-08 and .280 with 139- and 140-grain spitzers have plenty of reach for open country and enough moxie to drop distant game as big as elk.

.30 MAGNUMS FOR THE LONGEST SHOT

The crowded field of .30 Magnum cartridges dates to the World War I era, when the .30 Newton was driving 180-grain bullets 3,000 fps. This first high-performance .30 died for want of suitable rifles, strong soft-nose bullets, slow powders, and promotion. The .300 H&H came along in 1920 and met with success.

Actually, the .300 Holland—or Super .30, as it was fondly dubbed Stateside—didn't reach the United States until 1925. Its parent, the .375 H&H Magnum (introduced in 1912), had already made a name for itself in Africa. The necked-down version incorporated no other changes. Its long, tapered case with an $8\frac{1}{2}$-degree shoulder was shaped to accommodate long sticks of cordite powder. Hunters liked the way it chambered, but not many hunters favored the .300 H&H during the Depression. No domestic rifles were bored for it until 1936, when Winchester included the Super .30 as a charter chambering in its new Model 70. Ben Comfort had brought the cartridge into the spotlight by using it (in a custom-barreled 1917 Enfield) to win the 1,000-yard Wimbledon Match at Camp Perry in 1935. The M-70 and

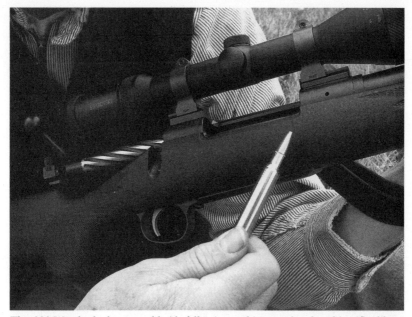

The .300 Weatherby has a worldwide following and is now chambered in rifles like this Ed Brown.

the Remington 721 introduced 12 years later had mechanisms long enough to accommodate the 3.60-inch .300 H&H cartridge, but other rifles had to be opened up.

The .300 H&H has been upstaged by short belted and now shorter rimless rounds. Remington lists no factory loads for this cartridge. Winchester loads a 180-grain Fail Safe at 2,880 fps. It kicks 3,315 foot-pounds out the muzzle and delivers about 1,500 to 400 yards. Given a 200-yard zero, this bullet strikes 8 inches low at 300 steps, 23 inches low at 400. Federal's Premium Safari load launches a 180-grain Nosler Partition to deliver the same performance. At one time, you could buy .300 H&H ammo with 150-grain bullets at nearly 3,200 fps, and 220-grain bullets at 2,620 fps. The 180-grain spitzers shoot 15 percent flatter than those from .30-06 loads and deliver a 10 percent edge in the wind. You'll feel about 26 foot-pounds of recoil shooting a Super .30, but only 17 for a same-weight .30-06. You may not find the difference noticeable, however. The .300 Holland seems to recoil less violently than most other .30 Magnums.

In 1945 Roy Weatherby expanded the Holland case, using more powder and boosting the speed of 180-grain bullets by 300 fps. This was one of the last of his original line of cases with minimum body

Steve Giordano aims a Dakota rifle in .300 Dakota, a rimless round with .300 Weatherby punch.

taper and radiused shoulders. Unlike the .257, .270, and 7mm Weatherby Magnums, the .300 was not shortened for use in .30-06-length actions. It featured the full-length .300 H&H case (2.85 inches) blown out. Loaded by Norma to higher velocities than later appeared in American-manufactured ammo, the .300 Weatherby beats the .300 H&H by nearly 400 fps (though handloaders can improve on Super .30 figures).

But into the 1950s, there was no .30 magnum short enough for the Springfield and other actions developed around the .30-06. A. B. Norma Projektilfabrik of Amotfors, Sweden, was the first to act on this omission. In 1960 it announced a cartridge much like the .30-338 wildcats that riflemen had been using since Winchester trotted out its .338 Magnum two years earlier. The .308 Norma Magnum had a case 2.56 inches long, with a .318 neck and a 25-degree shoulder. Well designed and positioned to fill an obvious market gap, it got a slow start because for 18 months Norma offered only unprimed cases. Just as frustrating was the lack of commercial rifles in .308 Norma. Eventually, they popped up here and there. Among the most memorable was Browning's classy High Power rifle, a commercial Mauser beautifully stocked.

Winchester's .300 Magnum arrived in 1963. Contrary to predictions, it did not mirror the .308 Norma or the .30-338. Its case measures 2.62 inches, with the neck a stubby .278. Deep bullet seating lets you load it in magazines designed for any short magnum. Perhaps Winchester decided to snare all the capacity it could—although both the .308 Norma and the .300 Winchester can be loaded to launch 180-grain bullets at 3,150 fps. Maybe the firm decided to take advantage of the .308 Normas and .30-338s floating around. Rechambering for a longer case was a simple matter of running another reamer—easier than rebarreling or lopping the shank to short-chamber—then retrofitting the stock. Whatever the reason, sportsmen welcomed this new cartridge. Generations had gone by since the .30-06 was considered obscenely powerful. The 7mm Remington Magnum was on its way to stardom, and hunters were using the .375 H&H for Alaska's bears.

If you don't think the .300 Winchester is a match for an irate grizzly, you'll laugh at anyone who packs a .44 Magnum in bear country. The .300 with a 180-grain bullet develops more than 3,500 foot-pounds of muzzle energy, three times what you'll get from even a long-barreled .44 Magnum. The .300 Winchester delivers more than a ton of energy to 300 yards—25 percent more than the .30-06 at that

The author shot this red stag in New Zealand with a Ruger Frontier rifle in .300 WSM, close up.

range, and 12 percent more than Remington's 7mm Magnum. The .300 Winchester packs half again as much punch as the .303 British, the Canadian service round that for decades killed more moose and grizzlies than U.S. hunters shot with all cartridges combined. And the .300 holds up—with streamlined bullets, you can toss a ton of energy to 400 yards. That's three times the payload of the .303 and nearly 30 percent more than you'll manage with a .30-06. In fact, at long range, the .300 Winchester beats the .375 H&H handily—and not just in foot-pounds. Expect a 270-grain .375 bullet to drop about $2^{1}/_{2}$ feet getting to 400 yards with a 200-yard zero. A 180-grain spitzer from Winchester's .300 loses only about 19 inches.

The 7mm Remington Magnum is justly praised for its versatility, but it's hardly a match for the .300 Winchester Magnum. Most 160-grain 7mm Magnum bullets are factory loaded to about 2,950 fps, or 100 fps slower than 180-grain bullets from the .300. Figure 20 percent less energy from the 7mm. A 150-grain bullet from a .300 Winchester

At the bench before elk season, the author zeros a Weatherby Mark V in .300 Weatherby.

Magnum at 3,290 fps moves out 180 fps faster than a 7mm Magnum bullet of the same weight—though at long range, the superior ballistic coefficient of the 7mm narrows the gap, and at 350 yards, they're traveling about the same speed. So the .300 is in top form with bullets of 165 grains or heavier. It can launch 200-grain softpoints at 2,825 fps, faster than most 165-grain .30-06 bullets.

With around 30 foot-pounds of recoil in an 8-pound rifle, the .300 Winchester kicks about as hard as most hunters want to be kicked. But it is significantly less brutal than a .338 Magnum and has as much reach. Less costly to shoot, with more load choices, it follows hard on the heels of the .300 Weatherby in ballistics tables. And it's available in almost every bolt rifle that chambers belted cartridges. It's not surprising that in my surveys of elk hunters for the Rocky Mountain Elk Foundation, the .300 Winchester Magnum was one of the three most popular rounds. Only the .30-06 and 7mm Remington Magnum beat it—the .30-06 largely because of its longevity.

I've shot more elk with the .300 Winchester than with any other cartridge and have great faith in it. For a decade I also guided elk hunters and found the .300 Winchester well represented. Of course, elk are tough, and you can't expect four hooves in the air as soon as a rifle comes off recoil, no matter the chambering.

Once, a client and I crept up to a small band of elk foraging on an open hillside. His tag was for a cow. I pointed out the biggest as he settled into prone about 300 yards distant. It was a longer shot than suits me, but we had no way to approach.

"Take your time," I crooned softly. "We have the wind. Let her get broadside and by herself."

He settled into the rifle and pressed the trigger. The cow crow-hopped and stood. She'll topple, I told myself. But she didn't. The others milled. My client cycled his .300.

"Shoot again," I hissed. "Same place." He fired again. "Keep shooting. Adjust your hold down slightly. I'll try to spot." Dust spurted from the ridge behind after each explosion, but I couldn't tell where the bullets had passed. At last the commotion drove the elk off, our target animal trailing. She collapsed at the edge of timber. We found her dead, and riddled. She had just outlived the first bullet.

Another time, a hunter and I were climbing out of a canyon at midday after a long, hot morning. In a closet of aspens below a spring, we stopped for a shade break. Suddenly, a fine six-point bull erupted from the long grass and dashed off. "Shoot!" I yelled. To his credit, my client deftly shouldered his .300 Winchester and laced a Nosler into the bull's ribs. The big animal collapsed in midstride. Grinning, the hunter lowered his rifle and turned to me. "Reload," I told him. "Be ready to shoot again." The animal was up before the bolt closed. Boom! The elk had almost vanished in the aspens when a third bullet landed. The bull staggered and dropped. When we reached him, he required a finisher. "Good grief," the hunter said. "Three in the vitals and he was still motoring!"

It didn't surprise me. But as tenacious as elk can be, they're also mortal, and even at long range a .300 Winchester Magnum is always enough. I favor 180-grain Nosler Partition, Trophy Bonded, Swift A-Frame, and Winchester Fail Safe bullets at 3,000 fps. I got that with 75 grains H4831 in the 1963 Model 70 Winchesters I foolishly sold when you could still find them for around $500. Because the cartridge came out just before the 1964 raping of the Model 70 by company account-ants, relatively few pre-64 .300s were made, and those had the smaller checkering patterns and ho-hum wood of the era. Mine, remarkably, wore stunning tiger-tail wood. A .300 I still own also has fine walnut. It's a Ruger Number 1B that shoots minute of angle.

The best shot I've seen with the .300 was on a last-day hunt in cold rain after a grueling week. My client and I, wheezing like steam

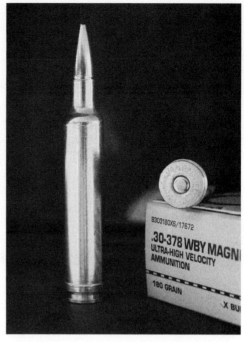

The .30-378 is more .30 than most hunters need (or can shoot well). But it remains a best seller.

engines, were toiling up a long hill when my binoculars picked up an elk slipping through the trees. A trailing fork told me that there were seven points on that side "Shoot!" I screeched. My companion swung his rifle like a shotgun. He fired as the bull's shoulder appeared briefly in an opening. The 200-grain Nosler ripped through the vitals and floored the animal. It scored 352 points. What a climax!

The longest shots I've made with the .300 Winchester have been on deer—a buck at about 400 steps that I hit poorly because I shot poorly, and another at about 300 that I drilled through the heart with a quick shot from the sit. The .300 Winchester Magnum is a fine deer round because it has its way with wind, and you needn't fret about shot angles. My favorite deer bullet is a 165-grain open-point Sierra boattail.

The .300 Winchester Magnum has grown increasingly popular. In the early 1990s Hornady and Federal drew from military work to boost the performance of this and other rounds. Hornady presented its Light Magnum ammunition as ordinary cartridges that performed like magnums but at standard pressures. Federal followed with High Energy rounds, including belted magnums. Hornady countered with

From left: *.30-06, .300 Winchester, .300 and .30-378 Weatherby. The Winchester is a civil hot rod.*

a Heavy Magnum (belted) line that included the .300 with a 180-grain InterLock bullet at 3,100 fps. You get 3,840 bone-crushing foot-pounds at the muzzle, and 1,700 at 500 yards, where the bullet is still clocking nearly 2,100 fps. Federal's High Energy 180-grain load kicks a Trophy Bonded Bear Claw downrange at 3,100 fps. A steep ogive reins this bullet in behind the Hornady, but its terminal performance on tough game is peerless. Federal also markets 200-grain High Energy ammo—a Nosler Partition that exits at 2,930 fps with 3,810 foot-pounds. Those 180- and 200-grain bullets carry momentum that extends the effective range beyond 400 yards.

The .300 Winchester's competition comes from many quarters, but no .30 Magnum is as popular. In 1992 Dakota introduced its own beltless .300 on a shortened .404 Jeffery case. With a case capacity just 3 grains shy of the .300 Weatherby, it has as much to offer and still anchors the Dakota line. On its heels came the mighty Lazzeroni 7.82 Warbird. No .30-bore is more potent, but its blast can rattle distant windows, and the recoil without the brake can turn clavicles to mush. Lazzeroni then embarked on a new project: short cases fashioned from his full-length rounds. The versatile 7.82 Patriot pushes 180-grain bullets at 3,180 fps.

This Freudenberg-built .30-338 is accurate. The round mimics the .308 Norma and .300 Winchester.

The need for faster .30-caliber bullets is debatable, but in 1997 hunters got a match for the Warbird in Weatherby's .30-378 Magnum. Development had begun in 1953, after the debut of the .378 Weatherby Magnum. Apparently, Redstone Arsenal asked for a cartridge that would accelerate a bullet to 5,000 fps. Ray Speer's bullet for the wildcat .30-378 reportedly reached this mark. But the .378 required an oversize rifle action, so shooters poking holes in 1,000-yard targets focused on the .300 Weatherby case, necking it to 6.5 and 7mm. The appearance of a .30-378 Weatherby rifle generated a lot of interest. A cavernous one-third bigger than the .300 Weatherby hull, the .378 case holds 136 grains of water. It's big enough to launch a 180-grain Barnes X-Bullet at 3,450 fps, about 200 fps faster than from the .300. Most shooters who stormed gun shops to buy .30-378s didn't care that the 6 percent boost in speed cost 25 percent more powder. Oddly enough, the market for this giant cartridge was not instantly satiated. Eight years after its appearance, Weatherby's Mark V in .30-378 was still the best-selling version of the firm's flagship rifle.

For years bereft of a lane in the .30-caliber race, Remington at last decided to challenge the .30-378 in performance, but with a case that would fit a Model 700 long action. The .300 Ultra Mag, ready for testing late in 1998, offered 13 percent more powder capacity than the .300 Weatherby. A 30-degree shoulder was a compromise between the smooth-feeding 25-degree shoulder on the .300 Winchester Magnum and the capacity-boosting 40-degree angle on Ackley wildcats. With a 180-grain Nosler Partition bullet at a velocity of 3,300 fps, the Ultra Mag beats the .300 Winchester by 200 fps. Like the Dakota, the case derives from the rimless .404 Jeffery hull, modified so the base fits the magnum (.532) bolt face on a Model 700. The .300 Ultra Mag fits any bolt action that handles a long magnum hull. Its body is bigger in diameter, which can mean premature cartridge release from magazines not specifically built for the round. (Slow cycling can leave a cartridge free to spin off the follower before the bolt can push it into the chamber.) Remington rifles factory-chambered for the Ultra Mag feed reliably.

More efficient than the .30-378 Weatherby but with no more assets than the .300 Weatherby, the .300 Remington Ultra Mag fits into a narrow niche that some riflemen don't even recognize. However, the rimless case follows the .300 Dakota and 7.82 Lazzeroni in bucking the tradition of using belted brass on high-performance cartridges. Theoretically, rimless cases cycle a bit more smoothly, and there's less case stretch on the first firing—although you can headspace belted cartridges on the shoulder after the first firing by neck sizing only. The rebated rim has its critics. Hunters in Africa have whined about the rebated .425 Westley Richards since its introduction in 1909. The .425 fits a standard Mauser bolt face, but forward of the extractor groove, the web is bigger in diameter than the rim. The top round in the magazine must come up higher than would an ordinary rimless case to provide the bolt enough rim to catch. If the bolt overrides the rim, it snags the case forward of the groove, shoving the cartridge ahead with the rim underneath the bolt. Result: a jam. The Ultra Mag case is less severely rebated, and there's no override problem.

The practical difference between the .300 Winchester and the .300 Ultra Mag isn't great. The Remington's extra 200 fps gives you about 4 inches less drop at 400 yards: 16 rather than 20. At that range, the difference in remaining energy amounts to an impressive 500 foot-pounds. But there, the .300 Winchester is still packing 1,800, or about what a .30-30 turns up at the muzzle. You'll deliver more than enough impact with the Winchester to open even stoutly jacketed bullets and drive them deep. If you don't yet have a .300 of any kind, however, the .300 Ultra Mag makes sense. Its case is as big as you can stuff in

Hunters buy .30 Magnums to put big antlers on the ground far away. This bull fell at 320 yards.

Similar tendencies with different loads hint at a bedding or barrel-heating problem in this .300.

an ordinary bolt action and has been offered in nine of Remington's Model 700 rifles. Factory loads (with Nosler Partitions and Swift Sciroccos) are more affordable than Norma-loaded .300 Weatherbys.

I once got a chance to carry a Remington rifle in .300 Ultra Mag in Alaska. A fellow with whom I shared a tent in those mooseless hills managed to shoot a grizzly bear with his .300 Ultra Mag. Two quick hits put the bear down. After the postmortem, we fired a few of the Swift Sciroccos into the carcass to assess bullet performance. One of the polymer-tipped bullets drove through the chest cavity after smashing the forward shoulder knuckle. Another ended up in the off-side ham after pulverizing a hip. Such trials have limited value, because live animals affect bullets differently. I decided to run the "spruce test" on Ultra Mag ammunition as well. My first bullet sailed through a 4-inch tree, my next through a 6-inch. An 8-inch spruce finally stopped the feisty Scirocco, but barely. (A side note: Grizzlies can be good to eat. We butterflied the straps, pan-fried them over a Coleman stove in a light dusting of seasoned flour, and fought over the last piece. I'll admit to being astonished, as this bear was on a carrion diet, and because black bear meat is one of my least favorite entrees.)

While Remington was promoting its still-new Ultra Mags, it was developing shorter cartridges on the same rimless case. To its later chagrin, it decided to delay announcement of these Short Action Ultra Mags to give the longer versions more traction in the market. But Winchester had a similar project under way and grabbed the headlines with its .300 Winchester Short Magnum. Slightly longer and, with a .532 base, not quite as broad as the Lazzeroni Patriot, the .300 WSM behaves like a belted .300 Winchester Magnum (the "short" magnum introduced in 1963 now seems quite long). At 2.76 inches, a .300 WSM loaded round barely clears the mouth of the .300 Winchester case. The .300 Remington Short Action Ultra Mag is loaded to the same speed (2,970 fps) but is slightly shorter, to fit a Model Seven bolt action.

Whether you're a fan of the .300 Holland or one of its derivatives, or favor the later rimless .30 Magnums, you're equipped to tackle all but Africa's biggest game at ranges that test your marksmanship. Across alpine basins and on the 1,000-yard target range, a big .30 pushing a 180-grain bullet 3,000 fps gives you a near-perfect combination of flat flight, manageable recoil, and a willingness to buck wind that would turn lesser missiles. These are truly versatile long-range cartridges.

BIG BORES: PRACTICAL AND TACTICAL

The 1958 debut of the .338 Winchester Magnum brought no flood of orders. It came out in a Model 70 that wore an inch-thick recoil pad and had a 25-inch barrel. Appropriately called the Alaskan, this rifle had modest appeal to deer hunters, most of whom considered the .30-06 a very powerful cartridge. Close on the heels of the .338, Winchester announced its .264 Magnum in a new Westerner version of the Model 70. This new rifle lacked a recoil pad but wore the 26-inch barrel common to 70s in .220 Swift and .300 H&H Magnum.

As I recall, you could buy a .338 Model 70 for $154 in 1958, the same price as the .264. Whatever the price, it was too low to last. But in 1958 I didn't have that much money. Like the .458 Winchester unveiled in 1956, the .264 and .338 were derived from the .300 H&H case cut to 2.50 inches to fit standard actions. The .458 African attracted attention largely because it was so potent and expensive. Nobody on my block would have considered spending $310 for a rifle that fired 500-grain bullets. Model 70s in .338 and .264 were a bit more sensible for North American game, but still seemed excessively violent.

Big-bore rifles don't get much bigger than a .50 BMG. The bullet has great reach but less versatility.

But whereas the .264 has been buried by the 7mm Remington Magnum, the .338 has developed quite a following. As shooters seek more and more reach from their cartridges, standards change. In my youth, .30-30 carbines held sway for whitetails. Now many hunters use magnum rifles that generate twice the horsepower of traditional deer guns and shoot much flatter. Elk camps during the 1950s and 1960s bristled with surplus 1903 Springfields and 721 Remingtons in .30-06. Model 99 saddle guns in .300 Savage killed a lot of bulls. Now a lot of elk hunters assume that they need a cartridge that carries a ton of energy to 300 yards.

The .338 is often thought to be less versatile than 7mm and .30 Magnums. The rifles and bullets are heavier than needed for deer, and the recoil is punishing. But deer can be killed neatly with .338s. A buck I shot while hunting elk showed less meat damage than if I'd used a .270, because my bullet, designed for elk, opened less violently.

Four years after Winchester announced the .338 Magnum, Weatherby came out with a full-length .33 that drove 250-grain bullets at nearly 3,000 fps. I saw my first .340 Weatherby rifle long ago on an Oregon mountain, as a bleak November afternoon faded into night. I

John Lee readies his .340 Weatherby Mark V for an Alaskan bear hunt by boat.

was utterly spent. The knee-deep snow and jagged route along the ridge had shoved me farther and farther behind the two bull elk I'd been trailing since noon. Descending in the dark, I still had three trail miles between me and a sleeping bag when lantern lights pierced the night. The camp in the clearing was a big one. It had tables and chairs and gun racks in the tents. Outside a huge white awning, hunters swarmed around an old man in a plaid wool coat, perched on a camp stool above a Dutch oven half buried with coals. He lifted the lid so I could see his orange rolls. He said that they'd be done in a minute and I could have one. I sat down. One of the hunters in camp came over to show me his rifle. He was a small man, not much taller than his long-barreled Weatherby. "It's a .340," he said reverently. I remember that rifle's lovely red Claro stock and long, slim barrel almost as vividly as I remember the hot orange rolls with the bubbly frosting.

If ever there was a cartridge made for elk hunting, especially for shooting elk at long range, the .340 Weatherby Magnum is it. But you still see few elk hunters with rifles chambered for this round. Weatherby's own .300 outsells the .340 Magnum 13 times over. This leggy

The author shot this Alaskan mountain goat with a Model 70 in .325 WSM and AccuBond bullets in Winchester loads.

.33, the seventh in Weatherby's line of commercial cartridges, arrived after the introduction of the Weatherby Mark V rifle. Early in his career, Roy Weatherby had used any bolt rifle long enough to accept Holland-length magnums. In 1956 he standardized rifle production on new Mauser actions made in Belguim by Fabrique Nationale. In 1958, prompted by the development of the fat .378 and .460 Weatherby Magnums, the new Weatherby Mark V action supplanted all others. Designed by Roy and engineer Fred Jennie, the Mark V is a Mauser derivation with nine locking lugs set in three rows 120 degrees apart. Roy made his own barrels at first, and chambered barrel blanks he bought from Parker Ackley. With the advent of the Mark V, manufacture went to West Germany, where Sauer used the then-new process of hammer forging to rifle Weatherby barrels. These were the first rifles with hammer-forged barrels to sell in the United States.

Right after World War II, the only way to get Weatherby ammunition was to roll your own or buy some of the limited number turned out by Weatherby's shop people on hand presses. Then in 1953, Norma of Sweden agreed to manufacture the ammunition. Still Weatherby's sole supplier, Norma has since moved production to the

Sables are tough animals; professional hunters recommend bullets of substantial weight.

United States. It now produces seven loads for the .340, with bullets weighing 200, 210, 225, and 250 grains. A 200-grain Ballistic Tip launched at 3,221 fps is still traveling over 2,100 at 500 yards. Zeroed at 300 yards, it drops 25 inches at 500, with a modest 4-inch rise above line of sight at 200. A 210-grain Nosler Partition traces nearly the same arc. The higher sectional density of the 250-grain Partition shows up at long range. Although it exits at only 2,941 fps, it gains on the 200-grain Ballistic Tip and at 500 yards is only 100 fps behind. Its heavier bullet hits harder at all ranges, delivering 2,286 foot-pounds at 500 yards, 260 foot-pounds more than the 200-grain and as much punch as you get from a 220-grain .30-06 bullet at 100 yards. At 300 yards, a 250-grain bullet from a .340 is moving almost as fast as it would from a .338 Winchester Magnum at the 100-yard mark.

Factory loads of 250 grains for the .340 Weatherby edge .338 Remington Ultra Mag ammunition by about 100 fps. The Ultra Mag shows no indication of topping popularity charts, despite its long reach and availability in Remington 700 rifles. Like .338 Winchester and .340 Weatherby, it kicks hard. But there are more powerful .33-bore options. The Lazzeroni 8.59 Titan and Weatherby .338/378 Magnum might have qualified as artillery in another time. They shoot 250-grain bullets as fast as a .270 shoots 130s and unload a ton and a half of energy at 400 yards. They're very unpleasant to shoot without muzzle brakes, however. If the recoil doesn't throttle your practice with these beasts, paying $100 a box for ammo might. Elk hunters who set up for super-long shots are evidently keeping these cartridges in production, but the heavy rifle actions required don't lend themselves to extended treks.

A more palatable alternative is John Lazzeroni's 8.59 Galaxy. A short-action round that delivers the ballistic package of the .340 Weatherby, it is one of my favorite cartridges. So is the rifle Lazzeroni designed for it on a McMillan action. He added a bigger Sako-style extractor and a three-position safety and installed a Jewell trigger, Schneider barrel, and new bottom metal. The L2000 Mountain Rifle weighs less than 7 pounds.

"Expect that Galaxy to outshine your .338 Winchester," said Lazzeroni, when he shipped the rifle. My chronograph showed lower-than-average variation in velocities, which averaged 3,005 fps for a 185-grain Barnes X Bullet, 2,970 for the 200 Nosler Ballistic Tip, and 2,760 for a 225 Nosler Partition—a close match to the .338. Predictably, accuracy was best with the Ballistic Tips: $3/4$ inch at 100 yards. The Partitions and Barnes X Bullets stayed just outside an inch. "We load Lazzeroni ammo by hand," explained John. "Powder charge weights are held to within 0.1 grain." Lazzeroni also sells brass, made by Jim Bell of MAST Technologies.

On an Alaska hunt, the Mountain Rifle shed rain as expected. ("Just leave it outside the tent; water can't hurt it," Lazzeroni said.) The long, slim grip is a delightful departure from the tighter grips that show up with increasing frequency but are slow and awkward to handle. The stock's svelte lines hide the wide three-round magazine, which feeds the fat hulls as if pumping syrup. Fit and finish are first class, down to the polished bolt face and mechanical ejector. The 8-40 mount base holes are standard on all Lazzeroni rifles, to give mounts more purchase than with traditional 6-48 screws. This rifle balances and handles like a fine shotgun. The rifle comes with medium-height Leupold rings on Leupold bases or Lazzeroni's quick-detach mounts fashioned by Talley Manufacturing. Both have the NP3 finish to match the rifle.

I took the Lazzeroni rifle afield in Montana after elk and found a herd early one morning as the animals climbed a burn toward thick bedding cover. Hustling up the back side of an adjacent ridge, I

The author shot this fine hartebeest at 310 yards using a wildcat .338/308 and 210 Nosler Partitions. The cartridges appeared recently as the .338 Federal.

Winchester's .325 WSM is an 8mm round with the ballistic credentials of a .338 Winchester.

The short, rimless Lazzeroni 8.59 Galaxy more than matches the .338 Winchester ballistically.

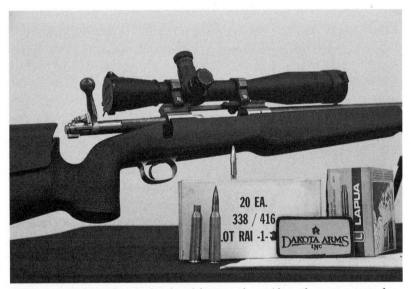

Dakota's tactical Longbow is chambered for several cartridges, the most potent of which is the .338 Lapua.

caught the last few animals in the open as I stalked crosswind at timber's edge. From the sit at 100 yards, I aimed at a three-point bull quartering toward me and pressed the trigger. The 200-grain Nosler Ballistic Tip struck just behind the shoulder, driving through to lodge in the off-flank. The bull stumbled, then tried to keep up with the cows dashing toward the forest. But I cycled the bolt quickly and broke both shoulders. The elk died right away. The heavy-jacketed .33-caliber Ballistic Tips penetrated better than I expected.

Winchester's .325 WSM, an 8mm round that appeared in 2004, can't quite match the speed of the 8.59 Lazzeroni Galaxy, but it's available in Model 70 and Browning rifles and delivers the punch of a .338 Winchester Magnum. One elk season, four hunters and I, all using the .325 WSM, packed out five bulls. Each was taken with one shot. I followed up with a goat hunt in Alaska, snatching a billy with the .325 from the teeth of an approaching blizzard.

Big-bore cartridges for military use are relatively new. The .30-40 Krag was the first smokeless round designed for issued rifles and carbines. Close on its heels came the .30-06, followed a half century later by the .308. In Vietnam, while infantrymen carried lightweight 5.56mm (.223) ammo, snipers such as the lethal marine Carlos Hathcock used .30s. His pet was a Model 70 Winchester in .30-06, but Remington Model 700s in .308 and .300 Winchester Magnum also delivered the accuracy and trajectory to match the optics and tactics of the day.

Post-Vietnam developments in sniping have emphasized reach. Chamberings vary from the standard .308 to the .50 BMG (Browning Machine Gun). Dating from 1918, it hurls a 750-grain bullet 2,700 fps. A very high ballistic coefficient gives this bullet extraordinary range. But in hand-held rifles, the Big Fifty kicks like a team of mules in synchrony. Boosting weight and adding a muzzlebrake help a great deal, but the violence is palpable no matter how you rearrange it. Several commercial firms have courted the government with heavy bolt-action .50s. Now military loads include armor-piercing saboted bullets with a starting speed of 4,500 fps.

The .50 BMG has few sporting applications, but a culture has grown up around it. Aficionados hold 1,000-yard matches that test the wind-bucking ability of the 750-grain spitzers (and 647-grain bullets at 3,000 fps). To date, the tightest five-shot group at that range measured just 5 inches. A few elk hunters have taken bolt-action .50s afield, setting up on canyon rims and zeroing powerful scopes on trails threading the opposite wall.

A 300-yard shot with a .338 Winchester and Nosler Partition bullet gave Ron Holden this bull.

A more practical tactical round for sportsmen is the .338 Lapua, developed in 1983 by the U.S. firm Research Armament Company. The ballistic target was essentially .340 Weatherby performance: a 250-grain bullet at 3,000 fps to extend the sniper's reach beyond that afforded by .30-caliber bullets. Engineers settled on the .416 case, a rimless hull that was necked to .338 and soon produced in quantity by Bell Extrusion Labs, Ltd., of Bensenville, Illinois. Hornady made the first bullets; Research Armament built the rifles under contract with the navy. When Sweden's Norma and Finland's Lapua started loading the new round, it earned CIP (Commission Internationale Permanente) and SAAMI sanction. Dakota's 14-pound tactical Long Bow was one of the first commercial rifles to chamber the cartridge, but Sako followed with a fine and affordable bolt-action sporting rifle, the TRG. Now other makers have added the .338 Lapua to their lists of chamberings in rifles that accommodate the big case.

Velocity, energy, and trajectory values for hunting bullets in the .338 Lapua match those for the .340 Weatherby Magnum. Target loads by Lapua flatten the trajectory still more. Sierra makes a 300-grain boattail hollowpoint with terrific long-range numbers, and the cartridge is inherently accurate. A colleague, Steve Comus, once joined

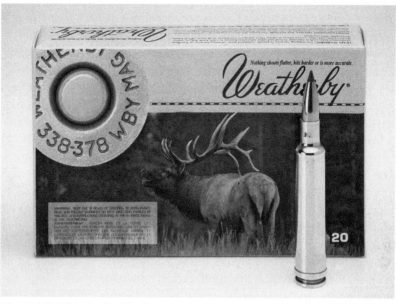

The .338-378 Weatherby, like the Lazzeroni 8.59 Titan, delivers 2¹/₂ tons of muzzle energy.

five other riflemen taking turns at the trigger of an 18-pound .338 Lapua rifle marketed by Erma. Each shooter fired five rounds at a target 1,500 meters (about 1,640 yards) distant. The aggregate 30-shot group measured only 9 inches. "It was the most accurate rifle I've ever shot," recalls Steve. "At 100 yards the bullet holes just stacked. You could hardly mike the displacement."

The most recent of the long-range headliners is the .408 CheyTac (for Cheyenne Tactical). Developed by Dr. John D. Taylor and William O. Wordman for military use, the .408 cartridge is midrange in size between the .338 Lapua and .50 BMG. Launched at 3,000 fps, its sleek 419-grain bullet maintains supersonic flight for over 2,200 yards. That bullet (and a 305-grain spitzer that can approach 3,500 fps) is a product of Idaho's Lost River Technologies, a company that began life making controlled-expansion hunting bullets. The .408's missiles are CNC lathe-turned from copper-nickel alloy. While the .338 Lapua is often described as a 1,500-yard cartridge, the .408 CheyTac crowd claims minute-of-angle accuracy to 2,500 yards for "soft target interdiction"—that's a mile and a half! The .408 CheyTac compares favorably with the .50 BMG, outpacing it in supersonic flight and delivering more energy to the target beginning at 700 yards (the .50 packs 11,200 foot-pounds at launch, compared with the .408's 7,700). CheyTac ammunition is lighter to carry: seven cartridges to a pound instead of just four. Shooters endure less recoil with the .408 as well.

Predictably, CheyTac Associates, a group of firms and individuals who contributed to the .408 project, were compelled to design a rifle to shoot it. The case, after all, is too big for ordinary rifle mechanisms. A bolt-action Target/Law Enforcement M310 features a heavy fluted barrel and an adjustable comb and bipod on a beefy synthetic stock. The Model 200 is of modular construction, with a skeleton butt and monopod and a bipod-equipped AR-style handguard up front. The Picatinny rail holds a Nightforce 5.5-22x56 NXS scope (or a Leupold Mark 4). Night-vision attachments are standard. The detachable box magazine holds five rounds. An OPSINC suppressor with mirage-busting thermal cover blankets the rifle's nose. At 55 inches and 27 pounds, the Intervention M200 Military is no woods rifle, and the carrying handle that's (properly) slung under receiver and handguard makes sense. CheyTac markets the fully equipped M200 rifle with a Kestrel 4000 sensor and a computer that helps the shooter figure out where to hold under various conditions—and not only with the .408. It includes data for other rounds of military bent, from the 5.56mm NATO to the .50 BMG.

CheyTac also builds tactical rifles on other platforms, for cartridges as petite as the .223. You can also order a CheyTac M400, an autoloading .408 with 10- and 20-round magazines. Available with both steel and carbon-fiber-sleeved barrels, it weighs $16^1/2$ pounds with the steel tube, 2 pounds less in carbon fiber.

HANDGUNS IN TALL COMPANY

Not long after the .357 Magnum cartridge appeared in 1935, sharp-shooter and fast-draw wizard Ed McGivern tested the reach of a Smith & Wesson (S&W) Model 27 revolver. From a rest, he lobbed .357 bullets into targets as far away as 600 yards. Once he learned the correct hold, he shot remarkably well. Man-size targets were sure to be perforated, though not with every shot.

Handgun hunting and long shooting with revolvers had intrigued shooters even before the .357 appeared on cartridge lists. Smith & Wesson's double-action revolvers were so favored by target shooters and law officers in the 1920s that the firm began engineering a .22 rimfire on the .38 Special frame. The K-22 Outdoorsman

Quartering elk call for heavy bullets that penetrate deep and drive straight through bone and muscle.

The longer .454 Casull predated the .480 Ruger. Background: Bullets recovered from a railroad tie.

appeared in 1930, a six-shot, 35-ounce revolver with a 6-inch barrel, checkered grips of Circassian walnut, target sights, and a crisp trigger that broke at 3 pounds. Advertised to shoot $1^1/_2$-inch groups at 50 yards, it sold as briskly as the Depression would permit. In 1939, following a production run of just 17,000, S&W overhauled the K-22, giving it a faster mechanism and micrometer rear sight. The new K-22 Masterpiece listed for $40 in 1940, just before it was dropped to accommodate wartime gun building.

A big-bore, N-frame rendition of the K-22, the .38-44 Outdoorsman, also came out in 1930 (as did a service revolver on the same frame, the .38-44 Heavy Duty). Suitable for the stiff .38 Special loads that approached the upper limits of handgun performance in that day, it featured target sights, a $6^1/_2$-inch barrel, and walnut grips. While factories continued to load the .45 Colt and .44 Special to traditional levels, Phil Sharpe urged Smith & Wesson to explore a supervelocity .38. Winchester Repeating Arms joined in the project, which resulted in a case $^1/_8$ inch longer than the .38 Special's. A hefty powder charge pushed a 158-grain bullet at over 1,200 fps—faster by a third. S&W N-frame revolvers for Winchester's new round sold for $60, complete with certificate and factory-zeroed at 200 yards. In 1938, after 5,500 revolvers and a growing backlog of orders, the company dropped the certificate as it struggled to build 120 guns per month.

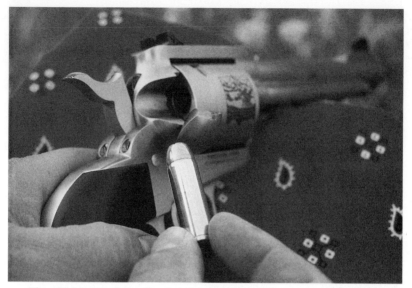

The .475 Linebaugh in a Freedom Arms revolver delivers a handful of recoil.

Meanwhile, Ed McGivern was testing the .357 beyond the range of most rifles.

Despite the new cartridge's success, the Depression shackled profits at Smith & Wesson. Then Carl Hellstrom, a consulting engineer, became the company's fifth president. Taking command in 1946, he pushed the development of new handguns. Four years later, civilian revolver sales had paid for a new 270,000-square-foot plant. About this time, Elmer Keith appeared, a short Idaho cowboy in a tall Stetson. A gun guru who lived in truly wild country, he lobbied Smith & Wesson to come up with a magnum revolver like the .357 but chambered for a .44-caliber round that would perform like the frisky handloads he'd developed in his .44 Specials. He lobbied hard for a super-velocity .44, and in 1954, Remington's R. H. Coleman brought to Smith & Wesson a new .44 round, $1/8$ inch longer than the .44 Special. The revolver to shoot it was the Model 1950, with a heavier barrel and a modified frame. The S&W Model 29 followed in 1956. It weighed 7 ounces more than the 1950 and became an immediate hit. More than 3,100 Model 29s sold in its first year on the market. Keith used it on big game, including a deer that he says took a finishing bullet at 600 yards.

Hunters have argued for decades about Keith's 600-yard shot. Was it possible? Sure. Did it occur? That doesn't matter. What's important is that the .44 Magnum gave handgunners a truly potent

The .500 Smith & Wesson X-Frame revolver dwarfs the company's .44 Magnum N-Frame.

round, one with the reach to take big animals handily at 100 yards. With cartridges like the .44 Magnum, the revolver was no longer simply a short-range gun for defensive purposes and target shooting.

When, years later, Clint Eastwood aimed his Smith & Wesson at the lens and rasped, "Go ahead, make my day," he sold more .44 Magnum pistols than the manufacturer could have done by adding a vacation package to Honolulu with each Model 29. Dirty Harry made people who had never heard of Elmer Keith aware that the grizzled gun writer's brainchild was still (after 40 years) the most powerful handgun in the world.

At the same time, Dick Casull was loading the .45 Long Colt to higher pressures than were safe in traditional single-action Colts. P. O. Ackley acknowledged the .454 Casull Magnum cartridge in 1959, the year Ruger announced Super Blackhawk revolvers in .44 Magnum and the Blackhawk in .45 Long Colt. The stout Blackhawk was a natural for the Casull. Dick replaced the six-shot cylinders with five-round versions for increased wall thickness between chambers. Not until the mid-1980s did the .454 Casull get its own revolver, a tightly fitted single-action built in the small rural town of Freedom, Wyoming. The .454 launches a 260-grain bullet at 1,800 fps, a 300-grain at 1,625. Essentially a "stretched" .45 Colt, it uses a small rifle primer to light

A scope extends the effective reach of any hunting handgun. This is a Smith & Wesson Custom Shop M629.

the fire under a .451 bullet, bigger than the .44 Magnum's .429. The .454 does not fall under SAAMI regulation, and loads can exceed 50,000 CUP. Delivering nearly twice the energy of the .44 Magnum, it is factory-loaded by Winchester with 260-grain Partition Golds and Platinum Tips, by Remington with 300-grain Core-Lokt Ultra bullets, by Federal with a 360-grain CastCore, and by Hornady with 240- and 300-grain XTPs.

Though the .454 would eventually find its way into other handguns, Freedom Arms revolvers would earn enduring respect from shooters. Still widely considered the best single-actions ever produced, they are both strong and as finely fitted as a watch. They're also incredibly accurate, as shown by their popularity among metallic silhouette competitors. "We own the line in that sport," chuckles FA president Bob Baker. "More than nine out of ten winners now shoot Freedom Arms guns."

Ruger's first handgun round, the .480 Ruger, followed the .454 Casull. The 325-grain .475 bullet is heavier than any that is commonly loaded in the Casull, but muzzle energy comes in midway between that of the .44 Magnum and .454. Here's how they stack up on the velocity and energy charts, and in tests to determine penetration. The guns were Ruger Redhawks with 7½-inch barrels. I chose Hornady ammo because the company loads all three cartridges with its XTP hollowpoint. My target was a length of railroad tie 8 inches in cross section.

Cartridge, Bullet weight (grains)	Velocity (fps)	Energy (ft-lb)	Penetration (inches)
.44 Remington Magnum, 240	1405	1110	3.5
.44 Remington Magnum, 300	1150	880	5.0
.454 Casull, 240	1800	1730	7.5
.454 Casull, 300	1585	1685	8.0+
.480 Ruger, 325	1420	1455	6.5

Chronograph speeds for some loads strayed far from catalog listings. The 300-grain .44 Magnum load matched catalog speed, but the 240-grain bullets flew 55 fps faster than the 1,350 fps claimed. Ruger's 325-grain .480 bullets bested the tables by 70 fps. At 1,800 fps, 240-grain Casull bullets clocked 100 fps shy of Hornady numbers, while 300-grain Casull loads fell 65 fps short. Those differences are significant, given the modest launch speeds of pistol bullets. These bullets lose or gain about 20 foot-pounds of energy for every 10 fps change in speed.

The heavy .44 Magnum bullets showed that weight counts for more than speed in penetration. All bullets drove deeper than I expected, with most Casull bullets exiting the railroad tie. The .480 Ruger came close to that mark, with an average penetration of more than 6 inches. The .44s punched more than halfway through the tie. To my surprise, none of the bullets showed expansion—only a slight bulge at the nose. Ballisticians tell me that as violently as hollowpoints upset in flesh, they can act like solids in wood. The cellulose delivers no hydraulic action inside the cavity. Instead, the nose is instantly plugged, while the tremendous pressure exerted by the wood surrounding the bullet keeps the jacket from rupturing.

The .454 and, to a lesser extent, the .480 Ruger and potent .475 Linebaugh have surely drained public enthusiasm for the .44 Magnum—much as magnum rifle cartridges have grabbed the spotlight from the equally useful but more shootable .30-06 and .270. Breaking through the traditional energy ceiling for handgun rounds led in 2002 to the .500 Smith & Wesson.

Handgunners shoot at a distance from the Creedmoor position. Note the pant leg protector.

S&W product manager Herb Belin and engineer Brett Curry were bent on recapturing the "most powerful" title. They ignored dimensional limits imposed by N-frame revolvers, starting from scratch to design a revolver for a .50-caliber cartridge that would hurl a 400-grain bullet as fast as the .44 Magnum launched a 240. The result: an X-frame gun with a five-shot cylinder $2^{1}/_{4}$ inches long. Its sleeved barrel features a frame-to-yoke cylinder latch, plus a muzzle cap with top porting that reduces barrel climb and felt recoil. Hogue-designed Sorbathane grips further soften the bite, as does the revolver's mass. The X-frame S&W weighs 72 ounces, 19 more than an N-frame .44 Magnum with the same $8^{3}/_{8}$-inch-long barrel.

Meanwhile, Cor-Bon was also tackling the new cartridge. Peter Pi and Terry Murbach came up with a case 1.625 inches long and three loads under a pressure lid of 48,000 psi (20 percent lower than for the .454 Casull). Their .500 Smith & Wesson pushes a 275-grain Barnes X at 1,675 fps, a 400-grain Hawk JSP at 1,650 fps, and a 440-grain hard lead cast bullet from Cast Performance at 1,625 fps. The heavy bullet delivers an astonishing 700 foot-pounds more energy than the .454 Casull, and twice as much as a .44 Magnum.

This isn't meant to demean the Casull, the .480 Ruger, or the .44 Magnum. All still qualify as big-game rounds, chambered in revolvers of modest weight and bulk. But the .500 certainly has a ballistic edge, and it's not that brutal in recoil. In fact, a 4-inch S&W 329PD with scandium frame and titanium cylinder hurts me more. This .44 Magnum scales a scant 27 ounces; the first Model 29 weighed 47 ounces.

If you want a pistol with more reach than a .44 but can't abide the bulk or heft of a .500 or have no affinity for revolvers, you'll want to investigate single-shots. Start with Thompson/Center's Contender. This now-classic pistol design came about in the mid-1960s, after Warren Center joined the K. W. Thompson Tool Company on the skirts of Rochester, New Hampshire. Barely able to keep his foundry going year-round, Ken Thompson agreed to manufacture the odd-looking handgun that had emerged from Center's basement workshop. The Contender, announced in 1967, cost more than many revolvers, but a broad choice of chamberings and easily interchangeable barrels soon endeared it to the public. Now the cartridge offerings range from .22 rimfire to .45-70, with barrel lengths from 10 to 16 inches. The most popular hunting rounds? "The .30-30, 7-30 Waters, .35 Remington, .375 Winchester, and .45-70 cap the list in the Northeast," says veteran handgunner George Dvorchak. Unabashedly fond of the T/C, he points out that it is sturdy, accurate, and versatile, "and it has a fine trigger." Compared with the best of current hunting revolvers, it is also quite affordable.

Dvorchak's pet deer round is the .338 JDJ (after J. D. Jones, who established a line of wildcat pistol rounds on the .444 Marlin case). He once killed an elk at 250 yards with a 270-grain Speer from the .375 JDJ barrel of his Contender. "With a rest, that's not too far," he says. "A pistol barrel is just as accurate as a rifle barrel, if not more so. It's stiff. In a single-shot pistol, you can use pointed bullets that shoot flat and hit hard at long range. Of course, I use a scope. My pistol is essentially a rifle without a buttstock."

The same can be said of the G2, an updated Contender that needn't be opened to reset the trigger mechanism if you lower the hammer after declining a shot. This super-accurate pistol is available in more chamberings than you could ever want. I used one of the first G2s in 6.8 SPC to take a Kentucky whitetail. That day at the range, the 10-inch-barreled 6.8mm put three shots into a $5/8$-inch group at 100 yards. Another pistol from T/C's Rochester plant is the Encore—a Contender on steroids, with more weight and bulk. Chambered for cartridges such as the .308 and .270, whose pressure lids exceed 50,000

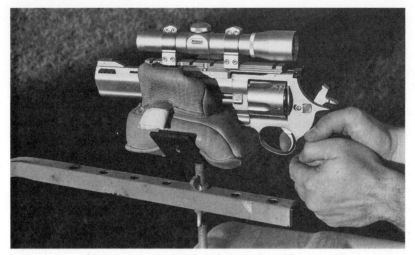

A pistol rest enables you to zero precisely at long yardage. The gun: a Taurus in .454 Casull.

psi, its lockup differs. You can interchange barrels between Contenders and G2s, but Encore barrels are unique to that mechanism.

Just before the T/C G2 appeared, Savage tapped the high-power pistol market with its bolt-action Striker pistol. Like Remington's legendary XP-100, the Striker has a midaction grip. This 5-pound gun balances nicely in the web of your hand. It features laminated or synthetic stocks and a 14-inch barrel in .223, .243, 7mm-08, or .308, as well as .22 LR, .22 WMR, and .17 HMR rimfires. Savage upped the power ante by augmenting that list with the .270, 7mm, and .300 Winchester Short Magnums. All versions come with a bipod provision, and some have an adjustable muzzlebrake. Magna-Porting (cuts in the top of the barrel) keeps the muzzle down but reduces recoil by only 20 percent or so. A brake can trim it 40 percent. At this writing, the Savage Striker has been dropped from the line—a fate that has befallen other long-range single-shot pistols. Some have returned.

Long-range pistols require much of the shooter. Recoil and blast alike draw your attention from the fundamentals of marksmanship to the anticipated violence. With no buttstock, you have no brace to counter the effect of twitching nerves and quivering muscles, no way to counteract that impulse to jerk the trigger and get the shot over with. To shoot well, you must be free to concentrate on sight alignment, says Phil Johnston, a handgun hunter of long experience. "Sight alignment means focusing your eyes on the front sight of an open-sighted handgun and aligning it in the notch of the rear sight so they are level across the top, with the same amount of light showing on both sides of the front sight. A small error in alignment shows up as wide bullet displacement at the target."

Johnston concedes, though, that open sights are for young eyes. Like Dvorchak, he pegs a practical limit for open-sighted guns at 50 yards. "Beyond that, it's hard to shoot at a spot on the animal rather than the entire animal. A 2x or 4x scope will help you reach to 100 yards. Single-shot handguns with longer barrels chambered for rifle cartridges can use more magnification. I have four long-range tack-drivers that keep five shots under half an inch at 100 yards. The best five-shot, 100-yard group that I've managed measured .385 inch, center to center. With a Burris 3-12 power variable scope, that 6mm BR Remington XP-100 has taken prairie dogs beyond 400 yards. At such range, you need a powerful scope just to see the targets."

Johnston says that trigger control is one of the most difficult of the fundamentals. "While a rough pull will move a rifle bullet out of center, jerking the trigger of a handgun will drive bullets clear off the target. The trigger squeeze must be slow and deliberate, and when the hammer drops it should all but catch you by surprise." He recommends dry firing and, at the range, having someone else occasionally load your gun for you, out of sight. "Give them the option of leaving the chamber empty. If, when you pull the trigger, the handgun recoils almost as much as if it had been loaded, you're due for more dry firing!"

Breathing matters even when you're not shooting, but you must control it carefully when pressing the trigger. Inhale deeply a couple of times as you bring the sights onto the target, then let about half the air out as you start the trigger squeeze. If your hold gets wobbly, don't hurry the shot. Start over. Rushing your cadence is bound to result in missed and crippled animals.

Bigger, more powerful cartridges have extended the limits of our range and made handguns lethal for all North American game. But as with rifles, they must be used skillfully to ensure clean kills. To shoot well is to finish a hunt successfully. Whether you play Hercules with a .500 Smith & Wesson or stay with the .44, whether you're shooting far with a .22 centerfire or fitting a big-bore barrel to your Contender, marksmanship matters more than bullet size or speed. Remember Ed McGivern's 600-yard stunts with the .357. Getting a bullet to the target is the first step in putting the target down.

After a long stalk, the author shot this pronghorn at 90 yards. For a handgun—even for this .500 Smith & Wesson—that's far enough.

WYOMING STRETCHES THE .500 S&W

Handguns built on stout bolt-action and hinged-breech frames are relatively new and, over the last 40 years, have changed the way hunters think about short barrels. Chambered for cartridges with truly long reach, short, stiff barrels can deliver tighter groups than many rifles. Of course, field results depend more on marksmanship than on load or gun design. And it isn't often that your only shot exceeds the lethal range of a revolver round, especially that of the .500 Smith & Wesson. When this muscular cartridge and a new thigh-length handgun to shoot it appeared in 2002, I was lucky enough to carry both on a wild hog hunt in Florida. The pigs, I decided, were in trouble.

Billed as the most powerful revolver in the world, the .500 S&W cartridge hurls 440-grain bullets with enough speed to register a ton and a quarter of energy at the muzzle. Oddly enough, the first thing I noted about the .500 was its understated profile. Herb Belin, whose team developed this 72-ounce revolver, managed to make it elegant. The sleeved $8^3/8$-inch barrel and full-length extractor shroud complement a cylinder that's long enough to swallow a $2^1/2$-inch cartridge, but neither makes the pistol look "stretched." The mechanism is unmistakably Smith & Wesson. Although K-frame grips would seem an odd choice, they fit this big frame as if designed for it.

Guide Pete Dube and handgunner Bill Booth zero in on distant game near Buffalo, Wyoming, on a hunt that tested the S&W .500.

The shooting in Florida was short and, at times, hectic. Thick brush, spooky pigs, and enthusiastic hounds precluded any accuracy trials at distance. Iron sights would have sufficed. The next time I holstered the .500 on a hunt was in eastern Wyoming. Pete Dube runs Bear Track Outfitters northwest of Buffalo. We'd be out on the open high plains after mule deer and pronghorns, where a scope would be a definite advantage. But affixing optics to hardware as violent as the Smith & Wesson .500 can be a challenge. Bill Booth, who represents S&W through Blue Heron Communications, told me on the way to camp that he'd had to replace all the mounts at the last minute. "The cantilevered base under our Bushnell 2-6x scope was actually flexing in recoil," he said. "So the forward end contacted the barrel. Warne got right to work and provided a base with a reinforcing block. Problem solved. We installed the new Warne base on all four guns." Those guns were mine, his, Frank Miniter's, and Tom Taylor's. Frank works as an editor at *American Hunter* magazine; Tom was then newly posted as vice president for marketing at S&W.

Wind and a touch of rain followed us to the Buffalo shooting range, where Bill and Tom sent their first shots into bull's-eyes the size of a silver dollar at 100 yards. "Good bullets," said Bill of

The author fired his S&W .500 to drop this mule deer as it rose from its bed 93 yards away.

Cor-Bon's sleek new 385-grain hollowpoints. Cor-Bon had been part of the .500 project since its inception, with three initial loads: a 275-grain Barnes X at 1,675 fps, a 400-grain Hawk JSP at 1,650, and a 440-grain hard cast bullet from Cast Performance at 1,625. The Barnes X, though lighter than the other two bullets, is also harder and has a long bearing surface. To keep pressures in check, the Barnes was throttled a bit more than would have been necessary with lead-core bullets of that weight. What you get in return is deep penetration, something to consider in a cartridge that matches the short-range ballistic performance of many rifle rounds.

The .500 Smith & Wesson as loaded by Cor-Bon generates 20 percent less breech pressure than the .454 Casull, but recoil depends mainly on bullet weight and speed. The 440's kick borders on brutal; however, the other two initial loads are surprisingly manageable in the heavy pistol. The 385 HP has a long ogive for flat flight and is, to my mind, the best game bullet—heavy enough to drive deep, but with the legs for kills beyond 200 yards (not that I'd attempt one that far; the accurate reach of this cartridge far exceeds my own!).

"The secret to good shooting with this gun is a high grip," said Bill, coaching me at the bench after Frank had centered a two-minute group. "You'll also absorb recoil better with the web of your hand well up toward the hammer." My first bullet landed at 6 o'clock, the next at 3. I fired another at 7. The fourth drilled the middle, and a fifth struck nearly 3 inches out at 8. I felt like a rookie. Then as my gun cooled, Bill nailed a steel chicken at 160 yards. Oh well, someone has to ride drag. I slunk to the far end of the line, paid attention to my grip, and squeezed off two more cylinders, adding eight clicks of elevation. My last four shots printed a 2-inch group, the final pair in one hole. Good enough.

Bill and I teamed up with guide Mark Kirby to hunt a series of hills creased with deciduous brush and studded here and there with pines. I stalked an old buck, circling a ridge to get the wind, then padding down deer trails through a suburb of beds to intercept. The plan worked. At 120 yards, I poked my daypack ahead of me and bellied into position behind it. But in a classic display of sixth sense, the buck stopped ambling toward me. He paused, seemingly lost in thought. Then he turned away and fed into a draw. Two junior bucks with him remained on my ridge, obviously puzzled. Illogical behavior helps deer grow old.

We saw lots of other bucks that morning, some with tempting antlers. At midday, Bill spied a fine deer bedded in scattered pines well up on a knob. Glassing to plan a stalk, I was astonished to find him in the center of a herd of does. His neck was swollen too. Early in October, we had expected bucks to hang out by themselves or in bachelor groups; rut was a month off.

Mark and I lost no time looping to skirt the knob. We climbed a finger ridge crosswind and peeked over the crest. Presently I found pieces of deer in my 8x32 Pentax. Then Mark whispered, "Buck!" The animal had stood up, exposing himself through a gap in the pines. But all I could make out were antler tines. Mark rolled to the side as I squirmed to his spot and pushed my pack under the extended .500. I guessed the range at 95 yards. When the crosswire quivered to a near standstill tight behind the deer's shoulder, I pressed the trigger. Boom! Recoil obscured the slope, but the hit was audible. As deer squirted from the pines, I saw the great buck lunge, recover, then tumble down the steep grade, trailing dust and rubble. He tried once again to regain his footing but failed. He was dead when we reached him. The Cor-Bon hollowpoint had struck exactly where I had aimed,

In Florida a year before the Wyoming hunt, the author tested the S&W .500 on wild pigs.

Bill Booth shows the form that enabled him to shoot a mule deer at 200 yards with his .500, the first x-frame Smith & Wesson revolver.

scrambled the lungs, and exited. No rifle bullet would have killed more surely. Mark's Bushnell rangefinder pegged the shot distance at 94 yards.

Over thick pork chops at camp that night, Frank sheepishly showed us a bandaged hand. He had sneaked to within 170 yards of a dandy pronghorn buck, taken a rest, and made a fine shot. The stricken buck ran, and when Frank shifted position to fire again, he unwittingly loosened his grip on the .500. Recoil from the next shot brought the hammer back into his hand, giving a Buffalo intern some stitching practice. "It's a lesson I'll remember," Frank grinned ruefully.

The next morning, Bill was on the docket, and Pete took over as our guide. But hours of hard glassing brought little in the way of antlers. We broke the spell by leaving to ogle antelope in another hunting unit. Returning to mule deer country, Pete spied an outstanding buck at the hem of a deep draw, but the animal had seen us and trotted off before we could think about closing the distance. We watched it cross a sage flat and slip into another draw. After circling to catch the wind, we eased into the mouth of that ravine.

"Pssst!" Pete, up front, ducked and pointed. We backed down, then eased to a sage-covered knoll and peeked over. A four-point buck lay in the sun next to a rock overhang. "A hundred yards," said Pete. Bill nodded as he drew the .500 from its DiSautis shoulder holster. Squirming forward to the knoll's crest, he steadied the revolver over his pack. Then Pete said what we were all thinking: "It's not the big buck. This one's chewing his cud and lying in the sun. That deer's been in bed since the rock shaded him."

We backed out, then moved slowly up the draw, confident that the deer we wanted was still ahead of us. Had he blown out the bottom, he'd have taken with him the deer we'd just passed—as well as the two bucks we soon spotted asleep under the lip of the ravine. We gave them space and climbed. "Nuts!" The thump of hooves was bad news. Pete saw the big buck only after it rocketed from the draw. We watched in exasperation as it raced across a sage flat, then melted into the earth a mile away.

Seemingly jinxed, we shuffled to the truck, then motored to find pronghorns. Our luck improved. In the shadow of a bluff we spotted a sprawling herd. Two hours later, with a red sun setting directly behind me, I bellied to a small bush in the antelopes' path. We had trailed them for more than a mile, and I had bungled a long shot at the only buck. Now the cross-wire steadied as that buck quartered to me. I milked the last ounce from the trigger, heard the explosion, and felt the big gun lift through a shower of sage leaves. Thwuck! My pronghorn hunt was over.

But Bill's deer quest was not, despite the failing light. Easing out of the valley between two bluffs, we spotted a fine four-point buck, statue-still 200 yards crosswind. "I can make that shot if he'll give me a moment," said Bill, matter-of-factly. "He's not going anywhere," whispered Pete. Twilight had come, and with it that sense of security deer show in alfalfa fields beside highways. This buck watched as Bill lowered himself to a sit, bracing his back. Several times he adjusted his position, clamping his knee with his wrists. When at last he fired, it was double-action, the long, smooth pull keeping the gun on target. "I shoot as well or better that way," Bill said, "especially with stiff-recoiling guns. There's no static resistance to leave you pressing ever harder, anticipating a sudden break. I don't jerk with a double-action pull." The Smith boomed. The sound of the strike reached us as the deer collapsed into the grass. A fine shot, it demonstrated not only the .500's reach and power but also Bill's skill with a handgun.

Tom finished out our week with a 90-yard last-day shot after slipping up on a bedded buck from below. "I'd like to have seen more of the ribs behind the curve of that hill. Luckily, the shot was perfect."

Smith & Wesson followed the original .500 with a shorter version. Although a 4-inch barrel is handy, the muzzle porting that mitigates recoil makes even more noise on the short tube. Ear protection is a must with both .500s. I used soft plugs plus muffs at the bench and soft plugs in the field (a good idea even with lesser handguns). The 8^3/8-inch barrel is my pick for this pistol, because it delivers higher bullet speeds and puts the blast farther from my face. The greater inertia at the muzzle helps with aiming and recovery.

You'd think that after letting 46 years pass between the introduction of the .44 Magnum and the debut of the .500, Smith & Wesson might take a breather before fielding another high-performance round. Not so. In fact, development of another cartridge for the X-Frame revolver was under way before the .500 had even made its way into the firearms press. The .460 XVR appeared in 2004, chambered, five to a cylinder in the 8^3/8-inch S&W revolver I had used with its .50-caliber cousin. Featuring a case even longer than that of the .500, the .460 was initially offered with five loads. These velocities are experimental, recorded over Oehler chronograph screens and published by Wiley Clapp in *Guns & Ammo* magazine (August 2004).

Hornady 200-grain SST: 2,211 fps
Cor-Bon 200-grain Barnes X: 2,291 fps
Cor-Bon 250-grain Barnes X: 1,821 fps
Cor-Bon 325-grain A-Frame: 1,591 fps
Cor-Bon 395-grain Hard Cast: 1,511 fps

Hornady's 200-grain SST reaches 100 yards clocking 1,772 fps and packing 1,395 foot-pounds of energy; at 200 yards, it registers 1,373 fps and 837 foot-pounds. Sight in to hit 3 inches high at 100 yards, and you're just 3.8 inches low at 200 yards. Both the Hornady and Barnes bullets have a long ogive and pointed nose, so they fly much flatter than most pistol bullets. With launch speeds that match a .30-30's, they offer reach previously found only in handguns with a fixed breech and rifle chamberings.

Another distinctive feature of this 73-ounce revolver is its gain-twist rifling. That is, rifling pitch at the throat is 1:100, or a slow one turn in 100 inches of forward travel. But the pitch steepens to 1:20 at the muzzle, a more appropriate rate for a pointed or long-shanked handgun bullet. The reason for gain twist? It allows the bullet a gentle start in rotation. A nonrotating bullet suddenly forced to spin once every 20 inches of forward travel (or, put another way, spun on steel rails to 1,400 rpm) undergoes a great deal of stress. The jacket can tear, and the lead core can suffer deformation. Pressures rise because rifling not only imparts friction but also imposes a brake as the lands cut across the path of travel.

Gain-twist rifling is nothing new, but it was costly to produce in the nineteenth century, and experiments with rifles failed to show better accuracy than rifling with uniform twist. As new revolver cartridges pushed pressure ceilings ever higher, gain twist got less attention than did load refinement in keeping frames and cylinders intact. Changes in ammunition are far easier to make than a switch to gain-twist rifling. And load experiments are easier to conduct than rifling trials.

For revolver aficionados, the .460 XVR offers a big long-range advantage over traditional rounds, even the most powerful. It is more comfortable to shoot than the .500 S&W, and you can zero for 200 yards without fearing a miss high at midrange. There's plenty of killing energy for deer-size game as far from the muzzle as most hunters can print Frisbee-size groups from a rest. With heavy bullets, the .460 hits as hard as a .45-70 handloaded for modern lever rifles. Elk are fair game.

Several loads are available for the .500 S&W. This Winchester offering is among the best.

I thought about such prospects as we skidded Bill's deer off that Wyoming knob. Dusk had settled on the high plains, blackening the horizon under a purple sky. You could say that the handguns made this hunt special, but that's not true. Hardware comes off the S&W line every day. But each sunrise happens only once. The leaves and creek water fall only once. People age and drift away. Whatever guns and cartridges make the news, they will never be remembered as fondly as the stories of their days afield.

8 Sights and Sighting

Foolproof, streamlined scope with windage and elevation adjustments built into the mount. . . . Factory sealed with nitrogen, changes in altitude or temperature cannot cause condensation or fogging. Nothing to get out of order . . . made to last a lifetime.

—ad for the Leupold Pioneer, circa 1950

SCOPE FEATURES THAT COUNT

You can shoot only as well as you can aim, and you can aim only as well as you can see. Optical sights help you see farther and in greater detail, but they can cost as much as your rifle. To get the most for your optics dollar, it's a good idea to find out what really matters in a scope.

As with spotting scopes and binoculars, you're smart to insist on fully multicoated lenses (every glass surface treated with several microscopically thin layers of compounds to limit light loss across a spectrum of wavelengths). Beyond that, any modern rifle scope will deliver a sight picture bright enough and sharp enough for hunting. If you anticipate long shooting, you'll want more scope power. And if you anticipate shooting in dim light, a big objective lens makes sense, to counter the light-throttling effect of magnification. You'll find that an adjustable objective (AO) lens delivers sharper focus while eliminating parallax at the shot distance you specify. It's a must, in my view, at magnifications higher than 8x. Incidentally, AO dials mounted on the turret are handier than traditional AO sleeves on the objective bell.

Scope tube diameters have grown since the World War II era, when snipers used sights with $7/8$-inch tubes. The Noske and Lyman Alaskan, among others, sufficed as compact, low-magnification scopes for hunters who'd teethed on iron sights. During the 1950s and

Adirondack Optics makes SmartScope; an internal digital camera snaps a photo at the shot or can be used as an ordinary camera, viewfinding through the scope.

1960s, the 1-inch tube became standard issue in the United States, while 26mm scopes (1 inch is 25.6 mm) held sway in Europe. Now there are many sights with 30mm tubes, and Schmidt & Bender catalogs a 34mm series. Do the big tubes give you a better picture? Only if they're matched with bigger lenses in the erector assembly. Commonly, erector units designed for 1-inch tubes are placed in 30mm housings, for no optical benefit. Remember that exit pupil (the point at which light rays form a magnified, circular image) is determined by the diameter of the objective lens, not by internal lenses. The only advantage of an oversize tunnel with standard erector elements is the extra room inside, so you have greater latitude in adjusting windage and elevation. The 30mm scopes are stronger, all things being equal, but in my experience, 1-inch tubes are more than stout enough. Of course, some big tubes are fitted with big erector lenses, which deliver an optical edge. Before you pay extra for a 30mm sight and additional bulk, however, assess the true benefits of that particular scope.

The same caveat applies to front lenses the diameter of manhole covers. Yes, they boost the exit pupil diameter and, consequently, light transmission. But they come into play only in dim conditions

The author adjusts elevation on a Nightforce scope. Adjustments should be crisp and predictable.

and at high magnification. A scope with a 40mm objective lens has all the brightness you're likely to need, even if you're peering into a shaded meadow fringe at dusk. That's because at 8x (high magnification by most standards), it still delivers a 5mm exit pupil. Long-range specialists shooting at 10x or higher power might want a 50mm lens. European hunters who wait for wild pigs over bait at night commonly favor 8x56 glass because under those conditions the human eye is fully dilated. The extra weight of such sights is no liability if you're sitting on a platform, but it's a problem if you hike the hills to find game. Additional bulk defies both easy trail carry and rifle scabbards. Big front glass mandates high rings that coax your cheek off the stock.

Fog-proofing has become standard treatment for rifle scopes (it's accomplished by evacuating the air inside and replacing it with nitrogen or argon gas). Waterproofing isn't universal, so you might want to check that specification if you routinely drop your gear in streams. Waterproof or not, most optics worthy of a hunter's consideration are so tightly sealed that rain, snow, and even the occasional dunk won't

This Shepherd scope is a range-compensating sight with reticles in both fore and aft focal planes.

affect them. Fogging or water on the exterior lens surfaces is actually a more common problem. When you shoulder that rifle in cold weather, try not to exhale into the scope's eyepiece. Rain is best kept off outside glass, but if you're still-hunting during a drizzle or get caught in a downpour, you may find new coatings a real blessing. Bushnell pioneered RainGuard, a hydrophobic sheath that beads water, giving you a clearer sight picture. Leupold's answer is a hydrophilic coating that causes water to sheet, for a similar result.

A rangefinding or range-compensating reticle helps you hit at a distance. The simplest comprise two horizontal stadia wires. The space between them subtends a specified measure at a given range. Stadia wires might, for example, subtend the 16-inch depth of a big buck's chest at 100 yards. If a buck fills half the space, he is roughly 200 yards off. An ordinary plex reticle without stadia wires can help in the same way. Just bracket the target between the intersection and the top of the bottom post. Of course, you have to measure the subtended distance before the season, marking a paper target at 100 yards. Most variable scopes sold in the United States feature reticles in the rear focal plane, so the subtended target changes as you change power. Reticles in the front focal plane (popular in Europe) change apparent size with power shift but stay in constant relationship with the target, so the subtended target measures the same at all magnifications. The European system thus makes rangefinding easy because you needn't stick to one power setting on your scope. Most hunters Stateside like the rear-plane reticle, however, because it covers less of the target at high power, allowing for greater precision, and it is easy to see at low power, when you must take fast aim at a deer close up. Front-plane reticles get skinny at low magnification and thick when you crank the power up, just the opposite of what you want.

Redfield once had a rangefinding reticle designed to read accurately at any power. You bracketed the deer between the stadia wires by changing power, then read the range on a vertical scale at the bottom of the scope field. Shepherd scopes have two reticles, one in the front focal plane and one in the rear. They are superimposed, appearing as one. You get an aiming reticle that doesn't change size, but a rangefinding reticle (a series of circles that does not interfere with the aiming reticle) that changes size with power—the best of both worlds. Shepherd thoughtfully packages this sophisticated reticle and high magnification in a sleek tube with a 40mm objective so that you can use low rings.

In an all-around scope, look for adequate field of view. Your chance may come up close, quickly.

This Leupold 3.5-10x Long Range Tactical scope is one of an extensive line for hunters and snipers.

Leupold® Mark 4®
3.5-10x40mm LR/T™ M1
Front Focal

Another range-compensating scope is the Leatherwood ART (Auto-Ranging Telescope). This sight got its field baptism largely on sniper rifles, but the company has since marketed sporting models under the Leatherwood Hi-Lux Optics brand. The M1200 features the trademark cam at the rear of the scope where it engages the special mount. Fit an 18-inch target between stadia wires by adjusting the magnification, then shoot. The 6-24x50 scope automatically ranges the target and adjusts scope angle (zero) from 300 to 1,200 meters. Of course, your bullet must track a predetermined trajectory for the scope to place each shot in the middle. The M1200 is predictably calibrated for flat-shooting rifles, but it will work for most hunting-weight spitzers launched above 3,000 fps. An M600 3-9x40 adjusts to bring bullets to point of aim to 600 meters.

Long ago I had a scope with a "lollipop" reticle—two circles that looked like a bull's-eye in the middle. It would have worked well for ranging targets.

Scopes without compensating mechanisms can incorporate stadia wires. On some, the stadia serve as alternative aiming points. The Ballistic Plex by Burris includes three hash marks on the 6 o'clock section

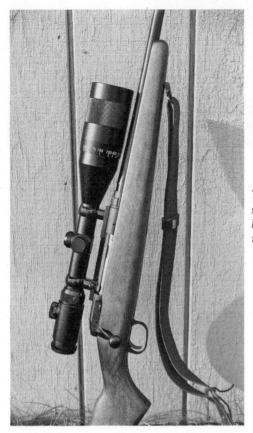

The big bell on this Nightforce sight gives a brighter picture at high magnification, but adds weight and bulk.

of the Plex reticle. Each gap between the marks is incrementally bigger than the one above it, so you get four subtended measures at any magnification. The differential spacing of the tics reflects the parabolic trajectory of bullets. If you zero at 100 yards with a 180-grain .308 bullet, you'll hit at the first hash mark (3 inches low) at 200 yards, the second mark (13 inches low) at 300 yards, and the third tic (30 inches low) at 400 yards. At 500 yards, the bullet strikes near the top of the bottom post. Faster bullets zeroed at 200 yards hit near the center wire to 250 yards. At 300 yards, your bullet will land about 5 inches low, or close to the first hash mark. At 400 yards, it will strike near the second mark, 18 inches low. The third tic serves as an aiming point at 500 yards (-38 inches). You'll hit 66 inches below center at 600 yards, at the top of the Plex post. The TDS Tri-Factor reticle on Swarovski scopes is similar to the Ballistic Plex. I've used the Burris reticle for

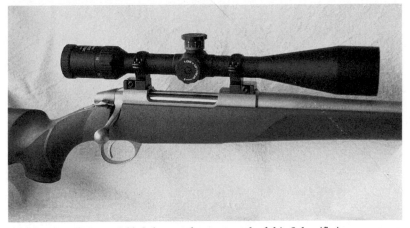

A high-power Zeiss variable helps tap the great reach of this Sako rifle in .300 Weatherby.

long-range target shooting and to take a fine pronghorn buck at 394 paces. I like its simplicity and efficiency.

The mildot reticle gets a lot of attention these days. *Mil* is an abbreviation for milliradian, $\frac{1}{6400}$ of a degree in angular measurement—that's 3.6 inches at 100 yards, or 3 feet at 1,000 yards. In a reticle, a mil is the space between $\frac{3}{4}$-minute dots strung vertically and horizontally along an otherwise normal crosswire. To employ this reticle as a rangefinder, divide target height in mils at 100 yards by the number of spaces subtending it. The result is range in hundreds of yards. For example, a deer 3 feet at the shoulder (10 mils at 100 yards) appears to stand two dots high in your scope. Divide 2 into 10, and you get 5; so the buck is 500 yards away. You can also divide target size in yards (in this case, 1) by the number of mils subtended (2) and multiply by 1,000 to get range in yards. The mildot reticle must be calibrated for a single magnification. In variable scopes, that's usually the top magnification or 10x, but some sights with very high magnification are calibrated at other power settings. After a bit of practice, the mildot is easy to use. In it, you have both a rangefinder and a way to compensate for holdover and wind drift. For short shots, just ignore the dots and use the reticle as a crosswire.

Mildot Master is a slide rule-like device (an analog calculator) with an instruction booklet that makes sense of what you see in your scope and helps you use mildots more effectively to ranges of 1,000 yards. It's available from Mildot Enterprises (P.O. Box 1535, Los

Scope covers, as on this Texas hunter's Burris, shield lenses from dust and rain. The rifle: a Ruger Number One.

Lunas, NM 87031) and from Lou Schwiebert (800-378-2174, or ballisti-cards.com), who also markets his own long-range shooting aid, Ballisti-card. This is essentially a pocket-size ballistics table for your favorite hunting or target load. You specify the bullet you're using and how fast it leaves the rifle, and Schwiebert's sophisticated computer pro-gram provides you with an all-weather laminated 3- by 5-inch card with the data you need for long-range hits. A three-card set has red, blue, and green headings: The green card contains baseline data; the red card covers the same bullet shot 100 fps faster, as might be the case if you hunted in very hot weather; and the blue card shows flight for that bullet pushed 100 fps slower, such as in cold weather. Ballisti-cards give you bullet drop (and quarter-minute clicks to compensate) at 50-yard intervals from 0 to 500 yards. There are also wind drift data and corrections for vertical shot angles of 15, 30, and 45 degrees, as well as lead values for running game. Ballisticard information is rou-tinely tested by Schwiebert's clients, some of whom are engaged as military snipers. "Hunters may not have time to consult even a sim-ple card when they see game," says Schwiebert. "But on stand they can prepare for a shot by ranging objects where game might appear and by doping wind. That's how tactical shooters operate." I have Ballisticards for a couple of loads, and I am impressed. Schwiebert can factor in the effects of elevation, temperature, and humidity where you hunt. A Ballisticard (with duplicate) costs about $30.

A most sophisticated and complex reticle was designed for the Marine Corps by Dennis Sammut. It comprises a crosswire with calibrated hash marks above, below, and to the sides of the intersection about a third of the way to the edge of the field. There are 13 crossbars on the lower wire. These vary in length and are themselves hash-marked and have mildots. In the upper left quadrant is a rangefinding grid with stadia wires for more precise rangefinding. On windy days, hold off using a tic on a horizontal wire as your aiming point. Horizontal wires are longer near the bottom of the field because as range increases and you elevate, you get more drift. Using the Sammut reticle in Schmidt & Bender scopes, shooters have claimed kills on vermin at ranges exceeding 1,100 yards. Besides helping you estimate range and maintain proper holdover; its multiple horizontal lines with hash marks enable you to correct for 90-degree winds to 30 mph. Also, you can quickly adjust after an errant first shot by using bullet impact as a grid marker and the subsequent aiming point. I mounted one of these sights on my Savage 110 tactical rifle in .300 Winchester and was soon planting 185-grain Berger Match bullets near target centers 700 yards away. But it's not a reticle for quick shooting. It makes you feel like an artilleryman.

Tactical reticles and tactical sights have earned a following among North American shooters who want to stretch their range. Markus Schwarz of the Austrian optics firm Kahles defined a tactical sight as one distinguished by (1) a matte or parkerized finish, (2) a mildot reticle, (3) a bullet drop compensating device that can be set for any given load, and (4) the sturdiness to meet demanding military specifications. Although some hunting scopes meet those requirements, companies marketing tactical optics are careful to separate them from hunting scope lines. At the same time, tactical scopes are getting more exposure. The prestigious German optics company Schmidt & Bender (S&B) markets a Police/Marksman line that includes a 10x42 fixed-power scope and several variables. The 3-12x50MIL has a steel tube (the others are alloy; all are 30mm). The MIL model is designed for shooting to 1,000 yards, as the bullet drop compensator shows. Quarter-minute clicks are standard on all but the MIL, which features half-minute windage increments and full-minute elevation clicks.

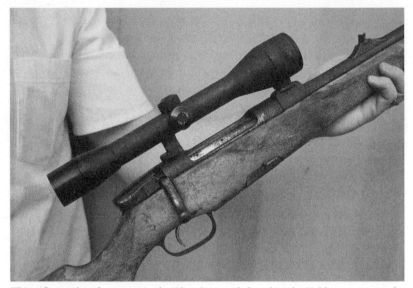

This rifle was lost for a year in the Alps. It rusted shut, but the Kahles scope stayed bright and fog free.

Each scope comes with two elevation rings: a neutral ring that lets you record settings for your particular load, plus a ring already calibrated for the 168-grain .308 Match load used in so many tactical rifles. The 1.5-6x gets a different ring for a 150-grain .308 load. There's also an S&B Precision Hunter series comprising a 2.5-10x56, a 3-12x50, and a 4-16x50. This line features 30mm tubes and bullet drop compensators (side mounted, like the 4-16x P/M). Schmidt & Bender offers custom-calibrated elevation adjustment rings for its tactical and Precision Hunter scopes.

It's noteworthy that tactical sights have traditionally been simple affairs—though electronics have become more accepted. Reliability is imperative in a tactical sight, and hunters would do well to make it a priority too. Remember that additional features can mean additional failures. Lighted reticles increase the weight and bulk of a scope, and they have little application on most hunts. High target knobs are prone to damage afield. Low-profile resettable knobs, in contrast, enable you to chase conditions but at the end of the day return to your original setting without fuss. They also bring you back home if you're using multiple loads with different points of impact. In 2005 Kahles got ambitious with an elevation mechanism that employs a

For quick adjustments to 1,000 yards, Leupold offers 1-minute elevation clicks in Mark 4 scopes.

Whether on helical threads or fine-threaded with a lock ring, the eyepiece adjusts reticle focus.

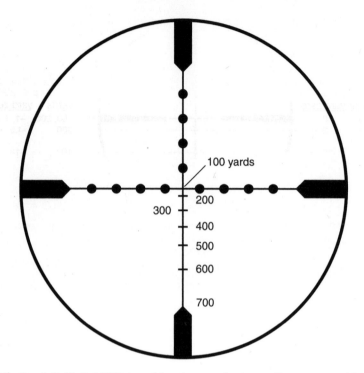

The Burris Ballistic Mil Dot combines two popular types of long-range reticles.

miniature clutch and mechanical memory so that you can register and return instantly to as many as five zeros. The unit is compact but costly. Sunshades can be useful on the front of a scope, and in 2004 Leupold announced a line of screw-on filters, much as you'd use on a camera lens, to fit late-model Leupolds. A clear filter has the firm's proprietary water-sheeting coating for use in rainy weather.

Leupold should know what's necessary in a scope. The Beaverton, Oregon, company has served surveyors, sportsmen, and military units for a century. The Mark 4 tactical scope series includes 10x and 16x scopes with 40mm objectives and a 10x40 M3 whose elevation knob incorporates a bullet drop compensator. The dial is calibrated to track bullet drop to 700 meters (1,000 on some models) with specific loads. One turn of the dial gives you enough elevation to bring you from 100 to 1,000 yards in one-minute increments. Windage graduations on the M3 turret are half-minute intervals. The two M1 models have target knobs with quarter-minute clicks. All Mark 4s feature 30mm alloy tubes and side-mounted parallax adjustments. You can

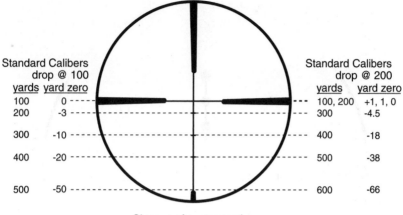

Standard Calibers drop @ 100 yards	yard zero		Standard Calibers drop @ 200 yards	yard zero
100	0		100, 200	+1, 1, 0
200	-3		300	-4.5
300	-10		400	-18
400	-20		500	-38
500	-50		600	-66

Closeup of center section

For hunters, the Burris Ballistic Plex and Swarovski's similar TDS reticle offer easy aim far away.

choose a mildot, target dot, or duplex reticle. Mark 4 scopes (called Ultra sights before 1990) have extra-thick walls to meet stricter durability standards.

Leupold also makes an LR/T (Long Range/Tactical) series that includes 3.5-10x40, 4.5-14x50, 6.5-20x50, and 8.5-25x50 variables. These scopes feature 1-inch alloy tubes and M1 target-style adjustment knobs. "Long Range scopes have 30mm tubes," explains Garth Kendig from Leupold's Technical Services branch. "That means they have about 30 percent more adjustment than in traditional scopes. For example, a standard 3.5-10x Vari-X III has 50 minutes of windage and elevation, but the Long Range model has 65 minutes. You can click up to longer distances. That's the main advantage of a Long Range scope: You don't have to hold over. Even beyond 500 yards, adjustment latitude helps more than does high magnification."

Kendig emphasizes the importance of shooting to familiarize yourself with any reticle you'll use as a rangefinder and advises that you verify bullet drop compensator numbers on targets. "Your rifle and loads may not match the data used to make the dial. We offer four dials for the M3 turret, each for a different trajectory. All are calibrated for sea-level shooting in 59-degree temperatures."

He adds that, besides servicing hunters, Leupold has outfitted police forces with its 3.5-10x40 scopes since the mid-1970s. Leupold later worked with the U.S. Army to develop a 10x scope now used by

An archetypal big-game scope in the West: Leupold's 3-9x40, here on a Mauser in .358 Norma.

the navy SEALs. The army incorporates 10x Leupolds in its Model 24 tactical outfit: a Remington 700 with an H-S Precision stock and Harris bipod.

Soldiers and big-game hunters can seldom use to advantage higher magnification than 10x, but if you're shooting prairie dogs or setting up across an 80-acre field from a deer trail that may give you just a piece of shoulder as a target, more power might help. But before you buy the biggest scope on the shelf, think about your shooting position, not just target size and distance. A 16x sight is all I can manage from hunting positions. That's because more magnification shows me all the little dips and swings of the reticle, movements I can't do anything about. You need to monitor the wanderings of your reticle so that you can shift position slightly to minimize them and keep them centered, but watching the gyrations caused by muscle twitch and pulse beat can impair your shooting. You subconsciously try to correct for wobbles too fast to anticipate; you try to wait out movements that never stop. You tire. The best moment for the shot comes and goes, and you're still working on the sight picture. High magnification delivers more mirage than you want on a hot day, too, obscuring your target. You want to be able to read the mirage, but you don't want targets drowning in it. Finally, scopes of very high power give you tiny fields of view. That means you'll spend more time finding targets and less time shooting. On a hillside showing

Before Alumina RainCote   After Alumina RainCote

Leupold® Alumina™ RainCote™

Leupold's various screw-in lens filters sheet water, add contrast, and change color emphasis.

many patches of yellow dirt, getting your reticle on the one that your partner said is hiding a sodpoodle can be frustrating.

For my money, the best scopes for all-around shooting at long range are variables, from 4x to 6.5x on the low end and 14x to 24x on the high end. A 5-15x Zeiss I used a few years ago combined an ideal power range with top-drawer glass in a relatively slim, lightweight package. If you're shooting from a bench, you might enjoy a 20x or 24x sight on clear, cool days. But you must have a steady hand to join the Metallic Silhouette shooters who use such sights standing. Even from a rest, magnification above 16x may not tighten groups unless the target is too small to see clearly at lower power. As with competitors who put bullets into melon-size groups at 1,000 yards with iron sights, if your sight picture is good, your shot will be too. Of course, target dimensions become more important at low power. One of the smallest groups I've fired with a hunting rifle came from a superaccurate Echols .375 and a 3x scope. It measured less than 0.2 inch.

Marksmen keen to make every shot count at long range insist on the best optics. Tactical scopes have nothing on the best sights designed for hunters, such as the Zeiss VM/V 6-24. This superb sight and high-power scopes by Swarovski and Nikon give you target images that Civil War snipers peering through dim, barrel-length

This Heym rifle in .270 is near zero at 200 yards. Next step: Find impact points at 300 and 400 yards.

tubes never dreamed of. Weaver's T-Series and long-range scopes from Sightron deliver fine value for the money. But you cannot buy the steady position and the disciplined trigger squeeze that makes each shot a center hit. Nor can you inherit an accurate read of the wind or a spot-on range estimate. Anyone can fire a bullet, just as anyone can slap paint on canvas. Gifted artists are few, and riflemen with polished long-range skills and the judgment to take only sure shots are rarer still.

THE LONG ZERO

I hit the buck twice through the forward ribs and just clipped vitals with a third bullet. It was a paper deer, and the holes were clearly visible. At 400 yards from prone, I'd like to have done better; but now I was sure of my zero—my hunting zero.

"You'll get tighter groups from a bench," said my friend.

"Not much tighter," I shrugged. "And the bullets will likely land in a different place."

Every rifle must, of course, be zeroed before you can hit with it. That's because a set of sights or a scope placed on the barrel is only roughly aligned with it. If you aimed at a distant target and fired without zeroing, only by sheer chance would your bullet strike close to the mark. Zeroing involves adjusting the scope so that your line of sight intersects the bullet's arc at a specific point—the zero range.

If bullets shot flat, all you'd have to do would be bring the line of sight almost parallel to the line of bore. By adjusting the scope to bring your aim to the point of bullet impact at, say, 500 yards, you'd hit very close to center out to the limits of your vision. If the scope's optical axis was $1^1/2$ inches above the line of bore—again, assuming that bullets shot flat—you'd hit closer to the point of aim as distance increased, out to 500 yards. You'd hit $1^1/2$ inches low at 1,000 yards.

But bullets don't shoot flat, not even for 1 yard. As soon as a bullet exits the muzzle it starts to drop at an accelerating rate of about 32 fps. After a full second in flight, a bullet would strike 32 feet below where the barrel is pointing. Of course, bullets seldom stay aloft for a full second. A 100-grain .25-06 bullet started at 3,150 fps will strike a deer 250 yards away in a quarter second, given deceleration that brings average velocity to 3,000 fps. During that quarter second, the bullet drops 3 feet (not 8 feet, because gravity has an accelerating effect, and the bullet drops several times as far in the last quarter of the first second as in the first quarter). A slower bullet drops the same distance during the same time; it just doesn't cover as much ground laterally. For example, if your 165-grain .300 Savage bullet clocks an average 2,400 fps over its first 200 yards, after a quarter second of travel, it would pass the 200-yard mark—3 feet below the bore line. Delay the bullet, and drop will increase at any range. Speed up the bullet, and it will stay closer to the bore line longer. Bullet speed doesn't affect gravity, but it does figure into a bullet's arc. It is true that if you dropped a bullet from your hand and simultaneously fired an identical bullet parallel to flat ground from a rifle the same distance above the ground, the two bullets would come to earth at nearly the same time, though far apart.

It's a common misconception that a bullet rises above the line of bore during its flight. It does not. It cannot—ever. The sight line is not parallel to the bore line, but at a slight converging angle. The line of sight dips below the bore line and the bullet's arc. Sight line and bore line never meet again, because both are straight. They cross and forever get farther apart. A bullet hits above the sight line at midrange, but only because the sight line has been purposefully angled down through its trajectory. The bullet falls back into the line of sight at greater range. If the sight line were parallel with the bore, it would

Danny O'Connell adjusts elevation on a Nightforce scope. Rifle: a Dakota Predator in .20 Tactical.

High magnification tightens groups, but how much depends on the target and conditions. Check zero with the power you'll use most.

never touch the bullet's arc. Sighting in or zeroing a rifle is simply adjusting the sights so that you are looking where the bullet hits. Zero range is the place at which the bullet crosses the line of sight the second time. You cannot change the impact point of the bullet relative to the bore (except by changing loads), but you can change the line of sight so that it intersects the trajectory at any range you choose. Of course, you must also adjust windage in the sight to ensure that the bullet doesn't strike to the side of where you're looking.

Zero range is not point-blank range. Shooting point-blank is shooting with no compensation for a bullet's trajectory. Point-blank range is so close to the rifle that there's no appreciable bullet drop, or it is close enough and at big enough targets that trajectory is of no concern. When hunting big game, you can ignore small differences between point of aim and point of impact because the animal's vitals may be the size of a large pumpkin. If you're willing to ignore a 3-inch deviation, a 200-yard zero will give your .30-06 a point-blank range of 250 yards or so, depending on the load. Maximum point-blank range is the distance at which your bullet falls so far below the line of sight that you must start compensating with a change in hold.

It's hard to overestimate what gravity does to any bullet at extreme range. A 168-grain .30 match bullet battles wind and gravity better than most pointed softpoints. Fired from a .30-06 zeroed at 200 yards, it still strikes 7 inches low at 300 yards. But at 600 yards, it lands more than 70 inches below the point of aim. If you think high velocity will pull your fat from the fire, note that the same sleek bullet driven at a scorching 3,300 fps from a .30 Magnum falls just over 5 inches at 300 yards and 10 times that far at 600 yards. That's better, but hardly as flat as a light beam. At 1,000 yards, the .30-06 load prints 328 inches (27 feet) low, and the .30 Magnum load 242 inches (20 feet) low. So much for those campfire champs who claim that they topple game routinely at half a mile by holding dead-on.

Hunting rifles with 200-yard zeros wouldn't do well at a 1,000-yard match because shooters would have to aim several feet over the target frame. There's too little elevation adjustment in many scopes to get a 1,000-yard zero. If you could crank in enough lift to achieve a 600-yard zero, you'd still have to aim 17 feet high to hit the bull's-eye with a .30-06 at 1,000 yards. Of course, a long-range zero comes with severe midrange penalties. The 600-yard zero would put bullets 2^1/$_2$ feet high at 300 yards!

Zeroing is an easy job, but it's also an easy job to bungle. Before you zero, make sure that your scope is mounted just where you want it and that the reticle is square with the world. A reticle that's tipped is said to be canted. It won't cause a miss, but neither will the bullet's path follow the vertical wire. Unless forced to the side by wind, the bullet is compelled by gravity to fall straight to earth. It's most convenient for you if it drops behind the vertical wire, especially if you're shooting long and must occasionally aim high.

Cant is induced by improper scope mounting. We tighten the scope rings around the tube before the reticle is properly oriented. "Close enough," we say after a few minutes of sqinting and twisting. But when shouldering the rifle days or weeks later, our eyes see the reticle afresh and are not so easily fooled. Because we want the vertical wire to appear vertical, we subconsciously cant the rifle so that it does. This is bad business and can cause misses, especially at long range, because a canted rifle puts the sight line to the side of the bullet's path. Instead of two intersections of the sight line and trajectory, you get just one. Hitting becomes exceedingly difficult at any distance

Horace Smith found the 200-yard zero on his 7mm Remington Magnum perfect for Colorado deer.

other than zero range. When mounting a scope, give yourself plenty of time. Install the tube with the ring screws snug. Close your eyes and lay the rifle down. Then, without opening your eyes, pick up and shoulder the rifle. Open your eyes. Does the reticle appear tilted? Repeat this exercise several times to confirm, then make any necessary adjustments.

When tightening ring screws, do so as you would the lug nuts on a car—incrementally, going from one screw to the next a turn at a time to ensure even pressure. Be especially careful with Weaver Tip-Off mounts. The inexpensive Weaver ring, which has been around a long time, is strong and lightweight. But because the top half hooks the base on one side and its two screws take up all slack on the opposite side, tightening a Tip-Off ring can rotate the scope tube down toward the screws. If they're installed on the right-hand side, you put a clockwise tilt into your reticle as you cinch them. You may have aligned the reticle perfectly with the rifle butt before installing the top part of the rings, but now the crosswire is tipped. Solution: Back off on the screws and twist the scope counterclockwise about as far as you think it moved. Tighten the screws again, and check the reticle.

Fire at various distances after you zero, and from hunting positions, to verify what the charts tell you.

Incidentally, although heavy recoil dictates that you mount a scope well forward of your eye, it's the right thing to do even when shooting mild cartridges. Your best shooting without a rest will be from prone and sitting positions that put your eye close to the rifle's tang. If you're lucky enough to find a rest in the field, it's no trick to snuggle a little closer to the sight to get a full field of view. Pulling your head back from a scope mounted too far to the rear results in poor shooting at best, and from sling-assisted prone, it's nearly impossible. Shooting uphill from prone or sitting, you're almost sure to plant even a properly mounted scope in your brow. I've been clobbered by enough eyepieces that I always check eye relief before I fire another shooter's rifle. I don't want that rear lens much behind the rear guard screw. Also, when you're straightening the scope reticle, make sure that you don't inadvertently pull the tube back.

Once you've cinched the scope in place, adjust the reticle focus by pointing the rifle at the northern sky (not at an object) and turning the ocular housing until the reticle becomes sharp. No more focusing should be necessary, even if you sharpen the target image with an AO sleeve or dial.

Burris ring inserts allow you to position the scope so that optical and physical axes mesh.

For me, zeroing begins at the bench with bore-sighting. After removing its bolt, I secure the rifle in a rest so that it points toward a target. Distance doesn't matter really, but far is better than close; 100 yards is fine. Then I shift the rifle in the rest until the target is centered in the bore. Without moving the rifle, I turn the windage and elevation dials until the reticle quarters the target. That's it. When I replace the bolt and shoot, my bullets will almost certainly hit near the target center. Bore-sighting isn't necessary, but it saves ammunition for what comes next. With a little repetition, I can get very close to bull's-eye accuracy with my first shot. Not long ago I bore-sighted a .223 that had just been scoped. After cranking handfuls of click on the turret, I fired two shots. They landed half an inch apart, just an inch above dead middle. With practice, you should routinely get first shots within 5 inches of center.

Unless you'll be hunting at woods ranges or you're zeroing a shotgun or muzzleloader, it's better to zero at 200 yards than at 100. Most modern rifle rounds shoot flat enough to keep a bullet within $2^{1}/_{2}$ vertical inches of point of aim out to 250 yards if you zero at 200. This means that you can hold where you want to hit without fretting over bullet trajectory to 250 yards. If you zero at a shorter range, you'll have to elevate at 200 yards or even closer. If you zero at 300 yards, at midrange—between 150 and 200 yards—you'll hit high

Even where very long shots are common, a 200-yard zero makes sense for most cartridges.

enough to matter. A lot of big-game animals are shot between 150 and 200 yards, so it makes no sense to adjust your sight such that you have to hold low at common shot distances. Very flat-shooting cartridges can be zeroed at 250 or even 300 yards, but you'll have to put up with about 4 inches of midrange rise. That may be acceptable if you're shooting big animals and you expect a lot of shooting around 300 steps and beyond.

When zeroing, fire slowly so as not to heat the barrel. Use the same ammunition you'll use on the hunt—or, to save money, zero with cheaper cartridges, then check with hunting rounds. You don't need to fire five-shot groups to move the sight. But once you've got the bullets hitting where you want them, shoot five rounds, cleaning the barrel and letting it cool between shots. The shot that counts on a hunt is the first one from a cold, clean bore.

If you're limited to a 100-yard range, sight in $2^{1}/_{2}$ inches high. Then, when you have a chance, go somewhere you can fire at longer distances. If you haven't shot at 400 yards, you have no reason to believe that you can hit at 400 yards. Yet every year, hunters blaze away at game farther than they've ever shot at a target. A lot of missing goes on, and a lot of animals escape crippled.

If there's no range in your part of the country that has long yardage, don't worry. The fact is, you need to check all zeros from hunting positions anyway—first, to ensure that a change in the way you hold the rifle off the bench doesn't affect the point of impact, and second, to put yourself to the test. You need to know not only where the rifle is hitting at long range but also whether you can hit consistently at long range. Shooting only from a bench, you won't know how your rifle will perform when cradled by your body, and there's no way to assess your own maximum range. So you can check long-range impact when you test your zero in hunting positions wherever you find a field safe to shoot over.

How you support a rifle affects where the bullet goes. That's partly why it's bad business to zero someone else's rifle or to accept someone else's zero. It's also why your rifle's zero can appear to shift over time and why it sometimes seems to "walk" bullets even when the barrel is relatively cool. If you're holding the rifle and your position changes, the point of bullet impact will likely change too, no matter that the reticle appeared to be on the bull's-eye when the trigger broke. Even if you're shooting from a bench, the rifle moves as you finish squeezing the trigger. Some movement comes from your pulse, muscle twitches, trigger travel, and the pressure of your hands and cheek on the stock. If the rifle is nestled in sandbags or all but locked onto a mechanical rest, there's less going on. However, as the striker drops, it sets up vibrations within the rifle. Ignition and the buildup of pressure in the case add movement. When the bullet enters the rifling, it transmits torque, and as it travels down the bore, the barrel shudders violently.

This all happens quickly, but a bullet hitting game expands quickly too. The difference is that a bullet sustains its transformation; evidence of upset is visible and permanent. After recoil, a rifle comes to rest just as it appeared the moment before firing. The chaos inside subsides more quickly than the sound of the shot, and you're left thinking that the only movement occurred during the bullet's release.

The mechanics of launching a bullet and the attendant violence are beyond your control, but the way you support the rifle is not. Consistency of support is the key to consistent rifle movement during the execution of a shot. It's also the key to fine accuracy and a reliable zero. Once, when zeroing a Ruger Number One in .300 Winchester, I benched a final group on the money at 200 yards. Using the same loads (75 grains H4831and 180-grain Speers), I bellied into prone with a tight sling and fired another group. The bullets landed 9 inches to

This hard-bucking .338 Lapua rifle wears three scope rings. Heavy scopes are more prone to slip.

7 o'clock. Sling tension had pulled the vertical lift out of my rifle's natural vibrations during the second session. Because this Number One had significant up-pressure at the forend tip, the taut sling made a big difference in point of impact. I later took pressure off the tip and bedded the forend using rubber washers around the screw where it entered the stud. The 9-inch disparity shrank to 4.

The old Model 70 .270 I use to shoot deer targets at 400 yards is less finicky. It shoots a tad to 7 o'clock with a taut sling. Incidentally, a synthetic stock won't ensure a constant zero after a change in position. Just like wood, synthetic materials flex. When barrel contact varies, so does bullet impact.

Just as a new position can affect point of impact, a different shooter may shoot to a different place. Practiced marksmen may apply similar pressures to a rifle if they're shooting from the same position, but seldom does any rifle behave the same way for one shooter as for another. Besides disparities in hold, shooters view the sights differently. Open sights leave the most room for personal bias. What's a fine bead? How much white do you see between post and bull's-eye? An aperture sight eliminates some error, assuming that the shooter lets his or her eye center the bead, where the light is brightest. The sight picture through a scope should look the same to everyone, but it doesn't, because we don't all have our eyes on the scope's axis.

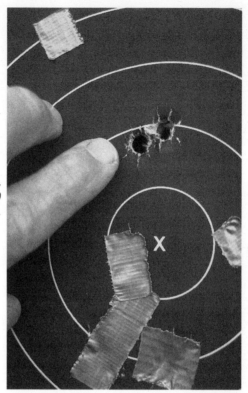

Two inches high at 100 yards, and you'll be on target at 200 yards with flat-shooting rounds.

I refine my zero by adjusting the scope so that my rifle hits the point of aim at 200 yards from the position I'm most likely to use. Bench targets are still useful, because they show me how to correct when I have the luxury of resting the rifle on a rock or log—padded, of course, by my hand. It's never a good idea to rest the forend directly on a hard object, because the surface will magnify the rifle's vibrations and cause it to shoot high. A rifle held against a vertical rest such as a tree typically tosses bullets to the free side. Barrel contact with any rest is especially heinous.

More recently than I care to admit, I was hunting from a plyboard blind in a southern state. A deer appeared in a clearing about 150 yards away. Resting the rifle on my hand on the window ledge, I fired. The deer ran off, obviously unhurt. Another came along a few minutes later, and I missed that one too. Vowing not to fire again until I had debugged the rifle, I spied a buck raking a tree at no more than 70 yards. It seemed too easy a shot to miss, but I managed. The whitetail stood, uncertain. In haste, I fired again, and he dashed away. I

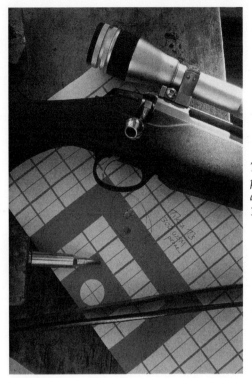

The author shot this group prone after zeroing the Tikka at the bench. Impact shifted 1 inch left.

searched that evening and the next morning for signs of injured deer but found nothing.

At the range, this rifle checked out. I had overshot. Even up close, a small animal is easy to miss if you aim high in the lungs, especially if you horse the trigger and are shooting off a hard rest. Any movement imparted to a rifle on a solid rest will likely result in a hop. I'm as apt to jerk when the rifle looks solid as when, offhand, the crosswire is bouncing like a fly off hot windows and briefly hangs still.

Consistent body support and sling tension go a long way toward eliminating zero problems. Many of the rifles that hunters claim were "knocked out of zero" while riding, cased, in the back of a pickup truck have never been bumped hard enough to spill water. And although changes in humidity and temperature can cause stock movement that affects zero, few are so severe as to push bullets off a sheet of typing paper at 100 yards. As a big-game guide, I've helped many hunters adjust their scopes. I suspect that few were ever properly adjusted in the first place. It's easy to sit at a bench for a handful of rounds; shooting from hunting positions takes more commitment, more ammo. Remind yourself before you case that rifle that a long zero isn't necessary for good shooting at long range—a consistent zero is. And you get that by training your body to act like a bench.

SHOT ANGLES AND THE LITTLE RED EYE

Some shots at big game must be taken at steep uphill or downhill angles. For distant targets, shot angle figures into your hold. It's as important a variable as range, because it affects range.

If you shoot horizontally, gravity acts perpendicular to the bullet path and thus has a pronounced effect on it. Gravity pushing down on the shank of a bullet is the equivalent of a strong full-value or right-angle wind. If the wind shifts to quarter toward or away from a bullet, it drifts less. Apply that principle to bullets fired at uphill or downhill angles, and you would expect less drop as gravity is forced to act obliquely. Think of a bullet fired straight up or straight down. In the absence of wind, neither would scribe an arc. The tug of gravity would be parallel to the line of bore, so there'd be no reason for the bullet to deviate from a straight path. A bullet fired straight up would travel until gravity and drag pulled it to a stop; then it would descend. The earth's spin would prevent the bullet from landing where it was launched, but touchdown would be very close to that spot.

Of course, you can't shoot a bullet straight down for any distance. But suppose you were able to drill a path for that bullet through the center of the earth. When you fired, the bullet would pass the center in a straight line, then slow as gravity from the other side of the planet retarded its forward motion. It would fall back just as would a bullet fired skyward.

Any shot angle between horizontal and vertical gives you a flatter trajectory than if you'd fired horizontally, whether you're shooting up or down. The effect of gravity on bullet speed—its pressure on nose or tail—is negligible. So you can hold the same, whether shooting up or down. But that hold will differ, especially at long range, from the hold you would want for a horizontal shot. Simply put, you want to aim as if the shot distance were the same as the horizontal component of the shot.

For example, say you were shooting at a mountain goat 141 yards away but at a 45-degree angle above you. You remember from high

For long shots, or to compensate for wind, you can adjust windage and elevation dials on Shepherd scopes without losing zero.

This early Swarovski laser rangefinding scope works but is heavy and bulky. Recently, new LRF scopes with trim profiles have surfaced.

school geometry that a right triangle with a 45-degree angle has a matching 45-degree angle and two legs of equal length. You also recall that the hypotenuse (the side opposite the 90-degree angle) is almost half again as long as either leg. Specifically, the leg length relationship is 1:1:√2. Now you know why I chose 141 yards for this shot: The square root of √2 is 1.41. A bullet path 141 yards long and angled 45 degrees from horizontal has a horizontal component of 100 yards (the vertical component is 100 as well). To hit the goat, you hold for 100 yards, because that is the distance over which gravity has an effect. Until ranges get really long, you can ignore the slightly longer flight time.

A 45-degree shot angle is very steep. Most of the time, the angles will be smaller, and at distances within the point-blank range of your cartridge, you may not want to compensate at all. For example, if the bullet path were 250 yards and the horizontal component 200, you could hold for 250. With a 200-yard zero, you'd hit 2 or 3 inches high, which isn't enough deviation to matter. The longer the shot, the greater the effect of shot angle, because as the bullet covers more ground, its arc gets steeper. My rule of thumb is to forget about holding off for shot angle out to 250 yards, then shade a hand's width low

Bushnell owns more than 90 percent of the laser rangefinder market, but others are challenging.

to 300 yards and two hand's widths at 350—assuming a shot angle of 30 degrees or less.

Compensating for shot angle is possible only when you know the distance to your target. In fact, at long yardage, you'll make good on horizontal shots only when you know the distance. But distance can be tough to gauge. Far away, target details are hard to see. Fog, back-lighting, mirage, and shadow all make the image less distinct and range estimation more difficult. Over most terrain, you see a smaller percentage of the intervening yardage than if the mark were close, but across canyons, you'll see much more ground than the bullet must traverse. Depending on the conditions and topography, a target that looks so small as to be 250 yards away may not appear much smaller than one 175 yards distant—or much bigger than one 325 yards away. But your bullet won't hit where you intend it if your esti-mate is off by 75 yards. A 30-percent goof seems huge, but it's easy to be short or long by that much. Remember that the bullet's arc gets steeper as distance increases. So where range estimates are most diffi-cult, they're also most critical.

Given a steep angle, up or down, figure shot distance as the horizontal component of bullet flight.

The lay of the land affects how you gauge yardage. A canyon that pulls ground away from your eye makes game appear far away because the vertical rise to the target is so visible. You'll likely guess long because you see so much of the opposite hill or canyon wall. Of course, your bullet doesn't care at all about the terrain, because it doesn't follow ground contours. Shooting uphill or downhill can also make estimates more difficult because the animal isn't showing you its side. Your eye registers a smaller image because, looking at the belly or back, you get a shallow profile. Your brain tells you that the shot will be longer than is actually the case.

Whereas canyons and mountains prompt us to overshoot, flat ground often causes us to underestimate distance to targets. If you shoot prone at a distant pronghorn on a Wyoming sage flat, your eye sees a severely foreshortened piece of prairie. "Not much ground to cover," says your brain. "That buck must be close." In fact, the animal may be many hundreds of yards away. The bright color of pronghorns can exacerbate the problem, because in the bright light common on the plains, it is a distinct target. The more prominent the target—the clearer it appears to your eye—the closer it seems. A whitetail silhouetted against snow or sky looks closer than one at the same distance that's partially hidden by brush or backlit in brown field stubble or standing in dim light against a background of shintangle.

When the size of individual animals varies a great deal, you can make big mistakes in estimating range. Black bears are notoriously deceptive in this regard. Although the relationships of ear size to head size and head size to body size change as bears mature, a little bear can look just like a big bear at long range. If you think the bear weighs 400 pounds when in fact it's a yearling, you'll overestimate the yardage. If the bear is larger than you think, you'll likely shoot low.

Many deer hunters think that deer are bigger than is actually the case. I was astonished when an experienced hunter told me that most deer stand about 5 feet at the shoulder. The truth is, most northern whitetails are closer to 3 feet. A deer standing 40 inches at the withers is big. If you think all deer measure 50 percent taller than they are, logic says that you'll overshoot a lot of bucks and pass up makeable shots as being too long. But my mistaken friend had killed a lot of deer and didn't miss often. Why? Because he didn't think in terms of target height when he aimed his rifle. He instinctively held where he'd held on other deer that had looked the same size in the scope and had dropped to his bullet.

Consider for a moment the stars. Any star in the night sky is bigger than most of us can imagine. It may be many light-years away, and we can't easily comprehend a light-year. A star is farther away than an unaided eye has any business trying to judge. Slight differences in the appearance of stars can reflect huge disparities in distance. Further complicating matters: Stars are not the same size, nor do stars of equivalent size deliver the same level of brightness. In sum, we'd fail miserably trying to figure the distance to a star by comparing its apparent size or brightness with the stars around it. Were we in fact "shooting for the stars," range estimation errors would be measured in light-years!

Knowing the distance to a star matters little to most of us. We cultivate the skill to judge closer and more meaningful distances: how far an approaching car is from a crosswalk, where a receiver will be when we release the football, the distance to that outside mallard decoy. Estimating short yardage is easier than estimating long, and we get more practice up close. Proficiency at estimating targets at long rifle ranges requires a lot of practice, especially if they're so far that we need magnifying sights to see them.

A shortcut to accurate range determination is the rangefinder. Optical rangefinders came about to assist not hunters but artillerymen. Soldiers intending to lob shells at a tank or mortar emplacement don't want to hit a church. Trial-and-error gunnery also exposes the firing position to the enemy. Rangefinders deliver first-round hits without a need for forward observers.

The first lightweight rangefinders for hunters came along after I was old enough to have missed several deer by overestimating the range. One buck, standing at what appeared to be many football fields distant, should have escaped. I held the reticle in the Weaver K4 just over its shoulder and fired. The deer looked up, then went back to foraging. Another shot brought the same results. In despair, I aimed where I wanted the bullet to go and fired my last round. The buck dropped instantly. Instead of pacing more than 300 yards, I strode only 160 steps to the carcass.

Apparently, other hunters had the same problem, because not long after that, a firm named Ranging was selling devices that helped hunters peg target distances. These "coincidence" rangefinders had two small windows. Looking through the sighting window, you'd see double target images. To get a read on the distance, you'd turn a dial that moved internal prisms to bring those images together. A scale

The author shot this Austrian chamois at a steep upward angle. But at 125 yards, he held center. The rifle: a Blaser in .222, with a Swarovski scope.

*Canting the rifle isn't a problem
if you do it consistently. This
spirit level tells you.*

showed the yardage. Bowhunters kept Ranging in business, but riflemen found that at long range—beyond 100 yards or so—accuracy
deteriorated.

In 1992 Leica broke ground with a new type of rangefinder.
The Geovid was both a high-quality binocular and a laser rangefinder. Laser units emit a laser beam, which bounces off a target and
returns to the instrument's internal electronic clock, which instantly
computes elapsed time. Since light travels at the constant speed
of 186,000 miles per second, time can be converted to distance.
The rangefinder runs this calculation and displays yardage on an
electronic display. A laser rangefinder is faster to use and, with an
accuracy level of plus or minus 1 yard, more precise than any split-
image (coincidence) model.

According to Jim Morey, former president of Swarovski, North
America, U.S. Army tank commanders had laser rangefinders in the
M-60 A3 by the mid-1970s. He notes that the technology became
available to the sport hunting market well before the first instruments
appeared. "Even in the army, hand-held units were not practical
for some time." Swarovski followed Leica's Geovid with a laser
rangefinder it labeled the RF 1. Unlike the Geovid, the RF 1 did not

Shooting downhill, hold the same as if the angle were uphill. Horizontal range is what counts.

incorporate a binocular. Consequently, it weighed and cost less. Still, both products retailed for more than $2,700, representing a substantial investment for hunters. And at 53 and 35 ounces, these 7x and 6x instruments weighed more than a big binocular.

Bushnell delivered the first lightweight, affordable laser rangefinders. The first of the Yardage Pro line came along in 1996. Designated the 400 for its maximum reach on a reflective target in dim light, it could be slipped into a coat pocket. The people at Bushnell have since improved that version of the Yardage Pro and added more sophisticated models. The 800 offers more reach; now you can get Yardage Pro 500 and 1000 models, plus Sport and Scout configurations. Yardage Pros weigh from 7 to about 14 ounces. Magnifications of 4x, 6x, and 8x let you see targets clearly. Some models have options that tell the laser to ignore interfering reflections from raindrops or solid objects closer than a specified distance. This enables you to find the range to a deer on the far side of a clearing while you hide among the oaks. By dint of intelligent and aggressive marketing, and with an expanding array of user-friendly rangefinders, Bushnell has captured 95 percent of the market. But Leica, Nikon, Pentax, and Swarovski have fielded tough competition. The trend is toward greater range and precision, more features, and lower unit cost.

The reflective properties of the target have a great deal to do with how well rangefinders work. All models perform best in flat or failing light. Bright days trim maximum range by up to 35 percent. A solid, smooth surface that's moderately reflective should give you an accurate reading all the time. The rib cage of a deer standing in the open under a hazy sky should bounce that laser beam back like a racquetball from a hard serve. A deer quartering away, or one partially obscured by thin brush, won't give you the same clean bounce. Glare can be a problem too. I suspect that most read failures result from the user's inability to hold the rangefinder's reticle on target. Improved reticles and more powerful lasers have markedly boosted rangefinder effectiveness, especially at long yardage.

Some hunters carry rangefinders routinely. I often do, to pass the time at midday. Even if you're hunting where long shots are rare, a rangefinder gives you quick, accurate readings to rocks, trees, and other things you might pick at random to test your eye. The latest rangefinders weigh almost nothing and fit easily in a pocket. Use one often, and your ability to accurately estimate yardage is bound to improve. When I guided hunters, a rangefinder often went along,

Gentle shot angles don't merit a change in hold unless the target is very far away.

More problematic than angled bullet flight is an unstable position. Practice making steep shots.

mainly because clients took comfort knowing that they could get correct yardage at the touch of a button.

Once, a friend and I spotted a buck on a hillside far away. Pressed by impending dusk, we raced across coulees, cutting a big arc in an approach that brought us within long rifle shot of where the buck had been, but we couldn't locate him. Inching forward and glassing until our eyes bulged, we found nothing. Then my partner spotted the deer bedded in low brush, in a shadowed pocket some yards off.

"How far?" he asked.

I gulped the bait. "Probably 280."

He pulled out his laser rangefinder and pushed the button. "Almost 400."

Good grief. I redeemed myself by slipping up behind the deer and catching him in the scope at 75 steps. It was the beginning of the hunt, so I let him walk.

Some hunters say that rangefinders encourage irresponsible shooting—that, like magnum rifles and powerful scopes, they encourage some hunters to shoot beyond reasonable yardage. That's no doubt true. But a rangefinder won't help you dope wind or hold a rifle still. It can only reduce aiming error.

$\textbf{9}$ Shooting Technique

Getting yourself ready for a shot is largely a matter of build-
ing your confidence, and that comes only through practice.
Nothing can take the place of practice.
—Lones Wigger, two-time Olympic gold medalist
in rifle shooting and setter of 29 world
marksmanship records

GET YOUR REST

This would be a quick shot, and my only one. The eland was
shielded, except for its head and neck and a window of shoulder. I
would have to shoot offhand, and I still had to catch my breath. Grab-
bing the tracker's tripod of shooting sticks at their binding, I settled
the rifle on my fist as I came above the thorn, triggering the Kimber
when my crosswire found the window. Because the sticks instantly
steadied the rifle, it was still the instant the striker fell. The eland
dropped. The range? Just 60 yards. But I still needed a rest.

Shooting at long range is just like shooting up close, except for
the little things that you can't get away with. A movement of the
muzzle that puts your bullet just 2 inches off at 100 yards means an 8-
inch miss at 400. Once you've determined the range and doped the
wind, hits depend entirely on your ability to hold the rifle still. A rest
always makes sense.

On the bench and in the field, if you can arrange the rifle's support so the sights spend more time on the target than off it, you've
improved your odds of a hit. Your best shooting will come when the
rifle doesn't need encouragement to point where you want the bullet
to go. When you're at the bench zeroing, a mechanical rest gives you
fingertip control on knobs that tune your sight picture. Some rests
have leveling devices and adjustable toe supports. Some, like the
Bench Master, feature a strap that arrests the butt during recoil. The

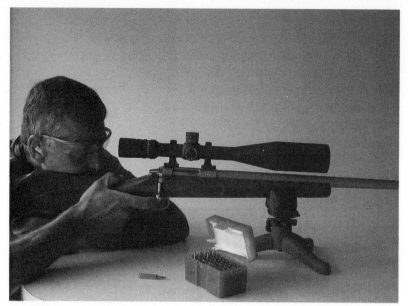

The author uses an affordable Caldwell front rest to steady a Dakota rifle in .20 Tactical.

A portable rest with sandbags helps Danny O'Connell zero in on woodchucks with a Dakota Predator and Nightforce scope.

Gunmaker and guide D'Arcy Echols fills this mule-ear bag with plastic pellets and straps it to a spotting scope for an instant rest afield.

Decker Gun Vise remains a popular rest in my part of the country (from Bill Hicks, 800-223-0702). Sinclair International, a favorite supply house for serious benchrest shooters, lists several types of bags and rests (sinclairintl.com). Cabela's offers myriad rests, many of them very affordable. It's also a one-stop source if you're looking for a bipod (cabelas.com).

The Lead Sled, a Battenfeld product marketed by Midway USA (midwayusa.com), is designed to hold shot bags that reduce rest movement and mitigate recoil. "It will take up to 100 pounds of shot," says Larry Potterfield, Midway's chief executive. "You won't need that much to make most rifles very comfortable to shoot." The Lead Sled is a one-piece rest that supports both the rifle's front and rear. It comes with a padded butt boot and an adjustable, padded U-shaped forend rest. The frame has rubber feet to protect your bench.

Also from Midway USA is the Caldwell Rock BR front rest. Made of cast iron, it weighs 16 pounds and has a 15-inch footprint. For heavy rifles and long shooting, the BR 1000 offers 3 inches more base and 8 pounds more heft. Both rests feature fine and coarse elevation adjustments, a finger-spin windage screw, and a bubble level. All machined parts, including the adjustable feet, are of stainless steel. There's a forend stop and wide, padded forend jaws that open to accommodate the beefiest forend. Midway's Caldwell Rock Jr. and Handy rests are economical, lightweight alternatives. Caldwell Deadshot and Tack-driver bench bags cradle your rifle without steel support. The Field Bag is designed to drape over a blind sill or pickup box.

A unique rest is the Ball Shooting System from Aim-Rite (theballshootingsystem.com). A modified bowling ball, with a clever rifle clamp affixed, is free to rotate in the padded socket of an oak base. Effortlessly, you can make minute corrections in elevation, windage, and cant. The ball's mass soaks up recoil. You don't even have to snug hard-kicking rifles to your shoulder.

One of the best benchrests I've used comes from Target Shooting Incorporated (TSI) in Watertown, South Dakota. Its proprietor, Wally Brownlee, is the kind of fellow you'd like to have with you in a prairie dog town. Self-effacing despite his linebacker build, he smiles a lot. Wally brought one of the first M500 rests to a sodpoodle shoot I attended in Montana. Stone-steady by design, it weighs just 11 pounds. The cast-alloy frame features rubber-booted feet so that you can use it on an automobile hood or picnic table without marring the surface. The V-block forend rest, amply padded with half an inch of felt, gives you more than 4 inches of bearing surface but rotates 360 degrees. A U-shaped buttstock support has the same padding and is adjustable for angle. There's even a rubber sleeve on its leading edge so that hard-kicking rifles won't ding their grips. Twin stainless rods connect forend and butt sections. There's generous clearance underneath, and the front assembly slides easily with the twist of a knob to give you just the right distance between front and rear. A set-screw knob allows quick vertical adjustment of the front block, secured and fine-tuned with a big, easily accessible wheel on threads.

A more sophisticated version is the M1000, with fine-threaded windage and elevation adjustments and silicon-treated sideboards up front that adjust for forend widths of $1^1/_4$ to 3 inches. The rest comes with a leather-covered rear saddle and a front-end attachment that converts the base for sandbag use. "We built our first rest in 1994," says Wally, who hawked it mainly on his own, logging 420,000 miles on a GM van. But he is quick to credit a Texas tool-and-die man with the rest's initial configuration. "I liked the device and sold a few for him, then made improvements and agreed to buy all my castings there. Still do." A friend in South Dakota helps with computer-aided design. A rural school became the TSI shop.

Besides steadying the rifle, this rest gets you low and hides you. Pad that rifle with your hand.

For long days in prairie dog towns, a collapsible table rest is hard to beat. So is a comfy chair.

Forend-enveloping rests like this from Midway USA grip the rifle and can be set up on any surface.

Wally counts himself "blessed with great people." And he's proud that all his products and their parts are made in the USA. Wally once clobbered a prairie dog at 589 yards with a .22-250. Shoot often enough, he says, and you get lucky. "I witnessed one hit at 879 yards, with a 168-grain match bullet from a .308." A good rest makes a difference, he concedes. Contact him at 800-457-2613 or targetshooting.com.

Sandbars are cheaper, but a pile of sandbags can shift and settle between shots, especially when you're pounding away with a powerful rifle. Fine accuracy depends on consistency in the details. To be fair, I've shot some tight groups over sandbags, and if you stuff them with granulated plastic, they're easy to transport afield. One of my friends stuffs a mule-ear bag with plastic pellets and straps it atop his spotting scope. When guiding hunters, he can offer an instant rest for clients.

Many hunters now carry a bipod attached to the rifle's forend at the front swivel stud. A bipod puts the rifle in contact with the ground, replacing slippery joints, pulsing arteries, and quivering muscles with a couple of dispassionate steel pegs that don't move. The best bipods allow some movement at the attachment point. The Harris bipod that I favor (Harris Engineering, Barlow, KY 42024) is cleverly designed to allow the forend to roll and swivel slightly so

A hunter in Idaho's Selway-Bitterroot wilderness steadies a Remington AWR for a shot.

This Weatherby varminter is set up on a fully adjustable rest common in bench-rest shooting.

that I can tune my aim quickly without mechanical adjustment. This flexibility comes with no loss of support; the rifle stays at rest until you exert pressure. The Harris's legs are individually and incrementally adjustable, so when you have to shoot from a place that isn't perfectly level, you can quickly extend the legs to accommodate your position and all but eliminate cant.

Shooting sticks are an alternative to the bipod. Buffalo hunters used crossed sticks to steady their heavy rifles. Lighter, stronger fiberglass versions are available from Stoney Point Products (P.O. Box 238, New Ulm, MN 56073). The firm's Steady Stix and taller Safari Stix collapse for carrying in a belt sheath. From the sit or kneel, plant the stick legs well forward and pull the intersection toward you as you lean into it. The rifle shoves the legs firmly into the ground as your hand (or a binding) keeps the sticks at a constant angle.

A monopod offers less support than crossed sticks because it permits left-to-right wobble. Mainly, it keeps your left arm from getting tired. It is easier to carry and quicker to deploy than a bipod or crossed sticks and is of considerable help when you're winded and the muzzle wants to dip and soar at each breath.

You'd think that a commercial rest, or even sandbags on a bench, would ensure tiny groups, but it's not so. You can still shoot poorly

Shooting sticks are popular on the African veldt, where tall grass prevents low positions.

from a rest. Jerking the trigger can move a rifle as easily as if you were holding it aloft with your hand. Aim through the corner of the scope, and you can introduce parallax error. Put your hands in different places, or exert variable pressure on the rifle from shot to shot, and groups will open up. One of the most common mistakes that shooters make when using sandbags is holding the rifle up front. Keep your left hand off the rifle unless the recoil is so violent that you must grasp the forend to control it. In most cases, you're better off with that forward hand on the rear bag, squeezing it to tune elevation.

In the field, you won't have sandbags or an adjustable rest. Seldom will an improvised rest be so secure and ideally situated that you can give your left hand a vacation. The trick is to use it to complement the artificial support. Try not to introduce tensions that move the barrel at the shot.

Whether at the bench or in the field, don't touch the barrel with your left hand or allow it to touch a hard surface. On any hard rest, pad the forend with your hand to cushion the rifle's bounce during recoil. Vibrations from the striker's fall and primer detonation begin traveling through the rifle before you feel the kick. They can bump your rifle before the bullet leaves the barrel. Padding is especially

Small-bore bench competitors use rests that can be fine-tuned with light finger pressure.

Shot bags filled with sand are not the ideal rest, but they're cheap, available, and soft against the rifle.

important when steadying a rifle against a vertical rest. In that case, the muzzle is pressured to move laterally instead of up, and without your fleshy palm as a cushion, the point of impact can shift.

The influence of pressure changes on the forend is easy to see if you shoot a rifle with a tight sling and then from the same position without one. At 200 yards, I've seen as much as 9 inches of deviation, firing ten-shot groups. The sling typically pulls my groups to 7 o'clock. It's a point worth noting when you zero. After shooting from a hard rest at the bench, try some groups with a sling (if you use one afield), or shoot offhand (weak support can also result in low groups). Lightweight hunting rifles are more susceptible to forend pressure changes than are target and varmint guns with their great mass. You're smart to shoot often before hunting season with the rifle supported as you're likely to hold it on the hunt, as well as from improvised rests. You might be surprised at how much a change in rifle support moves the point of impact and affects grouping.

Because I commonly shoot from a tight sling on hunts, I zero from prone. A few seasons back, I crept to a knob above a herd of elk working their way up a timbered draw in Montana's Bitterroot Mountains. Diffuse gray light slowly painted over the stars as I wriggled into a prone position, sling tight and my left hand hard against a rock. The sling and the rock together stilled the crosswire in my 3-9x Leupold. It hardly shivered as I waited. Dawn followed the elk up the hillside, and by the time I could verify the bull's antlers and get a clear shot, I'd been poised to shoot for several minutes. The rest not only kept the rifle from moving; it also kept me from tiring. This 300-yard shot was longer than I like to take, but the rock and sling made it easy. Had the elk been a quart jar, I'd have hit it.

Although the rock ahead of my forward elbow helped me make that shot, in truth, I can shoot almost as well from prone with a sling alone. A proper sling is not a one-piece carrying strap but a 1- or $1^1/4$-inch leather shooting sling with an adjustable loop that snugs around your left arm above the triceps. The loop is adjustable independent of sling length. It hauls the rifle back toward you, transferring rifle weight from your left forearm to your left shoulder while snugging the butt into your right shoulder. If you simply wrap a strap around your arm, you tug the buttstock forward because the strap tightens behind your triceps as it does in front. Also, the pull on the butt is to the side, inducing a cant.

To my mind, Brownell's Latigo sling is the best commercial shooting sling (Brownell's, Inc., 200 S. Front St., Montezuma, IA 50171). It

Steady as a rock. The hand protects the rifle but also deadens rifle vibration that can cause a miss.

The Harris bipod, here on an H-S Precision .223, is an industry standard for varminters.

This Nesika benchrest rifle is properly cradled by a finely machined, fully adjustable forend rest.

has little hardware (a button and a ring), so it's quiet and lightweight. You can adjust overall length with a couple of tugs. A series of opposing holes gives you almost limitless loop adjustment. The Whelen-style sling is my second choice. It is less readily adjustable for overall length but offers the same advantages when you shoot. A recent development at this writing is an all-leather sling (no hardware at all) by IST in Bozeman, Montana (istdesigns.com). The hunter who designed it admitted that he'd had lots of free time one winter. But whatever its genesis, this sling is a fine alternative to the Latigo. It is a high-quality, clever device that's quick to adjust for overall length and solid when "locked in." There's no hardware, so the shooting loop is not an independent feature. Incidentally, the various nylon slings on the market, though less expensive, don't impress me. Under tension, they can slip.

A sling is quicker to use than a bipod and better for shooting on steep or uneven terrain. It adds no significant weight or bulk to the rifle and can be used prone, sitting, and kneeling. From prone, you should be able (with practice) to keep all your shots inside 3 minutes of angle. That means killing shots on elk to 400 yards. From the sit, some shooters do almost as well. Kneeling typically puts a 3 to 9 o'clock wobble into the reticle, but on a still day, a 4-minute kneeling

Curt Crum shoots a David Miller rifle from kneeling. The bipod is a great assist in prone.

group is surely within reach. One of my best sling-assisted prone groups with hunting hardware came at Kenny Jarrett's 600-yard South Carolina range. Shooting one of his super-accurate rifles in .300 Jarrett, I coaxed three shots into the scribed vitals of a paper deer target. The group size was less than 8 inches. With match rifles, groups like that aren't uncommon. Not long ago, I borrowed a friend's AR-15 and, with just a couple of sighter shots, put four of the next five shots in the X and 10 rings at 600 yards. A scope might have shrunk that group.

A rest can speed your shot because the rifle quickly becomes still. Aiming an unsupported rifle can take a long time as you fight the rifle into submission. Meanwhile, the animal may turn or walk behind a tree or a herdmate. The wind may shift suddenly. It is smart to shoot as soon as you can shoot well.

A BENCH OF BONE

Back in the days of 32-cent gasoline, when the Beach Boys were big and Zimbabwe was Rhodesia and secretaries pined for electric typewriters, I shot under the tutelage of a man who wouldn't let me fire until the rifle naturally pointed where I was looking. "You can't hit if the rifle wants to point somewhere else," said Earl, around the unlit cigar clamped in his teeth. Gangly, raw-boned, and with a mop of fiery hair that draped over bushy eyebrows, Earl would squat and silently assess my cross-legged sit while my back and thighs cried out for relief. Kneeling, my right foot would burn, then go to sleep as Earl studied the bend of my leg. "You need bone under that rifle, all the way down."

I would sometimes use all of two hours to empty a 50-round box of .22 cartridges. But even when my scores improved, Earl kept after me. "If you hit the 10-ring once, you can do it again," he insisted. "Take care with each shot, and you'll do it almost every time."

Since then, it has become clear to me that people who want to shoot well tend to their positions. In my years on the small-bore prone circuit, I watched accomplished marksmen set up as if their bodies were astronomical instruments or long-range artillery. They didn't point their rifles at the target; they aimed *themselves* at it. Shooting was a matter of controlling breath and trigger squeeze and of watching the wind. If the position deteriorated, these experts didn't muscle the rifle onto the target; instead, they refined their position to give the rifle bone support and keep their muscles relaxed.

"If you fight the rifle, it will always win," Earl had said. "Even before recoil and noise break your concentration, muscle tension puts extra movement into the rifle. At every lapse of pressure, the rifle's mass pushes it toward its natural point of aim. When you see the sight wander or jump, you try to correct with more muscle tension. When the trigger breaks, your muscles twitch, again releasing the rifle." Earl told me that the rifle would spend a lot of time on target if I organized my bones to keep it where it wanted to be in the first place. "Remember," he'd chide, "*you* aren't holding the rifle. Your *position* is."

He was right. Still, I've missed a lot of easy shots at game. I have never missed because the sight was off or because a guard screw was loose, and never (to my knowledge) because of faulty ammunition. I have never missed because I forgot about elevation, the barometric pressure, or my horoscope. OK, I have on occasion misjudged wind and yardage and in 35 years afield clipped two or three branches with bullets. But almost all my bad shots have resulted from bad shooting. We miss when our concentration fails and our technique falls short. Hitting once—or a few times—is not marksmanship; it is happy coincidence. Missing comes easy. Nobody is born a marksman. You may

The prone target (left) *shows a steady hold. But so do the sitting, kneeling, and off-hand shots* (right). *The author printed these groups at woods ranges with a Ruger M77 Frontier rifle in 300 WSM.*

be blessed with fine vision, quick reflexes, and exceptional hand-eye coordination, but to shoot accurately, you must learn how to hold a rifle steady and how to control your breathing and trigger squeeze.

A rest that steadies the rifle gives you more time to shoot and reduced amplitude in sight motion. Because the sight spends more time in the center and never strays far from it, you'll shoot better. You get a great deal of confidence from a rest, just watching your sight quivering expectantly right where you want the bullet to go. Alas, on the hunt, you won't always have access to a rest when you see the animal you want to shoot, so your body must suffice. Intelligent rifle practice starts with a solid position.

An underpinning of bone is the foundation of every good shooting position. Bones, not muscles, best support you and the rifle. Muscles are elastic, and they tire. Muscles contain blood that surges, nerves that twitch. Bones are like two-by-fours: If you can align them so your muscles don't have to work to keep joints from slipping, you'll build a platform that's as still as the human body can be. Bone

No matter how solid your prone, sitting, or kneeling position, a shooting sling makes it steadier.

alignment must allow the rifle to point naturally at the target. If you force it on target with your muscles, you'll have the same problems as if you relied on muscles to support your body's weight. When the trigger breaks, your body wants to relax. If you have muscled the rifle where it doesn't want to go, it will come off target at the shot.

Bones can be arranged to help you shoot better from all positions. The most stable is prone, the lowest of your options. It gives you the most ground contact and puts your center of gravity mere inches above the earth. Your left arm (for right-handed shooters) should be almost directly under the rifle. Although arm muscles secure the elbow at the correct angle, they should not support the rifle. Count on your bones for that. A tight sling will reduce the strain on arm muscles to near zero. Limit stomach contact with the ground by cocking your right leg, rolling your body onto your left-side ribs. Those bones then support your torso while your stomach is held clear of the ground to mitigate pulse bounce. Your right elbow acts like the leg of a tripod jammed into the ground. No muscle tension is necessary here, because your trigger hand on the rifle locks in the elbow angle.

The author demonstrates prone. Bones bear the weight. Sling tension does, too, and deadens the pulse.

Sitting is not quite as steady as prone but is more versatile because it puts your muzzle above grass and low brush, and it allows you to swivel to follow moving game. It is useful on uneven terrain because of its small "footprint." I often fire from the sitting position, my legs tentlike in front of me, heels hard into the ground. It's important in this position to lean well forward, with the rear flat surfaces of your elbows against the fronts of your knees. Muscles in the small of your back apply tension to hold those elbows in place. But the lumbar stretch is not conscious muscle work; it's forced by bone contact, elbow to knee, so your back is also in its default posture and won't shift as your muscles react involuntarily to the trigger break. Your body rests on your tailbone. Rifle weight loads your left arm, held by friction and muscle tension (and a sling) against your knee. Leg bones support a lot of forward weight, but your leg muscles are relaxed, the bones held at their proper angle by the solid contact of heels and buttocks on the ground.

Alternative sitting positions are the crossed-leg and crossed-ankle variations. Competitive shooters like them, but they're not as useful on uneven ground. They also put the rifle on a lower plane, which can fill your sight picture with tall grass and brush. Although crossed-

Janet Nyce practiced a great deal with her .280 before heading for the hills. Result: a lovely ram.

leg sitting can give you the best results on paper, it requires a great deal of practice to stretch thigh and back muscles and may be impractical if you're bundled in heavy clothing. The crossed-ankle option is faster and more flexible.

Kneeling delivers a higher sight line than sitting. It is fast to assume but not as steady. Keep your weight over your bones; fight the urge to lean forward. Center your torso weight on your tailbone, squarely on the heel of your right foot, which is bent underneath to contact the ground through sole and toes. A vertical left shin should carry about 35 percent of your weight and support the rifle. Your left elbow rests on the forward face of your left knee. As with sitting, if you put the point of your elbow on your kneecap, you'll get wobble. The sight typically moves in an elliptical pattern from 9 or 10 o'clock to 3 or 4 o'clock. To minimize horizontal sway when kneeling, angle your left foot so that it's parallel to your right leg, comfortably to the side and bearing little weight (ground friction will hold your foot in place, despite muscle tension in your calf). Place the rifle butt high in on your clavicle, so you can look straight ahead through the sight. Given proper bone alignment, an erect kneeling position is easy to maintain. As with prone and sitting, a sling is invaluable.

Kneeling is quick to assume and high enough for shooting over most brush—and it's steadier than offhand.

The author shoots offhand with an Ultra Light rifle. Note the arm positions. No help from a sling here.

Standing, or offhand, is the position of last resort, because your center of gravity is very high and you have little ground contact. Your left arm has no anchor to the ground or your knee, so a sling is almost worthless. For all its failings, however, offhand is both flexible and fast and thus worth practicing. Start at ground level by planting your feet shoulder-width apart, with equal weight on each and a line through your toes at about a 30-degree angle to the sight line. Stand flat-footed with slightly more pressure on the balls of your feet. Keep your knees straight but not locked. You may feel steadier or more comfortable with different foot spacing or with your base at a different angle to the target. To find the natural point of aim, tack several targets side by side on a backing board. Aim the rifle at the center target, close your eyes, shoulder the rifle, relax, then open your eyes. Note where the sight is. Repeat. If the rifle is pointing consistently toward any target other than the one in the middle, change foot position until the reticle naturally finds the middle bull.

Gary Anderson, an Olympic shooter who's won two gold medals in 300-meter offhand events, told me that "a lot of top shooters lean back and slightly right to counter the rifle's weight. They support the rifle by bracing the left arm against their ribs." Try that with a heavy rifle, and you'll agree. But hunting rifles lack the mass to stay still with your left hand supporting the forend far to the rear. Wind and heartbeat bounce a lightweight rifle resting against your ribs. You'll probably get better results holding the forend near the midpoint, where you can actively direct and steady it.

Lones Wigger, another Olympic gold medalist, stands as straight as a new corner post and says that you should too. "Hunching over the rifle puts you off balance and adds tension to your back muscles." Keep your head upright, even if bringing the stock to your cheek puts the rifle's butt above your shoulder. You see best when you look straight ahead. Hold your right arm horizontal. Although that puts some strain on your wrist, the muscle tension is held by the friction of your hand on the grip. A high (horizontal) right elbow also puts a pocket in your shoulder, a place for the butt to nestle. Grip the forend with full hand contact. Pull the stock more firmly with your right hand. Your left elbow most effectively supports the rifle from underneath, not out to the side. Pulling that elbow left strains your shoulder muscles and tires your arm. In my offhand position, the point of my left elbow is almost directly above my left little toe.

Sitting, with a tight sling, may be the most useful hunting position. Practice stretches the muscles.

Whatever your shooting position, point your feet before you aim. Bring the rifle smoothly to your cheek (not cheek to rifle) as you breathe deeply to bring oxygen to your brain and eyes. Shoot with both eyes open if you can, pressing the trigger as you exhale gently. Hold about half a diaphragm of air. Keep up the trigger pressure when the sight is on target. Maintain pressure when it wanders off or if your position falls apart. The rifle should fire when your lungs are emptied but not purged. Don't jerk. You'll disturb the rifle if you try to nail the target with the sight diving toward it or on a brief, quivering sojourn at center.

You won't like shooting at paper from unsupported positions. It's easier on the ego to shoot little groups from the bench. But to shoot well in the field, you must practice with only your body as a platform, doing everything right, every time. Good shooting follows established habit. When a buck catapults from cover, or an elk gives you one last pose on a distant ridge, you won't have time to think about shooting. Your body must be conditioned to react reflexively in the right way.

A word about tempo: Speed and precision are mutually exclusive. You cannot be extremely fast and extremely accurate at the same

The author shoots sitting. Note the sling, tight and flat across the hand, and the elbow in front of the knee.

time. But you can be slow and inaccurate. On the hunt, you'll profit from practice that forces a cadence fast enough to leak the occasional poor shot.

Acceptable aim is what you're taught for defensive shooting, where center shots aren't necessary and speed can be crucial. It's also the mantra at Gunsite Academy's hunting rifle school, where instructors Eric Olds and Il Ling use timers to expose targets only long enough for "first-picture" shooting. "Begin the squeeze as soon as the sight is on target," says Olds. "The longer you hold, the more you wobble. The more you wobble, the longer you'll take to squeeze, the more likely you are to jerk."

You're less likely to feel pressure for a quick shot at long range than when you're tracking game into thickets. Still, you'll do well to practice fast shooting, because conditions can deteriorate quickly. In small-bore matches, fickle winds favor shooters who can send volleys downrange during a lull or a brief return to "zero" conditions. The only chance you get at a big buck might come and go in a couple of heartbeats.

For practiced riflemen, shooting too fast is more often a symptom of poor judgment than a flaw in technique. You won't blunder if you

On the prairie, a slight rise may allow you to shoot prone, the steadiest position by far.

stay calm and think through each shot and if your shooting routine has become automatic through practice. Triggers that pull like the starter cords on chain saws are unlikely to go away soon. Like wind and branches, tough shot angles, cold hands, and your own labored breathing, a lousy trigger is an impediment to good shooting, but it is no excuse for bad shooting.

Beyond good form honed by repetition, hitting at extreme range hinges on sound judgment. Some shots are so difficult that you're courting a miss when you pull the trigger. In bull's-eye competition, you do the best you can and try not to eat any rounds waiting for better conditions. When hunting, you're not compelled to shoot. To fire at an animal without assuming that you'll kill it is irresponsible. You're as likely to cripple as to miss. My own rule of thumb is that if I don't feel I could make a first-round hit 9 times out of 10, I don't fire. It's better to try for an easier shot or to leave the animal for another day.

BANDITS, BUCKS, AND BULL'S-EYES

When Pancho Villa and his bandits pillaged Mexican farmsteads at the turn of the last century, rivalry among the bandits gave rise to contests. Legend has it that after one raid, marksmanship became an issue, so a couple of hapless steers were rounded up and staked far away.

Ken Nagel settles into position for practice with a Dave Smith rifle. Shoot more to shoot better.

Shooting livestock at long range soon caught on. Dr. Mario Gonzales wrote about a fiesta in Jalisco where contestants fired at chickens 100 meters away—with pistols. Any hit drawing blood claimed that chicken for the shooter. In 1946 Gonzales joined a club in Guadalajara for weekly chicken shoots. Turkeys were added as targets at 150 and 200 meters, pigeons at 50 meters. Riflemen could shoot at chickens 200 meters away and try for turkeys at 400. Sheep were staked 500 meters downrange.

This sport didn't last long. Animal suffering had less to do with its demise than did cheating. Shooters learned that you could hit a big rock next to a small target to draw blood with shrapnel. Bribed judges overlooked blood from a previous hit, attributing it to a later contestant. Animals were not the same size, and some moved more than others.

In 1948 Don Gonzalo Aguilar organized a rifle match in Mexico City, substituting metal silhouettes in the shape of animals. Four years later, Mexico held its first national Siluetas Metalicas championship. The course consisted of 10 shots each at *gallinas* (chickens) at 200 meters, *guajalotes* (turkeys) at 385, and *borregos* (sheep) at 500.

Coyote hunting keeps many hunters sharp-eyed during the off-season.

Riflemen with .22s could shoot *palomas* (doves) at 50 and 100 meters and pint-size steel *gallinas* at 150.

In 1967 Roy Dunlap and others at the George Paterson Rifle Club of Nogales, Arizona, imported the sport. The targets were like those used by Mexico's Northern League, but Dunlap put horns on the sheep. The club added a bank of javelinas (pigs) to be shot at 300 meters. On April 12, 1969, the first American Metallic Silhouette match happened at the Tucson rifle range. An entry fee of 30 pesos, or $2.40, included all the pit-barbecued beef you could eat. Matches that followed Stateside were for centerfire rifles only; the maximum weight changed from Mexico's 4.0 kilograms (about 8.8 pounds) to 4.6 kilograms (10.2 pounds) to accommodate scope sights. Still, all shots had to be taken offhand (standing), without a sling or artificial support.

Metallic Silhouette shooting has since grown. The National Rifle Association (NRA) has developed courses of fire for blackpowder cartridge rifle, long-range pistol, short-range pistol, small-bore (rimfire) rifle, and even air rifle and air pistol. Rules are similar; guns, target sizes, and distances vary. In the popular centerfire and rimfire rifle matches, competitors fire 40, 60, 80, or 120 shots in five-round strings, with no sighting shots. Targets are taken left to right; any hits out of sequence are counted as misses. A second-round hit on target #3 would be a double miss because target #2 is safe and the hit on target #3 cannot be scored. No coaching is allowed. If wind knocks down a target, you skip it and return to the far left remaining target for your last shot. Equipment failure may qualify you for an alibi string, 30 seconds per shot, at the close of that relay. Ties are broken by sudden-death shoot-offs. The only cartridge restriction in the centerfire event is a bullet 6mm or larger, but most shooters favor bigger bullets, because *borregos* hit low can be hard to topple.

Shooting at long distance offhand doesn't make much sense on the hunt, but Metallic Silhouette matches get shooters off the bench and compel them to hone skills of little import over sandbags. Breathing, hold, trigger control, and follow-through become much more difficult when you're supporting a rifle by bone and muscle 5 feet off the ground. Because your only chance at a trophy may come when you have no rest or opportunity to find a low position, practice in offhand matches can salvage a hunt that gives you one imperfect opportunity.

For some shooters, the allure of Metallic Silhouette shooting has a lot to do with the audible, visible target reaction. Like the steel plates in Action Pistol matches, they fire for effect: a chicken spun off its

The author practices with a Boyd's-stocked Legacy Mauser and Zeiss 4-14x50 Conquest scope.

This Kimber rifle is easy to carry and lift, but any lightweight rifle is hard to steady.

Pancho Villa allegedly inspired Metallic Silhouette shooting, a great game for hunters.

pedestal with a resounding clang, or the faint bong that follows a *borrego* melting into the mirage. In my youth, gallery shooting was still part of each county fair. The parade of moving ducks always had a line of youngsters eager to watch targets topple to their shots. Few urchins would have coughed up nickels to shoot black bull's-eyes.

The truth is, though, that paper targets are by far the most useful. They tell you where each bullet struck, exactly. You can call your shots and see instantly if your call was accurate. You can measure groups and track scores as you progress. A steel target can be laid low with a hit on the edge; a black bull's-eye is brutally honest: full credit for center shots only. Shooting paper appeals to shooters who are serious about honing their marksmanship.

The "black bull's-eye" matches that have defined traditional rifle competition in the United States are conducted mainly by clubs affiliated with the NRA, which has published rule books governing all its sanctioned events. Venues vary widely, from BB gun matches at 5 meters to High Power competitions at 1,000 yards. The National Match Course includes 200-yard offhand and rapid-fire sitting stages, plus prone stages at 300 and 600 yards, all with iron sights. Service

Practice from hunting positions is far more valuable than bench time. The author aims a 6.5/284.

rifle and target rifle categories accommodate soldiers and civilians. Sporting rifles have their own events, some of which allow optical sights. International rules regarding rifles, targets, and courses of fire are generally more stringent than NRA rules. One Olympic event is Free Rifle, described in the "International Rules" booklet provided by the NRA. It consists of 40 shots prone, 40 offhand, and 40 kneeling at 300 meters with an iron-sighted centerfire rifle. At 105 minutes, the standing stage of Free Rifle gives marksmen more than $2^{1}/_{2}$ minutes for each round. That's much more generous than in the 300-yard timed-fire prone stage of the National Match course, when riflemen get just 70 seconds for the ten-shot string.

Several courses of fire exist for .22 rimfires, including three- and four-position matches, prone matches, and team events. A two-day prone match comprises 160 record shots each day at 50 yards, 50 meters, and 100 yards. The first day is shot with iron sights, the second with a scope. Placings are for individual matches (four each day), subaggregates, and aggregates. Some riflemen who've competed in both rimfire outdoor prone and High Power National Match courses

A tight group in the middle. It's about time the shooter got off the bench and practiced offhand.

liken the challenge of hitting a 1-inch X-ring with a .22 bullet at 100 yards to the task of drilling the much bigger 600-yard center with .308 ammo.

Both Metallic Silhouette and paper-target position shooting help you immensely in the field. Any hunter who says that he's deadly on game but doesn't shoot well on the range is full of prunes. On the range, you know the distance, can dope conditions, and usually have more time than when an animal appears at meadow's edge during the last few minutes of daylight. On the range, you're not winded or physically drained. If you can't hit a bull's-eye under ideal conditions, you're not going to shoot well consistently at big game.

Recently, I spent an afternoon shooting long on the Tri-County range south of Portland, Oregon. The first targets, at 200 yards, were no easier than the 300- or 500-yard targets, because the bull's-eyes were sized to demand the same level of accuracy. Mercifully, the breeze that swung from 11 o'clock to 1 o'clock had insignificant effect even on .223 bullets to 300 yards. At all ranges, my .308 drilled center with center holds, after I adjusted the scope for distance. Of the 60 rounds I fired that day, none were from the bench. At 500 yards, firing

In Sweden, hunters are required to pass a shooting test on running moose targets.

at human-silhouette police targets, all 12 prone shots and all 8 from the sit struck "in the black." Discounting 3 or 4 hits close to the edge, it was an acceptable tally. But the session pointed up my need for faster shot cadence and greater care with the trigger squeeze.

Just honing your ability to assume a steady position quickly can help you a great deal when you have little time for a shot at big game. Once in Namibia, I duck-waddled and scurried on all fours to get within 400 yards of a herd of hartebeest containing a trophy-class bull, but it was still too far. Then, feeling the pressure of time, I chanced a dash toward a small hill. I gained 100 yards, but a cow spotted me, and the bull trundled off just as I began the squeeze. He stopped, half hidden, at 350 yards—too far. Despairing of a shot, I caught a glimpse of another bull running to the south. Exposed and side-lit, he was vulnerable. Prone, I let the Model 70 sag against the sling. He stopped. The crosswire steadied; I crushed the trigger. A 200-grain Ballistic Tip from the .338 wildcat crashed through his ribs. He ran and died.

As Pancho Villa's ruffians knew, range is not the only variable that makes a shot difficult. Target size, conditions, position, and your own physical state matter. So does the time you have to shoot. In terms of distance, any shot that you might bungle more than 10 percent of the time is too long. I've missed big game well inside 50 yards, so shooters who brag that "anything inside 300 yards is dead" set me on edge. Under good conditions, with a tight sling in prone, I can drill pumpkin-size targets all day long at 400 yards. But offhand and winded from a climb, aiming at a small patch of rib in a thicket while an alpine wind gusts in from the side, I might decline a 60-yard shot.

Months after the hartebeest episode in Namibia, as a wintry front drifted in from Canada, I was hunting mule deer that ranged Montana's northern hills. It was a place that held exceptional deer, and I let many bucks walk. But on the final day, it seemed time to turn predator. Still-hunting into lodgepole cover, I spied the nose of an old buck. Slowly I raised the rifle. My shot sent the deer reeling, but after a dash downhill, he recovered and climbed. I followed huge hoof gashes in the snow, occasionally spotted red. He almost beat me, but across a broad clearing at the hill's crest, I saw him making for timber. Quickly, from an impromptu sit, I fired twice. One hit echoed back. The buck turned, ran, and collapsed. I flopped prone. The morning sun blasted through my Redfield, all but obscuring the target. I held

This moving deer target, rigged by Kenny Jarrett, hones practical field-shooting skills.

high on a sliver of deer and squeezed. The last 154-grain Hornady from my .280 Improved struck both shoulders.

You might think that the shots that killed the hartebeest and finished the buck, both around 300 yards, were not particularly long. Many longer hits are on record, and many more have been claimed around campfires. But at 300 honest steps from the rifle, deer-size animals look small. Even from a steady position, the reticle will likely quiver. If you don't know the exact distance or can't accurately assess the effect of wind, you'll introduce error. If your trigger squeeze isn't smooth or if a shoulder twitches slightly at the shot, the rifle will move just when it must be still. A small glitch in hold or shot execution can put your bullet outside the vitals.

It's a common misconception that long shooting requires special equipment, that marksmen who "gear up" can hit much farther than they could with ordinary rifles, sights, and ammunition. In truth, the limits of effective shooting have little to do with hardware. They're imposed by the shooter: his or her inability to judge range and wind, his or her failure to hold the rifle still while executing a shot. There's

A Finnish hunter practices kneeling at a range. Take care with each shot, or you'll be practicing to miss.

nothing complicated about becoming a better marksmen. The fundamentals of shooting are simple, but if you want to shoot well, you must commit the time and effort to master them. A crack shot is not someone who makes an astonishing hit, because anyone can get lucky. Even consistent success on hunts fails as a gauge of marksmanship, because big game gives you big targets. An accomplished marksman is one who can consistently hit small targets from unsupported positions, one who knows and adheres to his or her limits.

Hunters who have chalked up enough kills to become ambivalent about killing know that their effective range isn't one yardage. A host of variables affects every opportunity. There's no such thing as a sure shot. Every one requires a decision. Ask yourself: Can I make this shot 9 times out of 10? Some opportunities you'll pass. Shooting when you're not confident of a lethal hit is risking a crippling hit.

Often I hear tales of big bucks and bulls drawing fire from hunters "because I knew I'd never have another chance at antlers like those" or "because it was the last day" or "because the animal was

Il Ling, an instructor at Gunsite shooting school, demonstrates kneeling. Note the animal targets.

You probably won't get many chances at game like this. Practice to make that important first shot.

headed out of our unit and we'd never see it again." These conditions have nothing to do with the one variable that should be crucial to your decision: the likelihood that you'll make a killing hit with your first round. If you cripple a big bull with a chancy shot, is that better than crippling a little bull? Is it more permissible to lose a buck on the last day than on the first? The only thing that justifies a decision to shoot is your ability to make the shot. If you can't make it 90 percent of the time, you have no business thumbing the safety forward.

Veteran marksmen not only shoot well at distance; they also let game walk when the shot is at the edge of their reach, no matter how close that is.

10 Modern Long-Range Masters

You can't make any money selling to people as poor as you.
—Kenny Jarrett, rifle guru and Carolina philosopher

ROY SELLS THE LONG SHOT

When the .270 Winchester and .300 Holland & Holland Magnum hit the shelves in 1925, hunters had the fastest, flattest-shooting big-game cartridges to come off ammunition lines Stateside. Thanks in the main to Jack O'Connor's high praise, the .270 became an instant and enduring success. The .300 H&H got a slower start because its long, tapered hull and big, belted base required a leggy action and a magnum bolt face. Besides, hunters of the day were quite confident that the tremendous blow delivered by the .30-06 was more than enough to put any North American animal out of commission. You didn't need a magnum that whacked your clavicle, pounded your gums, and left you with throbbing temples.

Twenty years later, however, those hunters were changing their minds—or, more to the point, they were persuaded that bullets faster than the '06's and heavier than the .270's made a lot of sense. Given the advances in optics over the intervening period (including coated lenses, courtesy of Zeiss), long shooting did seem more feasible. The prophet to preach that gospel and sell long-range rifles and ammunition as a form of salvation was California insurance salesman and amateur wildcatter Roy Weatherby.

Postwar prosperity had put Hollywood in the spotlight. Weatherby took note and recruited celebrities to carry his message. He placed himself in photos with actors such as Roy Rogers, world-

John Lee shot this big Alaska black bear with a .340 Weatherby. The 7 1/2-foot boar died quickly.

traveled hunters such as Elgin Gates, and foreign dignitaries such as the shah of Iran. He shared the lens with Elmer Keith and Jack O'Connor, with Jimmy Doolittle, Joe Foss, and Robert L. Scott. He parlayed associations into success because he believed what he preached: The Weatherby rifles could extend your reach and bring you more game. He told customers that owning a Weatherby allowed them to join elite company. The subliminal message: Weatherby will help you become more than you are. Certainly, it helped Roy.

But this quintessential salesman didn't come by his fortune easily. Born in 1910 to a sharecropper in central Kansas, Roy knew poverty. He and his nine brothers and sisters moved a lot. The family had no automobile, no electrical service or indoor plumbing. Roy recalled walking behind an aging plow horse, watching enviously as a neighbor pulled five bottoms three times as fast with a Fordson tractor.

In 1923 his father, George, opened a one-pump filling station in Salina. Then there was the move to Florida, "nine of us in a four-passenger Dodge, camping in a tent along the way." George laid bricks, while Roy hauled mortar. Growing up, Roy clerked in a music store, sold washing machines, and drove a bread truck. He later enrolled at the University of Wichita, where he met Camilla Jackson.

The .257 Weatherby Magnum was one of Roy's first commercial rounds and a personal favorite.

They married in 1936, and Roy got work at Southwestern Bell Telephone. Not long thereafter the couple headed west, winding up in San Diego. Employed by a local utility, then by the Automobile Club of Southern California, Roy was soon making very good money: $200 a month.

Since his boyhood days trapping opossums, Roy had indulged an interest in the outdoors. He liked to hunt, and he liked to experiment with guns. Working in his California shop with rudimentary equipment, he reshaped the .300 Holland & Holland case to increase its capacity. He reduced body taper and gave it a double-radius shoulder. The full-length version became the .300 Weatherby, but his first magnums were necked to .257, .277, and .284 and shortened for .30-06-length magazines. In 1946 he pledged everything he owned to get a $5,000 business loan from the Bank of America. It was a start, but for the first couple of decades, Roy Weatherby's custom rifle enterprise teetered, and bankruptcy was a constant threat. Nevertheless, Roy pushed ahead. Then one day, while behind the counter at his small retail store, he watched Gary Cooper walk in the door. It

In Sonora, a Coues deer hunter takes aim with his .240 Weatherby, essentially a belted 6mm/06.

was a pivotal moment. Soon Roy met other Hollywood stars. He wrote an article called "Overgunned and Undergunned" for a magazine. Sheldon Coleman saw it and became a customer.

Although the legend of Weatherby's salesmanship and the colorful characters who helped him achieve success are well known, the company's beginnings owe much to the work of a wildcatter named R. W. Miller. In 1940 Miller was experimenting in his California shop with the .300 Hoffman, a round that had been dropped from Western Cartridge Company's line seven years earlier. Western claimed that the sharp Hoffman shoulder caused high breech pressure and that, when loaded to acceptable pressures, this .30 wouldn't exceed the velocity of the .300 Holland from which it derived.

Miller reasoned that if he replaced the angular juncture at the case neck and shoulder with a rounded, or radiused, one, the powder gas would flow more smoothly, directing more of its energy at the bullet base. He also lengthened the throat on his rifle to ease the bullet's start. Miller wrote letters to the *American Rifleman* about his work, and the magazine sent authority E. Baden Powell out to take a look. Powell advised Miller to straighten the case body, thus reducing bolt thrust and preventing premature escape of powder gas. The new

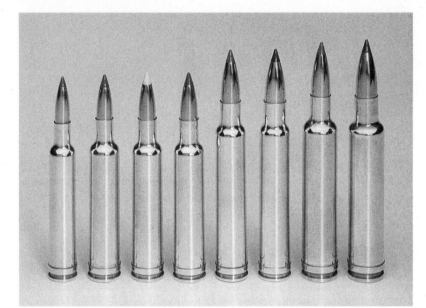

Weatherby cartridges for long shooting at big game. From left: .240, .257, .270, 7mm, .300, .340, .30-378, .338-378.

cartridge was called the PMVF: Powell Miller Venturi Freebore. In 1944 the two men went into business, marketing their product under the name of Vard, Inc., but they ran short of money and in 1945 sold out to Hollywood Tool and Die. Hollywood renamed the cartridge CCC, for Controlled Combustion Chamberage.

About this time, Roy Weatherby was designing his own wildcats. He carried a .270 PMVF on a deer hunt and liked it. Weatherby asked Miller to help incorporate the radiused shoulder on his rounds, but Miller demurred. Weatherby went next to George Fuller, a machinist friend who had fashioned the reamer for Weatherby's .220 Rocket. Fuller argued that a radius at the bottom of the shoulder would be hard to tool for, but he finally capitulated. Weatherby followed with a marketing package that would bring his company lasting success.

By 1949, Weatherby's hard work had produced a larger shop and store, but he needed more capital to put the company on the next rung. Business partner Bill Wittman agreed to incorporation, and in May the two men offered $70,000 in stock. One of the company officers was Herb Klein, a wealthy Texas oilman who owned a .270 Weatherby Magnum rifle. Klein bought $10,000 of that stock and

New Mark Vs with test groups of less than 1 inch at 100 yards merit the designation SUB MOA.

would later become a key source of business acumen and additional capital.

Roy Weatherby's sales pitch to hunters earned him the moniker "High Priest of High Velocity." A lightweight bullet driven fast, he said, delivered an effect out of proportion to its size, and you could hit easier with it at long range because it flew flat. The .220 Rocket, one of Weatherby's first efforts, did not go commercial, but the .257, .270, and 7mm—shortened, blown-out versions of the .300 H&H—developed loyal followings beginning in the early 1940s. The full-length .300 Weatherby, which came along in 1945, made the biggest splash and has long been the company's best seller. In 1953 Weatherby devised the huge .378, bigger in diameter than the standard .300 Holland round. Until the Mark V came along four years later, it found a home in Shultz & Larsen actions. The .460, a necked-up .378, appeared in 1958. Weatherby's diminutive .224, just slightly less ambitious than the .22-250, arrived in 1963, a year after the .340 on the .300 hull. In 1989 the company brought out a .416 on the .378 case, followed in the 1990s by the .30-378 and .338-378. Most recently, Weatherby reintroduced its namesake .375, a blown-out .375 H&H that died decades ago as the .340 and .378 bracketed its place in the lineup. No

Renowned for hunting rifles, Weatherby has gone tactical with the Mark V Threat Response Rifle.

matter what bullet diameter you name, if Weatherby has a cartridge to fit, it's one of the most potent, if not *the* most potent, for that bore.

Roy Weatherby built his first rifles on Mauser actions. In 1957 he and company engineer Fred Jennie came up with an action of their own: the Mark V. They engaged Germany's J. P. Sauer & Sohn to produce it. Since then, this mechanism, with its low-lift, interrupted-tread, lug-diameter bolt, has remained essentially unchanged. In 1971 rifle manufacture moved to Japan, then came Stateside in the 1990s. Now all Weatherby rifles are built in the United States.

During the 1990s, a six-lug Mark V appeared. This scaled-down action weighs 26 ounces, about 10 ounces and 28 percent less than the Mark V Magnum. Teamed with slim, fluted barrels, this receiver better fitted .30-06-size cartridges and enabled Weatherby to build rifles as light as $5^3/_4$ pounds. It became the nucleus of several hunting models and heavy-barreled varminters. For the Ultra Lightweights, Weatherby did not chop the barrel to pare ounces. That ploy would have reduced bullet velocity and impaired rifle balance. Barrels for the Weatherby Magnum rounds remained at 26 inches; those for standard cartridges and the 7mm Remington and .300 Winchester Magnum measure 24. Button-rifled Criterion barrels from John Krieger's shop are cryogenically treated. That is, barrel temperature is lowered to -300 degrees F to relieve stresses bound in the steel by manufacturing operations. The treatment and precise machining enable Weatherby to maintain its $1^1/_2$-inch, three-shot guarantee. It is not unusual for Weatherby Super Varmint Master rifles to shoot $1/_2$-inch groups at 100 yards.

Weatherby moved off the trodden path with a .338-06 Ultra Lightweight rifle. An offshoot of the .333 OKH developed in the early 1940s, the .338-06 was not adopted commercially until Weatherby chambered a lightweight Mark V for the round and added it to the list of Weatherby ammunition. The rifle weighs 6 pounds with a

24-inch barrel, a few ounces more than its Ultra Lightweight siblings. Reason: The Krieger barrel is of slightly greater diameter to leave enough metal in the flutes around a .33 bore. Larry Barnett at Superior Ammunition in Sturgis, South Dakota, provided the first .338-06 A-Square ammo, with 210-grain Nosler Partitions at 2,765 fps—only 65 fps shy of chart values for these bullets in the .338 Magnum.

The SVM and .338-06 were followed by the Super PredatorMaster, a $6^{1}/_{4}$-pound "walking" rifle for varmint hunters. PredatorMasters sold better than expected in .243, 7mm-08, and .308. Weatherby's marketing crew decided that the buyers weren't all shooting woodchucks and coyotes, so the company came up with a lightweight Super Big GameMaster on both the six- and nine-lug actions. The SBGM weighs $5^{3}/_{4}$ to $6^{3}/_{4}$ pounds. All barrels are stainless and handlapped, with six flutes and an 11-degree crown on a .583 muzzle. The trigger is adjustable, with .012 to .015 sear engagement. Like its predecessor, the Super Big GameMaster wears a stock of aramid, graphite, and fiberglass. Its T-6061 aluminum bedding block ensures precise recoil lug seating and stiffens the box mortise. In many ways, the SBGM is the modern version of Roy Weatherby's original Mark V rifle, stocked in nicely figured Claro walnut and listing, in 1964, for $285. There are now so many rifle models built on that action that keeping track of the subtle differences can leave you longing for the days when there was one Mark V and your only choice was chambering.

Tactical rifles have come of age, not only for police and military agencies but also for civilians with the yen to shoot far. The Weatherby TRR (Threat Response Rifle) has a beefy varmint-style stock with an optional Picatinny-style rail. Its 22-inch, superstiff barrel mikes .839 at the muzzle and comes chambered in .223 or .308. An alternative: the Custom Shop TRR Desert Magnum with a longer Mark V action and a 28-inch heavy, fluted barrel. It wears a target stock with adjustable comb and butt; you can order any chambering. The Custom Shop, incidentally, has grown to offer a broader range of options (including conservative stocks).

Beginning in 1954, Roy Weatherby conceived Imperial scopes to equip his long-range rifles. Built by Hertel and Reuss of Germany, the line comprised $2^{3}/_{4}$x, 4x, and 6x models, plus 2-7x and $2^{3}/_{4}$-10x variables. In the early 1960s constantly centered reticles in the second focal plane appeared. The Hertel and Reuss design didn't lend itself to other changes, so in 1972 Roy asked Asia Optical, a Japanese firm,

Roy Weatherby in his office. The sharecropper's son from Kansas found success in Hollywood, selling rifles.

to build a new Premier scope. In 1984 that was replaced by the Supreme series, also from Asia Optical. Soon thereafter, Weatherby stopped marketing scopes. Gone too are the Maynard Beuhler mounts that graced early Mark V rifles. Weatherby bought manufacturing rights to the Beuhler design and briefly offered the mounts under its own name. Roy's son Ed, now the chief executive, revived Weatherby scope mounts by contracting their manufacture with Gary Turner of Talley Manufacturing. The elegant steel Talley rings are embossed with a big "flying W."

Weatherby's Vanguard, a popularly priced alternative to the flagship Mark V, has come and gone since the early 1980s. Built on a Howa action in chrome-moly or stainless steel, it was reintroduced in 1994 and upgraded later. The 2004 Vanguard arrived in 12 chamberings, including Winchester Short Magnums and the .257 Weatherby Magnum. This hot .25, firing an 87-grain bullet at 3,825 fps, was one of Roy's first belted magnums and a personal favorite. But for decades it was factory chambered only in the costly Mark V. The Vanguard is much more affordable. Still, it boasts a fully adjustable

Rocky Gibbs claimed magnum velocities from .30-06 parent cases, suited to light-weight rifles.

trigger and a hammer-forged 24-inch barrel. A one-piece, fluted bolt slides easily in a forged and machined receiver over steel and alloy bottom metal with a hinged floorplate. An injection-molded Trico stock is standard. Weatherby's Custom Shop will replace it on order with a pillar-bedded Bell & Carlson stock of aramid, graphite, and fiberglass.*

THE GIBBS PHENOMENON

In March 1955, during a snowstorm, Rocky Gibbs moved from Richmond, California, to Viola, Idaho, 8 miles north of Moscow. He'd purchased a 35-acre tract laid out to accommodate a 500-yard rifle range. In his shop, Gibbs reestablished his California business: Gibbs Rifle Products. Until his death from leukemia at age 58 in 1973, Gibbs hawked his wildcat cartridges based on the .30-06 case. He left no hard evidence of how he achieved his eyebrow-raising bullet velocities, because his family, following his instructions, burned all the

---

*The early growth of Weatherby's company is well chronicled in the book *Weatherby: The Man, the Gun, the Legend* by Grits and Tom Gresham, Cane River Publishing.

After moving to Idaho, Gibbs developed high-speed rounds for hunting in country like this.

records. Gibbs had a flair for the dramatic, and he was openly concerned about other wildcatters pirating his know-how.

Rocky wasn't born Rocky. Christened Manolis Aamoen Gibbs, he
grew up with only one functional eye, having lost the sight in his
right one during a childhood bout of typhus. Soon after graduating
from high school in Gainesville, Texas, he boarded a train for California. As the story goes, he had it in his head to be widely remembered
and decided that another name would be a good first step. He asked
the train conductor about the mountains looming in the distance. The
Rockies, he was told. There in the coach he assumed the name Rocky
Edward Gibbs.

The California sojourn brought Gibbs in contact with other gun
enthusiasts who were not quite satisfied with standard ammunition.
A match at the local Richmond shooting club fueled his search for a
cartridge with exceptional reach and a violin-string trajectory. Each
year, the match winner would earn his crown by shooting groups at
100, 200, 300, and 400 yards, but group size wasn't all that mattered.
Part of the score derived from bullet drop measurements at 400 yards.
Flat-shooting rifles had an edge. Gibb's Model 721 Remington in .270
had plenty of sauce to kill deer as far away as he cared to shoot them,
but in the rarefied company of wildcatters, it lacked panache. Gibbs
followed his gunsmith's advice and rechambered to .270 Ackley
Improved. Discouraged by extraction problems, he sold the Remington and bought a Winchester Model 70 in .270. With it, he finally finished at the top of the chart. But his quest for a more potent cartridge
had just begun.

Rejecting the 40-degree Ackley shoulder, Gibbs ordered a reamer
with a 35-degree shoulder from Keith Francis in Talent, Oregon. He
called the cartridge the .270 Gibbs. Unlike the Ackley, Gibbs's wasn't
an improved case. The neck measured only .250 in length, so you
couldn't headspace a standard .270 round in a Gibbs chamber. It had
to be formed in a die or fire-formed in steps. The payoff: greater case
capacity.

Apparently, Rocky Gibbs set a record with his cartridge at the
next Richmond match. That was in 1953; a year later, he had six more
cartridges in a line that would change little. He stuck with the .30-06
as the parent case largely because in the 1950s there was still a surfeit
of military brass.

By the time he migrated to northern Idaho, Gibbs had something
of a reputation as a gunsmith and cartridge designer. He published a

The speed and energy of sharp-shouldered Gibbs cartridges made them suitable for long shooting at elk.

booklet entitled *Front Ignition Loading Technique,* which treated the subject of duplex charges developed by Charlie O'Neil, Elmer Keith, and Don Hopkins of OKH fame. Unfortunately, just three years after Gibbs had set up shop in Viola, a fire demolished the family's home, and with it all the undistributed booklets. Gibbs never reprinted the treatise, but his family of cartridges and his enthusiasm for wildcatting survived the blaze.

The .240 Gibbs, most easily formed from .25-06 brass, is among the most enduring of the Gibbs wildcats (though Rocky made relatively few rifles so chambered). He recorded over 3,600 fps with 75-grain bullets, 3,500 fps with 85-grain bullets, and 3,250 fps with 105-grain Speers. Rocky described the .25 Gibbs as the only wildcat that shot flatter than his .240 and compared it with the .257 Weatherby. His records showed 3,900 fps from 75-grain bullets, nearly 3,550 fps with 100-grain spitzers, and 3,330 fps with 117-grain bullets. The .25 Gibbs became quite popular, outselling the more versatile 6.5 Gibbs.

Rocky called his .270 Gibbs "the best all-around cartridge for a handloader." Even Jack O'Connor acknowledged its merits in *Outdoor Life:* "As far as I can tell, Brother Gibbs doesn't do it with mirrors." Launching a 130-grain bullet at 3,400 fps put the Gibbs in league with

Rocky Gibbs in his shop. The inventor/wildcatter reworked the .30-60 case into a series of high-performance rounds. He died at age 58.

the .270 Weatherby Magnum and a class above the .270 Winchester. Although Gibbs put a lot of stock in his 7mm and claimed 3,300 fps with a 139-grain bullet, this wildcat never sold particularly well.

The .30 Gibbs earned some notoriety as a poor man's magnum. Rocky managed 3,000 fps from 180-grain bullets, a match for the modern .300 Winchester Magnum and .300 WSM. Certainly the .30 was much more popular than the 8mm Gibbs, which Rocky considered a good use of 8x57 Mausers that made their way Stateside after World War II. Driving 170-grain bullets at 3,200 fps and 220s at 2,800 fps, the 8mm Gibbs certainly qualified as a killer of moose, elk, and big bears. But like the 6.5, it suffered from the curious American aversion to metric numbers.

Rocky added the .338 Gibbs to his line after 1958. By this time, the appeal of surplus rifles and ammo had worn thin—partly because the supply of both was drying up. The .338 Winchester Magnum had just appeared, and the .340 Weatherby was still a few years off, so .33-caliber barrels were special orders. An entrepreneur who could see the sunny side of any situation, Gibbs might have thought that the .338 would bring him more ink from the likes of O'Connor and Bob Hutton. But he knew that demand would be small; after all, he'd

Gibbs tested his cartridges on his 500-yard range near Vida, Idaho.

advertised the 6.5 Gibbs as "a vicious big game rifle, fit for gophers to grizzlies." Who needed a .338, with its brutal kick? Given the popularity and versatility of the .30 Gibbs, the .33 was a long shot indeed. And Rocky himself preferred 250-grain bullets in that bore—a tough assignment, given the magazines of the .30-06-length actions he used for his wildcats. Even though he claimed 3,050 fps with 200-grain bullets and 2,700 fps with 250s, Gibbs couldn't drum up enthusiasm for his .338. He dropped it after two years.

Many criticisms have been leveled at Rocky Gibbs and at his data. Like many wildcatters who sought to proselytize the unwashed, he may have embellished a bit when describing what his cartridges could do. He measured pressures, probably in copper units, but he appeared unconcerned with keeping them at what are considered reasonable thresholds today. His velocity readings were taken from barrels that may have been a couple of inches longer than his stated measure, because he considered only the bore, not the chamber, in that measure. Finally, like many handloaders, he remembered and repeated bullet speeds at the top of the range. Averages didn't impress prospective buyers quite as much as top velocity readings did.

Still, Rocky Gibbs brought high-performance cartridges to many shooters before the .264 Winchester and 7mm Remington Magnum were duking it out, before the .300 and .338 Winchester Magnums defined long-range punch for big, tough game. From a surplus Mauser or Springfield, a secondhand Remington 721 or Winchester 70, you could build a rifle with great reach and feed it with cartridges fashioned from GI hulls. Manolis Aamoen Gibbs got shooters to think beyond the limits of ordinary deer rifles and test their bullets and skills far along the arc.

BETTER ACROSS THE BEANFIELD

You can't tell an accurate rifle at a glance; you can't pick it from a rack the way you might Grandpa's old Enfield or a Weatherby .378. An accurate rifle identifies itself only when you fire it—and, to be brutally honest, sometimes not even then. Accurate rifles won't reveal themselves to inept marksmen. If you can't hold in the same place for consecutive shots, you'll find that accurate rifles scatter bullets as capriciously as rifles that can't keep their shots in a paint can. If you don't shoot well, accurate rifles are a waste of money.

Because most shooters consider themselves crack marksmen, rifles trumpeted as accurate sell briskly. Some companies go so far as to guarantee accuracy: $1^1/2$ inches at 100 yards, perhaps even a minute of angle. A smattering of these rifles get sent back to the factory, with notes from owners convinced that the hardware is flawed. Patiently, technicians punch out additional groups and offer telephone therapy. Convincing the incompetent that they are is a big headache, which is why anyone would be nuts to guarantee half-minute groups. Kenny Jarrett does.

Jarrett, 52, is a fourth-generation soybean farmer from Jackson, South Carolina. He grew up on the 10,000-acre Cowden Plantation, then owned by his uncle, J. M. Brown. After high school, Kenny went to work at Cowden. Then, in the late 1970s, he bought a lathe and opened a gun shop. Jarrett's perception of accuracy had already been molded by travel on the benchrest circuit. Building a rifle that consistently shot competitive groups, he found, was exceedingly difficult.

Texas gunmaker and benchrest shooter Harold Broughton took a shine to the lad and tutored him. Jarrett still credits Broughton for setting him on track to build truly accurate rifles. The next stop was Jerry Hart's barrel shop. By 1979, Jarrett had invested heavily in the gun business and had given up farming. His first year building rifles,

Whitetails are commonly shot up close in woodlots, but farm fields can offer long shooting.

he grossed $17,000—enough to encourage expansion. Favorable press in major gun journals gave Jarrett the traction he needed to establish himself as an industry icon. The red beard, golf-ball wad of tobacco, bib overalls, and Bubba wit all seemed an odd match to machine-work tolerances as fine as .0001. At first, that very incongruity helped sell stories about Jarrett rifles. It was the late Art Carter, I believe, who coined the term beanfield rifle to describe the deadly long-range effect of those rifles on southern whitetails. Hunters took note. By the time Jarrett's shop was a decade old, gross sales had topped $500,000, and he'd hired 13 people. The 2,200-square-foot shop, built from home-sawn cypress lumber and roofed with cedar shakes, had sprouted four additions, nearly tripling the space.

Meanwhile, Jarrett's rifles had risen in price to cover the over-head. In 1991 his least expensive rifle sold for $2,850—even though the finish was, by most standards, rough. Accuracy was the Jarrett hallmark.

"Lots of people tried to tell me early on that hunters just wouldn't pay for the level of accuracy demanded by benchrest competitors,"

Kenny Jarrett examines one of his rifles in .300 Jarrett, a flat-shooting, full-length magnum.

Jarrett recalled at that time. "I set out to prove them wrong." A top-rung benchrest shooter himself, Jarrett knew that building such precision into lightweight hunting rifles would be costly. He also figured, rightly, that for some hunters, accuracy is the defining element of a rifle—even one to be used on targets as big as deer. "It isn't that you need a half-minute rifle to shoot deer," he pointed out. "You don't pay a premium to kill. You pay the extra because accurate is what a rifle should be, and you can't abide a rifle that doesn't measure up."

For years, Jarrett built rifles on actions that the customer supplied, or he'd furnish a Remington 700 or, for large cases, a Weatherby Mark V. After truing the lugs by surface grinding and hand fitting, he chased the receiver threads so that the barrel and bolt axes lined up perfectly. Jarrett used Hart barrels for cartridges of .30 caliber and under; bigger rounds went in Schneider tubes. Along the way, he developed several of his own wildcat cartridges, from the .220 Jaybird to the .338 Kubla-Kahn, a .378 Weatherby necked to .33. One of his favorites is the versatile .300 Jarrett, on the 8mm Remington Magnum

*Even fast bullets drop. Kenny
Jarrett shows the impact below a
600-yard target (200-yard zero).*

case. By the early 1990s, Jarrett's shop held 68 chambering reamers. Seventy percent of his customers were then opting for wildcat rounds, the .280 Ackley getting the most play. Jarrett also developed a switch-barrel system for the Remington 700.

McMillan provided all the early Jarrett stocks. Kenny does not think that walnut has any place on an accurate rifle. "Stability is crucial to accuracy," he states simply. "Walnut walks." He pillar-beds all rifles and shoots them to make certain that they pass muster. In 1991 that meant $1/2$-inch three-shot groups at 100 yards for rifles 25 caliber and smaller, $3/4$ inch for larger bores. At the time, 85 percent of the Jarrett rifles sold wore hunting-weight barrels. Hewing to such strict accuracy standards, and developing loads to deliver that accuracy, limited annual rifle production to about 125.

In 1992 Jarrett started making his own barrels, button-rifled in stainless steel. "We learned a lot during those years, rejecting 27 percent of our barrels." That figure later dropped to 6 percent, even though the accuracy bar had been jacked even higher. Now Jarrett

Jarrett's rifles are renowned for accuracy. A short-barreled .308 Tactical rifle printed this three-shot group.

demands half-inch groups from even his 30-caliber magnums. Hardware that doesn't perform is discarded. Once, after rebarreling an action several times and scrapping the tubes, Jarrett hacksawed the receiver and hung it over his workbench—no compromises.

During the late 1990s, Kenny Jarrett's business went flat. The flush of publicity that had fueled early sales had died. Some customers came back with repeat orders—one man racked up $46,000 in Jarrett rifles—but for others, one expensive, super-accurate rifle was all a marriage could tolerate. At the same time, Jarrett was busy designing his own action. Unveiling it to me, he acknowledged that he'd have been better off with an accountant at his elbow. "It's too good," he shrugged. "I made it too expensive." Bleakly, he wondered if it would ever see production.

It did. In 2004 I visited Jarrett's shop and the Cowden Plantation, which he now owns and operates as a farm. He also leases hunting rights to deer and turkey hunters and maintains a 1,000-yard range to test rifles after they've proved themselves at a 100-yard range in the back of his shop. We started the tour at the shop, where an electrical discharge machine (EDM) and a computer-controlled mill (CNC unit) carve Jarrett receivers from 515 stainless bar stock, Rockwell 34. The mechanism includes clever features such as feed rails designed for specific cartridges. They're replaceable, not integral. A collar at the rear of the bolt ensures bind-free operation. Three evenly spaced lugs offer a lockup that puts even pressure all around the case head and allows for a low bolt throw.

Barrels for the Jarrett action and his custom rifles made from other metal are all rifled in-house. Stainless barrels receive a copper bore wash to ease passage of the carbide rifling button. The copper must be removed later—not a problem at the Jarrett shop, because all bores are hand-lapped. "We want to keep bore diameter within .0001, breech to muzzle," said Jarrett. "And we air-gauge every bore to check. Such tight tolerances cause high rejection rates, but if a barrel gets chambered, we're very sure it will shoot well. Of course, we don't know until we do the range work. Every rifle gets a proof target. We fire 40,000 rounds a year." He pointed to 55-gallon drums full of brass.

Kenny's son Jay runs the stock shop, where composite shells are precisely fitted to the metal, and aluminum pillars are glued in with Marine-Tex, also used in the recoil lug mortise. Conservative, classic profiles, with straight combs and cheekpieces, are typically painted black. "Jay is part of the reason I've kept investing in the shop," Kenny told me. "He and Rissa, who pretty much runs the office, deserve a shot at this business. They're not only my kids; they produce and sell my rifles."

Jarrett's most popular cartridges generate a lot of recoil, so Kenny designed his own muzzle brake. "It's effective because it has lots of holes and just .001 clearance for the bullet," he explained. Behind the well-equipped loading room at the 100-yard range, I found a prototype of the American Heritage Elk Rifle, built in limited numbers for the Rocky Mountain Elk Foundation. A few shots with this .300 Jarrett showed that the brake did indeed soften the kick. Accuracy? My first three Ballistic Tips nipped out a half-inch group.

Other rifles were promptly trotted out: a Tactical Rifle in .308, a long-barreled customer loan in .243 Catbird (Jarrett's own 6mm/.270 that drives 65-grain Shilen bullets fast enough to leave a hole in humidity), and Kenny's own .300, with the 200-grain Bear Claw loads he used to shoot a huge moose. The first three-shot group from the .308 went under 0.2 inch. The first three-shot group from the Catbird measured about 0.3 inch. At nearly 0.8 inch, the Bear Claws seemed naughty, but to miss a moose with a rifle that delivers $3/4$-minute accuracy, you'd have to be shooting at over 4,000 yards.

A Jarrett rifle that Kenny designed for the Rocky Mountain Elk Foundation shoots sub-minute groups.

"Let's shoot long!" Jarrett said, reading my mind. But the wind was up on the 600-yard range, and twice we had to staple backers that had been blown off by gusts that swayed the tall pines and flattened the grass beneath them. A row of trees would shield bullets somewhat over their first 350 yards of travel from the bench. Jarrett called the quartering breeze as I triggered three shots from the Elk Rifle: 8 inches. I fired three from the .308, keeping them under 5. Any thoughts that the tiny .243 Catbird bullets would be swept away by the gale were laid to rest by a sub-4-inch group at 600 yards. Drop, of course, was another story. All the bullets hit quite low. "That's why our backer is as tall as an outhouse," Jarrett explained. "At this range, even the hottest loads yield to gravity."

I settled into prone with a tight sling and fired another group with the Elk Rifle, holding high and doping the wind myself. Two bullets landed in the 8-inch target square; the third was a hand's width out. A prone volley with another .300 Jarrett equipped with a 6-24x Swarovski scope delivered a grapefruit-size group in the center of the vitals on a life-size deer target. With knowledge of the range and a handle on the wind, a practiced shooter with a Jarrett rifle has a long arm indeed!

"Addicting, isn't it?" Jarrett grinned.

It was a treat too, partly because ranges like the Cowden Plantation's are scarce, and partly because few—OK, none—of my hunting rifles can be counted on for $3/4$-minute groups at 600 steps. A truly accurate rifle impresses you the way a truly fast, quick-footed sports car impresses you. It imposes a responsibility too. Knowing that the rifle can shoot into one hole, you put your marksmanship on the line. Triggering a Jarrett with Kenny watching, you feel compelled to perform as well as the rifle. Good luck!

The Jarrett product line is smaller than it once was, thanks to some number-crunching and a commitment to make the 20-person shop more efficient. That quick turnaround is important for cash flow, too, Jarrett added. "Three of our rifles—the Signature, Windwalker, and Professional Hunter—already account for 90 percent of sales. We are a custom shop, and we'll continue to offer many options, including walnut and laminated stocks soon. But there's no sense slowing production and boosting costs with catalog items that interest only a few people."

Jarrett's customer base is small. "Of 1.3 million rifles sold annually in the United States, we figure about 5,000 are custom built," he said. "And our rifles are not cheap." Still, Jarrett has had tides of demand, and to ensure 90-day delivery, his shop capacity tops out at 200 rifles a year. He likes to think that his rifles go to people who appreciate their accuracy. "Back in the 1980s, a local youngster saved his summer hay money for three years to buy a Jarrett rifle. I threw in a Leupold scope on that deal."

Kenny Jarrett has shaved his beard and given up tobacco. But he still takes the measure of a rifle in tenths of an inch between impact centers. He'll tell you it's a good way to size up shooters too.

Beginning in 2004, Jarrett began marketing ammunition as well as rifles. Because Jarrett handloads already serviced 75 percent of his rifle customers, "we saw a need for ammunition to match our loads. We picked the .243, .270, 7mm Remington Magnum, .30-06, .300 Winchester Magnum, and .300 Jarrett for the first run." Assembled with Norma brass and the most popular big-game bullets, the ammunition comes in special 10-round boxes designed for one-handed, no-spill opening. Each includes a card with ballistic data: bullet velocity, energy, trajectory, wind drift, sectional density, and ballistic coefficient. Accuracy standards and velocities both exceed what shooters can expect from ordinary centerfire ammunition.

From beanfields to the Kalahari, Jarrett rifles are favored by many hunters who want to reach far.

DAVID MILLER'S FORMULA FOR DEER TOO FAR TO SHOOT

"Too far? I've shot several deer at over 500 yards." Such claims raise the ire of many riflemen who find long shooting irresponsible. Crippling can result when you fire at game from so far that you can't hit vitals consistently. But David Miller, rifle maker and avid Coues deer hunter from Tucson, Arizona, is unapologetic. "I may shoot farther than most hunters. But I don't shoot farther than I can hit." He's also ready to explain his super-long shooting.

"First, you need good equipment. I'm fortunate because Curt Crum and I build rifles for a living. We've done it for more than 25 years, so we know something about how to make rifles accurate. We use the best barrels and install the best sights and experiment with handloads. We're obsessive about intrinsic accuracy, because it is the cornerstone of field accuracy. You can shoot only as well as your rifle."

Miller concedes that for ordinary deer hunting, a rifle that shoots 2-inch groups past 400 yards is unnecessary. But he and Crum aren't ordinary hunters. "We focus on Coues deer, and we go for trophy-class bucks. You won't see many of those in a season—perhaps only one. Rarely will old deer let you get close, and sometimes your only chance to kill comes at a distance most hunters think unreasonable."

So Miller practices at those distances. While most hunters are rummaging for the box of cartridges they got with the rifle five years ago, Miller is sorting polished cartridge hulls by weight and reaming flash holes. He spins bullets on a concentricity gauge and sets aside for practice those with unacceptable run-out. Bear in mind that he is not using cheap bullets, but Sierra MatchKings and Barnes Triple-Shocks. "To get the best accuracy, you have to mind details. Accuracy is a measure of uniformity. The more you make each shot the same, the more likely you are to hit where you did before. Miking bullets to the fourth decimal and hand-scaling powder charges is tedious. But we know our ammo is as accurate as we can make it." It's not unusual for Miller to reject more than half the bullets or cases in a given lot. One batch of 500 match-grade bullets yielded only 50 that met his standards for hunting bullets. He uses a Bonanza Co-Ax Indicator to check run-out to .001 but concedes that variation to .003 is hard to detect on targets.

Miller says that the Internal Concentricity Comparator made by Vern Juenko of Reno is one of the best tools for sorting bullets by shape, weight, and concentricity. "It can even detect voids in the bullet core."

Safari Club International executive director Tom Riley used a David Miller rifle to kill this Coues buck at 375 yards.

Miller moly-coats his bullets, first cleaning them with denatured alcohol, then tumbling them for two hours in a container of hard shot pellets and molybdenum disulfide powder. The steel pellets help drive the moly into the softer jacket. Then the bullets are tumbled for one minute in a cleaning mix of ground corncobs. After that comes a two-minute shake in a jar of steel shot and carnauba wax, followed by a minute in the corncob mix for a final polish. The bullets emerge slate gray and slippery. Miller has found that moly bullets shoot measurably flatter than uncoated bullets and, with a 400-yard zero, rise only 4 inches above the sight line at 200 yards. They're not as quick to foul the barrel either. "My groups start opening up after 20 rounds with ordinary bullets," says Miller. "Moly-coated bullets deliver first-rate accuracy for up to 30 shots. And the cleaning is a lot easier behind moly."

In his early years as a rifle builder, Miller specialized in elaborate bolt rifles. Then, to satisfy his own need for a long-range Coues deer gun, he fashioned what he dubbed the "Marksman." A friend saw it and had to have one. Soon Miller offered the Marksman to customers as a low-cost alternative to his from-the-ground-up custom Classic.

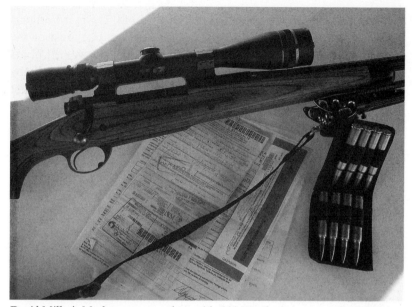

David Miller's Marksman reposes here with .300 Weatherby ammo and a Sonoran hunting license.

Expense, of course, is relative. The Marksman still costs as much as a used pickup truck. Miller takes no shortcuts in building a rifle and insists on the best components for both his rifles. "We have only one standard for accuracy," says Miller, who guarantees minute-of-angle accuracy with factory loads. Whereas the Classic's barrel is round, the Marksman's is fluted. Miller is willing to chamber the Marksman for wildcat rounds, but he prefers standard cartridges in the Classic. "We don't tell the customer what he should want," he grins. "But we're good at making him want what we're willing to build."

The Marksman wears a laminated, uncheckered stock, glass bedded to the action. Save for paper-thin gaps on either side of the barrel, the wood-to-metal fit matches that of skin on a peach. A Harris bipod comes standard on the Marksman, as does Miller's own scope mount, machined from a solid steel bar.

Like the Classic, the Marksman is built on a Winchester Model 70 Classic action. (David Miller was one of several prominent shooters who lobbied Winchester to bring back the Mauser-style extractor that was jettisoned to cut costs in the rifle's infamous 1964 makeover.) Both rifles get extensive work to make them more beautiful, smoother and more reliable in operation, and more accurate. The rear bridge is cut away on the right-hand side for easy loading, but most of the changes are inside. The entire magazine is Miller's design. It holds four magnum cartridges, not three. The follower has a detent so the bullet doesn't scrape it, and its shoulder is on the right so that the first cartridge ducks easily under the left rail. The follower spring has less tension than most; brand-new rifles cycle as if they were well used, but there's no trace of looseness. Parts on the Marksman move with the smooth precision of a Maserati gearshift.

This rifle was designed for the trail, not a presentation case. Its beauty derives from clean, graceful lines, and an impeccable fit and finish. The laminated stock is cut from Miller's own pattern. The medium-heavy 26-inch barrel from Krieger (or a maker of equal talent) has enough beef to mitigate muzzle jump and deliver accurate repeat shots in hot weather. Miller prefers to chamber for the .300 Weatherby Magnum. "It drives 168-grain Sierra MatchKings at 3,400 fps. They shoot flat, buck the wind, and hit hard enough to kill little deer as far as we can see to aim at them. We get fine accuracy at long range too."

To better equip the rifle for long shooting, Miller installs a Leupold 6.5-20x scope. It features Miller's own rangefinding reticle, a standard cross-wire augmented by two stadia wires below the horizontal wire. At 20x, they bracket 12 inches (the average depth of a Coues deer chest) at 400 yards. They also provide aiming points that, with the bottom post of Leupold's Duplex, enable you to hold on or very near the point of intended impact out to 600 yards. The Miller reticle includes two thin vertical lines on either side of the center wire (12 inches at 20x at 400 yards) to help with hold-off for wind at long range.

My first trip afield with a Marksmen amounted to a lot of sitting with it behind high-power glass. "You don't walk for big Coues deer," Miller said. "You stay in one place and look very carefully into spots that might hold bedded deer—pockets of shade just a bit too small to conceal a whole deer. Don't spend too much time looking at big patches of brush that you can't see through. Focus on smaller coverts; look for pieces of the animal. At dawn and dusk, and occasionally during the day, scrutinize the edges of bigger clumps to catch deer that are moving around. We stay out all day, because Coues deer can get up and nip at browse or stroll to the nearest water at any time."

Miller emphasizes that spotting a buck is hardly a guarantee that you'll be able to stalk it. Ocotillo and other desert plants can hide

Curt Crum fires while John Mullins spots. Shooting at Coues deer can be very long.

David Miller (left) and Curt Crum examine one of their Marksman rifles in the field.

Long hours spotting often bring only one long shot. Miller and his .300 Weatherby are ready for it.

these small deer as soon as you come off your vantage point. Shots taken from a hill or across a canyon or from a slope down to a flat can be long. Some are very long.

My hunt was almost over when we finally spied a buck to shoot. Actually, I spotted it, moving slowly along the foot of a ridge nearly a quarter mile away. It was dawn, and he was headed to bed. Even before Miller hissed, "Shoot!" I was prone, steadying the Marksman on its bipod. Centering the second wire on the deer's chest to adjust for bullet drop from the 300-yard zero, I squeezed the trigger. The deer vanished. We paced 410 yards to the buck, shot squarely through the lungs.

The next morning I grabbed a handful of cartridges and hiked into the desert to shoot the Marksman at paper. Groups from 100 to 500 yards included one three-shot cluster at 400 yards that measured an inch.

But intrinsic accuracy is not the whole trick. To kill game at very long range, you must shoot well. Miller doesn't just flail away at distant deer with his .300. He shoots very deliberately, and he shoots only when he's pretty sure that he'll hit. He can't abide the popular mantra: If there's a bullet in the air, you have a chance. That's irresponsible thinking, and it leads to irresponsible shooting. Miller puts the onus on the shooter, not on luck: "If you have a plan, you have a chance."

Miller always has a plan. He's not only an ace rifle builder but also a wizard at marketing his wares to the people most able to afford them. He's managed to hunt for bongo, mountain nyala, and forest elephant and spend weeks each winter chasing Coues deer in his beloved Sonoran hills. His collection of record-book Coues bucks is a remarkable testament to his rifles and his perseverance. Miller is not wealthy. He's sometimes lucky but always looking for opportunity. When he finds it, he comes up with a plan. "Any forward-thinking, detail-oriented person can succeed in business," he says. "And in shooting."

Miller plans for hunting season by shooting a lot at long range. He knows that deer seldom show up within 200 yards, so he doesn't waste time shooting there. "I like to zero farther out, and practice most at 300 to 500 yards. I shoot farther too." Practice, he says, makes an accurate rifle lethal.

Once, while hunting in Chihuahua, Miller spied a Coues buck in a place that denied him an approach. It was bedded far from the nearest place that offered a shot, so Miller hiked there and ranged the dis-

David Miller took this splendid Coues buck in 1991. "Big deer always show up far away," he says.

tance at 550 yards. Then, even though the deer was now hidden by brush, Miller waited—for hours. Finally, the deer stood. Miller shot him, then fired again, scoring two lethal hits at double the distance most hunters might consider a long shot. "It was farther than I like to shoot," he says. "Closer is always better. But there was no question in my mind I could kill that deer if conditions stayed favorable. I've shot this rifle at little targets out to 600 yards. I know where the bullets land and how big the groups are."

Miller stresses the importance of practicing under different conditions—not just in wind but also in varied lighting and from every hunting position you'll use afield. If you typically set up on a Harris bipod, use it in practice. But the next shot you get may be in brush too tall for a bipod, so you'd be smart to throw a few shots downrange from a sit or a kneel. A sling helps a great deal in these positions; it also affects the bullet's point of impact because it pulls the forend away from the barrel and counters the natural rise of the barrel during recoil. "Until you shoot at long range under specific circumstances, you can't predict the result of a shot at long range under those circumstances," says Miller. "So you're not qualified to take it."

There's no doubt in Miller's mind that shooting at extended yardage before hunting season enabled him to take his best Coues deer. During the late 1980s and through the 1990s, he killed six bucks that made the Boone & Crockett record books. The closest shot he got at those six stunning deer was 450 yards. He calculates that he's killed a buck for each of his 55 years and attributes much of that success to diligent and constant practice at targets too far for most riflemen to hit without walking the bullets in. "When Curt and I draw down on our practice targets," he says, "we shoot as if one bullet was all we had. We know that if we don't hit a deer fatally with the first bullet, it's a lost opportunity. We'll probably never see the deer again."

At the range, Miller uses the smallest target he can see. It is easier to quarter with the fine cross-wire and 20x magnification, and small targets encourage you to concentrate. "Just shooting is not useful," says Miller. "Practice sloppy shot execution, and it will become a habit and you'll shoot poorly when you see a deer. Every shot in practice must be the best you can make. Take your time at long range. Pick up the cadence only when you can do so without compromising accuracy. Remember, your goal is to make shots you can predict and repeat." A good plan, that.

THE LONG ARM OF LES BAER'S AR-15

Soldiers in Vietnam didn't all like the M-16, but it remains the official U.S. battle rifle. It has since challenged service rifle competitor who, in the National Match course, must shoot at ranges up to 600 yards. Heavy, match-grade barrels and tuned triggers have improved AR-15 scores out to the 300-yard mark. Beyond that, heavier bullets have made the "Mattel" a truly competitive rifle. Match bullets of 60 to 77 grains launched from barrels with rifling as steep as one turn in $7\,^1/_2$ inches maintain their speed better at long range and more effectively resist wind deflection.

In late fall 2003, Ruger and Hornady announced a new cartridge. Based on the .222 Remington Magnum case, the .204 Ruger has the same .378-inch rimless base. Trim length of 1.84 inches is within .01 of its parent's. You could say that the .204 is a necked-down .222 Magnum, with a 30-degree shoulder replacing the Magnum's 23-degree slant. Overall loaded length for the .204 is 2.26 inches, essentially the same as that of the .222 Magnum's.

On a windy range, 32-grain Hornady .204 bullets shoot very accurately and with surprisingly little deflection from the Les Baer AR.

The .222 and .223 Remington share the base dimensions and shoulder angle of the .222 Magnum. At 1.70 and 1.76, respectively, their cases are shorter—but not by much. The AR platform would no doubt accommodate the .204. Shooters speculated that if anyone could make a Mouse Gun shoot the .204 well, it would be Les Baer. Baer's Hillsdale, Illinois, shop is noted for producing accurate guns, both its AR rifle series and a fleet of sophisticated 1911 pistols.

Baer was even quicker than some had predicted in bringing a .204 AR to market. A prototype I fired in early 2004 at PASA Park, not far from the Baer digs, delivered X-ring-size groups on National Match targets at 600 yards. That day, I shot slowly to avoid drift in 10-mph gusts. The 32-grain Hornadys drilled the breeze with much less deflection than I'd expected.

Veteran long-range shooter Kenny Jarrett would not have been as surprised. Earlier that year, I'd been shooting at 600 yards on his Carolina range with a .243 Catbird, which looks like a .204 Ruger on steroids. "You'd think those 80-grain 6mm bullets would yaw in the slipstream of a sparrow," remarked Jarrett. "But they shoot plum straight." The target proved him right. Vigorous full-value drafts bent the pines lining the north side of the range, while the Catbird printed

Les Baer is known for building AR-type rifles that shoot like bolt guns. Not all shooters can tap that precision.

a 5-inch group. "It'll do better on a still day," noted Jarrett. "Three inches at 600 is my standard."

The Les Baer .204 prototype went back home before I had a chance to tap its potential. The better part of a year passed before a production rifle became available, but when the box arrived at my office, I tarried not. Tossing ammunition and targets into the pickup, I motored under a bright sun 5 miles along the south shore of the Columbia River, then turned up into the bluffs. There, with my help and countless rounds of ammunition, my friend Danny O'Connell has chewed a trench into the cliff behind the target frame in back of his house. Someday, someone will mine lead there. This day, I was out to pulverize more basalt.

What impresses you before you even load a Les Baer rifle is its finish and the way the parts snick and snap, click and thunk—no rattles, no hangups. The flat surfaces, impeccable detailing, and near-seamless fit of the parts tell you that this is no military rifle. Ease the bolt open; back it comes as if on hydraulics. Spring grinding? Hah! Does the gearbox in a Porsche talk back? *Schhhink.* A round whisks into lockup.

The heavy barrel of a Les Baer rifle steadies you offhand. The uniform bore begets bull's-eyes.

I stuffed a handful of Hornadys into a magazine and pushed it home. The Les Baer Super Varmint Rifle (SVR) settled nicely into the bags. Slowly I pressured the trigger. Bang. The barrel hardly moved. The allure of the .204 is its apparent lack of recoil, so you can stay on target and see the animal's reaction to hits. You don't need a brake to keep most .204 rifles lined up. My first five-shot group miked an even .70 inch. Subsequent strings showed this rifle capable of the half-minute precision Baer claims. Proof targets provided with this SVR were one-holers measuring less than .30, center to center. A bolt-gun junkie should approve of such performance, even if he doesn't cotton to the Mouse Gun feel of an AR. Still, I found the SVR surprisingly easy to aim and operate, on and off the bench. It balances well. A beefier rear grip aids control. Les Baer has made the rifle seem lighter than it is.

No matter the mechanism, you won't get one-hole accuracy without a first-quality barrel. The Les Baer 416-R stainless barrel is cut-rifled, air-gauged, and available in lengths from 18 to 24 inches. A note inside the gun's padded case explains that the chamber is cut for Hornady ammunition only. Baer told me that this cautionary missive

Les Baer's .204 feeds Hornady ammo smoothly from five-round magazines.

allows him to keep chamber dimensions near minimum and to hew to tight tolerances.

The two-stage Jewell trigger on a test rifle broke at 2 pounds 14 ounces, following a long, easy takeup. The Jewell is standard, as are a Picatinny rail, aluminum gas block with Picatinny top, chromed National Match carrier and extractor, titanium firing pin, slotted free-floating handguard with adjustable handstop-swivel, custom grip, and all-weather "Baer Coat" finish on metal parts except the barrel (and you can add it there if you wish). Included too is a Versa Pod bipod. Just snap it onto the rifle's forward stud and adjust the legs to your prone or bench position. Close the legs, and they swivel upward to lie out of the way, parallel to the barrel. Enough play has been engineered into the bipod's base to let you tweak the rifle's cant.

The price for this ultra-small-bore ordnance is well below the $3,000-plus you might expect to pay for such an extraordinary piece of equipment. What you pay depends in part on which extras you order—such as camo finish and special rifling twist. The base rifle lists for under $2,000. A couple of rifle-scope packages are available, including a $3,075 option that includes a Leupold 8.5-25x50mm Vari-X III scope with a side-mounted focus dial. This is the outfit I used.

The SVR weighs just over 13 pounds with scope and lightweight bipod. It is certainly a state-of-the-art autoloader. Although bolt rifles still excel at yanking hot, sticky cases from chambers and deliver more reliable performance in dirty conditions, cycling in the test rifle was unfailingly smooth and positive, with no stoppages. The SVR matches the precision of most traditional target rifles and shoots smaller groups than many of them. It wears a trigger that truly justifies a "match" label and feels like a rifle that wants to shoot well. Although some shooters might pick walnut over plastic and favor the profile of a prewar Mauser or Model 70, they'd find no edge in performance. Danny and I were mightily impressed with the SVR in .204. Brian Kelly, a local rifleman who'd recently bought an entry-level AR, needed no convincing. His only comment: "Do you think folks in Illinois would notice if we sent back mine and kept the Les Baer?"

Although some shooters still think of the AR-15 as simply an M-16 out of uniform, many hunters are finding the heavy-barreled target versions the ideal rifle for varminting. The notion that ARs aren't accurate enough to deliver consistent kills to distant prairie dog towns died when Mouse Gun enthusiasts started winning on the National Match course. With the SVR, you could say that there's no reason to manipulate a bolt except personal preference. Beyond precision, the Les Baer AR offers faster shooting, an asset when you locate several prairie dogs. Survivors often stay aboveground just long enough for another trigger squeeze. But they won't linger if you let them watch you manipulate a bolt. Staying still between shots is not only good for hunting; it's also less telling on old muscles. When

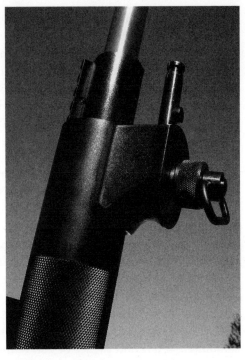

To accommodate competitive shooters, Les Baer offers a hand-stop and other match accessories.

you're prone, even cycling a bolt becomes work. It can also affect your position to the extent that you must refine it before the next shot.

AR-15s don't carry as comfortably as bolt rifles do—at least not on the shoulder. But once the action starts, a box with 20 rounds that nose into the barrel by themselves gives you lots more shooting for less effort than does a bolt-action magazine fed by hand or a loading platform begging for one round at a time.

The Les Baer rifle comes in .223 as well as .204, but I'd order the .204 in any new varmint rifle. It's not that I'm entertained by the mayhem caused by high-speed hollowpoints detonating rodents. A better view of the results of the shot is less appealing than the simple comfort of shooting a mild cartridge that has such astounding reach. Hornady's original 32-grain .204 bullet leaves the muzzle at an advertised 4,225 fps, a tad faster than a 40-grain bullet from a .220 Swift (4,200 fps) and a .22-250 (4,150 fps). But it is neither as loud nor as violent in recoil as those hot rods. It shoots just as flat, dropping only 4.1 inches at 300 yards, given a 200-yard zero. At 100 steps, the .204 strikes only .6 inch high, and at 500 yards, it's still tracking just above the arc of both the .22-250 and the Swift.

Hornady's 40-grain .204 load clocks 3,900 fps. This bullet, too, flies flatter than 40-grain .22-250 spitzers at long range, dropping 4.3 inches at 300 yards, compared with 4.5 inches for the Varminter and 5.5 inches for the Hornady 40-grain .223 load. The .204's heavy bullet is traveling faster at 200 yards than a 35-grain spitzer from the .22 Hornet clocks at the muzzle. With a higher ballistic coefficient than same-weight .22 bullets, the 40-grain .204 combines killing weight and laserlike flight to give you point-on lethality to 300 steps for most small game. It's less wind-sensitive than the 32-grain .204 bullet (which it passes at around 225 yards). It shoots flatter than even a Swift to 500 yards, and that is a very long shot.

TEXAS LIGHT

I like Texans. They think expansively and grin a lot. When talking with you, they toe the ground gently, as if to reconnect with the dirt. They're salt-of-the-earth, easygoing, but independent people. If it had a postal service, Texas would be a country. Texas has its share of oil, cattle, and mesquite. It has lots of dry acres and a long coastline. It has more Chevy Suburbans, probably, than California and New York combined. You'll find plenty of gun enthusiasts in Texas too—or, as they say there, a passel.

Certainly, there's enough firepower in Texas to equip an army. Some of that hardware in the hacienda is ordinary, but Texans can be picky about what they shoot, which is why some of them order custom rifles. They don't have to send out of state, because Texas breeds gun-makers—among them: Lex Webernick of Rifles, Inc., in Pleasanton; J. Earl Bridges, who works under the Hill Country Rifle Company ban-ner out of New Braunfels; and Charlie Sisk of Sisk Rifles, near Dayton. All three of these firms qualify as small semi-custom shops ("semi" means that you don't get to make *every* decision when you order a rifle, but you pay a lot less than if you insisted on that prerogative).

The lightweight hunting rifle is hardly new. Winchester brought out a sub-6-pound rifle in 1924. The selection of superlight commer-cial bolt rifles now rivals that of breakfast cereals. For the most part, these deer guns are good-looking, accurate, and affordable. What, then, can a semi-custom firm offer? "A stock better fitted to the shooter," says Lex Webernick. "Barrel lengths and weights, finishes, and stock colors to order. Tighter tolerances. A bolt and receiver truly aligned with the bore. Mostly, you get better accuracy." He and Char-lie Sisk and J. Earl Bridges concede that many factory rifles shoot or

Demand for custom-shop lightweights resulted in 6-pound rifles from Kimber (left) and Remington.

can be tuned to shoot close groups. "But accuracy is guaranteed when you have a rifle built from scratch to shoot well."

Webernick, who operates his shop with his wife, Lina, and one employee, has long specialized in lightweight rifles. He mates Winchester 70 and Remington 700 receivers to synthetic stocks, installing the customer's choice of barrels. "We prefer Liljas," he says. Like all the best custom makers, he trues the action so that bolt, barrel, and

This Model 70-based sporter in .270 WSM came from the Hill Country Rifles shop.

receiver share the same axis and the bolt lugs mate squarely with their seats.

Rifles, Inc., produces several models of bolt guns. Introduced to them on a caribou hunt long ago, I used a very lightweight Webernick rifle in .260 Remington. With it, I trekked over many acres of tundra and came to appreciate its wandlike handling. I crawled with it in one hand and held it steady for several minutes as a herd of caribou fed toward me, a sea of animals exposing the target bull too briefly for a safe shot. When the herd had passed, I trotted after it, sun to my back. As caribou do, these animals seemed to pick up speed without breaking out of a shambling gait. I jogged through a depression, out of sight. On the far side, a young bull spotted me. The caribou with the huge bez points and massive shovel was beyond him, probably 250 yards off. My chance for a sneak had evaporated, so I decided to sprint. Clutching the .260, I galloped toward the astonished rear guard. Ten yards, and all the animals had become aware. Twenty, and they were thinking. Luckily, it takes caribou a long time to think. I'd covered 80 yards and found an alley in the herd before the first bovine muzzles went in the air and the wariest animals began to prance off. But the target bull didn't leave soon enough. Breathing hard, I snugged my sling even as I dropped to a sit and leveled the rifle. One shot, and the bull was down. A truly portable rifle, I reflected, can help you kill game.

That rifle wore a Webernick stock that's truly one of the lightest in the industry—"11 ounces," claims Lex. It has a very slim wrist that's a tad short for my hand. In a fit of economy, Webernick kept the forend just long enough for a comfortable grip. He put the swivel stud on the end so you aren't cramped if you use a sling. A stud here doesn't catch on gun cases either. To keep the overall weight around 5 pounds, Webernick mates that stock to a slender barrel and a receiver machined to remove excess ounces. The rifle balances nicely and comes to your shoulder like a grouse gun. Most of these super-light-weight sporters wear muzzle brakes because, even in standard cham-berings, the lack of rifle inertia makes for quick, sharp recoil.

Webernick designed and manufactures his own short muzzle-brake, contoured to match the barrel and so unobtrusive that you must look hard to see the seam. It's among the smallest and quietest brakes, but also one of the most effective. "Many hunters want the reach of magnum rifles," Webernick says. "But they won't shoot them enough to shoot them accurately if there's no brake. However well-proportioned the stock, 30 foot-pounds of recoil will make a 5-pound rifle jump!"

Webernick's rifles have equipped women in my outdoor skills program, High Country Adventures. The slim grips fit small hands. A thick, soft buttpad from Rifles, Inc., mitigates recoil.

A couple of years ago I hunted with another Webernick rifle, this one built to my specifications on a stainless Winchester Model 70 Classic action. It has a 24-inch barrel of slender but not feathery con-tour, bored to 6.5x55. The stock is a McMillan of conservative profile. At just over 6 pounds, it has enough heft to aim easily when I'm winded but is still light enough to carry all day. There's no brake, because even quiet brakes savage my ears. Besides, a 6.5 Swede is a gentle cartridge. I asked Webernick to color the stock a deep red. It came out plum and, to my surprise, nicely complemented the satin stainless metal.

That rifle went with me to Sonora, where, from a hill swathed in cholla and ocotillo, I spied a buck on an equally inhospitable ridge. While stalking it, I lost sight of the deer. When I crested, there was no Coues whitetail in sight. Just then, the deer rocketed away, almost from underfoot. I fired as if at a quail and missed. The antlers floated

A long, open grip makes this HCR stock easy to handle, especially for someone with big hands.

periodically above bushes as he raced toward the valley floor. I slinged up and sat and had just trained my crosswire on the widest gap in the brush when the buck appeared in it. He stopped to look back uphill. I pressed the trigger, angling my 129-grain Hornady into his off shoulder. He collapsed.

I would later decline a long shot at a magnificent Coues buck that surely would have scored in the Boone & Crockett book. The 6.5x55, I had to remind myself, is not a .30 Magnum. Then I botched a relatively easy shot at a buck almost as big. I just wanted him too badly and jerked the trigger.

Most Webernick rifles are chambered to magnum cartridges. "About 60 percent of custom orders are for .300 Magnums of some sort," says Lex. "The .300 WSM was hot for a while, but I'm getting lots of requests now for rifles in .300 Winchester Mag. It's a great round, much more widely available." The bulk of his rifles not chambered to .30 Magnums go to shooters enamored of various .270, 7mm, and .338 rounds. Webernick says that the .270 Winchester is still popular, but he sells very few .30-06s. The 6.5/284 accounts for some orders, as do such unlikely candidates as the .264 Winchester. "We're

Lex Webernick built this super-lightweight rifle with a slim 11-ounce stock.

selling quite a few walking-weight varmint rifles in .204 Ruger now," he adds. Whatever their preferences, one thing his customers share is a desire to combine reach with portability. Nine out of 10 Webernick rifles are built on Remington 700 actions, "because they're available, affordable, and easy to bed." Webernick pillar-beds all rifles and will install an aftermarket trigger if the customer wants it; about 20 percent do.

He also offers a safari model with an express rear sight and barrel-band front sight and swivel. "I recommend the M70 with its powerful extractor for dangerous-game guns," he tells me. On all rifles, Webernick prefers stainless steel. It's less prone to interior rust than is chrome-moly. "I doubt it's any more accurate; you may get a little more life from the throat."

Mostly, the customer calls the shots when ordering a Webernick rifle. Specify a blind magazine, checkered bolt knob, fluted barrel, or special color in the Teflon (applied in-house and by a contractor), and Rifles, Inc., will accommodate. Lightweight scope mounts are a Rifles, Inc., specialty. Webernick machines rings with integral bases from alloy; they're clean and handsome. He agrees with me that big objective bells on rifle scopes have spoiled the balance of trim rifles and made stocking a headache. "The bigger the front lens, the higher you

A Rifles, Inc., 6.5x55 helped the author down this Sonoran Coues deer. The scope: a 6x Leupold.

have to mount the scope, and the higher the comb you need to put your eye on the scope's axis." But long shooting has become a passion for many hunters, and they want extra magnification for long shots. Wide front glass gives them an edge in dim light.

You'll spend at least $2,800 for a Webernick rifle, not counting the receiver. But you'll find it as accurate as it is appealing to the eye. Webernick breaks in every barrel. At least one test target must show three shots inside $1/2$ inch (1 inch for magnums) at 100 yards.

Such strict standards also apply at Hill Country Rifle Company (HCR), established in 1996. Like Webernick's, the shop's specialty is high-quality bolt-action rifles built on commercial actions, mostly supplied by the customer. "For synthetic-stocked rifles, about 60 percent of our clients prefer Remington 700s, the rest Winchester 70s," says J. Earl Bridges, an accomplished metalsmith who also builds several walnut-stocked rifles annually. Pick French, English, or Turkish wood checkered 24 lines per inch and oil finished; Claro and Bastogne are available too. "For walnut rifles, 9 out of 10 clients provide a Model 70 action," adds Bridges. He points out that Model 70s, with their Mauser-style extractors, are preferred for dangerous-game rifles too. These are typically stocked with a standard McMillan handle that's bedded and installed at HCR. Lilja, Hart, and Krieger remain top barrel choices. Actions are pillar-bedded, the barrels free-floated.

Bridges studied under Jerry Fisher, D'Arcy Echols, and Don Klein. In 1987 he bought Echols's Precision Machine Inletting Service, then began teaching at a gunsmithing trade school. In 1993 he and wife Charlene formed the Colorado Gunsmithing Academy in Lamar. They developed a curriculum and operated the school for six years. Hill Country Rifles was their next stop, where Bridges is the chief rifle builder there. HCR owner and president Dave Fuqua, who designed and manufactures the firm's muzzlebrakes, does much of the barrel work. Hector and Irene Herrera, a brother-sister team, serve customers with an accurizing service. "They've been at it for 20 years," says Bridges. "We finish 350 to 400 rebarreling jobs a year, and more accurizing projects. If you send a gun in for that, Hector and Irene glass-bed and install pillars, float the barrel, recrown the muzzle, lap the scope rings, and adjust the trigger to a crisp $3^{1}/2$ pounds. Of course, some triggers don't let us take that step." They lap the locking lugs on about half the rifles "But only if we can do so without changing headspace," he adds. The guarantee is impressive: You'll get groups half as big as you did before HCRs' work. Cost for accurizing at this writing is $295. Shooters who revel in long shooting find the expense reasonable.

Every year, Hill Country builds about 120 Classic rifles with synthetic stocks of Bridges's design. I got one for testing—a stainless Model 70 in .270 WSM. At first glance, I immediately liked it. The trim, long grip felt as good as it looked. Especially slender when viewed from the top, the grip swiveled and pivoted in my hand without costing control. The 18-lines-per-inch checkering had mulled borders, and although I prefer it a bit sharper and finer, it was both attractive and functional; ditto the shape of the forend and cheekpiece. Textured but not abrasive, the stock was finished with a properly dull paint. I liked the sage green color on this .270 WSM. It would complement matte blue as well as it did satin stainless metal. The barrel crown appeared perfect, adequately recessed. The action cycled snappily but with enough stiffness to indicate that it was still new. The trigger and safety could have been smoothed up to work with less effort; however, that could easily be done, and no doubt some shooters prefer a bit more resistance than I do.

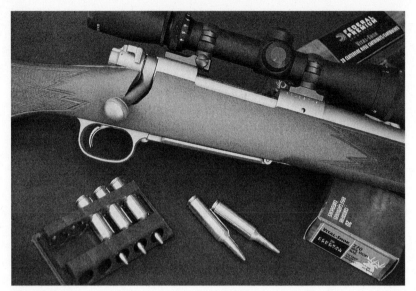

This Model 70 in .270 WSM was restocked by Hill Country Rifles. It wears a Burris 4-12x scope.

The .270 WSM functioned without flaw, but the first groups were disappointing. I suspected a scope problem and replaced the variable with another of a different make. Groups instantly shrank. Don't discount the possibility of a wandering reticle if your rifle seems inaccurate.

Walnut-stocked American Classic rifles offer more options than HCR's synthetic-stocked model, including Sunny Hill drop-box bottom metal, Biesen steel buttplate, Fisher skeleton grip cap, contoured cross-bolts, barrel-band front sight and single-leaf adjustable rear sight, extended extractor, checkered bolt handle, and bolt release. For these, Bridges fashions his own scope bases, contouring them to the receiver with near-zero dimensional tolerances. "Our guarantee is the same," he affirms. "Three shots inside half an inch with recommended factory ammunition. Slender, lightweight rifles can still be accurate."

"How about I ship you a .300 Ultra Mag?" Charlie Sisk suggested, after he'd introduced himself on the telephone. "Just finished it, and it'll shoot flies off the wall." I'm a sucker for southern hyperbole.

The deeper the snow, the more appealing a lightweight rifle. Brian Kelly scans rimrock for deer.

In due course, I got a metal box big enough to hold a half-grown Texas heifer and heavier than a tractor wheel. The rifle was not made to my specs, but it showed intelligent design. The Model 700 Remington action wore a 26-inch Hart barrel of substantial weight (.700 at the muzzle). Sisk uses other barrels too; Lilja is a favorite. "They're all air-gauged and will not vary more than .0001. I also inspect each bore with a borescope. My chambering is done with match-grade live-pilot

Charlie's railroad. The boxcars behind his customers constitute a Texas-size shooting tunnel.

reamers. Chamber concentricity and bore uniformity go hand in hand to ensure accuracy. I want my rifles to shoot itty bitty groups."

Working up loads for the .300 Ultra Mag (this was prior to published data), I added 10 percent to charges for the .300 Weatherby. It seemed a reasonable thing to do, given the 13 percent edge in capacity. Mostly, I came close to reaching target velocities. Sisk told me that he'd had good luck with Sierra Match bullets in front of 90 grains IMR 7828. I did too: They drilled a sub-half-minute group. Berger 185s pushed by 89 grains Accurate 3100 also shot into half an inch. Most of the loads tested gave or promised minute-of-angle accuracy, attesting to Sisk's good work and the high quality of the 26-inch Hart barrel.

Not long thereafter, I asked Charlie Sisk to build me another, more civilized rifle: a 6mm BR on a Remington Model Seven action. The 6mm BR dates to the 1960s, when wildcatters necked down the then-new .308x1^1/$_2$ developed by Frank Barnes. In 1978 Remington's Mike Walker standardized 6mm BR dimensions. (Incidentally, the 6mm BR chamber is not the same as for the 6mm BR Norma, developed by that Swedish ammunition company in 1996. Although case dimensions are identical, Norma's was designed for VLD 100-grain

At Sisk Rifles, Charlie has little time to shoot just for fun. But then, "all shooting is fun."

missiles used in 1,000-yard competition, so throat specs differ. Remington had initially envisioned the 6mm BR as a bench round launching 70-grain bullets. The company's factory-loaded 100-grain softpoints were shorter than boattail spitzers designed to reach the 1,000-yard mark clocking 1,400 fps. According to CIP, Europe's equivalent of SAAMI, any change in chamber dimensions requires a new cartridge label—hence, two 6mm BRs.)

Short and squat, the Remington 6mm BR resembles the 6mm PPC, derived from the .220 Russian case by benchrest competitors Lou Palmisano and Ferris Pindell during the 1970s. Remington 6mm BR factory ammunition (a 100-grain bullet at a modest 2,550 fps) came out in 1988, a year after Sako began loading 6mm PPCs. The BR case has a thin front end for ease in forming and a small rifle primer. Larger in diameter than the PPC, it holds roughly 10 percent more powder. "And there's the problem," Sisk drawled. "That fat, stubby hull won't feed."

That isn't a worry for benchrest competition but is a liability in a hunting rifle. I said that I'd like the rifle anyway, and Sisk sighed. A couple of months later, about the time I thought he might be phoning to discuss barrel dimensions or tell me that he just didn't want the project, he called me. "It's done," he said.

"What's done?" I asked.

"The 6 BR. I need to get it off my bench." Sisk is not one of those craftsmen who promise delivery sometime in the next millennium. He's fast as a florist, but that doesn't mean he rushes things. Accuracy matters to Sisk, and he burns lots of ammo making sure the rifles that leave his shop shoot little groups. In fact, his extensive testing brought complaints from the neighbors, so, true to his upbringing, he fixed the situation with a covered shooting range. His budget wouldn't brook a tunnel, so he bought half a dozen railroad boxcars, cut out the ends with acetylene, and positioned them end to end in his backyard. He is the only gunmaker I know who owns a rail line.

The 6mm BR arrived shortly. Its Model 700 short-action receiver sported a black finish, matching that of the 22-inch Hart #4 stainless barrel. Sisk had trued the receiver threads. "That's really the place to begin," he said. "Then I face the receiver so it's square with the threads. As it comes from the factory, a 700 bolt head rarely lines up with the bolt body or the receiver ring, so I square the bolt face and hand-lap the lugs." Dave Kiff at Pacific Precision Grinding fashioned the reamers. According to Sisk, "He's always my first choice. Dave cuts reamers not only for the trade but for big commercial gun firms." Leade angle in this barrel, Sisk told me, was $1\frac{1}{2}$ degrees.

The Sisk rifle wore a clean-breaking Timney trigger and a High Tech Specialties stock with black spider webbing over paint the color of the ocean: saltwater blue with a glimmer of green. Sisk had glassed it at the recoil lug. The forend was beefy but not beavertail. I scoped the rifle with a 6-18x Swift.

The 6mm BR Lapua cases that arrived were uniform in dimension, the flash holes nicely centered. Winchester small-rifle primers snapped smartly into the pockets. Lapua, a Finnish company, imports to the United States through Kaltron-Pettibone, a firm that also supplies shooters with Vihtavuori powders. Although the .243 Winchester and 6mm Remington have room for 100-grain bullets, lighter bullets make sense in the squat BR case. Because it has a long (.32) neck, Sisk hadn't extended the throat. I'd seat .1 off the lands, as is my custom, over powders with a medium to medium-fast burn rate. I chose Redding dies because they show superior machining and finish, which can mean better accuracy.

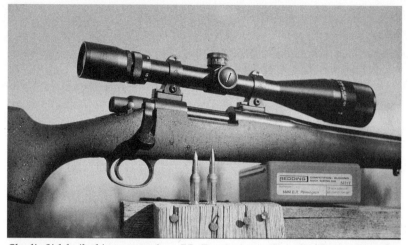

Charlie Sisk built this accurate 6mm BR. Despite its squat profile, the round has great reach.

Groups from the Sisk rifle averaged around ³/₄ inch. Lightweight bullets in this 6mm BR fared a bit better than 90-grain pills; still, the 1:12 twist stabilized all bullets fired. Hot loads shot well.

Charge (grains) / Powder	Bullet weight (grains) / Type	Velocity (fps)
Remington factory load	100 SP Core-Lokt	2810
32 Benchmark	75 Hornady hp	3265
30 H322	75 Hornady hp	3170
28 RL-7	75 Hornady hp	3240
32 N133	80 Remington Power-Lokt	3348 (warm)
32 RL-12	80 Remington Power-Lokt	3020
31 Accurate 2230	80 Remington Power-Lokt	3115
32 BL-C2	85 Sierra sp	3020
31 RL-12	85 Sierra sp	3000
31 W748	85 Sierra sp	2955
31 RL-15	88 Berger hp	3015
30 Accurate 2460	88 Berger hp	3050
30 IMR 4064	88 Berger hp	3030
31 N133	88 Berger hp	3240 (warm)
29 Accurate 2230	90 Speer sp	2900
32 BL-C2	90 Speer sp	2915

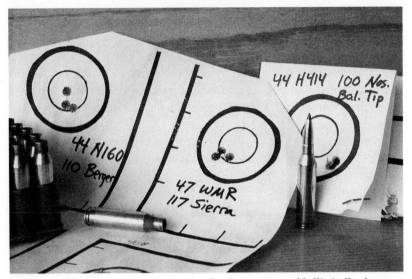

The author's Sisk-built .25 Souper is exceedingly accurate and ballistically close to the .25-06.

Extreme spread for three shots was often less than 10 fps—uncommonly low variation. Although you can get tight groups with high extreme spread readings, the lower the numbers, the better. These indicate that the powder burns efficiently and uniformly. Efficiency is a hallmark of the 6mm BR, which accelerates 85-grain bullets to 3,000 fps with just 30 grains of fuel. The .243 Winchester swallows 15 to 20 percent more propellant to reach the same speeds. The compact fuel cell of the BR also performs well in short barrels.

Does the rifle feed? Only from the top deck. "Sometimes you just don't get lucky," Sisk said.

My next Sisk project gave the Texas gunmaker no trouble at all. "How about a lightweight, open-country deer rifle chambered to .25 Souper?" I asked. Necking a .308 to .25 (or, more easily, a .243 case up to .25) gives you an efficient and practical deer round that's more potent than .250 Savage and .257 Roberts ammo. In short actions, the 2.015-inch .308 case is also a better fit than the Roberts, which derives from the 2.235-inch 7x57 hull. My yearning for a .25 Souper dates back decades. The late *Field & Stream* shooting editor Warren Page may have written the first text I read on it.

Sisk soon came up with a short Remington 700 action, a High Tech Specialties stock, and a 24-inch Lilja barrel with 1:10 twist. He squared the bolt face, lapped in the lugs, and trued up the receiver face and barrel shank. Before assembling the metal, he installed a Timney trigger and one of his own recoil lugs.

"It looks like a Remington washer," Sisk explained. "But instead of being stamped out, mine are machined from 416 stainless steel, then bored and surface ground by CNC so they're flat and true."

Sisk favors Brownell's Acraglas for bedding, and he used it on this 700. "My father had an old Farmall tractor whose radiator sprung a leak. Rather than pulling it for repair, we mixed up some Acraglas and dabbed that on the hole. It's held for more than 20 years." Sisk concedes that if Acraglas failed as a bedding compound, he'd keep it around only for tractors.

This .25 Souper shoots exceptionally well. Recoil, as you might expect, borders on the negligible. The rifle feels like a .243, but the .25 Souper accommodates heavier bullets. Here's how this quarter-bore compares to its competition, and how it performed with handloads I assembled for the Sisk rifle.

Cartridge	Load	Muzzle velocity (fps)	Group size (inches)
.250 Savage	Remington factory, 100 PSP	2820	
.257 Roberts	Remington factory, 117 SPCL	2650	
	Hornady factory, 117 SST	2780	
	Federal +P factory, 120 Nosler Partition	2780	
	Hornady Light Magnum factory, 117 SST	2940	
.25-06	Federal factory, 90 Sierra Varminter HP	3440	
	Remington factory, 100 PSPCL	3230	
	Remington factory, 120 PSPCL	2990	
	Hornady Light Magnum factory, 117 SST	3110	
.25 Souper	41 IMR 4064, 87 Hornady	3335	.75
	43 H380, 87 Hornady	3200	1.50
	44 H414 100 Nosler Ballistic Tip	3170	.05 (best)
	48 RL-19 100 Nosler Ballistic Tip	3325	.35
	46 H4350 100 Speer	3240	.85
	40 Vihtavuori N-150 100 Sierra	3090	.85
	39 Varget 100 Sierra	3077	1.15
	43 H4350 115 Nosler Ballistic Tip	3097	1.00
	44 H4831 115 Nosler Partition	2917	1.10

Cartridge	Load	Muzzle velocity (fps)	Group size (inches)
.25 Souper	46 RL-22 115 Nosler Ballistic Tip	3030	1.50
	44 WP Big Game 110 Berger VLD	3145	.75
	44 Vihtavuori N-160 110 Berger VLD	3020	.35
	47 WMR 117 Sierra flatbase	2885	.25
	45 NMR 120 Hornady	2945	.50

The Sisk .25 Souper gave me seven three-shot groups at or under .75 inch during sustained slow fire. I did not let the barrel cool or clean it during the trials. Loads were tested beginning with the lightest bullets and ending with the heaviest. The last 14 shots from a hot barrel showed me that this rifle is one of those sweethearts that wants to shoot. Incidentally, no signs of high pressure surfaced on the Winchester cases or primers. I got no sticky bolt lifts with these loads—although they should be approached cautiously.

Index